AMERICAN CHARACTER

to Deborah,
on the day
I first heard
you sing
"Kill the Indian."

Mark

AMERICAN CHARACTER

THE CURIOUS LIFE OF
CHARLES FLETCHER LUMMIS
AND THE REDISCOVERY OF THE SOUTHWEST

MARK
THOMPSON

ARCADE PUBLISHING • NEW YORK

FIRST EDITION

Unless otherwise indicated, all photographs are courtesy of the Southwest Museum, Los Angeles. Archive numbers are as given.

Library of Congress Cataloging-in-Publication Data

Thompson, Mark, 1956–
    American character : the curious history of Charles Fletcher
Lummis and the rediscovery of the Southwest / Mark Thompson.
        p. cm.
    Includes bibliographical references and index.
    ISBN 1-55970-550-7
    1. Lummis, Charles Fletcher, 1859–1928. 2. Authors,
American—19th century—Biography. 3. Authors, American—
20th century—Biography. 4. Social reformers—United States—
Biography. 5. Journalists—United States—Biography. 6.
Southwestern States—Biography. 7. Southwestern States—
History. I. Title.

PS3523.U49 Z89 2001
818'.409—dc21
[B]   00–50248

Published in the United States by Arcade Publishing, Inc., New York
Distributed by Time Warner Trade Publishing

Visit our Web site at www.arcadepub.com

10 9 8 7 6 5 4 3 2 1

Designed by API

EB

PRINTED IN THE UNITED STATES OF AMERICA

For my parents,
Rhodes and Lois Thompson

Contents

Acknowledgments

I owe a special thanks to Kim Walters, director of the Braun Research Library of the Southwest Museum in Los Angeles, and to Michael Wagner, also of the library staff, for their help during the many weeks I spent there, just scratching the surface of the Lummis manuscript collection and other materials about the history of the Southwest in the library's collections. And thanks also to Keith Lummis of San Francisco, Charles Lummis's youngest and last surviving child, for permission to quote from *Charles F. Lummis: The Man and His West*, the book he and his sister wrote about their father. A lucid ninety-six years old at the start of the twenty-first century, he was no stranger to his father's faults, but had immense respect for his legacy. He had only one request, which I have tried to fulfill: "I hope you'll give the old man a fair shake." I am grateful to my faithful agent, Eileen Cope, and my diligent editor at Arcade Publishing, Webster Younce, whose enthusiasm for Lum and unwavering support for my work helped immeasurably as I labored to see this project through to completion. My wife, Roya Mina, and my daughters, Sara and Amanda, learned first-hand about the effort involved in writing a biography, as I disappeared for long days in libraries and on jaunts through the Southwest. I owe them my thanks for their support as well.

AMERICAN CHARACTER

Prologue

On December 3, 1901, Charles Fletcher Lummis passed through Chicago on a train trip from Los Angeles to Washington, D.C. He had a few hours to spare in the Windy City, so he dropped by the studio of sculptor Lorado Taft to meet with a small group of the local literati. Even those who had never met Lummis had heard enough about the eccentric journalist and editor to be intrigued by his visit. Lummis didn't disappoint. Though he stood just five feet six inches tall, he dominated the gathering from the moment he walked into the room, dressed in his trademark ensemble: a well-worn Spanish-style corduroy suit, red Navajo sash, and soiled Stetson sombrero.

The impression he left wasn't entirely favorable. "He was reeking with sweat and his hair was tousled into wiglike tufts. He looked like some half-Mexican rancher," observed the novelist Hamlin Garland, one of those who had gathered to greet him.[1] Lummis cursed the Chicago weather, pronounced all cities "monstrous, destructive, and futile— Chicago the worst of them," and headed back to the train station to resume his journey east, leaving a somewhat befuddled group at Taft's studio in his wake.

Perhaps the most surprising thing about Lummis was the proudly declared purpose of his journey. Though he hardly looked the part of presidential advisor, he had been summoned to Washington to confer with President Theodore Roosevelt, who had been sworn in less than three months earlier following the assassination of William McKinley. Preparing his first annual presidential message to Congress, which would help set the tone for his presidency, Roosevelt wanted to hear what Charles Lummis thought he should say about the West, and about Indians, a group Lummis knew intimately from having lived in their midst for four years.

For his part, Garland, who had grown up on the northern plains and fancied himself something of an expert on the region, believed Lummis's "bluff, rough-and-ready manner" was to a degree an affectation designed to mask his New England upbringing. And yet he had to admit that Lummis's knowledge of the West, particularly the Mexican borderlands and the brown people of those parts, was unsurpassed. "He amused me at the same time that he won my respect," Garland wrote in his memoir *Companions on the Trail*, published in 1931, three years after Lummis's death. "Without in any degree defending his manner of dress and his outlook on life, I valued his knowledge of the Southwest and of Southern California which made him helpful to the President." Still, while Garland admired Lummis's "truculent nonconformity," he questioned whether it paid to be "picturesquely crumpled and dirty. Couldn't a man think just as well in a presentable suit and clean collar?"

Roosevelt, for one, didn't mind. Lummis had on the same outfit he was wearing at Taft's studio when he reached Washington at noon two days later. He usually wasn't self-conscious about his appearance, but Lummis was disheveled enough on this occasion to call the White House from the train station to offer advance warning of his condition. Roosevelt insisted he should come immediately anyway for a luncheon with a handful of dignitaries that was just getting under way. Afterward Lummis stayed for a private meeting with the president, the first of four he would have that week.

A year younger than Roosevelt, Lummis, then forty-two, had first achieved a measure of national fame seventeen years earlier during a widely followed "tramp across the continent" from Cincinnati to Los Angeles. Since then he had distinguished himself in a remarkable succession of careers. Poet, journalist, photographer, archaeologist, editor, champion of Spanish heritage in the Americas, and Indian rights advocate, Lummis was a lifelong workaholic who always had half a dozen projects going at once and rarely got more than three or four hours of sleep a night.

He wrote sixteen books, ranging from a couple of volumes of poems and a chronicle of his 1884–85 tramp to a history of the Spanish pioneers and several collections of Pueblo Indian folktales. He churned out countless newspaper and magazine articles for many of the leading periodicals of his day. And he wielded influence behind the scenes with a manic outpouring of letters, tens of thousands of them over the course of his life, to thousands of people—leading writers, social scientists, artists, politicians, unknown admirers contributing a dollar to save one of the crumbling Spanish missions or to help the Indians. His love of life, generosity of spirit, and devotion to the causes he espoused permeated everything he wrote and did. As one of Lummis's closest friends, Stanford University president David Starr Jordan, put it, "He is a journalist by profession, a human geyser of the first water, bubbling with enthusiasm."[2]

Lummis's extraordinary career spanned a remarkable period in the history of the American West. During his lifetime, the nation went through changes that were dramatic even by the standards of recent fast-paced decades. The Apaches were still holding out against the U.S. Army and Los Angeles was a Spanish-Mexican pueblo without a square foot of pavement when Lummis first strode into the Southwest. By the time he died, tourists were flocking to the pueblos by automobile and Los Angeles had been transformed into a modern city, home of a thriving movie industry, with traffic jams and the first whiff of smog.

From the moment of his arrival, he was in love with the natural wonders of the Southwest. But Lummis was even more inspired by the rich and diverse cultural heritage he found. In a region where Indians and Spanish settlers had intermingled and intermarried for centuries, joined more recently by northern Europeans, blacks, and Chinese, he learned that his country was far more multiracial and polyglot than he ever imagined growing up in New England. He quickly became convinced that the United States was far better for it. He spent his career encouraging other Americans to tour the Southwest, hoping visitors to the region would have the same eye-opening experience that had changed his life.

As he had at Taft's studio in 1901, Lummis raised eyebrows everywhere he went in life. But he was never fazed by the criticism that he continually stirred up with his eccentric attire, bombastic pronouncements, and scandal-tainted personal life, which included three failed

3

marriages and widely publicized extramarital entanglements. Flaws and all, he was a genius, according to many of his devoted friends. They far outnumbered the detractors who considered him an egomaniac.

When Lummis died in 1928, the headline over his obituary in the *New York Times* called him "Apostle of the Southwest." Lummis "was one of the first 'discoverers' of the southwest," the *Times* stated. "Many a person had traveled through Arizona and New Mexico before he did. A few had written of it glowingly. But Mr. Lummis combined the skill and instinct of a journalist with a deep love of the country." His friend Harry Carr, in an obituary he wrote for the *Los Angeles Times*, came closer to capturing Lummis's own perception of his place as a chronicler of American history, though Carr too resorted to the word that Lummis shied away from. "Lummis was one of the first writers to realize that the history of the United States did not begin with Plymouth Rock; one of the first to discover the Southwest as a treasure trove of romance, history and archaeology," Carr wrote.

Lummis would have been flattered by the sentiment, though he would have quibbled with the wording. He took pride in the large part he played in raising awareness of the beauty and cultural contributions of a region he loved. But he once demurred, "I am convinced—despite keen maternal pangs to the contrary—that I didn't discover anything." The suggestion that he had discovered the Southwest was yet another example of the lack of respect for, and the ignorance of, the real discoverers—those he called the First Americans, who had a sophisticated culture in the Rio Grande Valley for more than a thousand years, and the Spanish, who brought European civilization to the heart of the North American continent in New Mexico a century before Anglo-Saxon settlers first erected their crude huts on the shores of Lummis's native New England.

Lummis would have preferred his obituaries to credit him with rediscovering the Southwest and telling its story to a nation with an often woefully narrow view of its past, present, and future.

Chapter *1*

The Restless Yankee

By the end of the first week of his final semester at Harvard, it was apparent that nothing less than a miracle would get Charles Fletcher Lummis to the finish line. He was unquestionably smart enough to graduate and with honors, if he had set his mind to that goal. After all, he had qualified for admission to Harvard two years before he was old enough to enroll. And despite his own spotty college record, Lummis was in demand as a tutor for other college students in subjects ranging from French, Latin, and Greek to rhetoric and moral philosophy. But judging from his behavior at Harvard, it seemed that his chief goal in college was to get kicked out.

To begin with, he was an incorrigible prankster. His partner in many of the escapades, as recounted in the memoir he was writing when he died, was Boies Penrose, a future senator from Pennsylvania.[1] In one of their more harmless stunts, they posed as "professional vagabonds" and made a 127-mile trek to Manchester, New Hampshire, and back over Thanksgiving weekend of 1879, begging along the way. Some of their pranks around campus were considerably riskier to their status as students in good standing. Lummis claimed they garishly painted college buildings in the middle of the night, scrawled "Death to the Faculty" on walls in paint so black that the words could still be made out a year later, and retaliated against obnoxious residence hall proctors by screwing the proctors' doors shut and nailing trip wires at ankle level across entrances to their quarters. They also stole signs from storefronts around town and stored them in a vacant dorm room.

Lummis usually succeeded in covering his tracks, but not always, and he was called in by administrators more than once to defend his behavior. On one occasion, an irate father complained about Lummis to college president Charles W. Eliot after finding some highly suggestive letters that his daughter had written but never mailed to Lummis. When Eliot called him in and demanded that he explain the "shocking, horrible letters," Lummis looked the distinguished president straight in the eye and told him the "cold facts," vowing that he hadn't touched the girl but admitting that he wished he had.

"I should play poker with that man!" Lummis marveled. "His face never changed in the whole hour." Lummis didn't hear anything more about the girl. "Since I was neither expelled nor suspended, I knew that he had believed me," Lummis said.

Lummis *was* suspended once. It's not clear why. In an autobiographical essay he wrote a year after the fact, he stated without further comment: "I was absent during the first half of my junior year, at Watertown," where his father was living at the time. "Cause—special vote of the faculty."[2]

As reckless as he had been, when the final semester of his senior year got under way, Lummis was still enrolled at Harvard and intent on finishing. The diary that he had recently begun keeping recounts his losing effort to stay focused.[3] Classes started on Monday, January 3, 1881. Lummis's diary entry for that day commences "The grind begun. Don't like it for a cent" and ends "Dull day."

On Tuesday, Lummis focused enough to turn in an assignment that impressed a professor, but he spent the entire afternoon walking the railroad tracks on the edge of town with his pistol looking for rabbits to shoot. He couldn't even find a pigeon, but when he saw several men trying to snag eels with a spear through a hole in the ice on a pond, he decided to give that a try, borrowing the spear and quickly bagging three of the slimy creatures. "Great fun. Must invest in a spear & try it myself," he noted in his diary. He spent the next two days collecting a debt to raise funds for a spear, buying the implement, catching thirty of the creatures, hauling them home, and skinning them. It wasn't until well after nightfall on Thursday that he turned to schoolwork. "Grind like the deuce for about 8 hours," his diary entry for that day ends.

The frenetic bursts of effort, however, weren't enough to make up for all the classes he was missing. Just six weeks into the semester, Lummis casually noted, "Went up to visit the Dean, agreeably to his invitation. He said that it will be expedient to attend all recitations for the rest of the year." The next day he "went to English VI today for the first time, and found it tolerably interesting."

But it was no use. For Charles Lummis, graduating from Harvard just wasn't meant to be. He made it through the rest of that semester without any major run-ins with the administration, but in order to graduate, he had to pass a series of exams. He passed all of them except those in trigonometry and analytical geometry. He could have gotten tutoring and retaken the exams, but Lummis apparently didn't even consider doing that. A few steps short of the finish line, he dropped out.

His seditious behavior in college was as close as Lummis ever got to rebelling against his father. The Reverend Henry Lummis was a Methodist clergyman and educator revered by generations of students in the succession of preparatory schools and colleges across New England and the upper Midwest where he served as an administrator and teacher.

Charlie loved his father. And he clearly appreciated the advantages that the caring but strict discipline at home gave him later in life. His father was "a marvelous man," Lummis wrote in a tribute to his father at his death in 1905. He was "one of the most beloved men I have ever known.... Father gave me my foundation." But perhaps Lummis wouldn't have been so insubordinate in college if he had enjoyed a little more freedom earlier in life. He suggested as much in his memoir. At Harvard, he wrote, "I found that for the restrained, encircled 18-year-old son of a Methodist minister, circumscribed by the atmosphere of the congregation, there were many other things to study than lessons.... From my cloistered life I had come to the Tree of Forbidden Fruit. I climbed that tree to the top."

His mother had an equally profound influence on Lummis, though in tragically different fashion. She died on April 24, 1861, leaving Rev. Lummis to care for two-year-old Charlie and his two-month-old sister, Louise Elma. Known as Hattie, the twenty-two-year-old mother was probably afflicted with tuberculosis even before Charles arrived on March 1, 1859. In her diary, she chronicled moments of elation about the baby she called Charlie Bird, interspersed with "moments of great sadness" when she sensed that the "months were hurrying me to life's close." Indeed they were.[4] Her second pregnancy, not much more than a year after Charlie's birth, sapped what little strength she had left. So she moved with Charlie to her parents' home in Bristol, New Hampshire a few months before her second child was due, and there she died. For the rest of his life, Charlie Lummis would always be in no small part a motherless child. Not that he lacked attention from loving and supportive adults. Members of his close-knit extended family tried to fill the void left by his mother's death. Since his busy father couldn't possibly care for two babies, Charlie and his newborn sister remained with their grandparents for the next four years.

Louisa and Oscar Fowler were faultless surrogate parents. And Bristol was an idyllic place to grow up. A picture-postcard New England village of perhaps four hundred people, it had a large open commons in the middle of town where Charlie and his grandfather once watched a company of newly enlisted soldiers marching off to the Civil War. The crystal clear Newfound River rushed past the village, over a dam beside a mill, and down a three-hundred-foot cascade.

Charlie's grandmother made unforgettable pies and doughnuts, and his grandfather, the village saddle and harness maker and part-time probate judge, introduced him to the avocation that Charlie would always rank as life's single greatest pleasure: fishing for trout. Judge Oscar Fowler also taught Charlie that even if he was smaller than most, he didn't have to yield to anyone on account of his size. Grandpa Fowler was just five feet six inches in height, which was as tall as Charlie ever got. But he was "as tough as nails," tipping the scales at 230 pounds "without an ounce of fat," Charlie somewhat improbably claimed. He went on to assert that at the age of sixty, his grandfather beat a dozen eighteen-year-olds in a footrace across the Bristol commons.

Those four years with his grandparents were perhaps the closest he ever got to living in what he considered a complete home. But it didn't last. In the fall between his fifth and sixth birthdays, at an age when formal schooling could begin, he moved to his father's house. At the time, Rev. Lummis was principal of the New Haven Female College in Tilton, New Hampshire. Just nineteen miles from Bristol, it was a dramatically different setting—particularly the school filled with tittering girls where his father wanted Charlie to start classes. The trauma of moving to a strange new home no doubt magnified the usual first-day jitters. But his reaction to school was more severe than that. He spent his first day, as he told it in his memoir, hiding under a table, refusing to emerge until his father arrived and coaxed him out. "I told father I couldn't learn that way and asked him to teach me himself," Lummis wrote. And he "did exactly that for the next ten years."

Within a few years of his return to his father's house, Charlie's little sister, Louise Elma, had rejoined the household, and a stepmother had entered the picture. She would eventually have five children of her own, giving Charlie one half brother named Harry and four half sisters, Harriet, Katherine, Laura, and Gertrude. So it was far from a lonely childhood. But his father's new wife, Jennie Brewster, happened to be the same teacher he had recoiled from on his first day in school. Jennie was probably the one whose job it was to see that Charlie completed the daunting lessons that his father assigned, which couldn't have helped them establish a warm rapport. "We were greatly unsuited for the relationship by temperament but our mutual love for my father went a long way," he stated in his memoirs, only hinting at the tensions that must have arisen. "While she caused me a great deal of unhappiness in my young years, it was not all her fault. She was a noble woman as well as a brainy one and a model wife to my father."

Over the next twelve years, the family made six moves to towns in New Hampshire and Massachusetts. Charlie took a few courses in the schools where his father taught. But most of his schooling took place at home under the direction of his father. It was an old-fashioned education even for those days. He was "well drilled in the 'common branches'," with a special emphasis on classical languages, starting with Latin at the age of seven, then Hebrew at eight and Greek at ten. He honed his skills in these tongues by translating verses of the Hebrew Old Testament and the Greek New Testament over dinner each night.

As for his father, Lummis never made public any hint of criticism. "I am grateful for each of the seven lickings he gave me—and they all left their marks," Lummis wrote. One licking was especially memorable, the only time in his life that he was "laid on his back" by another man, Lummis claimed. He had reacted to something his father said in a manner that the older Lummis interpreted as a sign of disrespect. "I am sure he was mistaken about it, for I never in my life felt a moment's resentment against him," Lummis wrote years later, even then excusing his father for what ensued. "But the next thing I knew I was on my back, four points down, ten feet back into the next room, with father astride of me and saying very softly, 'Charlie, don't you ever look at me that way again'."

He never defied his father again, except indirectly in college. He heeded his father's wishes at least to the extent that he enrolled, even though he had "no violent ambition for college. I went because Father had gone and because he had trained me with years of personal concentration. It was the cultural convention of New England." From the start, however, he proved to be a very unconventional student.

The rigorous training he had received at home left Lummis exceedingly well prepared for Harvard. He had already read nearly everything that was on the reading lists for the Latin and Greek courses at the university. Though he was indifferent about attending class and balked at assignments that didn't catch his fancy, he didn't shy away from academic challenges. Quite the contrary. To enter Harvard at that time under the newly adopted elective system, students were required to pass an exam in either French or German. With his solid grounding in Latin, Lummis figured French would be too easy. So he chose to enter in German, picked up a 3,600-word German dictionary, "swallowed it whole," and waltzed through the test. But academics never got more than part of his attention. His priorities in college, as he later put it, were poker, poetry, and athletics—a list to which he could have added pretty girls and pranks.

Within days of his arrival on campus, he made a name for himself as a pugnacious free spirit, according to a tale that he would repeat often in later years. The tradition at Harvard when he entered in 1877 was that freshmen had to cut their hair short. But Lummis, apparently alone among his classmates, refused to knuckle under. The sophomores weren't about to let that challenge go unanswered. The enforcers of the upper class posted an ultimatum on a campus bulletin board: "NOTICE: If Freshman Lummis doesn't get his hair cut, '80 will cut it for him."

Lummis, whose thick, curly hair fell below his ears, promptly posted a response: "Lummis '81 will be glad to meet all tonsorially inclined of the Class of '80 individually or collectively, at 16 Holyoke any time."

Lummis's favorite part of this story was the compliment that his audacity elicited from one particular sophomore, "an odd looking chap" who was "flat-chested, hatchet-faced, lantern jawed, with funny side whiskers." His name was Theodore Roosevelt. Ordinarily he would have had nothing to do with Lummis, being from an entirely different social stratum. He was "a patrician who chummed with the Minots and Cabots and Lowells" and was known as an unusually diligent student to boot, proud to rank nineteenth in his class of 230. Lummis, in contrast, was a self-described "callow pauper" prone to ditching classes. Yet Roosevelt, who had been a sickly child and had tried to overcome his physical deficiencies in many of the same ways that Lummis compensated for his height, admired the freshman's brashness. He "grinned at me across the Unfathomable Abyss," Lummis recalled. In that memorable booming voice of his, Roosevelt called out, "Bully! It's your hair—keep it if you want to. Don't let them haze you."

Both Lummis and Roosevelt would become famous for maintaining a crushing workload, a habit that for both became ingrained in college. Lummis also began "night hawking" in those days, getting some of his most productive work done in the hours well past midnight. He stayed up late practically every night to play poker for as long as others lasted. Then he would turn his energies to translating the works of obscure Greek, Latin, and German poets.

Lummis devoted most of his time at Harvard to athletics. He spent hours in the gym. Some of the feats he took credit for in the memoir written many decades later are improbable, to say the least. For example, he claimed to have run the hundred-yard dash in ten seconds flat, which would have been a world record at the time. But there was no doubt that he whipped himself into perfect shape in his college days, judging from a photograph of him wearing nothing but shorts. He is suspending himself in the air on a set of parallel bars, showing off his muscular arms, powerful thighs, and a taut torso entirely free of fat. For at least the next decade, published descriptions of Lummis routinely mentioned that he was a "trained athlete." That was no exaggeration.

Lummis's preferred methods of physical and mental conditioning were wrestling and boxing, sports that he enjoyed both as a spectator and as a participant. Prizefighting was just barely respectable in the Puritan culture in which he was born and raised, but the pangs of guilt he felt the first time he paid money to see a prizefight quickly passed.

"When the door opened my scruples fell off me like snowflakes in the sun," he wrote. He loved nothing better than to step into the ring himself, preferably with a larger opponent. It was great fun, he wrote with the bravado that would characterize some of his published work, "to stand up and have my face pounded off me by a man forty pounds heavier and with six inches more reach—if every once in a while I could jump around his kidney, or get him in the turn of the jaw, and cool off while they brought him to."

One of Lummis's problems was that he didn't seem able to confine his pugilistic interests to the boxing ring. He owned up to this character flaw in the autobiographical essay that he wrote at the start of his senior year of college. "I have always had the ill-luck to fall into fights and get maimed therein," he matter-of-factly wrote. "In a sophomore quarrel I was shot in the left side, the ball glancing a couple of inches from the heart. I have also been stabbed several times, thanks to an exuberant spirit which never allows me to keep out of any row I chance to see going on."

The diary he kept for a few months in the final semester of his senior year offers further proof that he was a pugnacious character indeed. In just one two-week stretch in January of 1881, he described how he sent one of a group of "muckers" sprawling with three quick punches to the nose after they tickled him with a straw while he dozed on a train, reported that he "slugged a fellow in a cigar store" for an unknown reason ten days later, and had "quite an encounter with two bogus cops" two days after that.

Lummis spent all four summers in his college years working at a resort called the Profile House in the White Mountains of New Hampshire. Situated on the shore of Profile Lake, it was named after the massive rock formation, called the Old Man of the Mountain, that loomed over the water with a distinct chin, nose, and brow.

Lummis burnished his reputation for daring athletic feats—and revealed a pronounced romantic streak—during those summers. He claimed to have set records for speedy ascents and descents of nearby mountain peaks, and once climbed as far as the forehead of the Old Man of the Mountain without ropes, extricating himself from that treacherous perch by traversing a six-inch ledge to safety. He added to his reputation for marching to his own rather peculiar drummer by, among other things, spending most nights in good weather sleeping in a birch bark canoe anchored just offshore.

He had a dream job as in-house printshop manager with responsibility for producing hotel menus, programs, and announcements. Lummis had been fascinated with the printing process ever since his grandparents had given him a miniature but fully functioning press for his twelfth birthday. He had displayed enough skill with it to get the plum job at the resort. He got his work done there efficiently enough that he had both the time and the leeway with management to use the hotel's printing equipment in a remarkably ingenious and audacious publishing venture of his own.

He had been a serious would-be poet for several years, a passion that blossomed on the shores of Profile Lake. He admitted that they weren't the best bits of verse, but he figured that if they were packaged attractively enough, they just might sell. So he decided to print a dozen of the ones with New England mountain themes on birch bark. Through a great deal of trial and error, he learned how to peel sheets of the papery bark into the thinnest layers possible, how to flatten and cut them into perfect two-by-three-inch sheets, and, hardest of all, how to thin ink to just the right consistency to stick to the bark. He printed the title on the cover, *Birch Bark Poems* by Charles F. Lummis. Then he bound up the booklets with thread and in the summer of 1879 offered them for sale in the Profile House gift shop for twenty-five cents each. By the end of the next summer, he had sold more than 3,500 of the booklets.

Displaying an early flair for publicity that would serve him well later in life, Lummis sent copies of the remarkable little volume to dozens of the leading writers and poets of the day, including Walt Whitman, Henry Wadsworth Longfellow, Charles Dudley Warner, and Captain Mayne Reid, as well as to all of the leading literary journals. Charmed by the booklet, a number of famous writers responded with personal words of encouragement, and the book got impressive reviews in a number of publications. *Life* magazine reviewed the book, noting that the poems weren't quite as original as the binding but that some of the better ones might endure. In a thank-you note to Lummis, Longfellow wrote, "It is very quaint and pretty in design; and I have read with much pleasure the poems it contains."

The most successful of the dozen poems in the book actually became a minor hit and was reprinted so widely that Lummis took care to have it registered with the U.S. Copyright Office. Called "My Cigarette," it combined two themes that would become favorites of his down through the years, in poetry and in life: tobacco and doting women.

> My Cigarette! Can I forget
> How Kate and I, in sunny weather,
> Sat in the shade the elm-tree made,
> And rolled the fragrant weed together?
> I, at her side, beatified
> To hold and guide her fingers willing:
> She, rolling slow the paper's snow,
> Putting my heart in with the filling!

The proceeds from the sale of *Birch Bark Poems* largely paid Lummis's way through Harvard. At the same time, the modest commercial success of the venture gave him all the less reason to stay in college. His growing reputation as a freelance writer increased the pressure that was welling up inside him to quit. By his senior year, he had sold stories, poems, and epigrams to more than three dozen publications as far away as the *Louisville Courier-Journal* and the *San Francisco Post*, as parochial as the *White Mountain Echo* and *Cottage Hearth*, and as famous as *Harper's* and *Life*. Harvard had nothing more to offer that might help him down that career path.

Years later he could look back on his time at Harvard and say, "I was glad then to be there; I am glad now that I went." But the three most important skills he claimed to have picked up there—boxing, wrestling, and running—showed that his gratitude had little to do with academic life at the university. He especially appreciated the opportunity that his college years gave him to socialize with a large group of his peers, "an experience of deep value to a boy who had been as alone as I had been," he said. "But so far as the Learning that really Works in Life—that is, Education, as opposed to mere Instruction—I learned more almost every year for the five after I left Harvard than for the entire four years I was there. My chief thankfulness about the whole matter is that four years of Harvard didn't make a fool of me."

By the start of his senior year, Charlie Lummis knew exactly what he wanted to do after he put college behind him. "I plan to visit Europe next fall, to see the country and the common people closely; and shall make the tour largely a pedestrian one as it is in this way only that I can study peasant life as accurately as I wish," he declared in the personal essay he wrote in the fall of 1880. "It is my plan to work as a newspaper correspondent during my stay abroad and on my return I shall probably plunge at once into journalism."

Lummis, of course, didn't graduate. Nor did he make it to Europe later that year. The plan to vagabond around Europe was sidetracked by a small matter that he acted as if he would like to forget: he had a wife. In fact, he had been married since the spring of his junior year, though only a handful of people knew it.

In April of 1880, Lummis had quietly—and apparently in a bit of a rush—married a Boston University medical student named Mary Dorothea Rhodes, Thea or Dolly for short. He had been tutoring her in French. It was never entirely clear why they kept their marriage secret, though gossips sowed theories about it for years after. Letters they wrote to each other in the early years of their marriage suggested that they had been caught in a compromising situation by someone who would have spread sordid rumors if they hadn't gotten married. Another possibility is that he was at risk of being forced into marrying another woman, and married Dolly to escape that threat. Even though they didn't live openly as man and wife after that, they seemed to be genuinely in love at least some of the time.

Over Christmas of 1880, they spent a lovely week together in Plymouth, Massachusetts, at the home of his aunt Susie, who may have been in on the secret. Every morning, Lummis stole away for one of his favorite pastimes: sharing a smoke with the local folk. On his first visit to the local general store, he enjoyed a "long smoke" and "astonished the countrymen" not only with the quantity and variety of pipes and smoking paraphernalia that he was carrying with him in various pockets but with his skill at blowing rings and then sucking the smoke back in. Two days later, he returned to the store for another smoke and this time "showed the countrymen some athletic performances."

Back at Aunt Susie's house one evening, he astonished the family with another daring move. On an impulse, he shaved off the full beard that was de rigueur for men in those days. When he showed his face in the parlor where the family had gathered, he "greatly shocked the crowd at my antiquated appearance." Except on several occasions when he didn't want to bother with shaving, he went whiskerless for the rest of his life, even when doing so was out of fashion.

By the summer of 1881, with college at last in the past, whatever mysterious reason they had for keeping the marriage secret had vanished. Probably sometime toward the end of that year, they made it official. Charlie and Dolly Lummis were husband and wife.

It wouldn't be long before Lummis developed a view of marriage that was as off-kilter as his attitudes toward college and other hallowed institutions. But he had enough sense to know that he would have to change his behavior in some respects. To begin with, he would have to get a respectable job. He had continued to pick up tutoring jobs around Boston and to hammer away at his freelance writing. But neither of those pursuits constituted a career. So when Dorothea's father offered Lummis a responsible job, he accepted it apparently without any protest, even though it was a far cry from the European adventure he had planned to make. The job was managing the Rhodeses' six-hundred-acre farm in Chillicothe, Ohio.

Undoubtedly he was planning his move off the farm even before he started. He continued to push ahead in his career in journalism by submitting poems and articles to the best magazines in the country—and, when they were rejected, rewriting them and sending them out again. He also continued to take orders for copies of his *Birch Bark Poems*. On trips back to New England to visit Dolly, he would load up on more bark to take back to Ohio with him. The most he would ever say of his stint as a farmer is that he "taught the bull to carry me on his back as though it were a privilege" and the Jersey cows to follow him everywhere. But the biggest thrill was finding Indian artifacts in the newly plowed furrows, particularly after a rain. Those discoveries sparked his lifelong fascination with archaeology.

Lummis lasted only a single season on the farm. At the end of the summer of 1882 an opportunity came along for a paying job in journalism, and he eagerly seized it. On September 29 he started work, at forty dollars per month, as the one-man news staff of a four-page weekly, the *Scioto Gazette*, said to be the oldest newspaper west of the Allegheny Mountains.

The stories he wrote for the *Gazette* ran the gamut from reflections on his summers in the White Mountains to literary criticism to hard-hitting coverage of Ohio politics. He didn't confine his apparently newfound interest in politics to his work on the paper. Within a year of settling down in Chillicothe, he became president of the Young Men's Republican Club, a position in which he had the privilege of introducing a future president, William McKinley, to his first Chillicothe audience.

In March of 1884 Lummis came close to throwing himself bodily into a political conflict. One hundred miles down the road in Cincinnati, a string of murders had crystallized simmering public discontent with the criminal justice system. The county jail at the time housed nearly three dozen murderers—a group that many local citizens believed should have been strung up as soon as they were convicted. When the perpetrator of one of the most recent murders was sentenced to twenty years in prison instead of the gallows, a substantial number of local citizens had had enough. More than 8,000 angry protesters headed for the jail, intent on getting the job done themselves. They were met by a brave sheriff, a Civil War veteran named Morton Lytle Hawkins, and 150 deputies who succeeded in holding back the mob that night.

Lummis was sympathetic with complaints about the criminal justice system. He believed that corruption might have been behind some otherwise inexplicable verdicts. But he had no tolerance for the mob violence that had begun to take over the city of Cincinnati by the second day of unrest. Turned away from the jail, the protestors stormed and burned down the massive Cincinnati courthouse.

By the third day of rioting, Lummis was prepared to join a militia to reinforce Sheriff Hawkins. But the National Guard, armed with a Gatling gun, got there first and put down the insurrection. More than fifty rioters died. Lummis was denied a taste of battle, which he most assuredly would have relished, but his editorializing on the turmoil gave him some feisty clippings for his files.

Those editorials would turn out to be Lummis's ticket out of Chillicothe. His plan to leave developed over a period of months. It began with newspapers mailed to his father-in-law by a lifelong friend, Albert McFarland, who had moved to California a year or two earlier. McFarland would eventually become treasurer of the fledgling newspaper that he was sending to Chillicothe. Called the *Los Angeles Daily Times*, it was published and edited by another former Ohioan, a decorated veteran of the Civil War, Colonel Harrison Gray Otis.[5]

Lummis was impressed with the paper. "I was struck by the personality, the upstanding courage and breeziness of that far western sheet," he reminisced years later. And so he began to correspond with Otis, sending him copies of his own paper. Knowing that Otis was a Grand Old Party warhorse, Lummis talked up his own Republican Party credentials and boasted about his willingness to come to the defense of the Civil War hero Hawkins. After a while he presented Otis with a bold proposition. He asked Otis for a job with the *Los Angeles Times*—and, dusting off the plans for his scuttled European tramp, added that he would make his way to the West Coast on foot, writing dispatches about his experiences along the way.

Ten days later Lummis had Otis's response. The colonel liked the combative spirit Lummis displayed in his writing. He was impressed that Lummis had been willing to take up arms in a good cause. He needed people like that on his staff. Though by some accounts Otis offered to send Lummis a train ticket so that he could get to Los Angeles without delay, he admired the gumption behind Lummis's plan to walk all the way, so he didn't try too hard to talk him out of that.

Lummis surely didn't need any other excuses to pack up his belongings and head west. But that August, he received another kick in the pants that pushed him toward California. He had an attack of malarial fever, endemic in the humid bottomlands of the Ohio River basin. So he quickly wrapped up planning for the trek west.

His employer at the *Scioto Gazette* apparently didn't react favorably to the prospect of being abruptly abandoned, which may explain why Lummis cut a deal with M. J. Carrigan, editor and publisher of the Gazette's rival weekly, the *Chillicothe Leader*, that would help pay for the trip and boost his profile as a writer in the process. Carrigan agreed to buy a letter a week for five dollars each.

Chapter 2

Tramp Across the Continent

What most struck folks in Chillicothe about Charlie Lummis's plan to walk all the way to Los Angeles, as much as the audacity of what he intended to do, was the set of clothes he chose for the trip. After some research and thought on the matter, he concluded that the ideal outfit consisted of a white flannel shirt tied at the neck with a blue ribbon, knickerbockers, red knee-high stockings, a wide-brimmed felt hat, and low-cut Curtis and Wheeler street shoes. Over it all, he would wear a large canvas duck coat.

The coat, at least, was an obvious choice. It had twenty-three pockets in all, and it was big enough to serve as a blanket at night if he got caught without a roof to sleep under before he reached Kansas, where a blanket roll, Winchester rifle, and other supplies that he had shipped ahead by rail awaited him. He picked the shoes because they fit him perfectly and were sturdily put together, and he believed that a higher-topped model would coddle his ankles, preventing them from getting as tough as they would need to be to propel him across the continent. As for the knickerbockers, he said he chose them because he didn't want two extra feet of trouser material flapping loose around his lower legs.

Lummis also must have known they would help attract attention to his tramp, which wouldn't hurt his stock as a young writer making a name for himself. The publicity about his odd attire might come at some cost to his dignity, but he knew that as well. Lummis just didn't mind if people poked fun at him. In fact, defying convention was part of the point, and ridicule came with that territory. In just two years in Chillicothe, he had become a favorite son, well known and loved for his eccentricities. People would have been disappointed if Charlie Lummis had set out for California without making some sort of splash. Carrigan, at the *Leader*, helped him ham it up.

A souvenir photo of Lummis circulated by the *Leader* before his departure depicted an earnest young man, shorn of his long, curly college locks and clean-shaven except for a trim mustache, dressed as if he were headed to a picnic in the Tyrolean Alps. The *Leader* commenced its coverage of "Lummy's" tramp with a tongue-in-cheek story about a local resident named Wenis who had just seen the photo when a reporter encountered him on Second Street in downtown Chillicothe convulsed with hysterical laughter. When he regained his composure, Wenis, who had worked as a cowboy on the range for several years and purported to know exactly what Lummis would face out west, explained, "I was just thinking what a picnic those fellows out on the plains would have with the seat of Lummis' breeches. Did you ever see one of 'em handle a bull-whip? Never did? Why, I tell you one of those fellows can stand off a distance of twenty feet and take those breeches off Lummy with one stroke."

Lummis came in for some more ribbing about his outfit on the night before he officially started his tramp. A friend took him out to the most popular beer garden in Cincinnati, where Lummis was subjected to quizzical stares before one patron asked him what baseball team he was on. At nine o'clock the next morning, September 12, 1884, Lummis started on his way. Until he caught up with the western gear that he had shipped to Kansas, he could travel light, not even bothering with a pack. The pockets of his duck coat held everything he needed: tobacco and his best meerschaum pipe, notebooks and a stylographic pen, a pedometer to tally every step he took, hooks and flies and fishing line, a small-caliber pocket gun, an eight-inch double-edged hunting knife, and a harmonica. Under his clothes he wore a money belt filled with three hundred dollars' worth of two-and-a-half-dollar gold pieces, figuring that showing any larger a denomination in the rough country through which he planned to pass might attract unwanted attention from highway robbers. He rounded out his kit with a "route-book" in which he had plotted a tentative itinerary through all of the towns along his line of march where former residents of Chillicothe had settled. He planned to visit as many of the former townsmen as he could find.

The first installment of his series of letters to the *Leader* was published September 15 reporting on his first two days on the road.[1] "Lummis' Legs," read Carrigan's headline. "How They Measure the Distance Between Cincinnati and Los Angeles. Sixty-three Miles Already Traversed and Only Three Thousand One Hundred and Thirty-Seven Yet to Walk." As he informed his readers, he had gotten an inauspicious start, somehow managing to sprain an ankle even before he left Cincinnati. In compensating for the pain, he had shifted weight to the other foot, and it too began to rebel under the strain of the unaccustomed monotony of taking seventy-five to one hundred thousand steps, or around twenty-five to thirty miles, per day. But he didn't let the pain knock him off his pace. His wounds would just have to heal en route. So he trudged ahead, wincing at every step. As the headline on his second dispatch five days later put it, the "editorial tramp" was "slightly disfigured but still in the ring."

Lummis created quite a stir in some of the midwestern towns through which he passed. More than six hundred people reportedly turned out for his arrival in Vincennes, Indiana. "Lummy's passage through that city just tore up the burg," wrote a former Chillicothe resident in a letter to the *Leader* about the Vincennes hoopla. "Charley Lummis is arousing the natives along his line of march to California to an intense pitch of excitement." The feeling wasn't mutual. As he summed up his trip to that point in a letter mailed from Vincennes, "There was very little along the way worthy of remark."

Lummis didn't have any pretensions to recreating the experience of the first explorers to blaze trails across the continent. He was content to follow the westbound railroad track, stepping aside several times every hour to let a train rumble past.

A few days beyond the crowded, smoky city of St. Louis, Lummis first began to notice that he was entering wilder country, a realization punctuated by his first brushes with danger. In western Missouri, a large dog leapt at him without warning. Lummis drew his hunting knife just in time to catch the lunging animal beneath the throat. He didn't stick around to explain the situation to its owners. "Folks hate to lose a dog like that," he observed. In the same vicinity, a couple of tramps tried to hold him up. This time merely flashing the menacing blade sufficed to chase them off.

Lummis reached Kansas City on October 4, and several days later there was no mistaking that he had reached the Great Plains. He had watched the forests slowly thin out across western Missouri, then drop away altogether not far past the Kansas line. He was overwhelmed by the emptiness of the plains, and by the silence. There were "no trees, no rocks, no nothing. Or rather, I should say an immensity of nothing."

As he got farther west, however, there were new sights to relieve the monotony. A week past Kansas City, "things began to grow more interesting, and new experiences crowded in upon me with delightful rapidity," he wrote. "All in one short day I saw my first [prairie] dog town, my first prairie chicken, my first sage brush, buffalo grass, cactus and ranches." It was in Kansas that Lummis also encountered his first cowboys. He gleefully informed his readers back in Chillicothe that he had survived the experience. To those who "feared that I will be eaten up by cowboys," he had this to say: "They are 'hot stuff,' but I still retain the knee-breeches, thank you, Mr. Wenis."

The conditions for walking were better than ever in the crisp fall weather on the flat plains. He began to click off forty or more miles a day, sometimes starting before dawn when the air was fresh and he could watch the sunrise, which "is nearly as fine as when viewed at sea. Indeed one feels rather at sea as he looks out over this strange country."

He had come west for the scenic wonders, but he was even more interested in the people, regarding every encounter as an opportunity to learn something new. He stayed with local people every night he could, either at a railroad section house, a bunkhouse for cowboys, or any other building where he could stretch out on the floor. The most dependable lodging places, the section houses spaced at regular intervals along the track, offered at best bare-bones accommodation. There were mattresses for rent in some, but they were often infested with fleas and bedbugs. An old gunnysack spread out on the floorboards would serve the purpose on such occasions, or he might make a hollow in the buffalo grass and curl up outside. Farther west, after he had retrieved his blanket, if he found himself at the end of a long day's tramp with no other shelter at all, he would dig a hole in the sand, put his blanket in the hole, tuck himself in, and then pile sand on top.

Lummis stayed with cowboys on a number of occasions. The ranch hands were congenial company, and their cozy quarters at night were a welcome respite from the solitude of the vast plains. He was struck by the depth of the camaraderie that could spring up among strangers whose paths chanced to cross in those lonely spaces. The people he stayed with were genuinely elated to have entertaining company, and no wonder, given their setting. "You can imagine how welcome they find anything new," he observed.

When looking for a place to stay for the night, he was sometimes greeted with suspicion. Normal people, after all, didn't walk across the continent. But singing, one of his favorite pastimes, regularly opened doors for him. "Those roughly rendered songs changed everything," he wrote. Lummis picked up many new songs on the journey, including a railroad tune that would become a lifelong favorite, "Jerry, Go Ile the Car." But the rowdy college songs he brought with him to the West were the biggest hits. Agents at the railroad section houses where he often spent a night took to wiring ahead to tell their colleagues up the line that an unusual "tramp" was headed their way and that when he arrived they should be sure to request a rendition of "Mush, Mush."

Along the way, he met some representatives of the upper echelons of Great Plains society, such as E. W. Wellington, a wealthy young Bostonian with a fifteen-thousand-acre spread in western Kansas. But Lummis didn't have any social conceits. He spent the night on the Wellington ranch in the bunkhouse, singing "until I could howl no longer." It was not until the next morning after he had shared breakfast with the cowboys that the master learned that the visitor who had arrived during the evening was a fellow Harvard man. He invited Lummis over to the "mansion" for a second breakfast, giving the ever curious correspondent a chance to get a rundown on the intricacies and economics of managing eight thousand sheep, three hundred registered cattle, forty horses, and thirty-five men on the Great Plains.

A bit farther west, Lummis spent several days with a forlorn cowboy named Bill Henke. He had just lost everything—money, pistol, even his pony—in a gambling debacle and was at his wits' end in WaKeeney when Lummis passed through. Lummis struck up a conversation with him and learned his story. Henke said he had a brother in Wallace who would "stake him" for long enough to get back on his feet. But Wallace was far to the west, and he had no way to get there. Wallace happened to be right on Lummis's route, so the journalistic tramp suggested that the down-and-out cowboy accompany him on foot. "Nothing could have been more distasteful to this man, who would rather ride an unbroken pony a day than walk a mile, but he seemed to 'cotton to' me, and finally assented." Lummis shared his blanket and provender with Henke for 131 miles to Wallace. He turned out to be a rather agreeable companion and Lum got his money's worth in information. "I found my cowboy a regular directory, and learned 'more than few' from his pithy discourses," he said. Lummis left Henke "in his brother's bosom at Wallace" and resumed his solitary march west.

A big part of the appeal of the plains for Lummis was the opportunity it gave him to hunt exotic game. "Fun with the rifle began" west of WaKeeney. The first sightings of strange new prairie wildlife and the first howl of a coyote soon after he entered Kansas had awakened the hunter impulse in Lummis and left him yearning for his rifle, which he finally picked up at the train depot in WaKeeney. The Winchester added ten pounds to his load, but he didn't mind.

Lummis practically ached for the chance to shoot a coyote or an antelope. But for the first few days after retrieving his rifle, Lummis had to content himself with blasting snakes, tarantulas, hawks, and prairie dogs. The latter he parboiled and roasted, if he was able to retrieve them before they managed, in their death throes, to tumble back into their burrows. He also shot jackrabbits and carried them along to trade for dinner at the next section house.

One morning shortly after crossing into Colorado, he set out into the prairie on a hunting excursion "innocently expecting in this wild country to knock over an antelope every few miles." He finally spotted three specks that he took to be antelopes several miles away. Even though he used every trick he had learned by hearsay about how to stalk an antelope, it took him all day to get close enough to squeeze off a few rounds. He managed to bag two of them but was sorely disappointed with himself for missing the third. He slung one over his shoulders and headed back toward the tracks. But after just a few steps under that load, Lummis made some calculations and realized that the sixty-pound animal would total some twenty-six million pounds by the time he stepped off the last of the twenty or so miles back to the railroad. So he cut off the horns of the two antelopes for souvenirs, carved out a three-pound steak, spent an hour scrounging up enough fuel on the bare plain for a fire, and had his dinner on the spot.

Even while he was fattening up every buzzard along his route with the carcasses strewn in his wake, Lummis found time to lament the decimation of the "noble buffalo." Vast herds had still blackened the Great Plains little more than a decade before he passed through. By the mid-1880s, there were a few stragglers left, and whenever one was found, it too was finished off. Just a week before Lummis was in the vicinity, an old bull was shot and killed near Cheyenne Wells. Traces of the age of the buffalo—deep-cut trails, and bowl-like depressions in the turf where the shaggy brutes had wallowed—were still abundant. But the "skin-hunter, the pot-hunter, and worst of all the soulless fellows who kill for the mere sport of killing, have thinned out this noble game almost to the limit of extinction." Lummis's lament undoubtedly was tinged at least in part by regret that he didn't have a chance to shoot one of the beasts himself.

Years later, when he encountered a stranger on a train who bragged that he had killed 9,980 quail in the previous year, Lummis was moved to remark that there is a difference between hunters and butchers. But he went on to admit that his urge to hunt knew few bounds. "The man is to be pitied," he wrote, "who has never known that splendid orgasm when, between two twinkles of the eye and two flashes of antlered fray amid the bushes, arms and eye and a little octagon of steel have leapt together and made a Conquest." As he put it in one of the letters during his tramp, "I suppose nothing short of a broken neck will ever hold me down when game is around." The sight of fresh animal tracks "wakes all the wild desire that has come down to us from the days when our forefathers lived by bow and arrow; when meat was the only food, and the passion of the chase was the essence and guarantee of life."

The letter that Lummis mailed to the *Leader* on October 16 was the longest yet. Carrigan gave it one of his usual chatty headlines: "Camping Out: 'Lummy' Begins to Realize the Charm of the Beautiful West." It went on for five thousand words, and even then Lummis lamented, "I can not begin to tell you half of the interesting things I encounter at almost every step. This letter is too long already, and I am just getting fairly started." Lummis mailed that letter from First View, Colorado, a town that, as the name implies, is supposed to afford travelers their first glimpse of the Rockies. Lummis pronounced the claim a fraud. "They showed me a little white cloud which they said was Pike's Peak, 150 miles away. If it was, then Pike's Peak is portable, for I saw that cloud float a mile."

To disabuse his readers of the notion that the Great Plains was a pastoral paradise, he had plenty of hardships to report. The region was a land of diabolical stinging plants, such as bull nettles, cockleburs, sandburs, and prickly pear, not to mention prairie fires and grasshopper plagues. And then there was the relentless wind. "What is here an everyday breeze would make all Chillicothe hunt for a cellar," he wrote.

Water was scarce. He had long since added a quart bottle to his baggage. And food for travelers was meager and expensive at best. A typical section house dinner consisted of tough corned beef, hard bread, muddy coffee, fermented molasses, butter "which needs no testimonial from me, being old enough to speak for itself," and watery potatoes. The cost: twenty-five cents, "or if it is unusually bad, 35 cents." The game he killed, therefore, was a welcome supplement to the dreary diet, though his compulsion to hunt went well beyond his need for sustenance.

Despite the hardships, just over a month into his trek to the Pacific he was stronger than ever, he reassured his readers. "I am robust as a young bison, myself," he declared. Sleeping outdoors is a "glorious tonic." He reckoned that his feet were so tough by that point that he could stand on a live coal and not know it. The trek had returned him to top physical form, arresting a decline that had been under way ever since he had left behind the daily athletic regimen of his college years. His razor-sharp vision, which had been "sawed short by years of burning the midnight oil," had been restored. "My lungs are expanding, my eyes are good for three times their ordinary range, and every muscle is strung like steel," he declared.

A few days later Lummis strode into Denver. Though it was only twenty-five years old, the boomtown boasted a population of 75,000, well over twice the size of his destination, Los Angeles. He checked into a relatively luxurious hotel, the Windsor, where for the first time on his tramp Lummis planned to rest for a few days. He had an excuse to linger. In Denver he and "Dr. Lummis" had plans to rendezvous, he told his readers. Dorothea, who was traveling with her mother and a friend, stopped off in Denver on the way to Los Angeles, where she intended to settle in and open her medical practice in advance of his arrival. Carrigan headlined the letter Lummis sent from Denver, "The

Journalistic Tramp Rests His Wearied Head Upon the Backbone of the Continent." There his lungs were "Inflated with Invigorating Mountain Air, and His Stomach with a Few Square Hotel Meals."

There was, to be sure, no word about fresh air in his descriptions of the Queen City of the Plains. "Abominable smoke" obscured any view of the mountains two-thirds of the time, Lummis observed. And the hotel food apparently made him sick. "My internal economy was completely taken by surprise by all the richness after 400 miles of scaly provender," he observed. But the moments of relaxation allowed him to reflect on how far he had come, and ready himself for the rest of the trip. "The backbone of the continent! Surely a phrase more accurately expressive was never coined," he wrote. "For six weeks tonight I have been toiling over the scaly hide of this insensate monster we call North America; and tonight I look up from my window to where the crescent moon lies like a tiny silver saddle on the vast, rugged, rocky vertebrae of the sleeping Titan."

He was 1,261 miles west of Chillicothe, though he had walked, by his pedometer's reckoning, 1,418 miles to get there, with his hunting detours included. His attire had fared well, he was happy to report. He was still swearing by his choice of footgear. Though he had worn out several pairs of soles already, he had no reason to believe the shoes wouldn't carry him all the way to the coast. He was also standing by his knickers. But he did make several concessions to his new environs. He traded in his .28-caliber pocket revolver for a hefty .44-caliber Remington six-shooter, which used the same size ammunition as his Winchester rifle. He also made another change, swapping the felt hat that had served him well back east for a western replacement, a fine new Stetson sombrero.

Beyond Denver, Lummis made a dramatic course correction in his tramp to the Pacific. He turned due south. In his letter to the *Leader*, he explained the left turn by noting that snow had blocked the westerly route he had been following, which would have taken him directly over the front range of the Rockies into Utah. But it's hard to imagine that he hadn't planned to veer south all along. Two men whom Lummis greatly admired—his favorite boyhood novelist Captain Mayne Reid and the offbeat but respected anthropologist Frank Cushing—had stoked his wanderlust with stories of their exploits in New Mexico. At that point in his career, Lummis could only dream of emulating Reid and Cushing. But he figured he could learn more about them by visiting their favorite haunts.

So, after seeing Dolly and her mother and friend off on a train for California, Lummis turned toward New Mexico and left behind the smoky pall hanging over Denver. He couldn't resist making a detour into the mountains east of Colorado Springs to catch trout and to put a feather in his cap by scaling Pike's Peak. Back out on the plains, he continued south.

In the vicinity of Pueblo, Colorado, Lummis gained a companion. It was a greyhound pup that had been abandoned by a miner at a railroad section house where Lummis spent a night. The mistreated, half-starved dog wouldn't let Lummis get anywhere near him, but the traveler took a liking to him and decided to take him along. The section hands were only too happy to get rid of the creature. So the next morning Lummis resumed his tramp dragging the unwilling dog on a string. Within a few days the two had established enough of a rapport that Lummis turned him loose. He earned a name, Shadow, by "tagging along at my heels in solemn gratitude."

South of Pueblo, Lummis set his sights on Spanish Peaks, a pair of summits that loomed on the horizon like "two great blue islands rising from the level distance of the plains, lovely and glorious." Soaring more than 12,500 feet high in the northern reaches of the Sangre de Cristo Mountains, they were an important pilot point in the days of the Santa Fe Trail, visible from a distance of a hundred miles out into the plains. When they drew near the peaks, wagons from the east turned south, skirting the mountain range and following a relatively flat route the rest of the way to Santa Fe. But when Lummis reached the foot of Spanish Peaks, instead of following the still-fresh traces of the Santa Fe Trail to the former New Mexico capital, he turned due west, intent on taking a more difficult route into New Mexico by way of La Veta Pass. Though he never mentioned it in any of his accounts of the tramp, Lummis almost certainly was influenced in this routing decision by Mayne Reid. One of Reid's novels, *The White Chief*, was set in an imaginary Mexican community called San Ildefonso at the foot of Spanish Peaks, and the opening scene unfolds in La Veta Pass.

Lummis never contended that Reid produced great literature. But he acknowledged a deep debt to the novelist. "We have better writers,"

Lummis remarked in an appreciation that he wrote years later. "But we have not yet had one who knew the land so well and loved it so deeply and could make his love so contagious."

An Irishman and the son of a minister, Reid had quenched his own youthful wanderlust by hopping on a ship to New Orleans when he was twenty. He served with the Texas volunteers in the Mexican War and lived among the Indians in the Red River country for five years—adopted as one of their own, it was said—before returning to Ireland, where he retired to the life of an author of adventure novels, most of them set in the American Southwest.

Reid died in 1883, but not before Lummis had a chance to exchange letters with his boyhood idol. He was one of the writers to whom Lummis sent a copy of *Birch Bark Poems*. Reid responded with a letter in May 1883, thanking Lummis for the "sweet appropriate verses printed in this quaint page of Nature." Aged sixty-five at the time and in declining health, Reid went on to tell Lummis, who had just turned twenty-four, how lucky he was. "America is . . . the land of novelties, as it is that of my love and longings; and you are to be envied—perhaps you know not how much—for being able to claim it as your home," Reid wrote. "I only wish—fervently wish—I could say the same for myself; but, alas! my disabled state may hinder me from ever again seeing that far, fair land of the West, so endeared to me by early recollection."[2] Reid died five months later, and less than a year after that, Lummis set out on his tramp.

Lummis first crossed paths with his other hero of the Southwest, Frank Cushing, two years before he began planning his trek to the Pacific. One of the first anthropologists sent into the field by the Smithsonian Institution's Bureau of American Ethnology, Cushing had gained considerable notoriety by the early 1880s for "going Indian" while he was based in the Zuni pueblo in western New Mexico. His white colleagues, dismayed and concerned that he had become just a little too close to the savages, had effectively abandoned him in 1879, leaving him at the mercy of the Zunis during a hard winter when he was cut off from supplies.[3]

The Indians had their own suspicions about the odd blond fellow marooned in their midst who carried a notebook with him and filled it with scribble and sketches everywhere he went. But Cushing proved his devotion—and value—to the tribe over time. He was an effective mediator in dealings with government officials and neighboring whites. And most impressive of all to the Indians, he didn't shy away from using deadly force to help fend off intrusions by Apache raiders and white horse thieves alike. Ultimately he was adopted as a full-fledged member of the tribe and was given the name Te-na-tsa-li, Medicine Flower.

Cushing was later inducted into the Bow Priesthood. Before he could enter that elite circle, guardian of the innermost secrets of the tribe, he was required to take a scalp, a task he accomplished when a Zuni party he was accompanying was attacked by a group of Apache raiders, two of whom were killed in the skirmish. Those exploits secured his status among the Zunis, who named him First War Chief in the fall of 1881.

All the while, Cushing continued to produce groundbreaking anthropological studies of everything about the Zuni from their bread-making methods to their creation myths. In the process Cushing, who could make arrowheads and practice other Indian crafts better than most Indians, pioneered the participant-observer style of anthropology used by generations of researchers who followed him.

Lummis first saw the anthropologist—and probably first heard of him—in the spring of 1882 when Medicine Flower paid a visit to Harvard's Hemenway Gymnasium. It had been nearly a year since Lummis had dropped out of Harvard, but he was still hanging around the campus, picking up odd tutoring jobs and juggling his strange marriage to Dolly. On the day he saw Cushing, he had gone to the gym to watch the boxing matches that were part of the Spring Meeting of the Harvard Athletic Association. Cushing had apparently been booked as a sort of halftime entertainment. He was only two years older than Lummis, but here was a man who had clearly found his place in the world.

"A slender young man with long yellow hair and an almost unearthly ambidexterity of utterance," Te-na-tsa-li entered the gym in full Zuni regalia with his bead- and feather-bedecked brown brethren in a single file behind him, beating drums and chanting in a rhythmic cadence, Lummis recalled.[4] After threading his way through the crowd to the ring, Cushing "harangued the multitude, and then promoted and presided over a strange ceremonial dance."

The "white Indian" and his band of Zunis were a big hit in New England that spring, and helped turn Lummis's thoughts toward a region that he may have never considered visiting before that. "His personal magnetism, his witchcraft of speech, his ardor, his wisdom in the unknowabilities, the undoubted romance of his life of research among 'wild Indians of the frontier' . . . all were contagious," Lummis wrote.

After returning to Zuni later that year, Cushing found himself on the Indians' side of a land war in which he angered a powerful U.S. senator, who leaned on the Smithsonian to recall Cushing. The order calling him back to Washington reached him at the start of 1884. So Lummis wouldn't have had a chance to meet him in the field. But on his tramp, he hoped to be able to swing through Zuni and see for himself where his hero had lived.

From Reid and Cushing, Lummis absorbed a thoroughly jumbled mixture of views about the people he would encounter in the Southwest.

Reid's Indians were mostly of the treacherous savage sort, though there were noble leaders among them. And yet all Indians, in Reid's view, were amenable to civilizing influence.[5] Some entire tribes of Indians, such as the Seminoles in one of his novels that was set in Florida, were morally superior to the greedy, bloodthirsty whites who invaded their homeland. Even the most primitive tribes could lift themselves to a level of social respectability under American leadership, Reid believed. The common enemies of both the Anglo-Americans and the Indians were the Mexicans and their oppressive Catholic faith. The Indians in *The White Chief*, for instance, realized that "their deliverers from the yoke of Spanish tyranny would yet come from the East—from beyond the Great Plains." In his life, Reid was something of a crusader for Indian rights, though he clearly believed that they would have to make their future on a continent that, fortunately for all concerned, had succumbed to American domination.

Cushing's Zuni Indians were cast more in the romantic-savage mold. But his view of Indians from in their midst wasn't nearly as simplistic as that of others who viewed them from afar. In his attitude toward the Zunis' age-old enemies the Apaches, for example, he could express his distaste in terms every bit as strong as the language used by the most genocidal of whites. But the Zunis were a different breed. Their ancient way of life was a repository of secrets about interpersonal relations and social organization that could save white society from its alienating and other self-destructive tendencies, he believed. And so in any future merger of the races into a common nation and culture, the Indians must be allowed, for the good of everyone, to retain something of their own identity.

There was no ambiguity in the lessons that Lummis had absorbed about Mexicans, Spanish influence in North America, and Catholicism. Many of Reid's southwestern novels had a brave and beautiful Mexican heroine who would fall in love with the American protagonist. His books also featured the occasional dignified Mexican aristocrat who would secretly ally himself with the Americans. But most Mexicans in Reid's novels were irredeemably bad.

Contempt for "greasers" had been a standard feature of reports sent back by American travelers from the southwestern frontier for years, ever since the newly independent Mexican Republic in 1821 opened its borders to trade with the Americans. Washington Irving and Frederick Law Olmsted, who published accounts of their travels in Spanish America in the mid-nineteenth century, had virtually nothing good to say about the Spanish-speaking denizens of the region. The American trader Albert Pike described New Mexicans as "a lazy gossiping people always lounging on their blankets and smoking cigarillos," a race "peculiarly blessed with ugliness." Another Santa Fe Trail trader, Josiah Gregg, added that New Mexicans lived "in darkness and ignorance" and had "inherited much of the cruelty and intolerance of their ancestors, and no small portion of their bigotry and fanaticism."

On his way up the mountainside toward La Veta Pass, Lummis could tell he wouldn't have any opportunity to relive the opening scene of *The White Chief*, in which the narrator gazes across the vast plains to the east, then turns to peer into the enchanted land of Nuevo Mexico to the west. When he reached the top, clouds shrouded the mountains and a "marrow-chilling" wind stung his face with sleet and snow. It was the first taste of hard winter weather that he got on the tramp. He could hardly make out the trail, much less the view of the surrounding country, so he didn't even pause at the summit as he hurried to the other side.

After a couple of days with some congenial American trappers on the western side of the pass, Lummis proceeded to Alamosa, Colorado, where he got his first look at the Rio Grande, spent a night in a hotel, and sent a letter to the *Leader* telling about his first impressions of Spanish America.

He had first noticed that he was entering a new world as he approached Spanish Peaks. "The day was full of interest to me, for in it, I stepped across the line from an alleged American civilization into the boundaries of one strangely diverse," he wrote. His first encounter with Mexicans in their native habitat, a settlement on the banks of Cucharas Creek, confirmed what Reid's novels had taught him to expect. "The Mexicans themselves are a snide-looking set, twice as dark as an Indian with heavy lips and noses, long, straight black hair, sleepy eyes, and a general expression of ineffable laziness," he wrote in his November 18 letter from Alamosa, concluding with an especially nasty joke. "Not even a coyote will touch a dead Greaser, the flesh is so seasoned with the red pepper they ram into their food in howling profusion."

Lummis reported that their dwellings were as pathetic as the people themselves. In that first village he came across, the Mexicans resided in a rambling "mud shed" surrounding a plaza. "In it, in lousy laziness, exist 200 Greasers of all sexes, ages and size, but all equally dirty." The building, "if it can be dignified by such a title," was an adobe, he explained.

What distinguishes Lummis from most other visitors to Spanish America who had published similar venomous attacks is that he changed his mind.[6] A dramatic transformation began almost immediately. His prejudices simply couldn't last, traveling the way he did on foot with little more than a blanket, a rifle, and a duck coat to protect him from the elements, depending on the willingness of strangers to provide him with food and shelter. Lummis knew hospitality when he experienced it, and he certainly wasn't getting it from the whites.

He got a dose of gringo-style hospitality a day before passing that Mexican adobe on Cucharas Creek. It was after dark in bone-chilling weather, but he was denied entry by the suspicious white occupants of one dwelling after another. Finally a group of Italian railroad workers who had taken shelter in a boxcar made room for him. "I looked at them rather sharply, for Italians don't bear the best reputation in the world, and then accepted their offer," he wrote. Lummis was astonished when one of the men loaned him two of his three blankets. "Any man who goes to running down Italians after that has me to climb. . . . It will be a long day before I forget the simple but honest kindness of my unknown Italian friend that cheerless night," he said.

By the time Lummis mailed his second letter to the *Leader* from Spanish America, he had been the recipient of similar acts of unexpected kindness from many poor Mexicans he encountered, and the transformation of his attitude toward that maligned race was well under way. "I find the 'Greasers' not half bad people," he wrote, distancing himself from the epithet by putting it in quotation marks this time. The white man "will share your last dollar with you," Lummis added. "The Mexican, on the other hand, will 'divvy' up his only tortilla and his one blanket with any stranger, and never take a cent." Within a week of his arrival in Spanish America he had begun to flesh out a theme that he would preach for the rest of his life, that Mexicans are "one of the kindliest races in the world."

Lummis's opinion of adobe also underwent an abrupt transformation. In his second letter from the Southwest, he sought to retract the aspersions he had cast upon the lowly-looking building material in his previous dispatch. "Don't let yourself be fooled by nincompoop correspondents who write back home about 'mud houses.' These adobes are made of baked dirt, it is true," he pointed out, but so are houses in the East. "The sole difference is, that you roast your clay with a fire, and these people let the sun do their brick-burning." Adobe was perfectly suited to the climatic conditions of the Southwest, he went on to explain. To cope with the extremes of temperature from day to night and from summer to winter, a three-foot-thick insulating wall of adobe bricks would "knock the socks off" any other building material in every respect but looks.

Lummis was slower to acquire a taste for chile peppers, though that came along soon enough. But he began to pick up Spanish immediately, a relatively easy feat for one who had been steeped in Latin from the age of seven. Two weeks after crossing over La Veta Pass, he could testify, "I have sworn in a posse of about twenty words, and handle them with the easy grace of a cow shinnying up an apple tree tail first." Even a limited vocabulary was invaluable in opening up doors to homes and hearts, but he was adding dozens of new words a day. He first dropped a word of Spanish on the readers of the *Leader* in his letter from Alamosa, which he concluded with "adios." A month later, he signed off "Buena suerte a todos," and two weeks after that, in his letter datelined New Year's Day of 1885, Lummis proclaimed, "Deseo a V. un muy feliz ano nuevo!"

Lummis's first contact with a group of New Mexico Indians came in a store in Espanola, twenty miles north of Santa Fe. They were an unimpressive bunch, crowding into the store to buy whisky and tobacco, "keeping up an incessant jabber." But the unfavorable first impression didn't have time to sink in. That night Lummis made it to San Ildefonso, a name that Reid had borrowed for his Mexican town at the foot of Spanish Peaks but that in fact was an ancient village of the Pueblos in the bottomlands of the Rio Grande. When Lummis asked around for a place to stay, he was ushered to the governor's house, where the odd white stranger was given the best place in the house to sleep— the floor in front of the stove next to the governor's children. For dinner, he was plied with platters of venison and red-hot chile peppers, tortillas, and coffee.

He couldn't recall a time when he was treated with such kindness. The Pueblos' homes, which in the ancient fashion were separate units in a sprawling, multistoried communal adobe, were "neat and attractive." Of these first Pueblos that he observed up close, Lummis said they were "the best looking Indians I ever saw," not to mention "intelligent, rather neat and industrious after their own funny fashion." He was especially impressed with how well-behaved and happy the children were, despite the fact that he saw no sign of discipline imposed by the adults. "I have seen 300 tiny Pueblos, and I never heard one of them screeching," he marveled.

He didn't explain how he was able to offer the following assessment after just a few days, but he added, "A loose woman is a thing unknown among the Pueblos." Shrewd but fair as traders, they were so honest that a package left unclaimed on a station platform in Pueblo country would stay there unmolested for weeks. "I wish they would send out missionaries to their American brothers," Lummis concluded.

Lummis walked into Santa Fe after dark on November 25. By then his tramp was a minor national sensation. His letters to the *Leader* had been picked up by a number of other papers. The dispatches were "a bonanza to the newspapers," as one editor put it.[7] "Somehow the articles have a strange, indescribable interest and people have got to talking about Lum all over the country. He is the most noted man in the West just now and carries in his shoes a pretty fair-sized circus."

His arrival in Santa Fe made the front page of the next day's *New Mexican*. "Mr. C.F. Lummis, an Ohio journalist with a penchant for athletic sports, tramped up San Francisco street at 8 o'clock last night carrying a rifle, a fishing rod, a gum coat and about 30 pounds of baggage," the story began.

The "journalistic tramp" was a "bold vigorous and spry writer" who had been zigzagging through mountains and valleys on his way to a job at the *Los Angeles Times*, never failing each Wednesday to send a letter back to the *Chillicothe Leader*, the story noted. "Small in stature, spare of figure, light hair, blue eyes, a dainty mustache, close cropped hair and a high forehead, wearing knickerbockers and red hose conveys something of an idea of the young man's general appearance. One remarkable feature is found in the fact that he has made the whole trip in low-quartered shoes, which must have been most trying upon the ankles. He has neither lost nor gained in weight. His legs are slender and his muscles are as hard as iron. At first sight he looks all forehead and feet."

Lummis was as taken with Santa Fe as the town was with him. It was the most exotic place he had ever seen, even though its heyday had come and gone. Five years earlier the Santa Fe Trail had been shut down for good when the railroad reached the Rio Grande valley. The railroad had further marginalized the aging territorial capital by establishing the nearest depot at a rail junction in Lamy, eighteen miles away. By late 1884 the town was underpopulated and many of its buildings were vacant. The best hope for a revival lay in plans to develop the town as a health and pleasure resort for easterners looking for a change of environment.

Santa Fe's somnolence must have given it all the more the appearance of a city that had popped up out of the earth. With its adobe walls made of the same material as the dirt streets, it looked like an "assemblage of mole hills," as a visitor in 1839 had put it. Echoing that assessment, Lummis described Santa Fe as a "flat little town of dried mud."

Lummis had a sizable welcoming committee in Santa Fe. A substantial little community of Chillicotheans had settled in the area. They had been reading of Lummis's march across the plains in copies of the *Leader* mailed from home, and they were eagerly anticipating his arrival. So from the moment that he presented himself at A. C. "Phon" Ireland's drugstore, he was treated like a hero come home. A stack of mail was waiting for him. That evening he had a shave, a bath, and a "bill of fare fit for a king."

The next day, on looking around, he found plenty of life in the little town, fascinating vestiges of an old and rich local culture. Intending to stay for a couple of days, Lummis ended up falling in love with Santa Fe and staying for more than a week.

The narrow, unpaved streets "were full of interest," he wrote in his letter from Santa Fe. He was especially amazed by the diversity of the town's inhabitants. "You meet so many different types of humanity—and some of them types that are new to you. And in a bunch you may run across Yankee, Frenchmen, German, Mexican, Spanish—for there are a few real Castillians—Indian and Negro, not to mention English, Irish, and Scotch representatives." There were also conspicuous numbers of a more obnoxious breed: eastern tourists. "I don't know why it is that folks who have good horse sense back at home in Boston, New York, or Cincinnati, can't get out here without turning to doddering imbeciles—but it seems they can't," Lummis wrote, describing how they gaped openmouthed at Indians and snapped up cheap trinkets thinking they were authentic artifacts.

Lummis was an eastern tourist, too, of course. But on the long, hard walk west, he had begun to shed his eastern skin—without losing all of his Yankee inclinations. He had a mixed opinion of the upper echelons of Spanish American society in New Mexico. It was not a particularly enterprising group, he observed, judging from the fertile but empty farmland that surrounded Santa Fe. All the region needed to become "one of the garden spots of the world" was some eastern capital and a few Yankees with the initiative to drill some artesian wells. The moneyed old families of Santa Fe had the resources to take on such a project, but the effort was more than they cared to be bothered with. They "are well enough fixed, and don't care to stir up new enterprises so long as they can sit still and loan their money at 12 per cent and upward," Lummis observed.

He summed up the story of how the Hispano elite's ancestors came to the Southwest in a few casual remarks about the Spanish Conquest. The conquistadors came in waves through the 1500s, and as their descendants settled in, they behaved just like "Southern Democrats, every mother's son of them, for they stuffed the ballot boxes, bulldozed the majority and kept the poor Pueblos down in regular slave fashion." During the bloody Pueblo Revolt of 1680, the Indians "ran their oppressors out at the end of a pointed stick." But twelve years later the Spanish returned and "gobbled" New Mexico once again.

Lummis's glib summary wasn't far off the mark. The Conquest had been brutal indeed. But that passage in his letter from Santa Fe turned out to be, for Lummis, a rare expression of unmitigated criticism of

Spain. Realizing within a few days of this arrival in the Southwest how skewed his own views of Spanish Americans had been, he took it upon himself to correct the imbalance by doing what he could to tip the scales in the other direction.

Already he was meeting exemplary representatives of the Spanish American elite through whom he could tell a different story about their role in the region's history. One was Pedro Sanchez, the U.S. Indian agent for the Pueblos. Don Pedro had a degree of sympathy for the Indians that few white Indian agents ever displayed, Lummis noted. "Unlike the average Indian Agent, whose highest use of the red man is to skin him alive, the Don is very plainly putting his whole energy and attention to such honest endeavor as is doing vast good," he wrote.

A few days later Lummis was introduced to the scion of one of the oldest and most influential Spanish American families in New Mexico, Amado Chaves, who had recently served as speaker of the Territorial Legislature. An eastern-educated liberal, Chaves took immediately to the brash and adventurous Lummis. Upon hearing that Lummis was fascinated by Indian artifacts, an interest that had been kindled by his finds in the fields around Chillicothe, Chaves invited Lummis to visit his family's estate in western New Mexico on his way to California. Chaves had recently discovered the buried ruins of an ancient Indian pueblo not far from his home. Perhaps Lummis would like to try his hand at excavating, Chaves suggested. Needless to say, Lummis could hardly contain his excitement. "This is apt to be the richest find on my whole trip, for the place has never been described nor even visited by scientists," Lummis exclaimed. It was a remark that would prove to be prescient in more ways than Lummis could have imagined.

Leaving Santa Fe "was as hard as breaking away from your best girl at 11:45 P.M., when she puts her soft arms around your neck and says, 'Oh, George, it is real early yet. Please don't go'," Lummis wrote. But other adventures beckoned as he headed out of the old New Mexico capital on December 3. Besides, he was starting to feel some pressure to complete his tramp. Otis had notified him that one of his editors had gotten sick. He was anxious to know exactly when he could expect Lummis to show up. And Dorothea had reached Los Angeles nearly a month earlier. Her first letter from his future hometown piqued his curiosity.[8] The air was "soft and warm and sweet," she wrote the day she arrived, though the town was "a kind of irrigated oasis in the sand," and in the surrounding countryside "one must resign once and forever all hopes of what we call greenness." The prices were "fiendish," Dorothea added, and as for Otis, she had learned that he was smart but unprincipled. She was also anxiously awaiting her husband's arrival. "You don't know, sweetheart, how much of the old and marvelous light of our early love and marriage still lives and lightens my sometimes weary and often worldly heart," she wrote, in the letter that was awaiting him in Santa Fe. "I know I was too romantic then. . . . Must I let it go? It is for you to say."

Back on the road after his eight-day respite, Lummis sported a new look. He was wearing "a handsome pair of buckskin leggins made for some Apache dude." He had changed his attire "with all due respect for the knickerbockers," he assured his readers. In fact, he was still carrying the knickers and reserved the option of donning them once again as soon as he reached the Mojave Desert. But now, even though it was still unseasonably warm in New Mexico, he knew hard winter weather would hit anytime. Crossing over La Veta Pass, he had been forced to acknowledge that the knickers simply weren't up to the challenge of a western winter. Besides, it was clear from his ardent description that his fascination with the Apache garment had quickly displaced his attachment to the knickers.

They were as soft as velvet and skin tight from the ankle up with a two-foot fringe of thong running down the outside seam of each leg. "I'd just like to walk into Chillicothe with my recent outfit and see the small boys skin over the back fences holding on to their scalps with both hands," he wrote. More pertinent to his immediate needs, he observed, "The wind might just as well try to blow open a burglar-proof safe as to get through these things."

Lummis reached Golden, the next destination he had marked in his route book, after a two-day walk. The town didn't amount to much, at least not yet. It had a population of several thousand, but many of those residents were scattered on mining claims that spotted the desert for miles around. Golden had been on Lummis's tentative itinerary since before he left on his tramp. Its chief claim to fame was a violent, protracted mining-rights dispute that had gained national notoriety. The villain in the story was the so-called Santa Fe Ring, a group of "unscrupulous and wealthy scoundrels" composed of many of the leading American politicians in the territory. They had taken advantage of uncertainty over the status of Spanish-era land grants to encroach on mining claims staked out by scrappy but politically powerless prospectors. The heroes, whom Lummis especially wanted to meet, were Colonel R. W. Webb and his wife, publishers of a crusading weekly newspaper, the *Golden Retort*, and the "champion of the miners, and the idol of every poor man in the territory," Lummis wrote.

With the *Retort* rallying support for their cause, the miners eventually won and were awaiting the formality of a final court ruling when Lummis arrived. The *Retort* had ceased publication a few months earlier and the Webbs had left town. So Lummis didn't get to meet the courageous editors. But he was looking forward to spending a day or two exploring the mines before moving on.

The weather changed that plan. The Southwest had been unusually warm and dry all fall. But on the day Lummis reached Golden, a massive cold front blew in from the west, and a "howling storm" descended on New Mexico. The snow didn't let up for more than week. By December 16 the *Santa Fe New Mexican* was reporting that the snowfall was the heaviest in memory. For the first time in the history of the Atchison, Topeka & Santa Fe Railroad, snowdrifts shut down the tracks. It took a locomotive fitted with a snowplow and five hundred men working for several days to break the blockade.

Lummis spent his time in Golden delving into the history of the war over mining rights. The little guys seemed to have won in that instance. But having learned of a similar dispute in Colorado with a different outcome, Lummis wasn't optimistic about the ability of miners to withstand determined monopolists. "Let the poor man strike it rich, and a hundred hands are outstretched to oust him from his claim," he wrote. "I believe that only violence will work the desperate remedy. Monopoly is a disease that does not cure itself. . . . Within a generation we will see something warmer than ink spilled."

As for Golden itself, the small town had "an 18-carat future," Lummis concluded after a brief stint in a mine. Even in his clumsy first attempt at mining—hauling buckets of ore out of a shaft, crushing and washing it—he ended up with a tiny but entrancing pile of gold dust. Lummis had studiously avoided overly effusive enthusiasm for the West—until then. At the sight of the telltale glint of gold in the bottom of a pan, he threw caution to the wind. Whole mountain ranges in the region were made of precious minerals and semiprecious stone, he wrote. He had seen for himself tunnels that were "gorgeously decorated" with glittering formations of copper, turquoise, and gold-bearing quartz. "Now is the time to come in here," he declared in his letter from Golden. Valuable claims could be bought "for a song." A miner with even primitive equipment would make decent money, but a "princely fortune" awaited anyone with the wherewithal to set up a hydraulic mining rig. Golden couldn't help but have ten thousand people in two to three years, Lummis predicted. In fact two years later, when he returned with Dolly, Golden was already headed toward becoming the virtual ghost town that it is today.

To get from Golden to his next stop, Albuquerque, Lummis could have backtracked to the Rio Grande valley and strolled down the tracks. But instead, on advice from locals, he chose a route to the south, looping around the back side of the Sandia Mountains through Tijeras to Albuquerque, which was twenty-one miles shorter and offered better scenery to boot. The choice nearly proved fatal, as Lummis would tell it in the book he wrote about his tramp six years later. In his letter to the *Leader* immediately after that leg of the trip, Lummis described the ordeal in less melodramatic terms. But clearly it was a hard slog through snow that was much deeper than the locals who had recommended the route realized.

A big disadvantage of his low-cut shoes quickly became apparent that day. As he plunged through ever-deepening drifts, they filled with slush. He found an old gunnysack in an abandoned miner's cabin, cut it into strips, bound up his shoes and ankles, and kept going, eventually breaking through and reaching Albuquerque. Lummis stayed for two nights, giving himself one full day to catch up on his writing at a borrowed desk in the office of the *Albuquerque Democrat*.

Leaving Albuquerque, Lummis headed thirteen miles south to the junction of the Rio Grande and Atlantic & Pacific Railroads adjacent to the pueblo of Isleta, which he explored for a few hours and pronounced "tolerably interesting." Then he followed the A&P tracks up the long grade of the Western Mesa out of the Rio Grande valley, resuming his twenty-five- to thirty-mile-per-day pace, stopping for the night in railroad section houses, pausing here and there for brief detours to inspect sights close to his line of march. He couldn't resist filling the empty spaces in the pockets of his duck coat with agates and chunks of petrified wood that were strewn everywhere on parts of the route, even though they weighed him down.

A few days west of the Rio Grande, Lummis spent several hours preparing his strangest clothing accessory yet. He had been itching to shoot a coyote for weeks but never got within rifle range of one. In western New Mexico, however, he managed to kill a coyote with poison that he mixed with lard and left outside a section house overnight. The next morning, he amazed the railroad workers by "casing" the animal, skinning it in such a way that the hide remained intact. He spent hours gathering enough dry grass in the barren desert to stuff it so that it would dry en route. Then, slinging the animal over his shoulders like a shawl, he continued on his way.

By this point in his tramp, Lummis no longer looked anything like the spiffy fellow with the felt hat and knickers portrayed in the souvenir photo handed out by the *Leader*. He had decided to forgo shaving until he reached Los Angeles, so he had a beard for one of the few times in his life. To cut down on weight, he had traded his ten-pound Winchester rifle for a second Colt revolver, so that he now had two of the six-shooters strapped around his waist. He had a skunk pelt dangling from his bedroll, a rattlesnake skin wrapped around the crown of his sombrero, the Apache leggings, and a stuffed coyote around his neck.

As he told it, he looked strange enough to upstage a colorful crowd of celebrants at the Laguna pueblo when he strolled into the village on Christmas Day. They were in full feathered regalia, performing the Corn Dance before an audience of a thousand Indians, when Lummis walked down the main street and took his place among the spectators to watch for a while. He amused the children by jiggling the coyote while making growling sounds. The people of Laguna must have thought that the "wild man of the plains" had dropped by for a visit, Lummis remarked. Lummis made no mention of the coyote after that. The uncured skin of a dead animal probably emitted a horrific stench after a day or two and was unceremoniously discarded after it served its purpose as a crowd pleaser at the Corn Dance.

A day later Lummis reached Grants, a depot on the train line due south of San Mateo, the town near the Chaves family home. Since the visit to their home was a detour that didn't contribute a single step to his forward progress, Lummis accepted a ride in a wagon filled with groceries that a family servant was taking back with him from Grants.

The wagon got stuck in a streambed along the way, and the servant had to fetch a fresh team of horses, so Lummis didn't reach the Chaves hacienda until well past midnight. His late arrival after that long, cold wagon trip must have made it seem all the more like an oasis of warmth and family hospitality.

Amado had been called away on business, so he missed Lummis's visit. But there were sixteen others members of the extended family on hand, including the elderly patriarch of the clan, Colonel Manuel Chaves. Amado had told them to expect the visitor, to treat him like a member of the family, and to show him to the nearby ruin. He had an unforgettable time. The letter that Lummis wrote describing his stay with the Chaves clan was the longest of the trip, more than five thousand words.

Don Manuel's great-great-grandfather was originally from Valencia, Spain, Lummis learned. As a colonel in the Spanish army, he joined an expedition to New Mexico in the 1670s, helping establish an outpost across the river from present-day Albuquerque. Don Manuel had spent his early years fighting Indians in the Mexican army, then fought with the Americans to help put down an uprising by Mexican loyalists after New Mexico became a U.S. territory. His body bore testament to his many exploits in war. "It is doubtful that a postal card could be laid on his body where it would not touch some ugly scar," wrote Lummis.[9] He was "a courtly Spanish gentleman, brave as a lion, tender as a woman, spotless of honor, as modest as heroic," known among the peons as Leoncito, or Little Lion.

There was another contingent in the household that Lummis found even more captivating. He met them at breakfast on his first morning there. They included "the most beautiful girl I ever saw" and two others who would be beauties in their own right, out of the presence of the first, Lummis reported. The sight of the three señoritas that morning sent him to the nearest washbasin after breakfast so that he could hack off his beard.

In his letter from San Mateo, Lummis went on at some length about the exceptional beauty of Spanish women. "Blue eyes are sweet and alluring," he wrote, "but for solid magnetism it takes two orbs of jet, framed in lashes and brows still darker, and showing the sparks of a fire that is set to blaze up at any minute." Mindful that his in-laws and their friends, not to mention Dolly herself, were among his readers, Lummis

acknowledged that he was venturing into "a rather risky line of literature." But he was unrepentant. "I wouldn't give much for any man who
wouldn't warm up a little under the demure glance of such beauty as
lights up the casa of Don Manuel Chaves."

Lummis spent his days at the hacienda exploring the immediate
vicinity and digging in the ruins of the collapsed pueblo nearby, where
he uncovered mounds of pottery pieces, arrowheads and stone imple-
ments, and even some human bones. He spent his evenings reveling in
the camaraderie of the household. As many as twenty-five people gathered around the dinner table each night. Afterward they all retired to
the parlor for singing and games. "One doesn't want to be a dumb post
in such a gathering. So I kept the mutilated Spanish flying," wrote Lummis, who enthusiastically joined in the games and songs. Lummis stole
the show with his rendition of "Three Black Crows," marked with frequent cawing. Summing up his stopover with the Chaves clan, he concluded, "I believe I could make a pretty good Mexican in a little more."

From San Mateo to the Pacific coast was by far the worst part of the
entire tramp. With nothing left to do but get to Los Angeles, Lummis
was having little or no fun anymore. The snow was so deep in western
New Mexico that Lummis had to abandon plans for a forty-five-mile
detour south to Zuni, "that most interesting of all Indian towns" where
Frank Cushing had lived. By the time he hit the Arizona line and bid
farewell to the red mesas of New Mexico, which had relieved the long
walks with majestic scenery, the tramp had lost practically every semblance of a journey of discovery and had become a grim test of
endurance. "The day was long and cold and dreary: red noses, cold wet
feet, chapped hands," he said of one day's trek in Arizona. Another day,
he confronted "as lonely a stretch of track as ever bored the eye." He
later said of that final six-hundred-mile stretch, "There isn't enough
gold in California to hire me to do it over again. But now that it is all
past and gone, I am glad it happened—one likes to know how much he
can stand at a pinch."[10]

Along with the terrain, the Indians turned less appealing and hos-
pitable in Arizona. He had left the land of the noble Pueblos and had
entered the territory of the Navajos, who sent him searching back
through the imagery from Mayne Reid's novels for descriptive adjec-
tives. The Navajos are "dirty, thievish, treacherous and revoltingly

44

licentious," Lummis wrote. He did have to admit, however, that they made fine jewelry and blankets that he pronounced the best in the world. He was so impressed with them that he traded his precious meerschaum pipe for a blanket a quarter-inch thick and woven tightly enough to hold water.

The weather, though not posing the mortal danger that it had in the Sandia range, got steadily more miserable. He had to walk into the face of a relentless, bitterly cold wind. The railroad was ankle deep with freezing mud, so he had to walk on the end of the ties, which were slick with snow. But those difficulties didn't begin to compare with the hardship he endured after an accident that befell him about fifty miles into Arizona. In an attempt to head off a deer that he had seen crossing the track up ahead early one morning, he had scrambled up the steep side of a mesa when a loose shelf of fragile shale on which he was standing suddenly crumbled, sending him tumbling twenty feet backward down the rocky slope. When he recovered his wits at the bottom, he could feel a broken bone beneath the skin of his left forearm. He had no choice but to set the bone himself or risk losing the arm. So as he described it, he tied his wrist to a tree with his canteen strap and threw his weight back against the restraint, forcing the broken bone into place. He fashioned a makeshift splint with two sticks, replacing that later with barrel staves that he found along the track, and resumed his westward tramp, which was suddenly grimmer than ever.

He covered the fifty-two miles to the next town, Winslow, in thirty hours of continuous walking in a cold, drenching rain "with that arm dragging at my side, heavy as lead, and jumping like a hollow tooth." When he finally stumbled into the town and found lodging, he had covered one hundred thirteen miles in forty-eight hours.

The *Los Angeles Times* hadn't been paying much attention to Lummis's tramp, perhaps because it was considered a stunt aimed at easterners who had never been west. The paper had reported on his departure in September by reprinting a story from the *Cincinnati Commercial Gazette* and had published just three of his letters since then. The others didn't appear in the *Times* until later that spring and summer. But the news about his broken arm warranted a story describing the gutsy reporter who would soon be joining the staff. "He is a remarkable young fellow, and as full of 'go' as one of the conejos de jack which he so frequently sights in the sage brush jungles of the limitless plains," the *Times*

45

informed its readers. "He is a vivid, graphic, and hilarious writer, and his letters breathe the spirit of the mountains and make luminous what were otherwise a dark and dreary waste."

By then Lummis was so intent on getting his tramp over with that he passed up a side trip to the Grand Canyon, a day's walk to the north of his route. There was only one major incident to write about the rest of the way to Los Angeles. It concerned a tragedy that befell Shadow.

The hound had shared his sometimes scanty provisions and his often inadequate blanket for more than a thousand miles of hard traveling. But the harshest terrain lay ahead—the Mojave Desert. The thirty miles or more of walking day after day and the meager supply of water had taken their toll on Shadow. Signs that something was wrong had been apparent for several days. But Lummis was still taken by surprise when suddenly the dog went mad. With froth dripping from bared teeth, Shadow lunged at Lummis. He pulled out his Colt revolver and fired. But shaking at the thought of "driving a bullet into a dear and faithful friend," he succeeded only in wounding the animal. He couldn't leave Shadow slowly dying alone in that wasteland. So he took aim and fired again, finishing him off.

In crossing the Mojave, Lummis did a lot of his walking at night to avoid the deadly heat. At one point he stumbled upon a bleached human skull gleaming in the moonlight, a reminder of the untold thousands before him who had perished in the attempt to reach the Pacific coast on foot. He ran out of water himself during one painful stretch when he foolishly decided to shave some miles off the trip by leaving the train tracks and striking off across the desert. But after five days in the Mojave, he reached the back entrance to the Cajon Pass. In the plain below lay the scattered settlements of Los Angeles County. Through the pass, part way down the other side, he ran into the first signs of habitation: orchards, tidy farmhouses, a trout pond, a "forerunner of the Eden I was entering."

He spent a night halfway down the mountain. The next day he walked through miles of farms and orchards past "beautiful Ontario" to "thriving Pomona," where he spent another night before proceeding through the bustling rural villages of Arcadia, La Puente, and El Monte to San Gabriel. The rains had been especially abundant that winter, a phenomenon that can make Southern California look, for a few months, as green as Ireland. Lummis saw no evidence of the barren deserts that

Dolly had described surrounding Los Angeles. In fact, he was convinced that he had found paradise. The air was "warm and balmy but not oppressive," he wrote. "Flowers nodded at me, and countless butterflies danced past. Crystal brooks sang down from rugged canyons, and upon their banks were houses and gardens, orchards and apiaries. The world was green with springing grass and full of the warble of a thousand birds. Do you know how that looked to one fresh from the hideous desert, and into that from Arizona snows? But that's a fool question—of course you don't."

The tramp had changed Lummis forever. He would write about the experience often in the years to come. He would explain hundreds of times why he walked all that way. It was "the longest walk for pure pleasure on record," he once said, though that remark was too flippant to capture the whole truth. In fact, he had a number of more serious motivations.

For one thing, the tramp gave him a chance to revive his obsession with physical conditioning. He got to put himself to yet another test of his endurance and tolerance of hardship.

He also firmly believed in the ability to transform oneself through sheer exertion of willpower. The human spirit was dwindling away under the pressures of civilization, of which he had this to say: "Its whole tendency is toward laziness for it is always inventing something to supplant work. . . . Yes, civilization is might fast ruining the race physically; and the mental and moral decay are inevitable corollaries of the bodily." He wasn't about to submit to that fate without a fight. No one could accuse Lummis of going soft, not after what he had just accomplished. He had taken 6,513,541 steps on the way from Cincinnati to Los Angeles, which amounted to 3,507 miles.

Lummis had another serious motive. "I want to see the country and you cannot see it from the car windows," he explained. He wanted to study the land, and particularly the people who inhabited it, up close. That mission had been accomplished.

The tramp was over. His first sight of the lights of Los Angeles drove that point home and it wasn't a happy thought. Though he was headed to a new life in a thriving city in which he would be surrounded by people, he feared that he would no longer experience the sense of camaraderie he had enjoyed with so many of the companions he had met on the road. "A little feeling of loneliness . . . rub[bed] against my diaphragm as I looked down from a little bluff, Sunday midnight, and saw the electric lights of Los Angeles at my feet, and remembered that I wasn't to poke out into the sand again in the morning, nor lay my bones by night along the soft side of a plank."

He had anticipated the bittersweet sentiment he would feel on arrival at his destination in a comment dropped into one of his letters a month earlier in western New Mexico. "The longer a man is a tramp," he wrote, "the easier it is for him to stay one."

Otis had sent word to Lummis that he wanted to rendezvous with him on the outskirts of town. He suggested a hotel in San Gabriel as a good place to meet. Lummis got there ahead of schedule, so he cleaned up, had a "metamorphosing shave" and a meal, and was "smoking a meditative pipe" when Otis, a "portly military looking man," entered, took a good look at the bandaged arm, and said, "Mr. Lummis?"

"Yours truly," Lummis replied.

Otis and Lummis walked together for the final ten miles to Los Angeles, and the two had a celebratory late-night meal at Eckert's restaurant on Court Street.

Otis wrote about Lummis's Sunday-evening arrival for the Tuesday edition, Monday being the one day of the week when the *Times* wasn't printed. "His garb was not reassuring to the timid," Otis remarked, ticking off a long list of the odd things Lummis wore or carried in the pockets of his coat. The proprietor of Eckert's "no doubt thought he was seeing a first class tramp." Indeed, the outfit was "calculated to excite the curiosity of the police."

"Mr. Lummis has made a trip that puts him in the first rank of American travelers," Otis concluded. "It was needless to say that he did not come here for his health, and he could hardly be called a tenderfoot. He has joined the staff of the *Times*, and has come to stay."

Chapter 3

On the Beat in El Pueblo de Los Angeles

L ummis had hoped to have a week off to unpack, unwind, spend some time with Dolly, and get acquainted with his new town. But the *Times* was seriously short-staffed. Otis needed his new man on the job without delay. Lummis obliged, showing up at the *Times* office at ten on Monday morning, ready for work, less than twelve hours after completing his 3,507-mile tramp.

The *Los Angeles Times* operated on a shoestring in those days. The office was in a plain two-story brick building on Temple Street. The editorial office shared the second story with the composing and job printing rooms. The business office was on the first floor and the press was in the basement. Practically from day one, Lummis was the "entire staff for local news," according to William Spalding, who joined the staff later that spring.[1]

A newspaperman looking for good stories couldn't have picked a better place and time than Los Angeles at the start of 1885. The town still bore strong markings of its Hispanic origins, the era of Spanish-Mexican rule having ended just thirty-eight years before Lummis arrived. But the process of rapid Americanization was well under way. Los Angeles was bursting at the seams, and seething with excitement.

One sign of the arrival of Los Angeles as an American city to be reckoned with was taking place that night. The world-famous Emma Abbott Company was opening a one-week engagement in the one-year-old,

1,300-seat Grand Opera House with a performance of *Lucia di Lammermoor*. Just a week earlier, it still hadn't been clear whether Abbott and her famously large entourage of eighty people including a full orchestra would bother to come to Los Angeles after a long engagement in San Francisco. But promoters had been successful enough with advance ticket sales—at ten dollars for the series of seven operas—to persuade her to make the detour. The event had drawn "liberal support as can only be obtained in a city of considerable importance," boasted the *Evening Express*. The fact that the incomparable Emma Abbott was gracing Los Angeles with her presence "marks the claim of our city to metropolitan dimensions and importance."

Perhaps as a reward, or as a way of showing Lummis what his new hometown had to offer in the way of finer pleasures, Otis gave his new reporter a plum assignment for his first morning on the job: interview the diva.

Colonel Henry Boyce, a co-owner of the *Times*, escorted Lummis to the meeting with Abbott and introduced him "in flowery language," as Lummis later recalled, "and wound up: 'He has the hardest legs in the world, Miss Abbott—just feel them!' That fine prima donna, against whom no breath of scandal ever stirred, was a 'good scout.' She pinched and marveled."

If Lummis wrote up his interview with Abbott, it never made it into the paper, which ran eight pages and was overcrowded with news in those days. But the experience thrilled Lummis, who from that point on had a soft spot for opera singers.

It wasn't the last time he crossed paths with Emma Abbott. Several years later, as he told it, he was standing on a station platform in the desert town of Mojave, waiting for the train to San Francisco, when he heard a musical voice behind him call out, "Here John, here is Mr. Lummis—he has the hardest legs of any man in the world!"

"I whirled around and there was Emma Abbott, bringing her husband for introduction." Her admiring remark about his legs "required explanation upon her part."

In his memoir, Lummis described Los Angeles at the time of his arrival as a "dull little place of some 12,000 persons" where the Spanish-speaking population outnumbered the gringos two or three to one. A residential district just a few blocks from downtown was so bucolic that he claimed he hunted rabbits and quails there.

In fact, that is a fair description of Los Angeles—as it was five years before Lummis got to town. During that half decade, however, the population had tripled to more than 30,000. And gringos had moved solidly into the majority for the first time since El Pueblo de Nuestra Señora la Reina de los Angeles de Porciuncula was founded by several dozen settlers from Sonora, Mexico, in 1781. The fact that a 1,300-seat opera house could nearly sell out seven nights in a row was one sign that the days of the sleepy pueblo were history.

The town was still plenty rough around the edges. At the start of 1885 there wasn't a square foot of pavement to be found. On the other hand, Los Angeles could rightfully claim to be the best-lit city in the country thanks to ultramodern, three-thousand-candlepower electric lamps mounted on masts that towered 150 feet over downtown, powered by steam dynamos fed with the crude oil so abundant under the city that it seeped to the surface and collected in pools at Rancho La Brea.

Signs of the old Spanish-Mexican town abounded. There were lots of old adobes standing near the plaza in a district that the Americans called Sonoratown. It was predominately Mexican. But a Chinatown had blossomed along several blocks of the district in the sixteen years since the Southern Pacific rail line from San Francisco was completed and hundreds of the Chinese laborers who built it settled in Los Angeles and moved into other lines of work. Some of the most prosperous businesses in Sonoratown were saloons, brothels, and gambling parlors concentrated along a street radiating out from the plaza that was known as Calle de los Negros in the days of Spanish and Mexican rule, presumably in recognition of the fact that several of the original group of Los Angeles pioneers had been part African. The Americans had informally renamed the street Nigger Alley.

In the American era, the commercial heart of the city was a quarter mile southeast of the old plaza. By 1885 a thriving commercial district stretched in a long plume to the southeast, fading into a comfortable residential quarter that reached as far as the five-year-old University of Southern California three miles south of the plaza.

Lummis, who would continue to send an occasional letter to the *Leader* for the next several years, wrote one about his new hometown on

February 8, just a week after his arrival. In it he focused on the dramatic changes under way in Los Angeles at the time. The letter showed that his prejudices against Mexicans hadn't been entirely erased on the tramp. The demise of the city's Spanish and Mexican heritage was a cause for celebration, he believed at the time.

"Los Angeles is a brilliant example of a tail that has come to wag the whole dog," he wrote. "In fact, it is hard to find the original dog, at all, so completely has the tail overshadowed him." The dog in this story consisted of "the queer precincts of Sonoratown, with its rickety adobes, quiet streets and general air of Mexicanization." It was a "diminutive, lazy and ill-conditioned pup 114 years old." In contrast, the tail "is only a few years old but she is the liveliest wagger going," he continued. "It is New Los Angeles, the metropolis of Southern California, six miles square and pretty as a peach. It is as wide awake and beautiful as the dog is neither, and makes more noise in a day than he does in a year. In half another generation there will be no dog left at all, his whole personality being merged and lost in that greedy tail."[2]

That glib and approving account of the Americanization of Los Angeles was a far cry from the nostalgic laments for the past that he would write in later years. But one early impression would stick: his rapturous assessment of Southern California's weather. Los Angeles, he declared in a letter to the *Leader* one month to the day after he walked into town, is the "gem city of the world." He couldn't help boasting to his friends back east about the paradise he had found. "This is the 1st of March, but I am sitting all night in a fireless room in my shirt-sleeves, with the doors and windows open. To-morrow I am going to steal down to Long Beach for a dip in the soft Pacific surf," he wrote, and "I'd like to take a few acres out of the heart of this county, and send it back to you, air and all, for a sample. In six months after its arrival, there wouldn't be a soul left in Chillicothe."

The relentless regimen of pacing off 75,000 to 100,000 railroad ties a day had left Lummis well prepared for the fourteen-or-more-hour days at the *Times*. Otis ran the office like a military campaign, demanding total devotion from his staff. Lummis delivered more than even Otis could have expected. "A more indefatigable or more conscientious worker in a newspaper office I never knew," Spalding recalled. "Every day he was at his desk an hour or two ahead of the required time and, before commencing his rounds, occupied himself in pasting in a big scrapbook and indexing every item of local news that had appeared in the paper that morning. This special work was entirely on his own motion and I used to regard it as an unnecessary labor of love, but must acknowledge that in looking up past events and getting the correct history of things that are ordinarily lost in the shuffle he had the bulge on any other newsgatherer I had ever seen."

There were plenty of stories to keep track of in the burgeoning city. In just his first few days in the office, a horse team that had been left untethered on a downtown street ran amok, sparking cries for enforcement of the city's hitching ordinance; a state senator said he would go to jail before submitting to a woman's demand for alimony; a stack of valuable otter skins stored on one of the nearby Channel Islands was devoured by wild hogs; a group of Mormons complained of discrimination; six white orphans were rescued from Chinatown, reportedly just in time to save them from being sold to China as concubines; a man found howling in the Arroyo Seco was declared to be incurably insane; a Mexican man hanged himself on Alameda Street; and 372 citrus growers turned in a petition calling for the county to be subdivided into pest control districts. Those were just a few of the smaller news items that appeared in the *Times*.

The big stories in the spring of 1885 included the first executions in Los Angeles in a generation. Two convicted murderers, Rodolfo Silvas and Francisco Martinez, were hanged one after the other on March 20, drawing an enormous throng that "blackened the hills" and rooftops around the low-walled prison compound. Men, boys, and even women jostled to get a better "glimpse of this tragedy of death." The macabre spectacle prompted the *Times* to run an editorial several days later remarking that the crowd was a "pitiful commentary upon humanity" and calling for private executions.

Less than two months later the Los Angeles City Council ousted the city's new police chief Edward McCarthy after a bitter battle that began with allegations of selective enforcement of laws against Sonoratown brothels and Chinatown gambling dens. Otis staunchly defended the chief for months. But prodded by Lummis, he finally withdrew his support after McCarthy and his son beat up a lawyer who was representing the councilmen seeking his ouster.

One of the most scandalous Los Angeles courtroom dramas of the nineteenth century was just heating up when Lummis came to town. On his third day in the office, the *Times* ran a long story about the case, which involved a pretty sixteen-year-old girl named Louisa Perkins and E. J. "Lucky" Baldwin, a wealthy thoroughbred breeder with a huge ranch in Santa Anita. Baldwin, who had parlayed mining stocks into one of America's great fortunes, had persuaded Perkins's mother to let him take the girl to San Francisco on the pretext of educating her. But instead, as the *Times* reported, he had seduced the girl and taken her into his bed on a promise that he would marry her. Then he had cast her off.

Upon her return to Los Angeles, Perkins lost her job as a sales clerk because of rumors about her affair with Baldwin. With nothing left to lose from airing the scandal, she had recently sued for damages. The *Perkins v. Baldwin* case would be a lurid running saga for the next three years.

The Chinese question was one of the more delicate issues that confronted the *Times* in 1885. An increasingly virulent anti-Chinese movement was gaining steam, demanding that the Chinese, no longer needed in massive numbers to build railroads, be driven out of California. The *Times* didn't support that movement, but Otis didn't want his paper to seem too pro-Chinese. While the *Times* called for fair treatment of those Chinese already in the United States, the paper argued for strict controls on further immigration. A week after Lummis started work, the paper carried an editorial that explained, "The worst feature of Chinese immigration to this country is the fact that these heathens come to our shores bringing with them all the vices of degraded heathenism, with no rein upon their passions, huddled and massed together like so many cattle, with no home life and no domestic relations to restrain or elevate them."

That was mild stuff compared with what the *Herald* published on a regular basis. On one occasion, the paper was enraged to discover that the eighteen-year-old daughter of a white saloon keeper had a Chinese boyfriend. "She fully acknowledged her partiality for the almond eyed Mongol," the *Herald* reported incredulously, heaping scorn on her mother who had evidently "encouraged the girl to carry on a most vile and shameless trade with a large gang of these heathen." In another story about a Chinese man who was lynched by a mob in Northern California for allegedly killing a white girl, the *Herald* observed that the grisly event "will doubtless have a salutary effect on the Mongolian mind."

An article that appeared in the *Times* in November 1885, quite possibly written by Lummis, offered a perspective on the Chinese in California that had rarely been seen in print before. The article was styled as a profile of "John Chinaman," a hard-working and thrifty vegetable farmer who brought his produce by cart through the white neighborhoods of Los Angeles each day. He had "velley good gleen peas" for sale and other immaculate vegetables. He never cheated his customers and freely gave them credit when they didn't have cash on a particular day. "He never begs. That is a feature of civilization he has not yet acquired." He offered his produce for rock bottom prices because he was so thrifty and efficient in the way he ran his farm. Where else would the housewives of Los Angeles get such beautiful produce delivered to their door if not from John Chinaman? the *Times* asked.

The *Herald* wasn't about to let that shocking story pass without comment. "It is evident that the *Times* is very much in love with the Chinese race, or some Chinaman is furnishing the editor of that paper with vegetables and taking it out in a large amount of gush over the Mongolians," the *Herald* snarled.

The *Times* also parted company with other papers in the region on black-white race relations. The issue surfaced early in 1885 when reports began to circulate that Lucky Baldwin was considering bringing black laborers to work on his eighty-thousand-acre racehorse farm in Santa Anita.

The *Santa Ana Standard* was aghast at the thought. A devastating earthquake "wouldn't be half as bad as a Nigger colony," the paper wrote, prompting a rebuke from the *Times*. "We see no reason why they may not prove to be a desirable class of laborers," the *Times* declared in an editorial. "It takes all sorts of people to make a world. . . . Give the black citizen a chance, say we."

The *Times's* attitude toward race relations was evinced by another apparent change in editorial policy implemented about a year after Lummis joined the staff. In most though not all cases, the paper began referring to the notorious Sonoratown street of gambling dens and whorehouses universally called Nigger Alley as Negro Alley.

*   *   *

Most daily news stories in the *Times* didn't carry a byline. So it's hard to tell from reading the paper exactly what Lummis was writing in his early days there. But he was the subject of a news event covered by the paper not long after he arrived. Apparently the "ill-luck" that had caused him to fall into fights in his college days had followed him to Los Angeles.

As a story in the *Times* on May 21 told it, Lummis was on his way to dinner the previous evening and was passing by the Nadeau Block when without warning a man lunged at him from out of the shadows. His assailant turned out to be one of the most renowned lightweight boxers of his day, Billy Manning, of Manchester, England.

The seeds of the altercation had been sown early in the morning the day before when Lummis was passing by the Palm Garden and heard a woman screaming inside. He entered to investigate and found Manning pummeling his wife. He "thrice pulled the brute away from the woman, at her wild screams for aid," as the *Times* account put it. "After Manning's third assault upon her, she begged the reporter not to go away, as she was afraid." So he stayed until the police arrived and quieted things down. He left, but not before Manning warned him that he'd face trouble if he printed anything about the incident in the paper. The threat didn't deter Lum, who wrote up the incident the next day.

Manning had recently taken up residence in Los Angeles and had been on the wrong side of the *Times* from the start. He ran "a disreputable sporting resort," which had been chased out of one building by tenants who were fed up with the disorderliness. And so he had moved to the Palm Garden, where he sponsored prizefights and an occasional wrestling match. "The police testify that the place has been and is a resort for thieves and roughs with but few respectable visitors," the *Times* noted.

Manning's attack on Lummis took place right in front of the police station in the presence of several witnesses, one of whom happened to be a reporter from the *Evening Express*. The report said Manning didn't try to hit Lummis. He might have missed even if he had tried, because Lummis, in an instinct for self-preservation, immediately dropped to the ground and grabbed his assailant's feet. A police officer and the reporter from the *Express* then piled on, eventually pulling Manning and Lummis apart. As the *Express* reporter told it, "Lummis felt elated that he had stood off the champion lightweight for a 10-second round without being knocked out, and with his face enveloped in a Fourth of July smile, he sauntered on toward his roast beef and gooseberry pie."

Lummis's moment of triumph was short-lived. On his way back from dinner to the *Times* office for the evening shift, Lummis was jumped outside the Palm Garden by Manning's wife. She too was a professional boxer, who fought under the name Madame Franklin. Unlike her husband, she wasn't inclined to go easy on Lummis even though she had a five-inch height advantage over the five-foot-six-inch reporter and outweighed him by more than thirty pounds. Lummis tried to hold her wrists, but he later said they were so thick he couldn't get a grip. She broke free, grabbed him by the neck with one hand, and landed eight or ten quick blows to Lummis's face with the other hand, administering what the *Express* called a "severe beating."

Both Manning and his wife were hauled into court the next day and arraigned on an assault and battery charge. They pleaded not guilty. Manning testified, "I only tried to scare the blasted, blooming fellow, you know." He claimed he was retaliating for negative remarks about his boxing camp that Lummis had published in the paper. The reporter was biased against him, Manning surmised, because he had refused to let him into a match for free.

Mrs. Manning told a different story, saying she was getting revenge against Lummis for "scandalizing" her with his report about the alleged marital tiff. She wanted to teach him a lesson about interfering in other people's family affairs, she testified.

Lummis's torn jacket was entered into evidence as Exhibit A. A scratch on his cheek was Exhibit B. Both Mannings were convicted of battery and fined twenty-five dollars each. Manning fished fifty dollars out of his pocket on the spot, and paid the judge, and the pair of pugilists went on their way.

There were no lasting hard feelings with Lummis. In fact, according to Lummis, Manning became "a very staunch friend for many years, willing to go almost any lengths for me."

Otis was delighted with his new reporter, as he had good reason to be. Lummis had certainly injected some vigor into the *Times*, and readers apparently noticed. While each of the city papers' circulation claims were routinely ridiculed by its rivals, during Lum's first year on the job, the *Times*'s circulation reportedly doubled.

Dolly had also adjusted quickly to her new city. Within weeks of her arrival in Los Angeles, nearly three months ahead of her husband, she was displaying the drive and ambition that had gotten her through medical school. She had set up home and office in the Hollenbeck Block, secured a California medical credential, and begun to run a daily classified ad in the *Times* offering her services as a homeopathic physician available for consultations in her room with hours of 8–10 A.M. and 2–4 P.M.

Not long after arriving in Los Angeles, Dorothea introduced herself to her husband's future boss, Colonel Otis, and worked out an arrangement with the *Times* to write reviews of theatrical performances around town. She exhibited a tough streak in her reviews, and Otis got complaints from time to time that she was too critical, but he always backed her up.

Dorothea also plunged immediately into various civic activities. On the Friday afternoon of the week of Lummis's arrival, Dorothea founded the Los Angeles County Homeopathic Medical Society. Within a few years she had taken leadership positions in several other leading associations. She was a founder of the Society for the Prevention of Cruelty to Animals and the Society for the Prevention of Cruelty to Children. And she was a charter member of the Friday Morning Club, founded by the leading women's suffrage advocate in town, Caroline Severance.

At this point, with his high-profile job and dynamic wife, Lummis could have found his own place in the civic milieu of his new city and settled into a life of domestic repose at home. But several issues intruded. For one, into the fourth year of marriage, Dolly still hadn't produced a child, and children were an absolute necessity for Lummis in his quest to create the sort of home that he felt he had never had. For another, Lummis had an affliction, which had only been exacerbated on the tramp: an incurable case of wanderlust.

During his first year at the *Times*, he had confided in a letter to friends back east, even though things had turned out better than he could have expected in a great job on a gallant young paper with a salty old boss who held him in high regard, he needed something more.[3] "I don't believe prosperity agrees with me," he wrote. "Here I am in the land from which it is generally supposed that the Lord got His plans and specifications for heaven; basking in eternal summer while you poor creatures are building fires under the thermometer to keep it from freezing. I am eating four meals a day, not to count a superabundance of the finest fruits, plugging away at work which fits my intermittent intellect like a pair of dude pantaloons, drawing a neat salary and fixed in just the swellest suite of rooms in the city with the furniture of domesticity—and still I am not happy. That is, I'm always happy anywhere—but there's a sense of something lacking. It is too soon yet to forget my old exultant careless life in the New England woods, called back so vividly by the experiences of the Tramp, and the full free blood and knotted muscles which grew from that life are not toned down enough yet to lie content between four walls. And so I sit and scratch at the offensive paper as if I owed it a grudge while my thoughts go drifting out of the windows and across the mountains to—well, I call it life."

Chapter 4

Defending the General
Pursuing Geronimo

Otis wanted to keep his star reporter happy. So he arranged for Lummis to make occasional excursions out of town—and flattered him with the paper's coverage of the trips. One of the stories Lummis wrote during his first year on the job, for example, was headlined "Lum Again Traveling to the Front." It wasn't much of a "front"—the mining town of Waterman in the Mojave Desert a hundred miles northeast of Los Angeles. But even brief stints away from the city helped him keep his wanderlust in check. Just nine months after Lummis reached Los Angeles, Otis turned him loose for a brief return trip to New Mexico with his wife. They revisited some of the places and people he had gotten to know on his tramp, and saw for the first time a few sites he had regretted missing, such as the "sky city" of Acoma, an eight-hundred-year-old pueblo perched dramatically on a mesa. Lummis wrote several stories about the trip for the *Times*, starting an annual fall tradition of travel-writing excursions to New Mexico with Dolly.

Lummis certainly didn't get completely free rein at the *Times*. In the memoir about his experiences at the paper, Spalding recounted an incident from early 1886 that showed that Otis wasn't averse to cuffing Lummis's ears when necessary. "Charlie was a little hard in the mouth sometimes," Spalding recalled. He had the misfortune of provoking the chief in some way or other just before the catastrophic flood of January

19 hit. A wall of water surged down the Los Angeles River sweeping the banks clean of all buildings and severely damaging every bridge from the Arroyo Seco to Long Beach. To punish Lummis for his infraction, Otis assigned him the City Council beat that day while sending Spalding out to report on the disaster, an assignment that ordinarily would have gone to Lummis.

"This must have been a heartbreaking business for Charlie. . . . I pictured him droning away his time with the stupid Council, and fairly gnashing his teeth," recalled Spalding, who was relieved that Lummis didn't hold it against him.

Lummis must have been unusually well behaved after that. A few months later, Otis gave him permission to take off in pursuit of a story that made his heart rush. It's not clear whether Otis proposed the reporting trip or whether Lummis dreamed it up. But it was an assignment beyond his wildest dreams: go to Arizona to cover the final days of the Apache War. Otis could hardly spare his one-man city desk. But he may have figured it would be a quick trip. By March 1886 the last hot Indian war in North America was expected to end any day with the capture of the infamous renegade Geronimo.

Besides helping keep Lummis content, the trip could serve a couple of other purposes, Otis may have reasoned. Lummis's reports would give the *Times* unsurpassed coverage of a controversial war that the whole nation was talking about, which would boost the paper's reputation and circulation. Otis also hoped Lummis's reporting would help shore up the eroding reputation of the regional U.S. Army commander responsible for catching Geronimo, Brigadier General George Crook.

Otis informed the readers of the *Times* about Lum's expedition in an editor's note that ran in the paper the day after he left. The note said Lummis was off to "Geronimo's stamping ground" where he would try to "throw a good deal of light on the much-vexed Indian question." Lummis would have been especially thrilled by the conclusion of the note: "Should the campaign continue he will probably remain in the field as long as his legs hold out and his scalp holds fast."[1]

There were just a few things about himself that Lummis took greater pride in than his hard legs. There was no chance they would give out. He could only hope he would be lucky enough to get so close to hostile Apaches that his scalp would be put at risk.

* * *

General Crook was a highly decorated Union veteran of the Civil War who had risen through the ranks to become commander of the cavalry in the Army of the Potomac by war's end. But the fighting did not end for him with the Confederate surrender at Appomattox Courthouse in 1865. Crook, who had fought Indians in the West before the war, returned to the frontier and spent the next quarter century in virtually nonstop war against Indians, becoming one of the most celebrated Indian fighters of his time.[2] Crook fought Chinooks in the redwood forests of Oregon, Blackfeet in the freezing Bitterroot Mountains of Idaho, and Shoshones and Sioux on the northern plains of Montana. But no tribe was more entangled in Crook's military career than the Apaches of Arizona, where he served three tours of duty spaced out over fifteen years. And no single Indian was a source of more consternation—or ultimately had a greater effect on his life—than Geronimo.

A member of the Chiricahua band, one of six distinct subgroups of Apaches, Geronimo was a medicine man by trade, a formidable warrior by necessity.[3] He earned his first battle stripes as a teenager fighting alongside the greatest Apache chief of all time, Cochise, and the almost equally legendary six-foot-eight-inch Mangas Colorado. After Cochise died of stomach cancer in 1872 and Mangas Colorado was captured and killed by U.S. Army troops two years later, Geronimo became the leading war captain of the Chiricahuas. He surrendered at least half a dozen times, twice to Crook himself, agreeing each time to stay on lands that had been reserved for the Apaches. But Geronimo and bands of followers repeatedly broke out and returned to their mountain homeland, surviving by attacking isolated homesteads, mines, wagon trains, and tiny villages from the outskirts of Tucson to the hinterlands of Fronteras, Mexico, butchering the inhabitants and then vanishing with horses, livestock, food, weapons, ammunition, and other supplies. Each time Crook was reassigned to Arizona, his mission was to put an end to the raids and recapture Geronimo.

Crook's latest encounter with the world-renowned Apache warrior was one of the biggest news stories of the day. Every newspaper in the country worthy of note had staked out a position on the way the general was handling the campaign. The longer Geronimo evaded capture, the louder grew the murmurs of doubt about his performance. By the spring of 1886 the majority of papers, from the *New York Times* to the

Tombstone Epitaph, had turned critical, with the degree of reproof ranging from the measured to the apoplectic. The *Los Angeles Times* was among the minority of papers in the pro-Crook camp.

Otis had written editorials in support of Crook's handling of the Apache Wars, arguing that no one was in any position to second-guess the battle-tested Indian fighter's judgment, and predicting that his tactics would be proved correct in the end. Whether Otis really cared about the issues at stake or not, he had a personal reason for coming to the defense of the beleaguered general. He had served under Crook in the Army of West Virginia during the Civil War and had warm memories of the fatherly commander, known to his Civil War troops as Uncle George. A quarter century later, with his age beginning to show in the color of his trademark billowing muttonchop whiskers, Crook was called the Gray Fox.

The end of the long struggle between Crook and Geronimo appeared to be days away when Lummis left for the front. Indeed, it almost ended too soon to suit Lummis. He realized what a close call it had been as soon as his train hissed to a stop in Tucson on the morning of March 30 and he grabbed a copy of the *Arizona Daily Star,* one of the few pro-Crook papers in the territory. Luckily the news hadn't broken the day before. If it had, Otis might have scrubbed the trip. "Geronimo and His Entire Band Surrender Unconditionally to General Crook," the headline read. "The Long and Bloody War at Last Over, and General Crook and His Policy Fully Vindicated." At least in the last line of the header, there was a glimmer of hope that Lummis might still find something to write about. "One Hundred and Five Captive Chiricahuas on Their Way to Fort Bowie," it said. After mailing a dispatch to the *Times* from Tucson describing his ride across the desert on a train filled with territorial politicians, he hopped right back on a train bound for Bowie Station, 110 miles east of Tucson and fourteen miles north of the fort where the captive Apaches were headed.

Of the six major subgroups of Apaches, each had a different dialect and predisposition. Geronimo's group, the Chiricahuas, who occupied the rugged mountains of southeastern Arizona, were by Crook's account the toughest foes he ever tangled with. In fact, the Chiricahua Apaches were arguably the greatest guerrilla fighters in history. Out of the hundreds of tribes that occupied North America when Christopher Columbus reached the New World, they were among the very last to succumb to onrushing European civilization. Their demise thus represented the final episode of a sad, bloody struggle that had raged across the continent for four hundred years. Lummis had arrived just in time to be an eyewitness to the historic event.

The first European incursions into Apacheria, by slave-gathering Spanish conquistadors in the 1530s, set the tone for the conflict with the Apaches, which steadily became bloodier in the centuries to come. The Apaches answered the brutality of the invaders in kind, often torturing their captives in unspeakable ways. When the borderlands of New Mexico and Arizona were transferred to U.S. control in the Gadsden Purchase of 1853, a legacy of more than three centuries of bloodshed between settlers and Apaches came with the territory. In excess of four thousand people died in the conflict over the next thirty years. About half the casualties were Apaches shot down like coyotes by the Americans, and the other half were troops and civilian settlers and fortune seekers who were ambushed, tortured, scalped, and in many cases tied up and burned to death by the Apaches.

By the 1880s, most of the Indians were confined to the San Carlos Reservation, two hundred miles north of their traditional homeland, and the killing had nearly ceased. But corrupt government agents made the lives of the Indians on that inhospitable reservation miserable. Even a grand jury of citizens of the Arizona Territory, a hotbed of hatred toward Indians, recognized the injustices, calling the agent in charge at San Carlos a "disgrace to the civilization of the age" in an 1882 report. But official acknowledgment of the problem didn't lead to any improvement in conditions. So bands of Chiricahuas led by Geronimo repeatedly escaped from San Carlos, returned to their mountain bastions in Mexico, and resumed their bloody raids on miners and settlers. Each time this happened, Crook was recalled to Arizona to track down the renegades and put an end to the raids.

This was easier said than done. In their rugged homeland, the Chiricahuas knew the location of every cool, forested hideout amidst the rocky peaks, and every tiny water pocket at the foot of every mountain range, scattered over an area as big as Europe. In any frontal assault on the renegades' mountain hideouts, the attacking troops would be shot to pieces in the steep, narrow, boulder-clogged canyons by a rear guard while the main force of Apaches would scramble over the mountain range, down the other side, and across the desert to another hideout. Six-year-old boys could ride a bronco all day, covering 110 miles in twenty-four hours if necessary, Crook said. He had seen his Apache scouts run 1,500 feet up the side of an impossibly steep mountain without breaking stride.[4]

Crook had come to the conclusion that the Chiricahuas would never be defeated militarily, at least not by white soldiers and certainly not with conventional military tactics. That belief was the basis for his increasing dependence on scouts, best of all friendly Chiricahuas, to track their wayward cousins. When troops under Crook's command located a hostile camp, a small group of scouts accompanied by one or two white officers would make the final approach unarmed to commence negotiations. Ultimately, Crook believed, to bring the war to an end, a bargain would have to be struck, a deal based on mutual respect and something else that the Apaches had rarely received from the European invaders of their land: promises that would not be broken.

When Geronimo and a large number of followers fled from San Carlos in 1883, Crook's scouts tracked them down and Crook himself entered the Apaches' camp unarmed to negotiate their surrender. He assured Geronimo that the promise of fair treatment on the reservation would be honored this time. Geronimo agreed to accompany Crook's troops back to San Carlos. Crook did not disarm the Indians after their surrender, a practice for which he was widely damned. But peace, at least for the moment, had been restored.

Back at San Carlos, however, conniving U.S. Indian agents were still in charge. Life for the Apaches was as miserable as ever. A bungled attempt at meting out punishment for a violation of the rules prohibiting alcohol led the suspicious Apaches to flee once again in May 1885. Frightened by a rumor that they would all be shipped to Alcatraz Island in San Francisco Bay, Geronimo led 130 Chiricahuas back into the rugged mountains of Mexico once again. They resumed their bloody raids on both sides of the border. Crook was called back to Arizona for a third time, and he set about carefully planning a final campaign against Geronimo.

In the summer of 1885 Crook spent three full months making careful preparations, placing special emphasis on building supply lines to support a long campaign deep into the Sierra Madre and stationing troops at every known water hole in southern Arizona to prevent incursions.

Crook's troops didn't take off after the renegades until August. Despite their best efforts to seal the border, an Apache war party from Geronimo's group managed to pull off a terrifying raid into Arizona that November. They covered an astonishing 1,200 miles in less than two weeks, killing thirty-eight people. No defeat of the renegades was in sight at the start of 1886, when Otis first began thinking about sending Lummis to the front. Popular patience with Crook was wearing thin.

The not-so-subtle undercurrent to the rising tide of attacks on Crook was that he was soft on savages, an Indian lover. It was an odd charge to hurl at a highly decorated general who had killed as many Indians as anyone else in the West. But in his decades on the frontier Crook had come to understand that the root cause of the conflict was the inexorable centuries-long invasion of Indian lands by Europeans, many of whom had less of a claim to being civilized than the so-called savages. He had found Geronimo and other Apache leaders to be more honorable than the sorts of whites who frequented the Arizona frontier.

Crook's approach was put to the test yet again in January 1886. After a relentless pursuit that lasted for months, one of his top field officers, Captain Emmet Crawford, leading a force of more than 150 Apache scouts and twenty U.S. soldiers, cornered Geronimo deep in the Sierra Madre two hundred miles south of the Mexican border. But instead of attempting a final assault on their camp and marching them in chains back to Arizona, Crawford sat down for a chat with the Chiricahua war leader. Geronimo said the women and children in his party, including his own wife and children, were beyond exhaustion and were ready to turn themselves in. They would accompany Crawford's troops back to Fort Bowie as a sign that he, too, was willing to talk peace. But he and his warriors would surrender only after a face-to-face meeting with the only American they still trusted, Crook himself.

They agreed to a rendezvous with the general two moons hence at the Cañon de los Embudos—the Canyon of the Funnels—a few miles south of the Arizona-Mexico border. Crawford, a faithful student of Crook's way of dealing with the Indians, took the wily Apache at his word and headed back to the United States with his exhausted troops and a crowd of forlorn Apache women and children, leaving Geronimo and his diehard band of braves in their Mexican refuge. Crawford was killed a few days later in an ambush by Mexican troops who claimed they mistook the Apache scouts for a band of hostile Indians. So the force that had spent months in pursuit of Geronimo limped back across the border not only without the renegade but with the corpse of their commander. The anti-Crook press was enraged, and the general's public approval and professional standing as a famed Indian fighter went steadily downhill from that point.

Crook's critics had no shortage of mouthpieces. In the late 1800s there were more newspapers in Arizona than there are today. No self-respecting boomtown was without one or two, most of them reflecting the views of their readers advocating extermination of the Apaches.

No territorial newspaper kept up a steadier barrage against Crook than the *Tombstone Epitaph* and its editor, J. O. Dunbar. The *Epitaph*'s pronouncements on the Apache War were funneled to newspapers nationwide by the regional bureau of the Associated Press, which was based in Tombstone but had no reporters of its own in the field. The paper regularly skewered Crook for trusting his scouts. Describing one raid on an outlying settlement by unidentified assailants—who easily could have been white rustlers, a menace then far more prevalent in southeastern Arizona than Apaches—the *Epitaph* observed, "It seems to be believed apparently on good grounds that the marauders are some of Crook's precious scouts, who have been discharged and now combine the cunning and ferocity of the Apache with the training gained under the careful tutelage of the 'Grey Fox'."

The *San Francisco Chronicle* was less hysterical but no less critical, reflecting a growing consensus about Crook's performance in the spring of 1886. His "mismanagement of the Apache campaign has cost him not only advancement in rank but a large share of his reputation as an Indian fighter," the paper declared.

All spring Lummis had followed the press campaign against Crook from his desk at the *Los Angeles Times*. There was no question about whose side he was on. He was itching to jump into the fray and fight back against the "venomous novelists" who were attacking Crook. With the news that Geronimo had surrendered at the Cañon de los Embudos as promised, all that was left for Lummis to do was mop up. The news was a "sad snub to the paper warriors" who had been hounding Crook for months, Lummis remarked in the dispatch he posted in Tucson before hopping back on the train on his way to Crook's headquarters.

Indeed, as Lummis made his way to Fort Bowie, the anti-Crook papers were already beating a retreat. Even Dunbar paid Crook a rare, though qualified, compliment. "General Crook, with all thy faults we love thee still," he wrote.

That afternoon when Lummis disembarked from the train at Bowie Station, he was shocked—and thrilled—by the astonishing news that awaited him. Contrary to what all the papers had reported that very morning, Geronimo hadn't surrendered after all. He had engaged in three days of intensive negotiations with Crook. But in the middle of a rainstorm the previous night, he had slipped away from the Apaches' campsite near Contrabandista Springs with nineteen of his most loyal warriors, six children, and thirteen squaws, sneaking undetected past the loose ring of Apache scout sentries who had staked out the hostiles' camp. Three-quarters of the renegades—seventy-five Indians including thirty braves—had remained in their camp, committed to completing discussions with Crook about the terms of their surrender. But the most infamous Apache of all was already dozens of miles deep into the Sierra Madre with a band of hard-core loyalists, continuing to open a gap between themselves and the party of Crook's scouts and soldiers that had taken off in pursuit.[5]

Any chance of a continuing thaw in the sentiment toward Crook by his critics in the press ended with that report. "The Territorial papers howled and damned Crook for a fool," Lummis wrote in one of his first Fort Bowie–datelined dispatches. The lunacy of every Apache fighting tactic that the unconventional general espoused was writ large in the murderous Geronimo's latest escape, his critics brayed.

As the *Epitaph* saw it, the gullible general had quite simply been out-witted yet again by the treacherous Apaches. "It is claimed by General Crook and other officers that this is the first instance on record where Indians have broken their words after formally pledging themselves to surrender," the *Epitaph* reported, a claim the paper scoffed at, recalling the other instances when the Apaches had fled from the reservation. Dunbar concluded with a remark that almost made it sound as if he felt sorry for the general, who surely now was so thoroughly discredited that his days as an Indian fighter were over. "Who will care for General Crook now?" Dunbar wondered.

* * *

Lummis spent the night of March 30 at Bowie Station awaiting an army orderly, who escorted him to the fort the next morning. The complex, at 4,780 feet near Apache Pass in the Dos Cabezas Mountains, consisted of a large parade ground surrounded by a couple dozen stone and adobe buildings and one Victorian-style wood-framed house that served as the commander's headquarters.

The lonely outpost was considered hard duty for soldiers, but for Lummis, Fort Bowie was almost heaven. It was certainly worlds removed from his desk in Los Angeles. It also afforded him a break from Dolly. The absence was long enough to rekindle the romance that had always been more torrid at a distance, sustained through correspondence, than it was after a few days of togetherness. To be sure, she missed him more than he missed her. "Will you laugh, my darling, way off there in the Apache war, that I sit up here desolate and alone, to write loving nonsense to you—your old married-up wife that is nearly thirty years old?" she wrote in one of her letters to him at Fort Bowie. Being apart from him clearly wasn't a new experience for her, and he had brushed aside her feelings many times before. But she made her plea once again anyway, using her affectionate name for him. "You see it's so different, this being a woman. Why Carl, do you know that I haven't had you that long—two whole weeks—for months, almost for years. . . . Please stay a little while with me, when at last you can come, so that all our youth won't slip away and leave me starved."[6]

Lummis was having too much fun to feel any pangs of loneliness. There was plenty to write about. The fort was a hive of military activity with squads of soldiers constantly on the move, heading out to resupply the troops who were back in the pursuit of Geronimo, returning with fresh, firsthand news from the front. There were dozens of exotic and mysterious Apache scouts hanging around the edges of the fort awaiting their next assignments, and the Chiricahua prisoners who had surrendered to Crawford in January, including the wife and children of Geronimo. They lived in the guardhouse at the lower end of the parade ground and spent their days in the dusty yard in front of the building, the women constantly busy with their hand looms, the children frolicking with their dogs and their balls fashioned from woven strips of cane.

The officer corps included several erudite men who became lifelong friends of Lummis's. There was Captain John Bourke, who had served on General Crook's staff since 1870 and would recount his experiences in an 1891 book called *On the Border with Crook*. He was delighted to have another writer around and would become a key source of information for Lummis. And there was also Lieutenant Leonard Wood, a twenty-six-year-old army surgeon who would become a general at the age of forty, win fame with Teddy Roosevelt in the Spanish-American War, and eventually become army chief of staff. The best prospective source of all, General Crook himself, was at the fort and there was always the chance that Lummis would get a chance to buttonhole him and ask a few questions.

Crook had returned to the fort the evening before Lummis arrived. He appeared unflustered by the fiasco at the Cañon de los Embudos. But he made a point of conveying to the Apaches who hadn't fled into the night his deep sense of annoyance. Even though about seventy-five of the renegades—including Chief Chihuahua, the hereditary leader of the Chiricahuas—still intended to surrender, Crook refused to resume negotiations with them. He sent word to Chihuahua and the others the morning after Geronimo's escape that they would have to come to Fort Bowie and turn themselves in. They were due to arrive the next day.

Crook was holed up in his headquarters, consulting with his officers, when Lummis and the orderly reached the fort. Later that day, the general spared a moment to greet Lummis and accepted a few questions but offered just a "few non-committal words" in response. "It is like pulling teeth to get anything out of him," Lummis lamented. He didn't allow the general's cold shoulder to color his first impression of Crook. He understood that this wasn't, to put it mildly, one of the better days in the Indian fighter's long career. "I like the grim old general," Lummis announced.

Much like Lummis, Crook was supremely self-assured, yet down to earth and informal to a flamboyant degree. He was, in short, like Lummis, an iconoclastic oddball. Crook and the troops under his command had killed countless thousands of Indians over the decades and had corralled tens of thousands of others onto reservations. He had dutifully worked his way up through the ranks of the military hierarchy, playing his career by the book. But at heart Crook had become a free-thinking humanitarian.

His unorthodox appearance began with the great cotton-candy mounds of gray muttonchop sideburns that covered most of the lower half of his face, above which protruded a strong, straight nose and piercing, deep-set blue eyes. Crook's chief sartorial hallmark was the fact that he almost never wore a uniform, preferring overalls or a canvas suit. He also had a peculiar preference in headgear—a conical hat such as that worn by a Japanese farmer at work in a rice field. In other departures from standard-issue Army gear, he carried a shotgun instead of a Springfield rifle and passed up a horse as his mount in favor of a mule, affectionately named Apache, an animal that he insisted was far superior to a horse in the arid, mountainous terrain of the desert Southwest.

It took a while for Crook to open up to Lummis, which was frustrating to a reporter who had come to rescue the "old gray wolf at bay." But Crook didn't care to rebut even the nastiest rumors hurled against him. In one of its broadsides against Crook, the *Epitaph* flatly contradicted the old story about how Crook had bravely led his troops to a heroic military victory in a 1872 campaign against the Tonto Apaches. Crook in fact "never saw a hostile Apache nor heard a gun fired," the *Epitaph* asserted. Another rumor that got wide currency in the anti-Crook press maintained that the supposed Apache War hero had in fact once surrendered to a band of Apache attackers before being liberated by his troops. Crook did nothing to set the record straight. "He is here to fight not to justify himself," Lummis wrote. Lummis would try to fight back for Crook, whether Crook wanted him to or not. "If ever there was an honorable task in letting in the light on a libeled career it lies before me now," wrote Lummis.

In his latest campaign against Geronimo, Crook was far more successful than his critics were prepared to acknowledge, Lummis asserted. Though Geronimo and a few die-hard followers were still on the run, "Crook has reduced the number of renegades by four-fifths within a fortnight without a single death in his ranks," Lummis noted in an April 7 dispatch. "[T]hey knew that Crook would give them fair play. This absolute confidence of the Indians in his honor is almost as important a factor in Crook's success as his matchless knowledge of their traits. The hostiles would not have surrendered thus to any other man." Members of "the blowhard fraternity of Arizona" who talked as if they knew better how to defeat the Apaches were rank failures as Indian fighters when given a chance, Lummis added.

Lummis's low regard for Arizonans sunk steadily lower the deeper he delved into the recent history of the Apache War. He soon came around to the view that many white citizens of the territory hated Crook not because they thought his tactics would fail to end the war. Their chief worry was that his strategy might succeed in laying the groundwork for a lasting peace with the Apaches. Certain members of the business elite in Tucson and Tombstone, Lummis wrote, had grown rich during the interminable conflict. Some of the very people who were braying for Crook's blood were the ones landing contracts to supply the army with food and other provisions. They would "sacrifice all their wife's relations to perpetuate their chief source of income," Lummis remarked. The group of politicians, businessmen, and other power brokers based in Tucson and Tombstone who were benefiting from the war were known as the Tucson Ring or Indian Ring. "When I get time I'll measure the diameter of this ring as closely as can be," he wrote in one of his first stories from Fort Bowie.

Within a few days Lummis had learned of an especially devious deed of the Tucson Ring. A member named Charles Tribolet, a Swiss-American trader long notorious in Tombstone for running a fence used by livestock rustlers, had played a crucial role in the sudden decision by Geronimo to flee in the midst of his negotiations with Crook. From a trading post that he operated four hundred yards south of the Mexican border, he supplied the Apaches who had come to surrender with five five-gallon kegs of grain alcohol and, as he would later boast, one bottle of champagne that he personally handed to Geronimo himself. Fully intending to sabotage the negotiations, he also passed on an incendiary tip, Lummis said. Tribolet told Geronimo and other Apaches, after they had been sufficiently lubricated with drink, that Crook had no intention of sparing their lives as he had promised. The gallows awaited them if they went through with the surrender, he warned his drunken and impressionable customers.

The Apaches didn't believe Crook would blatantly lie to them. But they had good reason to fear he would be ignored or overruled by higher-ups, as he had been on occasion in the past. While the liquor impaired their judgment, it didn't stifle their survival instinct nor their stealth. Without raising the alarm of Crook's Apache sentries in their midst, they slipped out of their encampment in a driving rainstorm, and by dawn Geronimo, though he must have been nursing a fierce hangover from Tribolet's alcohol, was many miles away, on the run once again.

The *Epitaph* denied that an upstanding citizen of Tombstone would have sold whisky to the hostiles. But according to Lummis, Tribolet bragged about it to a U.S. Customs agent investigating the incident, and explained, "It's money in my pocket to have those fellows out there."

Crook knew that Tribolet was guilty. He also realized nothing would be done to punish an act that the territorial business community secretly applauded. "We have no laws here," Crook told Lummis, in a conversation that was one of the first in which the general opened up to the reporter. "This is a country where the majority rules, and no matter what is on the statute books, no law can be enforced against the sentiment of the community."

Crook added that Tribolet should be shot like a coyote. Lummis suggested that he would meet a different fate. Tribolet "has made a lot of money," Lummis wrote, "but it would all melt, one of these days, if he could take it with him."

Lummis filed his story about Tribolet a week after he reached Fort Bowie. But his attempt to absolve Crook of blame for Geronimo's latest escape was too late to save the general. On April 2, the day after Lummis's arrival, word had reached Fort Bowie indicating that the anti-Crook drumbeat in the press had finally gotten through to President Grover Cleveland. Crook had been relieved of his command and had been ordered to relinquish his post at Fort Bowie as soon as his replacement, Brigadier General Nelson Miles, arrived in a couple of weeks.

While Lummis could no longer save Crook's job, perhaps he could help salvage the general's reputation for posterity. He set out to do that in a series of articles about Crook's views on Indian policy that he wrote over the next two weeks.

The lame-duck commander suddenly had plenty of time to talk to Lummis, though he was reluctant to go into much detail about military strategy. Lummis, however, was able to obtain a copy of Crook's final report on his recent activities in Arizona, and he drew on that for several stories.

Chasing the Apaches in their own homeland would have been a formidable assignment for any commander, Lummis noted. "Hunt the world over and you will find no more inhospitable and savage mountains," he wrote, exaggerating just a bit. "No campaign in the Civil War, or in any of the northern Indian wars, was ever so entangled and crippled by topographical cussedness."

Crook was fully justified in letting the Apaches keep their weapons, Lummis added. As the general explained in his report, "The disarming of Indians has in almost every instance on record proved a farcical failure." They would hide their best weapons and turn in inferior arms, if ordered to disarm. Moreover, Crook wrote, it was best to show that you were not afraid of them even when they were fully armed. The Apaches also needed their weapons for their own protection against "white scoundrels who, armed to the teeth, infest the border."

As for the loud chorus of calls for removal of the Apaches from Arizona, taken up even by Crook's more responsible critics such as the editorial writers of the *New York Times*, Crook pointedly noted that the suggestion was "in cool disregard of the fact that Arizona belongs to the Apaches, that they were forced to accept the small reservation in lieu of the whole Territory and that even the Reservation has been thievishly stolen from them and cut down five times to fill the pockets of grasping settlers."

Crook could commiserate even with the Apaches' infamous barbarity toward their enemies and civilian captives. For centuries they had been bred on warfare, with enemies ranging from the Spanish conquistadors to white settlers who were "as cruel as the beast," Crook said. For generations they had seen that their women and children were the first to fall under their enemies' merciless knives. As an inevitable result, for the Apaches "no act of bloodshed is too cruel or unnatural," Crook told Lummis, refusing to fault the warrior for that. "It is therefore unjust to punish him for violations of a code of war which he has never learned, and which he can with difficulty understand." Crook concluded that "sweeping vengeance is as much to be deprecated as silly sentimentalism."

Crook spoke "with an earnestness which showed how deeply his heart was enlisted in this perplexing question," Lummis noted. "You observe that Crook goes by the assumption that the Apache is a human being, after all. That's one of the reasons Arizona is down on him."

Lummis wasn't sentimental about the Apaches. He had gotten an earful about them from Manuel Chaves, who was covered with scars from his lifetime of skirmishes with Apaches and other Indians. The Apaches "were born butchers, hereditary slayers, a robber to whom blood is sweeter than booty," Lummis wrote. They had the "eye of a hawk, the stealth of a coyote, the courage of a tiger—and just as merciless."

Lummis didn't have to go far to find tangible evidence of their brutality. The cemetery in Fort Bowie, which contained thirty-three graves, was "full of Apache workmanship," he wrote in one story. "The dumb upheavals of its brown breast tell of the old stage creaking through a desolate canyon; the sudden little puff of smoke from behind yon innocent tuft of bear-grass, matched in a sickly curl from that rock and another from the aloe-bunch beyond; the sturdy driver tumbling from his perch; the tangled horses floundering in terror; the ashen traveler dragged from his concealment; and last of all a horrid bonfire, whose odorous smoke goes up with the tortured shrieks of a writhing form."

To be sure, an Apache occupied one of the graves, Lummis added. A marker indicated that the body beneath one small mound of earth in the cemetery was that of a three-year-old boy named Little Robe, who had died earlier that spring in the guardhouse. He was the son of Geronimo.

In his days at Fort Bowie, Lummis began to put the history of Apache atrocities into perspective. His conversations with Crook helped shape his opinions. But another important catalyst for change in his outlook was his firsthand experience with the seventy-five Apache renegades who surrendered to Crook. They reached Fort Bowie on April 2, two days after Lummis. Led by Chief Chihuahua, they were a disheartened bunch, though their mental and physical exhaustion was somewhat relieved by a joyful reunion with their family members who had been at the fort since January. They turned in their horses and weapons upon arrival, but Crook let them set up their camp half a mile west of the fort in the arroyo near Apache Spring.

In his first story describing the renegades' encampment, Lummis ridiculed their crude shelters made by stretching ragged blankets between bushes. But his opinion began to change the next day. He was present when Chihuahua and a handful of other braves gathered in Crook's headquarters to conclude the surrender discussion that had been abruptly terminated at Cañon de los Embudos a week earlier. Two Army mule tenders—one who could speak Apache and Spanish, and another who could speak Spanish and English—relayed the conversation between the two veteran warriors.

Chihuahua had participated in a number of the most gruesome attacks in southern Arizona in recent years. But Lummis was struck by how different he seemed from the barbaric killer that all of Arizona wanted to string up. "The old man has a very kindly face and musical voice," Lummis wrote. His speech to Crook lasted fifteen minutes. He said he was surrendering himself to the great general who rules the sun by day and the moon by night. He was willing to take whatever punishment Crook saw fit to impose, but pleaded with the general to treat him as a kindly master would a little dog. He was now at Crook's mercy and trusted that whatever he chose to do with the Apaches would be the right thing. But he had a special request. His children were distraught about the prospect of losing their pet horse. Could they take it along to wherever Crook was going to send them?

A few days later Lummis paid a second visit to the renegades' encampment, this time with a far more respectful attitude toward their handiwork. The women had cleared out the cactus, knotted the bear-grass into mats with strings of its own fiber, built windbreaks with mesquite branches, and constructed shelters with muslin stretched over frames made with the stalks of century plants. In a couple of days, Lummis observed, the squaws had turned the camp into a "work of art" while the braves, who spent their days gambling, "lent moral support."

Lummis was especially interested in gaining insights into how the Apaches could traverse hundreds of miles of rugged terrain in no time. He discovered that the soles of their feet were "as tough as a politician's conscience," an observation that must have influenced his decision some years later to force his own children to go barefoot as much as possible. He watched in amazement as a brave struck a match on the sole of his foot. "A strip of sandpaper couldn't have been more effective." He ended that visit to the camp by trading his boots for a pair of Apache moccasins.

That night Lummis and a few others from the fort were drawn back to the camp by an eerie spectacle. The Indians, who had learned that the next day they would be marched to the depot at Bowie Station and carried by a train somewhere far to the east, danced and sang all night long, surrounded by the mountains that their ancestors had occupied for countless generations.

On April 7, the day of the Apaches' departure from Arizona, whites who had heard the news came from miles around to gawk as the Apaches marched to the rail line accompanied by their horses and dozens of dogs. A total of eighty-seven Apaches were shipped to Florida that day, including Geronimo's wife and children, leaving thirty-seven of the tribe led by Geronimo still at large in the Sierra Madre. The captives were loaded into the railcars. As the train picked up speed, their dogs started yelping in distress. One reportedly chased after the train for twenty miles. But most of the abandoned pets were left wandering aimlessly around Bowie Station, where they served as target practice for the milling crowd of gleeful whites. The horses—including Chihuahua's children's favorite—were rounded up and auctioned off on the spot.

The crowd wasn't as large and hostile as it might have been. At Crook's request, Lummis withheld his report about the departure of the Apaches until they were gone. "There are plenty of alleged white men who would jump at the chance to signalize their bravery by shooting a captive squaw through a car window if they had received sufficient notice to brace themselves with brag and whisky," Lummis wrote in explaining his act of self-censorship.

The removal of the Indians was a triumph for Crook, as Lummis told it. They were not going back to the San Carlos reservation, as the Apaches had hoped. But neither were the warriors among them going to the gallows, an outcome that many Arizonans demanded. In fact on March 31, the day Lummis reached Fort Bowie, Cochise County sheriff Robert Hatch also rode into the fort for a meeting with Crook during which he presented the general with a warrant for the arrest of Geronimo and forty-one John Does. Crook turned Hatch away, telling him that the Apaches who were surrendering were federal prisoners of war and he had no intention of relinquishing custody.

Crook himself packed his bags and left Fort Bowie a week later when his replacement, General Miles, arrived to take charge of the ongoing pursuit of Geronimo. Lummis was sad to see Crook go. When he told the general so, Crook retorted, "I'm not." Lummis could only hope that the kindly general would win vindication in this life and not have to wait until the next, though that wasn't a foregone conclusion. "When the mongrel pack which has barked at the heels of this patient commander has rotted a hundred years forgotten—then, if not before, Crook will get his due," Lummis wrote.

As for Geronimo, the passage of time would raise his stock with many, including Lummis. In the final months of his life, stricken with cancer, knowing that his days were numbered and with dozens of unfinished projects, Lummis chose to expend his waning energy on completing his book of poems about the Southwest, *Bronco Pegasus*, and particularly the centerpiece of the book, a 256-line ballad, "Man-Who-Yawns," about the Apache war leader. Lummis had belittled Geronimo as the "gory Chiricahua" in his first dispatch to the *Times* from the Arizona Territory. But in the end Lummis saw Geronimo in an entirely different light, praising his fighting prowess in the opening stanzas of the poem, and concluding with an image of the Apaches as heroic figures whose demise symbolized the loss of much else about the Southwest that Lummis cherished.

> The Desert Empire that he rode,
> his trail of blood and fire,
> Is pythoned, springs and valleys, with
> the strangle-snake of wire.
> The Fence has killed the Range and all
> for which its freedom stood—
> Though countless footsore cowboys mill
> in mimic Hollywood.
>
> A Tragedy? What wholesale words
> we use in petty ways—
> For murder, broken hearts of banks,
> and disappointed days!
> But here an Epoch petered out,
> An Era ended flat;
> The Apache was the Last Frontier—
> The Tragedy is *that!*

Miles had virtually nothing in common with Crook. He was a by-the-book military man who reveled in all the pomp of his position as commander of an army. He also was much more committed to conventional military doctrine than Crook. He made it clear at the start that he had little use for Crook's tactics, starting with his predecessor's heavy reliance on Apache scouts, who he believed should have been shipped to Florida in the same train as the renegades. Typical of most army officers, Miles had unconcealed contempt for his savage foes. As would become apparent, he had little compunction about lying to the Indians. For all of these reasons, the *Tombstone Epitaph* and much of the rest of the territorial press couldn't sing his praises loud enough.

Convinced that the best white soldiers could quickly corral Geronimo, Miles announced soon after arriving in Arizona that he planned to implement a strategy of "vigorous pursuit" by units manned with the best athletes in the U.S. Army. A small contingent of Apaches would play a minor supporting role. His secret weapon was a network of heliographs, signal towers on the highest peaks that used mirrors to flash messages in Morse code. Miles's officers could use the communications network to send a message four hundred miles across deserts and mountains and receive an answer within four hours. The Apaches would be so awed by this astonishing capability and the tactical advantages it would give his troops that they would give up at the sight of the lights flashing from every mountain peak, Miles believed. His corps of elite troops would be capable of continuing the chase for months, but Miles said they should be able to bring the renegades to heel after just forty-eight hours of round-the-clock pursuit.

Lummis would have realized such a claim was ludicrous. He almost certainly disliked Miles even before the new commander reached Fort Bowie. As the *Times* had reported earlier in the year, Miles and his friends had been lobbying President Cleveland for months to remove Crook and give Miles the job. As his esteem for Crook grew, Lummis probably had grown to hate the man whose appointment gave such joy to the *Epitaph* and all others who had worked so hard to ruin Crook. But Lummis wasn't about to disclose his true feelings for the new commander. In fact, he put on a good show of liking the man, and did his best to flatter Miles and butter him up. In this Lummis had an ulterior motive: his request to join the troops in the field in the pursuit of Geronimo was now on Miles's desk.[7]

Lummis nearly got his wish. Miles, who unlike Crook understood the importance of courting the press, was "ready to give me every facility," Lummis informed Otis. On April 15, Miles notified Lummis to pack up and prepare to depart for Mexico. Knowing something about the difficulties the troops would encounter, Lummis planned for a three-to-six-month expedition. In an April 19 dispatch to the *Times* Lummis wrote, "By the time you read this I shall doubtless have jumped the picket fence of civilization" to enter the fabled Sierra Madre in pursuit of Geronimo. On the eve of departure, however, Miles got a telegram from Washington ordering him to hold off. U.S. diplomats had hit a snag in negotiations with Mexico for permission to send troops across the border. Otis seized the opportunity to order Lummis to return to Los Angeles, where he was desperately needed back on the badly overtaxed city desk.

Lummis was devastated. "I am victim of a cruel fate. The *Times* yanked me in to attend to some pressing work at home," he lamented later. Otis had promised Lummis that "whenever anything lively developed," he would send his reporter back to Fort Bowie. But once Lummis returned to Los Angeles, Otis kept him there, even though Miles sent four telegrams urging him to return and join the troops in the field. "I argued and orated, cajoled, damned and held on. But I couldn't get away to see the fun. It's a hard dose," Lummis said. "To be choked off and tied down to this dodgusted routine—isn't it enough to make anyone sick?"

Through the summer Geronimo made a mockery of Miles's "continuous pursuit" strategy. More than eighty percent of the soldiers in his units of tough white superathletes who went into Mexico in pursuit of Geronimo had to abandon their mission and limp back to Fort Bowie. By the end of the summer, Miles was forced to bring back large numbers of Crook's Apache scouts to continue the chase.

In September Geronimo finally turned himself in to Captain Charles Gatewood, one of Crook's protégés. He entered the Apache renegades' camp unarmed and accompanied by half a dozen Apache scouts. After lengthy negotiations, Gatewood agreed to escort the Apaches to Fort Bowie without disarming them until they got there. Without getting explicit permission from Miles, but convinced that Geronimo and his braves would flee otherwise, Gatewood promised them that they would not be turned over to the territorial authorities, who were itching to hang them high. Their lives would be spared and they would be permitted to joined their families and the rest of the Chiricahuas at Fort Marion in Florida, Gatewood said.

Miles would later try to rescind Gatewood's offer. But President Cleveland, under heavy lobbying from Crook, would uphold the promise to spare their lives. Miles was more successful in stealing credit from Gatewood for the surrender. No sooner had Gatewood returned to Fort Bowie than Miles transferred him to Kansas, to isolate him from the press, who, now that the Apache threat was finally over for good, descended on Fort Bowie to chronicle Miles's heroic final victory over the infamous Apache warrior. Mile's deceitful grab for glory would eventually catch up with him. Years later, when he and Crook were vying for the same promotion, army chief of staff Leonard Wood gave the nod to Crook.

Lummis would have to read of the final surrender of Geronimo that September and of the aftermath in the months that followed as the news reached the *Times* office through the wires of the Associated Press.

Chapter 5

Boom and Bust

By the fall of 1886 a full-blown land boom was starting in Southern California. The stage had been set a year earlier when the Atchison, Topeka & Santa Fe Railroad completed a line across the southwestern deserts to Los Angeles, breaking a monopoly that the Southern Pacific had enjoyed for sixteen years.

The first Santa Fe train reached the city on November 29, 1885. Fares began tumbling within days. When the Southern Pacific was the only way to reach Los Angeles by rail, the fare from Kansas City had been $125. By the end of 1885 the price had plummeted to $10, and in a promotional frenzy the next March, it hit $1. That unbelievable deal lasted for only a few days, but the fare stayed below $25 for a full year. Freight rates dropped as well, helping spur an economic boom by, among other things, boosting the value of the Los Angeles area's agricultural output. People surged into Southern California. At the height of the boom in 1887, hundreds of new settlers poured into the region each week. By the end of that year, the population of the city had doubled since Lummis's arrival less than three years earlier and the crossroads settlements that he had passed on the last day of his tramp had become boomtowns in their own right.[1]

Stores and restaurants in the city were so overcrowded that patrons had to wait in line for service. Every hotel in town was filled to capacity, and some set up cots in the parlors to handle the overflow. To lure prospective purchasers to picnics at newly opened subdivisions, brass bands paraded through the streets of downtown Los Angeles practically every day accompanied by boys handing out leaflets announcing the latest last-chance bargains for a piece of paradise. A street-paving campaign was going full blast. By the end of the 1880s there were eighty-seven miles of paved streets and seventy-eight miles of concrete sidewalk in Los Angeles, eliminating one of the chief banes of city life at mid-decade—the mud that formed after every winter rain and the dust that swirled up in the summer from the town's dirt streets. Work on the first cable car running up the hill on Second Street had begun in March 1885, and in just a few years an extensive network of electric cars had spread throughout the region. In 1887 the cacophony was so loud at times, with the huffing of the steamroller that was paving Court Street converging with the racket of the brass bands, that judges in the county courthouse had to suspend proceedings from time to time because the jurors couldn't hear witnesses testifying just ten feet away.

Describing the bustling street scene at the height of the land boom, the *Times* observed in its 1887 year-in-review issue, "Anyone arriving for the first time from the back country would imagine that a fair was in progress." Ironically, the sentence was borrowed verbatim from a story that had appeared in the paper in March 1885 about the crowd that jostled for position to witness the hangings of Silvas and Martinez in the adobe courtyard of the old county jail. Perhaps even the *Times* recognized, at least subconsciously, that there was something obscene about the land-buying frenzy that gripped the Los Angeles area in 1887. As settlers poured into the region, land prices went through the roof. In the community of Monrovia, fifteen miles east of downtown, lots that had cost $150 in mid-1886 sold for $5,000 to $8,000 a year later. Price increases like that inevitably gave rise to a new class of land buyer—speculators who expected to sell within months for a fat profit.

Notwithstanding any qualms they might have had, the region's newspapers did their part to sustain the frenzy, none more effectively than the *Times*. Ads for real estate ventures packed the pages of the paper, urging people to buy supposedly fast disappearing parcels. "The Boom at Alhambra! . . . Don't be slow if you want a bargain in the most desirable spot in Southern California," read an ad on December 26, 1886. "Talk Quick! Splendid opportunity to DOUBLE your money in THIRTY DAYS," proclaimed an ad the next fall touting parcels in another tract.

The news sections of the *Times*, on the other hand, carried hints of a grittier reality. Swindles of various sorts were commonplace. People down on their luck flocked to the region where everyone seemed to be getting rich, only to find themselves worse off than ever. Hardly a week went by without news of yet another suicide, and notices about the latest crimes filled the paper every day. But those downbeat news items weren't enough to take the gleam off the main story conveyed by the *Times* about the region: Southern California, the paper proclaimed, is heaven on earth.

The message was especially blatant in the annual year-in-review edition sold as a souvenir that tourists could send to friends back home. The boom years' editions carried page after page of descriptions of all of the fruits and vegetables that thrived in Southern California and the staggering yields that farmers routinely got. A doctor weighed in with an account of all the diseases that could be cured by the region's phenomenally beneficent environment. In an article entitled "Seventy Answers," addressing frequently asked questions about Los Angeles, the *Times* dismissed the popular misconception that earthquakes were a concern with the categorical denial "not at all." "Within the past year (a fair average) four shocks have been felt," the article stated. "The strongest would not spill any water from a brimful tumbler."

As for ethnic tensions, there were none of those either, nor for that matter was there much ethnic diversity except as a quaint relic. A history of the region dwelt on the romance of the Spanish colonial past, briefly recounting the years of Mexican governance. A few rapidly vanishing remnants of that era could still be found in the part of the city once called Sonoratown, more recently known as Chinatown. The Mexicans and their languorous way of life "have passed in making room for the more energetic Chinaman with his washee house, his notion store and meat market. But even these later occupants are but tenants of a day. This street is too important for a Chinatown. A break in the line of adobes shows a substantial brick business block. Another block with iron front and modern façade is in course of erection a little further on. Across the way a line of adobes is undergoing demolition. The ancient domiciles are going, going, and in a year or two will be gone. Thus," proclaimed the *Times*'s front page on New Years Day 1886, "the old type fades away for the new."

The *Chillicothe Leader* commissioned this publicity photo of Lummis before his cross-country "tramp" to California. Photo N22201

Frank Hamilton Cushing, here in Zuni regalia, whose visit to Harvard piqued Lummis's interest in the Southwest. *Photo N24856*

Lummis, here dancing with Nina del Valle, fell in love with the Southwest's Spanish heritage during his time with the del Valle family. *Photo N13622*

Lummis's first wife, Dorothea, was a doctor, part-time drama critic for the *Times,* and a leading member of several civic associations in Los Angeles in the late 1880s. *Photo N24316*

General George Crook, the army's most successful Indian fighter, whom Lummis defended against charges of being too sympathetic to the Apaches. *Photo N42641*

Unperturbed by the temporary paralysis of his left arm, Lummis learned to roll and light his cherished cigarettes with one hand. *Photo N22203*

Crucifixion of Penitente Santiago Jaramillo, Good Friday, Mch. 30, 1888.
Jose Salazar
Filomeno Chaves
Cuate
Cisto Baca.
-n Baca

Lummis's persistence eventually
won him the Penitentes'
permission to photograph the
secretive religious society's
annual crucifixion ritual.
Photo N22541

The famous archaeologist
Adolph Bandelier maintained a
close if fitful lifelong relationship
with Lummis. *Photo N36542*

While his left arm was paralyzed, Lummis learned to shoot rabbits with a rifle held in one hand. *Photo N42941*

Lummis in attire that would be his trademark: a green corduroy suit, red Navajo sash, and soiled Stetson sombrero. *Photo N42477*

Charles and Eve Lummis with their daughter, Turbesé, and Luis Abeita, one of the children whom Lummis liberated from the Albuquerque Indian School. *Photo N10276*

Richard Henry Pratt, head-master of the Carlisle Indian School, upon whose death Lummis wrote, "God absolve [him] for what he did, and credit him only with what he meant to do." *Cumberland County Historical Society, Carlisle, Pennsylvania.*

Administrators of the Carlisle Indian School took "before" and "after" photographs of Indian children to show the progress they were making in becoming "civilized." Henry Kendall, in the top row, right, of this "after" photograph, helped teach Lummis the Tigua language. *Cumberland County Historical Society, Carlisle, Pennsylvania.*

Amado Bandelier Lummis, Charles's oldest son, died of pneumonia two months after his father took this photograph. *Photo N42944*

The latest group of immigrants drawn to the region were as extraordinary as the region itself—progressive, adventurous, and dynamic simply by virtue of the fact that they had pulled up stakes back east or in the Old World and come to California. "It is a vast colony of intelligent and prosperous seekers for a residence where the conditions of life shall be more favorable." They are people "who demand to live in the garden of Eden," who would settle for nothing less than a "country where dreams come true."

Lummis probably wrote much of the copy in the year-in-review issues. He certainly wrote the article about the climate, introducing a theme that would become a favorite of his in the years to come. But at the time, he would have been hard pressed to prove that his own dreams were coming true. He hardly had time to notice the lovely climate. In a city bursting at the seams with more news than ever, and as the chief workhorse on the staff of a newspaper that was getting steadily bigger by the month to contain it all, he was working night and day.

The *Times* was already locked in fierce competition with the *Daily Herald*, a Democratic Party mouthpiece, and the *Evening Express*, a rival Republican paper. The fall debut in 1886 of a bitter new competitor, the *Tribune*, intensified the newspaper war. The *Tribune* was published by the former co-owner of the *Times*, Henry Boyce, who had been ousted during a business dispute with Otis that spring.[2] The *Herald* was "neighborly and journalistic" by comparison, Otis noted in one of his many editorial assaults on his former partner's new venture. For the *Tribune*, there was "no abuse too brutal, no falsehood too malignant for them to employ it with palpable delight." To be sure, Otis dished out more vicious abuse than he got, relentlessly attacking Boyce over everything from his lack of business ethics to his "malodorous" marital record.

By the summer of 1887 the *Times* had emerged from the financial difficulties that had precipitated the split between Otis and Boyce. With profits from all the real estate ads, the company had built a new headquarters, a three-story building of granite blocks, brick, iron, and copper, at the corner of First and Fort Streets. The paper commenced business in this impressive new home on July 1.

Over the previous year or so, the *Times* had grown steadily, both in the dimensions of the paper and in the number of pages, trying to keep pace with the galloping growth of the city. In the summer of 1887 the paper often ran sixteen pages a day. The staff had grown from perhaps a couple of dozen when Lummis had arrived two and half years earlier to just over a hundred. However, with the labor-intensive printing technology of the day, most were involved in setting type and operating the bulky printing presses. Only 7 of the 104 employees on the staff that August were engaged in gathering, writing, and editing the news. Lummis, who had been named city editor in September 1886, was the overworked linchpin of the editorial staff.

The stories that Lummis worked on weren't as exotic as his dispatches from Fort Bowie. But there was no shortage of scintillating subject matter in the burgeoning city.

The sensational saga of Louisa Perkins versus Lucky Baldwin was back on the front pages. Baldwin had filed a libel suit against one of the *Times's* competitors for reporting that his conquests had included not only Perkins but other young women, including one of his own relatives. Even a "decent dog wouldn't associate with him," the paper had said of Baldwin. As for Perkins, in a trial in 1886 she had won a jury verdict for $75,000, but the judge had set it aside as excessive. A new trial was scheduled to begin on Monday, July 25, 1887. Then, the Friday before, the *Times* got the scoop that the case had been settled for ten percent of the judgment amount. The report of the settlement turned out to be accurate, though the amount was not quite right. In a settlement finalized July 26, Perkins got $12,000 and immediately headed for Europe with her new lover.

The paper carried another love-gone-wrong story in the fall of 1887. An enterprising *Times* reporter noticed a young woman at the post office who seemed lost and alone, and distraught that there was no letter for her that day. Identifying himself as a reporter, the scribe asked if she needed help, and she told her story. She was a newlywed, brought to the strange city by a heartless husband who had promptly abandoned her. It made for a poignant front-page story about a confiding young wife "deserted among strangers in the city."

That phrase was an apt description of Lummis's own wife. Though by 1887 they had been legally married for six years, they had spent so little time together at home that it seemed to Dolly that they were newlyweds. To be sure, she hadn't depended on him to make a life for herself in Los Angeles. She was strong enough to go it alone, if that was her lot in life. In addition to her full slate of activities in various civic associations, she had built a successful medical practice. She made quite an impression around town, by one account making house calls in a light carriage behind a pair of fast horses, with an Irish setter by her side which had red hair that matched her own. But in her letters to him when he was out on another adventure, she regularly noted that, as a man, he had it better. "How I wish I could be a man o' days and a woman o' nights," she wrote in one letter to him when he was out on the road. "Then we could have comradeship and love, too, instead of my seeing you a scant week or two after all these months and then accepting the hardest part, that of waiting while you explore and tramp."

The best times she and Charlie had were on the several occasions when they traveled together to his favorite haunts in New Mexico. Otis, apparently happy enough with the stories Lummis had written about their visit to Acoma in the fall of 1885, freed up his key reporter for a few weeks in each of the next two years so that they could repeat the trip. Lummis produced a series of stories reminiscent of the tales from his tramp, which Otis presented in the paper, often on the front page, as the adventures of "Lum and Doc" in "Injun Country."

They rode by train and horseback through the land of enchanted light, broad plains, yawning canyons, and broken mesas colored in browns, reds, and grays. They found arrowheads and pottery shards, enjoyed the camaraderie of railroad workers in section houses, stayed in pueblos, and witnessed Indian dances accompanied by singing "with the sentimental aboriginal pathos which makes a man want to get his back up against something and see that his six-shooter is in running order."

When Lummis and his wife left for their tour of New Mexico in October of 1886, he was carrying a device that he had purchased just a few months earlier and was still learning how to use: a camera.[3] "One of the regrets of my lengthy paseo of two years ago was my lack of ability to bring away pictorial reminiscences of the countless places along the road," Lummis wrote. "It was always a pang to me, and at times a most cactus-pointed one. One little picture of the faithful dog that shared my hard bed and scanty board across the Rockies, through the snows of the southwestern mountains, and the fearful heat and thirst of Arizona's deserts—one poor little dingy likeness would be dearer to me than the rarest work of art." To prevent any further regrets of that sort, he had decided to "learn light-writing—the expressive name which photography has borrowed from a language that knew nothing of these later wonders." He took ninety dry plates with him on that trip and used up all but three.

By the time of his 1887 "Lum and Doc" adventure, Lummis had mastered the technical skills of photography and was working on the trickier art of snapping pictures of unwilling subjects. Writing from Acoma, he observed, "For these Pueblo towns one should have a lens which will focus itself, adjust a plate and make the exposure in about the millionth part of a second. The Pueblos share the superstition of the Navajos about pictures; and my appearance around a corner with the tripod and camera was the signal for such a scamper as nothing else short of a pack of wolves would be likely to cause. Children flew, women ran, and the most dignified men got an immediate 'move' on them. We had to be content with photographing such buildings as we desired, and then, planting the camera in some obscure corner, focusing it down the street and waiting for the unwary to happen along."

Lummis wrote with affection about his wife in those stories. But back in Los Angeles, all was not well between Charlie and Dolly. Friends of hers would later say she confided to them that she lived in fear of his occasional rages. In fact, she kept a carving knife by the bed in case she ever needed to dissuade him from attacking. And she kept a coat outside the house so that she would have something to wear if he ever kicked her out at night in her nightgown.[4]

Lummis's stressful job and ungodly hours at the office couldn't have helped his relationship with his wife. The strain that Lummis and others on the editorial staff were forced to work under at the *Times* was something that Otis actually bragged about. A lengthy story in the paper in the summer of 1887 about how the paper was put together each day and evening and shipped out to its readers across the city in the wee hours of the night spoke of the "severe and unseasonable toil" that characterized the exercise of producing a newspaper. The employees of the paper worked under a regime that was "military in its severity," the article boasted.[5]

"It is hard to say at which point the day begins for a daily paper, inasmuch as there is no beginning and no end of labor," the article explained. If you had to pick a time when the daily cycle started, it would be around half past three, when the last of the plates for that morning's edition were shipped to the pressroom. One side of the paper had already been printed, and the steam-driven press was ready for the final pages. The press run finished at 6 A.M. and the last papers were out the door by seven.

The editors and reporters arrived for work anytime between 9 A.M. and 2 P.M., depending on their particular duties. Lummis was always one of the last on the editorial staff to leave. And he was one of the first to arrive, beginning each day with his ritual of cutting up a copy of the paper and pasting the clippings in indexed scrapbooks. His plan for the day's paper was already mostly in place. He had given daily assignments to his reporters the night before, while holding some in reserve for breaking news. When reporters began turning in their stories in the afternoon, his day would begin in earnest. He pruned, elaborated upon, or boiled down the copy, wrote headlines, and then passed it on for the final approval of the chief editor.

The article in the *Times* observed, "Old Ben Franklin numbering the hours which should constitute a night's sleep said: 'Six for a man, seven for a woman, and eight for a fool.' Whether this rule is a good one or not—and there are excellent authorities who dispute it—newspaper writers rarely enjoy the luxury of ranking with Franklin's class of fools."

The article lends credence to a claim that Lummis often made about his time at the paper. "In my three years on the *Times*," he recalled in his memoir, "I never got more than two hours of sleep in the twenty-four and for the final newspaper year not over one."

Though Lummis was run ragged in his years at the *Times*, he never held it against Otis. He would always remain a devoted admirer of the Old Chief, the salutation he favored in his letters to Otis in the years after he left the paper.[6]

His admiration was based in part on the role the *Times* played in turning Los Angeles from a lawless frontier pueblo into a modern city. "Few people in Los Angeles realize today what they owe him," Lummis wrote in his memoir. "I don't exaggerate when I say as one who has known and studied this town for 44 years that it owes no other man so much as this rough old soldier."

In his years with the paper in the 1880s, the *Times* was virtually a lone voice standing up to the forces that were railing for a boycott of Chinese businesses. The paper was the leading proponent of "high license," a fiercely opposed regulatory mechanism that imposed a licensing fee and other controls on businesses selling liquor. The *Times* also supported the first municipal bonds that financed construction of a sewer system and helped beat back the attempt by the Southern Pacific Railroad to block construction of a city harbor in San Pedro, a port that competing railroads also served.

To be sure, Lummis wasn't blind to Otis's faults. In 1922 at a reunion of former employees of the *Times*, Lummis offered some frank comments on his former boss. "Colonel Otis was brusque, rough, suspicious, vindictive. . . . He made innumerable enemies quite needlessly, as well as a large number that were greatly to his credit. It was good that every scoundrel, every criminal, every low politician hated him. It was a pity that so many thoroughly good people disliked him. He could have done a great deal more good if he had not antagonized so many good citizens. However as he did more for the community than all other newspapermen put together, I presume we may forgive him this loss of further achievement."

In his final months at the *Los Angeles Times*, Lummis became personally involved in one bitter dispute that was a product of Otis's vindictiveness—the publisher's relentless vendetta against Boyce.

By the fall of 1887 the Otis-Boyce battle was once again in full fury. Otis was especially determined to prove a point he had made in passing earlier in the year about Boyce's sordid marital record. To back up his allegation, Otis had obtained a copy of the court file covering Boyce's divorce from his first wife in Lake County, Illinois, seventeen years earlier. As Otis gleefully informed readers of the *Times*, the first Mrs. Boyce had asserted that her husband had brought another woman to their home "for his own purposes" and had forced his wife to wait on them.

Boyce returned fire with editorials that were mild in comparison. In the November 30 edition of the *Tribune*, Boyce called Otis a "brute" and Lummis a "sneak" and a "little liar." That insult was more than Lummis was going to take. At 4 P.M. on the day after that editorial appeared, Lummis confronted Boyce in front of the Nadeau Hotel on Spring Street. Boyce was in a double-team wagon with several women passengers. Lummis let the ladies disembark and leave the scene before he leapt up onto the wagon and attacked. As Lummis matter-of-factly recounted the incident in his memoir, "I sought out Col. Smoothy and whacked him across the face with my leather cane."

Several eyewitnesses corroborated Lummis's account, but Boyce denied that Lummis hit him. The "excited little man" never got closer to him than ten feet, he told a reporter for the *Express*. The *Times*, which took great pride in the combative spirit of its reporter, insisted that Boyce "*was* struck, but made off in a hurry." Lummis's action, the *Times* added, was fully defensible in light of Boyce's libelous tirade "to which no sober person would think of replying in words."

Lummis, however, did not emerge from the fracas unscathed. The stress from the encounter may have been a final straw on top of tensions that had been building up through the fall of 1887. "For several months I had admonitory symptoms," he recalled. "My left forefinger went to sleep and stayed so. And sometimes the same crinkly feeling ran all around my heart." Then he felt an odd tingling sensation in his left leg. "But I laughed to scorn those who warned me to look out."

He couldn't very gracefully cut back, after Otis had so frequently and lavishly praised him for his selfless devotion to his work. "I worked without a thought to lateness or of health," he later recalled. "Having long before sent off my reporter or reporters (in the growing days when I had actually had any), I would put the paper to bed myself. At 5 A.M. I would get home. At 7 my wife—not daring to disobey my orders, for the smell of blood was in my nostrils—was shaking me violently and weeping." He would come to, shave, take a cold bath, and stumble into the office, where the adrenaline would kick in and he would be good for another twenty-hour day.

On December 5, however, four days after his attack on Boyce, that routine was abruptly interrupted. "I went home for supper and lay down for a few minutes on the lounge. I couldn't get up. I fought like a tiger. I knew what fighting was, too. Finally I did get up—but only to discover that my left side was helpless. I was paralyzed."

Chapter 6

A New Mexico Convalescence

By December of 1887 the bloom was off the rose in Los Angeles just as it was with Lummis's health. A Los Angeles–datelined report in the *New York Herald* that summer told a story that few in Los Angeles could bring themselves to admit. "It is not hard to see signs that the great real estate boom is in tatters," the New York paper gloated. Brass bands "have to toot louder and longer to get any excitement," even though the terms offered to purchasers were getting easier by the week. People who bought lots with the intention of flipping them for a quick profit began to run into trouble finding buyers.

For Republicans, the political climate also took an unfriendly turn. In the election of December 5, the day of Lummis's breakdown, the Republican Party, weakened by the defection of one core constituency to the Prohibition Party, lost its majority on the City Council. In a futile hope that the results would be overturned on a technicality concerning the time of day that the polls closed, Otis didn't accept the Republican defeat until weeks after it had become a reality.

Otis's distasteful war with Boyce was as nasty as ever and still had several years to run. Otis would eventually squeeze his rival out of business by buying the *Tribune's* printing plant. But in the meantime, working in the midst of that vendetta would be no fun.

Even the weather that was supposedly ever idyllic in Southern California took a dramatic turn for the worse that December. The *Times* tried to deny that as well, for a while anyway. Unusually heavy and persistent rains had begun in the final weeks of December. By the first week of the new year, it still didn't look like anything that the tourists packed into the city should bother to write home about, the *Times* breezily asserted. "Even during the past stormy days dwellers in tents, with well-laid floors, were comfortable here in Los Angeles," an article in the *Times* on January 5 observed. "Our winter is such in name only."

But the storm continued. A blizzard on January 2 in the mountain passes near Truckee leveled three miles of telegraph lines, leaving San Francisco almost entirely cut off from the East. Trains across the state were halted by landslides and washed-out bridges. Two schooners were lost at sea in a relentless storm that news reports began to concede was the "most severe which has visited the coast in years." By the middle of January, the rain still hadn't let up. When those reports began to appear in papers back east, the flow of winter tourists and would-be immigrants to Southern California slowed to a trickle. That was enough to nudge the already faded land boom over the edge and into what was undeniably a bust.

Lummis, likewise, was rapidly approaching a day of reckoning. For weeks after his breakdown, he continued to try to struggle to his feet. He succeeded in making it to the *Times* office a couple of times, but on each occasion had to be carried home. It wasn't until the end of January that Lummis finally came to accept that he would have to change tactics in his battle against paralysis. No more fighting it by trying to pretend nothing had happened. No more trying to drag himself back to the *Times* newsroom under the sadly mistaken impression that he was ready to resume a full day and night's work. Even he had to admit he was no better—in fact his condition had gotten worse. So he began to warm up to the idea that Dolly and the Chaveses had been pushing for weeks.

Dorothea had been keeping Don Manuel and Amado apprised of Lummis's steadily deteriorating physical and mental condition. They encouraged her to bundle him onto a train and send him to San Mateo for a quiet convalescence. Lummis eventually decided to accept the Chaveses' offer. Requesting a three-month leave of absence from the *Times*, he boarded a train February 5, bound for Grants. But he wasn't retiring to New Mexico to take it easy. Lummis didn't see the move as an admission of defeat. He was simply moving his grim war against his paralysis onto new ground. He had decided to "go to the wilderness and live outdoors till I'm well," as he later told it, "and off I packed to New Mexico, though I was barely able to waddle."[1]

Later, looking back on this period in his life, Lummis could portray it as an uplifting adventure. In *My Friend Will*, his autobiographical account of his struggle to overcome his devastating affliction, published in 1911, he went so far as to declare, "My paralysis was the luckiest thing that ever befell [me]." It reinforced one of the guiding principles of his life: that "man was meant to be, and ought to be, stronger than anything that can happen to him." The experience also taught him another lesson, one that came in handy during those times when his troubles appeared to have the upper hand. "If I couldn't have what I wanted, I decided to want what I had, and that philosophy saved me. . . . it turned my misfortunes into good," he explained.

There was no hint of an end to his misfortunes when he staggered painfully off the train in Grants at 3:20 on the morning of February 8. The trip should have taken a day and a half. But a landslide caused by the heavy rains had blocked the tracks in eastern Arizona, detaining the train and turning the ride into an ordeal of nearly three days. Lummis had mustered enough energy to haul his heavy camera tripod off the train to take three shots of the rock pile on the tracks. But by the time he reached Grants, he could hardly stand.

Amado had asked a friend of his, Emil Bibo, to meet Lummis. A German Jewish immigrant who owned a general store and Indian curio shop in Grants, Emil and his wife and brother were three of the couple dozen people in town, which occupied a single street about fifty yards long lined with a dozen structures flanking the train depot. Lummis slept in the Bibos' home for what was left of the night.

He looked worse than Amado had led Bibo to expect. His speech was badly slurred, his left arm was useless and his left leg nearly so. But he could cling to a saddle. So Bibo escorted Lummis on horseback for the four-hour ride over the worn lava shoulder of Mount Taylor to the Chaves family hacienda twenty miles northeast of the rail line near the village of San Mateo. In early afternoon, they reached the Chaves hacienda. Lummis felt like he had come home.[2] The sprawling adobe with its twelve-foot-wide central hallway, floors carpeted with Navajo blankets, windows covered with lace, roaring fireplaces, and fun-loving members of the extended Chaves clan, two dozen in all including several seductive señoritas—this was where, during his brief stopover as a tramp, Lummis's lifelong love affair with Spanish American culture had begun. But at the start of this visit, Lummis wasn't in a frame of mind to settle into the home life of the hacienda. He had another agenda. "I got out. As much as courtesy to my hosts would permit, I stayed out," he said.

In fact, on his first afternoon he took off across the prairie alone with a horse and rifle to hunt but, unable to hold the gun steady, he had no luck. Within several days, though, he had taught himself to "throw down" with his Winchester rifle while on horseback—in a single motion drawing and aiming it as if it were a six-shooter, steadying the gun in his one good hand. Soon, in the diary he had begun to keep, he was tallying a daily body count of animals he had succeeded in killing. Within two weeks of his arrival, the toll of rabbits was in the teens and he had bagged his first coyote.[3]

The village of San Mateo a mile away from the hacienda was a fertile field for Lummis's explorations. The town's rapid demise in the face of onrushing American influence was still a few decades off. In the 1880s it was "perhaps the most unreclaimed Mexican village in New Mexico. Not a dozen of its four hundred inhabitants spoke English," Lummis said. His Spanish, though still flawed, was much improved from his first visit. So he was able to make the rounds in town on his own, introduce himself, and query any who had time to chat about local lore. Within a week he had uncovered the life story of the county's resident witches and had photographed three of them. They would become fodder for dozens of newspaper and magazine articles and a chapter in several books. To hear Lummis tell it, there were four witches in the vicinity until just a year earlier, when one had been stoned to death for turning a man into a woman for three months and then back into a man.

The illiterate, superstitious villagers of San Mateo formed the under-pinnings of the most pervasive vestige of the region's Spanish colonial past: a sociopolitical hierarchy based on land grants awarded by mon-archs in Madrid two centuries earlier. Unassuming San Mateo was the hub of sheepherding operations in the thirty-thousand-square-mile northwest quadrant of New Mexico. The Spanish-Mexican peons who constituted nine-tenths of the local population tended the flocks for the landowners and gave most of their earnings back to their employers to pay for rent and for enough food and other necessities of life to keep them modestly happy and busily reproducing. It was a form of slavery that was officially outlawed in 1861. It still hadn't disappeared by 1888 but it was taking its last gasps.

The Chaves family, which could trace its lineage to twelfth-century Spain, was one beneficiary of the Spanish throne's largesse when land grants were first awarded in New Mexico in the seventeenth century. But the family had sold off much of its land and its flocks over the years. Amado's grandfather had one million head of sheep in the early 1800s. But his uncle had sold most of the family's remaining hundred thousand sheep a few years before. Though the family still had a modest herd of a few thousand, Amado had become one of the most influential opponents in New Mexico of the peonage system.

Another land-grant family with an ancestral home in San Mateo was decidedly more old-guard: the clan of Don Roman Baca and his eldest son, Liberato. The Baca family still had fifty thousand head, one of the largest flocks in the territory.

The two patriarchs, Don Manuel and Don Roman, had been blown by the winds of history down the same path. Both had been imprisoned briefly after the Americans occupied New Mexico in 1846, on suspicion that their sympathies lay with Mexico. Both proved their loyalty to the United States by fighting side by side in the bloody battle at Taos in the revolt by Mexican loyalists in 1847.

Though the families had begun to go their separate ways, Amado and Liberato had also followed similar paths. Amado had earned a law degree in 1876 from National University Law School in Washington. Liberato picked up his J.D. at Georgetown University two years later. Both had returned to San Mateo to learn the family business and launch careers in politics. In their late thirties, they were nearly a decade older than Lummis. On Lummis's second night in the Chaves home, Liberato dropped by for a visit. According to Lummis's diary, he played poker with Amado and Liberato all night long.

A week later Lummis got Don Roman, his wife, and Don Manuel to pose for his camera. The three are sitting ramrod straight, the men astride horses, the wife perched confidently on her horse in a Mexican sidesaddle. The men, lean and distinguished-looking with trim gray mustaches and suede hats, wear bemused looks. Don Roman's courtly wife is assessing the camera and its operator with a decidedly more suspicious gaze. She seems to have realized even then, a few days after he had staggered into town, that Lummis meant trouble.

The Chaveses tried to keep him close at hand the first week with an activity that had enthralled him on his first visit: excavating the ruins three-quarters of a mile from the house. For two days he burrowed through the rubble of a collapsed second story of the ancient pueblo and was awestruck by his discovery of a skeleton on the hard-packed clay of the first floor with bones that had apparently been shattered in warfare.

It wasn't long before Lummis was pining for more rigorous challenges. His arm was still dead weight and his leg had regained just a fraction of its full strength. But by March, a month after he had arrived, he could speak clearly again and he had regained enough mobility that the Chaveses obliged him. They put him to work running messages and supplies to the sheep camp at the northern edge of their land grant thirty miles away. Soon they felt confident enough to entrust him with ferrying wagonloads of supplies to the outlying camps. He nearly met with disaster on one such trip when rapidly rising waters caught the loaded wagon in an arroyo where the wheels had sunk into the sand. Lummis claims he saved the cargo by dragging two-hundred-pound sacks of corn and four quarters of beef up the sandy bluff with his teeth, digging out the wagon and its team of horses with his Bowie knife, and reloading it at the top.

Lummis subjected his body to other challenges. Rolling a cigarette with one hand was one of the trickiest, but for him one of the most essential, skills that he mastered. He told himself he didn't deserve a cigarette unless he could make it himself, and so he learned how, pinning the paper between his uplifted left leg and the dead weight of his left elbow, adding a pinch of tobacco, and swiftly twisting it into shape with his right thumb and forefinger, sealing the cylinder with his lips.

Lummis also took up a more physically taxing and riskier hobby: breaking wild horses. It is a task accomplished by saddling, bridling, and clinging to the back of a thrashing animal just plucked wild from off the prairie, holding on for hours and letting the horse run and buck itself to exhaustion. In all, Lummis broke twenty-four horses that spring including Alazan, a sorrel pony that would become his companion for the next twenty years.

By April Lummis was spending days at a time in the sheep camps, a suitably austere setting for the Spartan lifestyle that he figured would lead him back to full health.[4] The eighteen-by-thirty-foot stone cabin where he and the shepherds slept was made of stacked sandstone slabs with no mortar to seal the cracks. There were no coverings on the door and windows. There were plenty of sheepskins on hand to keep everyone warm at night, but the cabin was so drafty that the candles Lummis used to read and write by kept blowing out. So he lit a fire on the frozen ground outside, scooped up the thawed mud, and spent a day caulking the cabin.

At an elevation of eight thousand feet in March, it was cold enough to form a thick layer of ice on the small stream that ran past the camp. But that didn't stop him from sticking with a daily ritual that Dolly had urged him to take up before they were married: a cold bath every morning. And so he started each day in the sheep camp at 4 A.M. by chopping a hole in the ice over a deep pool and plunging in. For that and for his reckless refusal to limit himself just because only half his limbs worked, the shepherds suspected that he was either crazy or bewitched. But they liked Lummis anyway. They couldn't help but like a gringo who pitched in right alongside them, worked tirelessly all day, then huddled around the fire with them at night, singing their songs over and over again until he got the words and melody right, sharing with them some of his own favorite tunes.

One particularly foolish attempt at heroics helped hasten the end of his stint in the sheep camps. A mountain lion had been killing sheep, and Lummis took it upon himself to track it down. Following its footprints to a cave, he tried to lure it out by bleating like a lamb. When that didn't work, as he tells it, Lummis cocked his rifle, held it in his good hand out in front of him, and crawled a hundred feet into the cave, with a smoldering dead branch of buckthorn clenched in his teeth to light the way. He almost choked to death on the smoke. But worse than that, the cave was empty. Whether Lummis was actually that reckless or not, it's clear he took an enormous risk. Amado later wrote of the incident and recalled that he gave Lummis a serious tongue-lashing.

During his last month in Los Angeles, Lummis hadn't been able to grip a pencil. That was one of the final straws, convincing him to make the move to San Mateo. As soon as he arrived, he began to write again. At first he wrote no more than the half page allotted to each date in the pocket-sized diary he had begun to keep, resuming the practice he had started and then abandoned in college. His first entry was dated February

5, the day he left Los Angeles. With neat, tiny lettering in cryptic sentences—mostly in Spanish—Lummis jotted notes about where he went, who he met, what letters he sent and received, how much he earned and spent, and an odd assortment of other details of his daily existence. It was a habit he kept up with just a few lapses for the rest of his life. Within two weeks of his arrival at the Chaves home, his old passion for letter writing was rekindled. He began sending a constant stream of missives, some many pages long, often to half a dozen people a day.

When he left Los Angeles, Lummis apparently was under the impression that he had an arrangement with Otis that would enable him, as soon as his three-month paid leave of absence ended, to resume full-time work for the *Times* as a sort of roving correspondent in the New Mexico Territory. Dorothea waited until the end of February, when she thought he was strong enough for it, to tell him the truth. Otis had cut him off the payroll after just six weeks. His last paycheck, thirty dollars for the last half-month's salary, had been issued a month earlier. As for his contributions from New Mexico, what Otis had in mind was a letter every week or two for which Lummis would be paid $2.50 a piece.

Lummis was devastated. The news triggered a relapse of his paralysis. The entry in his diary for February 26 reads, "Can't walk except with much difficulty. What a devil of a day for me! I have lost all that I had gained and more." Three days later, March 1, his twenty-ninth birthday, he declared that he was "not worth anything."

In a cycle that repeated itself several more times over the next year, Dolly was so alarmed by the sudden despairing turn in his letters that she set aside her demanding medical practice and made the three-day train and wagon trip to New Mexico to check up on him and cheer him up. The visits drained Dolly. But they never failed to get Lummis back on his feet, back to looking for ways to turn his latest setback to his advantage.

If Otis hadn't kicked him out of the nest, he surmised in his memoir, "I would probably now be a superannuated hack on the *L.A. Times*." Instead, left to fend for himself in the wilds of New Mexico, he was forced to piece together a new career that turned out to be much better suited for him—with his eclectic interests and itinerant lifestyle—than a staff position at a newspaper. He became a remarkably prolific freelance photojournalist, one of the pioneers of the field.

Lummis had quickly recognized photography's potential both for preserving history and for helping him sell his written work. Recent advances in technology paved the way for his photographic explorations of New Mexico. The dry-plate process perfected over the previous decade liberated photographers from the need to haul around a portable darkroom, as Mathew Brady had been forced to do during the Civil War. Wet-plate negatives had to be prepared just before they were exposed, and the image had to be fixed immediately after. Dry-plate negatives, in contrast, could be purchased ready-made in bulk and stored for months. It took one-tenth as much light to expose them, which gave photographers a much wider range of shutter speeds. Brady couldn't venture more than several hundred yards from roads where his darkroom wagon could travel, and he had to struggle to get a crisp exposure of a corpse. A quarter century later, the technology had advanced to the point that Lummis could go practically anywhere he cared to lug his Dallmeyer lens, camera, and tripod, a kit that tipped the scales at a mere forty pounds. With a shutter speed of one-twentieth of a second, he could capture reasonably sharp action shots of events such as the Hopi Snake Dance.[5]

To make prints, Lummis favored the cyanotype or blueprint technique. Still used today to reproduce architectural plans, it was the simplest, cheapest, quickest, most forgiving way to turn negatives into positive images. The technique was tolerant of the impurities in New Mexican well water. And sensitive only to sustained exposure to direct sunlight, the paper could easily be prepared in the dim light of an adobe room.

In New Mexico he photographed the same people and places he was writing about and began submitting portfolios of prints with many of his manuscripts. The photographs eventually would help him make big sales and charge premium prices. Printing technology didn't yet permit affordable reproduction of photographs in newspapers and magazines, but publications commissioned artists to make facsimile engravings and published them.

As he had since his college days, Lummis aspired to write for the best magazines of the day, including *Harper's Weekly*, the *Cosmopolitan*, and *Collier's*. His submissions were rejected more often than not, though he made enough sales to encourage him to keep trying. He had better success at the outset with newspapers and began writing regularly for the *Chicago Inter-Ocean*, the *St. Louis Globe-Democrat*, and the *San Francisco*

Chronicle, in addition to his old standbys the *Chillicothe Leader* and the *Los Angeles Times.*[6]

No editor got more mileage out of Lummis's dispatches than M. J. Carrigan of the *Leader.* Lummis's move to New Mexico to fight paralysis was treated by the paper as an undertaking as daring and glorious as the tramp. Writing the headline for Lummis's first letter to the *Leader* since leaving Los Angeles, Carrigan was at his melodramatic best:

CRUEL FORTUNE

A Letter from Plucky Charley Lummis, the Trained Athlete, Who, a Few Years Ago, Was Strong Enough to Walk From Ohio to California,

But Who Now Seeks Rest and Recuperation in the Mountains of New Mexico From an Affliction of Which He May Never Recover

With An Arm Dangling Useless at His Side, and a Skull 'That Isn't Worth Two Bits on the Dollar,' He Still Retains His Nerve and His Desire to Shoot Jack Rabbits and Roll Cigarettes—

The First Installment of Another Letter from Dear Old 'Lum'

Life in San Mateo was a delight, Lummis let on. "If a contented animal could keep a diary it would be a good deal like mine. Hunting, riding, digging in prehistoric ruins, photographing beautiful landscapes, quaint habitations and quainter inhabitants, rounding up cattle, eating chile, frijoles and carne machado, talking rheumatic Spanish, learning the queer folksongs of the shepherds, and paralyzing them with Irish imitations, sleeping like a log and eating like a coyote—that's about the bill." He claimed that he no longer missed a functioning left arm. His paralysis wasn't going to slow him down—or still his pen. "Don't ask a newspaperman to divorce his pencil for keeps," he wrote. "Why the very corn on the inside of my right middle finger cries aloud for the old familiar pressure on it."

A major theme of the newspaper articles he wrote in his first months in New Mexico was sheep. He wrote a three-thousand-word dissertation for the *Globe-Democrat* on the history and economics of sheep ranching in New Mexico. He wrote other long stories about the shepherds and their music. More than thirty years later, in the introduction to his book *Spanish Songs of Old California*, Lummis described his days among these simple folk as very nearly idyllic and their heartfelt music as the most pleasing on earth. At the time, however, Lummis wasn't nearly so enchanted with the shepherds. "The life of a New Mexico shepherd is the most hideously tedious thing in the whole creation of dullness," Lummis wrote in an article for the *Globe-Democrat* datelined June 4, 1888. "With no society save that of the sheep and a fellow shepherd as stupid as himself, the pastor's lot is not a happy one." Even the music didn't offer much consolation at the time. The off-key singing accompanied by a twangy mouth harp constituted "alleged music," he wrote.

On one of his visits to the village of San Mateo in early March, Lummis stumbled upon a story that turned out to be far more interesting than sheep. His curiosity was piqued by an eerie shriek drifting down from one of the side canyons in the foothills flanking the village. When Lummis asked the townspeople about the noise, they tried to discourage his curiosity, but he soon coaxed an explanation out of them. The sound was made by a fifelike reed instrument called a pito, which was used in the religious rituals of the Penitentes.

A Catholic cult with mysterious roots, possibly reaching back to Spain in the Dark Ages, the Penitente Brotherhood had been entrenched among the peons of the Rio Grande valley for more than two hundred years. The group met a broad range of educational, social aid, and political organizing needs of its members, but the Penitentes were best known as devotees of self-flagellation. Designated members of the group whipped themselves bloody in private ceremonies every Friday night from Lent until Palm Sunday and then every day until Holy Thursday, when they began a round of public processions that ended with a re-enactment of the Crucifixion on Good Friday.[7]

When Lummis heard about this, Good Friday was three weeks away. It's not hard to guess what immediately crossed his mind. He knew he had in his grasp a shocking scoop that could ignite his freelance writing career: a firsthand account—accompanied by the first photographs—of a crucifixion on American soil.

When the Chaveses got wind of Lummis's plan, they tried to talk him out of it. The Penitentes were notoriously secretive. The Chaveses weren't certain they would tolerate even an unobtrusive gringo observer, much less a gringo pointing a large camera at them. The Brothers might well try to kill him if he tried to do that, the Chaveses warned. Lummis heard them out. He was aware of the risks. But that only steeled his resolve to get the story. Besides, the danger of it all would give him a better story to tell, a new episode in the legend of the intrepid Charlie Lummis.

As Lummis told it in one of his half dozen or so published accounts of his scoop, "As the midnight wind sweeps down the lonely cañon, the wild shriek can be heard for miles. It carries an indescribable and uncanny terror with it. That weird sound seems the wail of a tortured soul. I have known men of approved bravery to flee from that noise when they heard it for the first time. The oldest inhabitant crosses himself and looks askance when that sound floats out to him from the mountain gorges." But not Lummis.

"I had been watching feverishly for Holy Week to come," he continued. "No photographer had ever caught the Penitentes with his sunlasso, and I was assured of death in various unattractive forms at the first hint of an attempt. But when the ululation of the pito filled the ear at night, enthusiasm crowded prudence to the wall."

The next Friday he wandered through the fields and arroyos around San Mateo all night long chasing the intermittent sound before finally, up in one of the canyons a mile outside of town, he was rewarded with a fleeting glimpse of three figures ducking into a roughly built rock hut. It was the Penitentes' morada or meetinghouse.

On Holy Thursday, Lummis was up before dawn getting his camera gear ready to haul into town, not wanting to miss a moment of the first public procession, which would give him his first chance to shoot some photographs. He had already selected a vantage point, a small hill overlooking the graveyard, which he had learned would be one of the stops along the way. He was there and had set up his camera before the villagers began to gather at about nine in the morning. The sight of the camera "provoked ominous scowls and mutterings on every hand." But Lummis sent a clear signal that he wasn't going to be intimidated. He placed his pistol on top of his camera.

He stood there for hours, but there was no sign of any procession. The villagers, sitting in small clumps, rolling cigarettes, and chatting hour after hour, appeared to have settled in for a long wait. Lummis eventually got tired of guarding his camera, so he stashed it inside a "friendly house" until the procession finally arrived at two. It was "a sight which might grace a niche in Dante's ghastly gallery," Lummis wrote. "A fifer came over the ridge, followed by five women singing hymns; and behind them a half-naked figure with bagged head, swinging his deliberate whip, whose swish, thud! swish, thud! we could hear plainly two hundred yards away, punctuating the weird music."

Lummis took his first several shots from just inside the adobe gate of the friendly house. But when the procession entered the graveyard, Lummis carried his camera back to the hilltop to get a better view. At that, the crowd turned openly hostile, and it would not have ended well for him if Don Ireneo, Amado's younger brother, hadn't arrived on the scene with two well-armed friends. They stationed themselves on each side of the camera with their guns drawn, and they "held back the evil-faced mob" while Lummis exposed half a dozen plates of the strange scene below.

The first procession by then had been joined by a larger group. The assemblage of Penitentes now included four men whipping themselves bloody and three carrying heavy wooden crosses. Following behind the flagellants were the Hermanos de Luz, or Brothers of Light, the title claimed by the cult's leaders. They did not beat themselves, though they furiously whipped any of the flagellants who appeared to be easing up or who fainted from the self-inflicted torture. The procession entered the burying ground and the flagellants stooped to kiss the earth at each grave. When one of the cross bearers stumbled and fell on his face, the Hermanos de Luz beat him furiously, lifted him to his feet, and placed the heavy cross back on his shoulder.

Lummis survived Holy Thursday with himself and his camera in one piece. But given the hostility he encountered in taking shots of the procession from a respectful distance, he knew his plans for the next day would be a much tougher challenge. That evening, however, he got a chance to set the stage for his scoop. At the end of the day, the Penitente procession made its way to the Chaves family compound, a customary stop. The flagellants waddled on their knees into the small family chapel in the shade of two old oaks a hundred yards from the house and lay prone on the floor for an hour while the rest of the people in the procession sang hymns. Then the flagellants entered a room in the Chaves home, plugged the keyhole to prevent anyone from looking in and discovering their identity, removed their hoods, and ate a meal. The rest of those in the procession milled around outside for a couple of hours with nothing to do, which gave Lummis a "golden opportunity" to win over the leaders of the cult.

"Metaphorically collaring the Hermano Mayor, the Hermanos de Luz, and the pitero, I dragged them to my room, overwhelmed them with cigars and other attentions, showed and gave them pictures of familiar scenes—a Mexican finds it hard to resist a picture—and cultivated their good graces in all conceivable ways" Lummis wrote. "And when the Brothers of the Whip had supped, re-masked themselves and emerged, the Chief Brother and Brothers of Light were mine."

The next day, the entire village was on hand for the climactic rite. In the procession this time only one hooded man carried a cross, the cross-bearer from the day before who had the honor of being chosen for crucifixion. Several other men followed behind him, beating themselves with scourges, while another brought up the rear with a bundle of buckthorn bound tightly to his back with the vicious inch-long spines, tough enough to penetrate shoe leather, piercing his back in hundreds of places. Lummis fell in behind with his camera. When the procession reached the crucifixion spot, Lummis's diplomacy the evening before began to pay off. Many in the crowd still glowered at him. The two friendly villagers who had agreed to help him lug his tripod and camera around that day refused to proceed any closer than a quarter mile from the crucifixion site. But the Hermano Mayor was moved to return Lummis's hospitality of the previous evening. He walked a hundred paces away from the hole in the ground where the cross would be planted, drew a line in the dirt with his shoe, and said Lummis could stand behind it to photograph the event. He even posed for a photograph holding a statue of the Virgin Mary, looking like a tattered, bearded ruffian sheepishly cradling a homemade doll.

The man who had been chosen for crucifixion had a four-inch gash in his side. When he reached the spot chosen for the ritual on a hillside in one of the canyons back of town, several of the Penitentes lifted the cross from his shoulder and laid it on the ground. He lay back on it and his attendants cinched him to it with rough ropes around his legs and arms pulled as tightly as the bindings on a mule. As they tightened the ropes, the man on the cross "sobbed like a child," Lummis reported, not because of the pain but because he was ashamed that they were not using nails instead. "Ay! Que estoy deshonrado! Not with a rope! Not with rope! Nail me! Nail me!" he cried. Up until that year, the victims had been spiked to the cross. But that grisly practice was in decline as a result of bad publicity from the rising death toll. The year before, four men had perished while nailed to crosses in Penitente communities in southern Colorado, Lummis claimed.

The ropes were brutal enough. As Lummis watched and the minutes passed, the victim's arms swelled and turned purple and he groaned with pain. Meanwhile the Penitente with the load of buckthorn lay on his back at the foot of the cross with his head on a stone and another larger stone placed on his stomach, pressing him more firmly into the spiny backpack.

At one hundred paces, Lummis was too far away from the scene to get the shot he wanted. So he decided to press his luck by asking permission to move closer. "In gracious response to my request, the Hermano Mayor paced off thirty feet from the foot of the cross and marked a spot to which I might advance in order to get a larger picture," Lummis wrote. "And there we stood facing each other, the crucified and I— the one playing with the most wonderful toy of modern progress, the other racked by the most barbarous device of nineteen hundred years ago. What ambitious amateur ever dreamed of focusing on such a sight?"

The man was left hanging on the cross for several hours until sunset, when he was taken down and carried away barely conscious. The last leg of the procession ended at the morada, where, judging from the sound of the pito, the Good Friday commemoration continued until midnight. After that, members of the sect returned to their homes, not to gather again for a religious ceremony until the next Lent or until one of their number died. In their daily lives, some were devout and humble men such as the farmer who had borne the burden of thorns and by Lummis's estimate had given himself more than two thousand fierce blows on Good Friday and countless more on the days before. "The next day he was at work with his irrigating hoe!" Lummis marveled. Others are "good though deluded men," Lummis reported. But most of the Penitentes were of more dubious character. "The majority of them, particularly the Brothers of the Whip, are of the lowest and most dangerous class—petty larcenists by nature, horse-thieves and assassins upon opportunity—who by their devotions in Lent think to expiate their sins of the whole year."

Lummis started working on his account of the ritual as soon as he returned to the Chaves hacienda that night, no doubt staying up even later than usual, writing feverishly. He printed his photographs the next day, and that night he had the first version of his exposé of the Penitentes, a two-thousand-word manuscript, ready to mail to newspapers around the country.

The story ran in April in the *Leader*, the *Globe-Democrat*, the *Los Angeles Times*, and the *Boston Transcript* and was reprinted in a number of other papers over the next month or two. In all of the versions of the story that he published over the years, Lummis played heavily on his audience's presumed incredulity that such a spectacle could happen in the United States. "The most civilized country in the world! Of course! Everybody knows that," Lummis wrote, proceeding to describe a phenomenon that called that assumption into question: "a procession in which voters of this Republic shredded their naked backs with savage whips, staggered under the weight of huge crosses, and hugged the maddening needles of the cactus." New Mexico is a strange corner of the nation indeed, a region "where we still kill off an occasional witch; where in every Holy Week, you might see scores of marked men whipping their own naked backs till the blood flows in the streams, and winding up on Good Friday by the actual crucifixion of one of their number."

Lummis spent many days off and on through the rest of 1888 working on a much longer version of the newspaper piece, his magnum opus about the Penitentes, which he hoped to sell to a major national magazine along with a portfolio of his photographs. By summer he had finished a seven-thousand-word article about the cult and begun sending it to magazines, starting with his first choice, *Harper's Illustrated*. The response he got taught him a harsh lesson about the economics of freelance writing. The story, which went through a succession of rewrites, was rejected more than a dozen times over the course of a year before it was finally accepted by the *Cosmopolitan* and published in May 1889, fifteen months after the event. Lummis said he was convinced it was rejected so many times because, despite his photographic evidence to the contrary, editors refused to believe that the events he described really happened.

In the meantime Lummis was having better luck selling articles about the Pueblo Indians. In June and July of 1888 he wrote about the St. John's Day festival at Acoma for the *Globe-Democrat*, about Indian jewelry for the *San Francisco Chronicle*, and about the Sun Dance at Cochiti for the *Globe-Democrat*. The *New York World* published his four-thousand-word treatise on Navajo blankets. He also began to work on stories about Pueblo folklore and adventure tales for young people that summer, and he stepped up his output of poetry, some of which was accepted for publication in leading national magazines.

The Bibos, who were becoming good friends of his, maintained a mail drop for Lummis at their store in Grants. Every time he passed through, a stack of correspondence from editors across the country would be waiting for him. Most of them were rejection slips. He logged them all in his diary, keeping close track of which version of which story had gone to which magazine so that he could quickly repackage the rejects and send them right back out again. A slowly increasing percentage of the responses were letters of acceptance—and greatly welcomed checks.

Lummis was settling in quite nicely to his new life as a freelance writer in New Mexico, despite his paralysis. A tourist from Chillicothe named M. C. Swift who was passing through New Mexico crossed paths with Lummis at some point that summer and sent a status report back to the *Leader*. It was published under the headline "Lum In His Lair: An Amusing Account of His Bohemian Ways."

The folks in Chillicothe would have been especially amused that Charlie Lummis had recently taken on a new look. Apparently inspired by his residence at the Chaves family hacienda, which continued to serve as his base of operations between forays among the pueblos, he had adopted some of the habiliments of an aristocratic Spanish don. The glimpse of Lummis that Swift offered is one of the first accounts of a style of dress that Lummis would keep for the rest of his life.

"Lum dresses in a suit of purple velveteen or corduroy and wears a big sombrero with a broad blue leather band around it," Swift wrote. "He has pockets sewn in his jacket to suit his peculiar needs and his peculiar condition and in the most convenient pocket on the right side he carries a package of cigarette papers and his cigarette tobacco." Though his left arm was useless, he delighted in demonstrating that it didn't hold him back. Smith marveled at his ability to roll a cigarette with one hand. "The whole thing is done in a second and done so dexterously that one wonders where so far as the manufacture of cigarettes is concerned there is any use for two hands." His attachment to tobacco was stronger than ever. Lummis "smokes incessantly morning to night," Smith noted, even though he knew full well that it was harmful to his health. "He says that smoking is one of the few pleasures that life has to offer him. . . . He would sooner live 10 years less with his cigar and pipe than 10 years more without them."

Lummis spent a good deal of his time on the back of a horse traveling among the pueblos of New Mexico, Swift added. He had a splendid collection of turquoise, Navajo blankets, and other curios. He was a dead shot with his Winchester, which he could draw and fire "quick as lightning." As for his economic well-being, Lummis "earns considerable money, certainly enough to supply his own simple needs, writing for the best publications," Swift concluded. "He appears to live a very happy and contented life, wild and secluded as it is. Should he recover I do not think he would care to go back to the 'busy haunts of men'."

By the end of the summer of 1888, Lummis was on the trail of a story that was far more dangerous than his exposé of the Penitente ritual. It was a story about five unsolved murders committed over the previous couple of years in Valencia County, which in those days covered a vast expanse from the Rio Grande valley south of Albuquerque to the rangelands around San Mateo. Plenty of people knew who was behind the killings, but no one dared name the culprits. The opportunity to blow the story open was one Lummis simply couldn't resist. It didn't seem to faze him that the prime suspects were the Chaveses' neighbors, the heads of the family that had been intertwined with that of his hosts for generations, Roman and Liberato Baca.

At least Lummis was prudent enough to hold his fire while he gathered evidence. He knew that taking on the Bacas would put himself and maybe even members of the Chaves family in grave peril. And yet Amado apparently didn't try to discourage Lummis's interest in the story. The two old New Mexico families had been on slowly diverging paths ever since the American era had begun. With the generation of Amado and Liberato, the divergence was becoming a wide gulf.

109

Lummis himself had helped bring out the differences. The Chaveses adored their oddball gringo friend. They were inspired by his tenacity, fascinated by his wide-ranging talents and interests, and cheered by his enthusiasm for life. Tales of his audacious escapades and exploits were the talk of the Chaves family for decades to come. Lummis was certainly eccentric, as Amado once put it in a letter to a friend, but most geniuses are.

The Bacas, on the other hand, regarded Lummis with suspicion from the moment he arrived in San Mateo. They had good reason to be concerned, for although they had never met him, he had a reputation that preceded him. He was a troublemaker, an iconoclast who relished the chance to topple the high and mighty, and in San Mateo the Bacas were boss. They happened to be unusually vulnerable when Lummis showed up.

Following a long line of Bacas before him in elective office, Liberato was Valencia County's representative to the territorial legislature. But he faced a crucial election in November 1888, and for the first time in memory a Baca candidate was in danger of losing. The relatively recent arrival in Valencia County of sizable numbers of white Americans had begun to tip the balance that had favored the Bacas for generations. The newcomers were still vastly outnumbered, but unlike the quiescent Mexican majority, they had begun to ask pointed questions about the boss system that kept the Bacas on top. If enough disaffected peons cast their votes with the white newcomers, the Bacas knew they would be finished. Their first thought upon seeing Lummis pull into town at the start of the year had to have been how he might affect the delicate balance of power in the county. They quickly concluded that he wasn't going to help them.

It was no coincidence that Liberato dropped by to play poker on Lummis's second night at the Chaves home, nor that the senior Baca came the next day. "Don Roman va a casa por pregunta me"—he "came to the house to ask me questions"—Lummis wrote in his diary.

Lummis wasn't the first nosy American journalist who dared to take on the old guard in Valencia County. In the early 1880s a man name Thomas Kusz Jr. arrived and set about making a life for himself in the little town of Manzano, east of the Rio Grande at the eastern edge of the county. Born in Albany, New York, Kusz had struck it rich in the mines of Colorado, though his fortune apparently "took wings" with a wife of "uncertain character" before he came to New Mexico. But he had enough money left to start a cattle ranch, an assay office, and a more unusual business, a bilingual newspaper that he called the *Gringo & Greaser.* As the name implied, Kusz intended to skewer everyone in his sight.[8]

Kusz wielded an acid pen unrivaled in the annals of American journalism. Consider this commentary on an act of cruelty that offended his sense of decency: "Some lousy, fistulous, carrion-scented, worm-eaten and otherwise deformed human miscarriage, walking on its hind legs and having a remote resemblance to the animal man, has added another to the horrid list of his infamous acts by cutting off the nose of a colt, the property of Nicolas Candelaria! Such a wretch ought to be mashed to a jelly between two limburg cheeses without benefit of clergy, and the remains of his hideous cadaver chopped into sausages and fed to the dogs."

Kusz regularly leveled broadsides at Anglos who used legal trickery to grab portions of land grants. And the first issue of the *Gringo & Greaser,* dated August 18, 1883, led with an article expressing outrage at the murder of a member of the Spanish American old guard in a land dispute. So while Kusz didn't make it a particular mission in his career as a publisher to topple the social order that benefited the Bacas, he wasn't beholden to the bosses, either. Lummis figured that was reason enough for the Bacas to want to rub him out. He believed they were behind the crusty editor's demise, which occurred dramatically on the night of March 27, 1884. Two gunmen who were never caught fired through a window in his house, sending a pair of bullets through Kusz's brain.

Several other suspicious murders of freethinking gringos in Valencia County had occurred in the previous several years, including the especially vicious murder of jovial Old Man Barrett. But the killers weren't finished yet. Early in the fall of 1888, Lummis and Amado learned that their names were on the hit list. The word on the street in San Mateo, passed on by friendly villagers, was that Don Roman Baca had paid a hundred dollars to a peon from Mexico named Tiburcio to finish them off. Lummis found some consolation in the fact that Baca had been forced to import a hired killer. The local people liked him too much to do the deed, he figured, and those who weren't his friends were leery of him, suspecting that he might be bewitched.

By mid-October, with Election Day drawing near, Liberato's lead was as tenuous as ever. And Lummis was still alive and kicking, apparently to the Bacas' chagrin. Lummis said that on several occasions when he was out on the range on his horse, passing near a rock outcropping or a clump of brush, he heard the crack of a rifle and a bullet whistling past. The shots missed. So the Bacas stepped up the pressure. On October 17, Liberato officially joined the Penitentes. In a speech to his new brothers he added a new motivation to kill Lummis, reminding his audience how the "Americano malvado" had brazenly photographed them the previous Good Friday and had insulted their sacred rite in stories about the event for eastern newspapers. The Chaveses, Baca reminded his audience, were friends of the "wicked" journalist and had sheltered him in their home.

Lummis was flattered by the attention. The *Leader* could hardly contain its excitement at the dramatic turn of events. "Our old friend Lummis has been raising Cain among the Greasers, and has at last reached that enviable point in his adventurous career when he has a price set upon his head," wrote Carrigan, again at his melodramatic best, in an editor's note introducing a letter from Lummis that September. "He can ride about the country in that composed state of mind induced by the knowledge that he is liable to have the top of his head shot off, or a knife stuck in his back at any moment, and when his only hope of an existence of any duration depends upon the reliance to be placed in the Derringer at his belt, or the Winchester swung across his saddlebow. . . . Now, that's what we call genuine enjoyment."

To be sure, it soon got to a point where it wasn't such fun for Lummis. He didn't have a death wish, some of his conduct over the years notwithstanding. So he began to limit his rides in the vicinity of San Mateo and canceled some travel plans altogether. Amado was equally wary and spent a good deal of his time that fall away from San Mateo.

On November 6, Election Day, it became apparent that their precautions were warranted. It hadn't been a good day for the Bacas. At the polling place in San Mateo, Don Roman had been thwarted by a group of well-armed independents when he attempted to bring in twenty outsiders to vote for his son. That night the ballot counting was under way, under the supervision of six observers from different parties and a judge, when two men pointed shotguns through the window of the room and commenced firing. A French settler named Dumas Provencher, known for his kindness and generosity, was struck in the heart, took two steps, and fell dead. The other election observers might have been killed as well if one quick-thinking member of the team hadn't extinguished the lights in the room.

It was common knowledge around San Mateo that the killers had been sent by the Bacas, who believed they could order up an assassination without consequence to themselves. They were right. Though Liberato lost the election in Valencia County that fall, the territorial legislature, the county grand juries, the county sheriffs, and the magistrates were all firmly in the palm of bosses determined to protect one of their own. They wielded their clout within weeks of the Provencher killing to thwart the attempt by the U.S. attorney for the territory, Clifford S. Jackson, to bring two alleged triggermen to justice for the Provencher murder. The suspects weren't talking, but Jackson hoped the threat of a capital conviction might loosen their tongues. He succeeded in obtaining a federal indictment and held them behind bars in a neighboring county to await a trial. The territorial legislature quickly passed a bill preventing the suspects from being removed from the county in which the alleged crime occurred. The territorial governor, Edmund Ross, vetoed the bill. But the legislature immediately overrode the veto. The presumed killers were returned to Valencia County and promptly walked free.[9]

The Bacas' sense of invulnerability was apparent at Provencher's funeral. Liberato attended and sat confidently in the front row. As Provencher's wife leaned over to kiss her husband's still form, she saw Liberato and, according to a newspaper account of the funeral, "her eyes dilated like a tiger's. No queen of tragedy ever looked so impressive as that little, faded French woman as she seized young Baca by the throat and dragged him forward." Mrs. Provencher shrieked, "Look at your victim," and ordered Liberato to touch the hand of her husband's corpse. He refused and quickly left the church.

Amado Chaves never dared to implicate the Bacas in the murder. Without solid evidence, any such accusation would have given the Bacas the right, under the frontier code of honor that was all but recognized by the courts, to shoot him dead and plead self-defense. But Amado dropped broad hints about their culpability in two letters that he wrote to Governor Ross in the weeks after the murder. He mentioned the "most distressing" incident at the funeral between Provencher's wife and Liberato Baca. That killing was part of a broader conspiracy, Amado said, adding, "I have evidence in my possession showing in what manner and at what place I was to be killed." Amado pleaded with the governor to offer a large reward. "Money goes a long ways with the kind of men who are mean enough to murder men in cold blood," he wrote.

Years later, both Amado Chaves and Lummis apparently felt it was prudent to distance themselves from the suggestion that the Bacas were cold killers. Then, as now, the far-flung Baca clan was one of the most prominent families in New Mexico. In fact, a member of the Baca family was one of the pallbearers at Amado's funeral in 1930. In his memoir, Lummis left the name of the Bacas out of the discussion of the Valencia County killings, creating fictitious names to take their place. The masterminds behind the murders were "Adan" and his father "Tiburcio Coran," Lummis wrote.

But in the fall of 1888, Lummis had no such reservations. Four weeks after Provencher's death, Lummis told all in a story that ran in the *Los Angeles Times*, datelined December 2 from Grants. He mentioned the name that no one else dared let escape their lips, and it ran in bold type in the headline on the story:

A GRAN AMO

A Characteristic New Mexican Election Tragedy

The Iron Rule of the Bacas

A Reign of Terror, Leading at Last to Open Revolt

The Story of a Crime Thrillingly Told

The story about the "big boss" behind the Provencher murder, which ran in the *Times* on December 4, asserted that more than two decades after the Civil War, slavery as perpetuated by the peonage system was at last on its way out. "Today for the first time there is a cheering probability that these last links of bondage will soon be broken in fact as they long have been in the fiction of the law. For at last an organized effort is growing in New Mexico to clean out the old and arrogant Mexican bosses." Roman Baca, "a man of intelligence and courage but without

114

scruples," had kept Valencia County in the grip of "Baca despotism" for decades. But "a series of most atrocious assassinations and a high-handed course of tyranny on the part of the Bacas led at last to open revolt," Lummis asserted.

With that story out, there was no longer any question where Lummis stood. So on the day the story was published, he took another step in his personal crusade against the boss system. He met with U.S. Attorney Jackson to lend his support. The ambitious federal prosecutor didn't conceal his desire to attack boss rule at its root by prosecuting and imprisoning the bosses themselves for misdeeds that they had come to expect they could commit with impunity. But Jackson complained to Lummis that anyone who knew anything about the bosses' crimes was scared to talk anonymously, much less show up to testify in court.

Lummis said he told Jackson, "There's one who isn't afraid. I know where the evidence is to be gotten and I'll get it. But you know what they'll do to you if you push the case?"

Jackson answered, "You get me the evidence. I'll take care of the rest."

"So I got the evidence," Lummis said.

To help him in that effort, and also perhaps as a measure of self-protection, Lummis let Jackson swear him in as a deputy U.S. marshal.

Chapter 7

Refuge in Isleta

For months before his story about the Gran Amo of Valencia County hit the front page of the *Los Angeles Times*, Lummis had known that his days at the Chaves hacienda were numbered. He spent a good deal of time in the fall of 1888 looking for a new place to settle. He found what he was looking for in the Indian pueblo of Isleta on the banks of the Rio Grande fifteen miles south of Albuquerque. It took some doing, but he found a local family willing to rent him a one-room adobe house on the outskirts of the pueblo. He moved in on December 5, the day after his story appeared.

Lummis had passed through Isleta on his tramp. The village, one of the most unassuming pueblos he had seen, was just half a mile from the railroad track he had followed to California. Isleta had none of the multi-story, multiunit dwellings that had so impressed him in other pueblos. The houses were all one-story, scattered up and down an irregular grid of dirt lanes. The only notable structure was the Catholic church that still stands in an empty dirt plaza in the middle of the pueblo. Built in 1613, it has adobe brick walls ten feet thick at the base, sturdy enough to hold up the enormous tree trunks that serve as roof beams.[1] For more than 250 years, right up until the decade before Lummis arrived, the walls had occasionally protected villagers from attacks by roving bands of Comanches and Apaches who controlled the desert plains on both sides of the Rio Grande valley and periodically raided the prosperous Pueblo villages along the river for plunder and slaves.

During the Pueblo Revolt that started August 10, 1680, the church was a refuge for terrified Spanish colonists. Isleta was one of just two towns in the entire Rio Grande valley where pockets of Spanish settlers managed to survive the slaughter. Although most Isletans supported the revolt, the town developed a reputation as the most assimilated of the pueblos. When the Spanish reestablished control of the Rio Grande valley in the Reconquest of 1692, Isleta became the Spanish colonial capital of Rio Abajo, or Lower River, a region that encompassed the southern half of New Mexico.[2]

Isleta's day in the Spanish colonial sun ended with the advent of American rule in 1848. A district capital to the Spanish and Mexicans, Isleta was irrelevant to the Americans. The pueblo economy based on the sale of agricultural commodities and labor to the Spanish was rendered obsolete practically overnight after the railroad tracks reached Isleta in 1879. Adding insult to injury, the railroad construction crew plowed through a corner of pueblo property without the pueblo's permission, and the railroad company made a take-it-or-leave-it offer of compensation. The railroad also opened the spigots for a flood of cheap manufactured goods from around the world, further marginalizing the local economy based on handmade goods. By Lummis's day a new, somewhat humiliating, source of revenue had begun to trickle into Isleta: tourists on layovers at the junction who wandered through the pueblo gawking at the Indians and their mud houses. Tourists who didn't have time to leave the train platform could get a taste of pueblo life from the Indian women who greeted the trains with baskets of tiny wild plums and apples on their heads and displays of Indian pottery, blankets, and other curios at their feet.

Isleta had, in short, been a focal point in the sometimes violent convergence of European and native cultures in the Rio Grande valley for three hundred years when Lummis arrived on the scene looking for a place to live. By the late 1880s, though there was still a significant residue of anxiety about the dramatic changes under way all around them, the resilient and industrious Isletans appeared to be adjusting well to the new economic order.[3] As he sized up the pueblo as a place to settle, Lummis was impressed with the tidiness of the homes and the prosperity of the farms surrounding the village. His photographer's eye was already framing shots of doors draped with strings of dried red chiles, pretty maidens with piles of Indian corn, chubby children and happy dogs playing out front, and picturesque old folks with hand-woven serapes and weathered faces. Alongside many of the houses, protected behind breast-high adobe walls from the withering winds, were tiny gardens bordered by grapevines and plum and peach trees. The fields surrounding the village yielded a rich harvest of corn and wheat. Cattle and burros grazed in the brown meadows. Abundant water gurgled through an ancient aqueduct system from the Rio Grande, just beyond the fields past a grove of towering cottonwood trees. The waters of the river itself were dotted with ducks and geese.

The farmers of Isleta were prosperous enough that they had recently pooled their funds to buy a newfangled mowing machine to expedite the wheat harvest. But they still employed more primitive forms of technology. They processed their grain in small water-powered mills, and hauled supplies in ox-drawn wooden carts with wheels that were carved in one block from cross-sections of huge sycamore tree trunks. The mellow rasp of the millstones, the "greaseless shriek" of the carreta, and the church bells were the sounds that Lummis fondly remembered from his years in Isleta.

To be sure, beneath the bucolic surface of Isleta, there was more social turmoil than met the eye. The sense of dislocation that had begun with the end of Spanish rule was exacerbated in 1883 when the local cacique, the hereditary leader of the pueblo, became paralyzed. He was still alive when Lummis moved in but was only nominally in charge. Though he survived for another four years, he was the last of the life-appointed hereditary chieftains of Isleta. His role was filled a decade after his death by a democratically selected Pueblo Council.

The fact that no one was really in charge in 1888 goes a long way toward explaining how Lummis managed to slip in. The Pueblos have always been famously wary of outsiders—a suspicion born of centuries of repression and attack by outsiders. The pueblos generally made exceptions for foreign traders and priests, but not for the likes of Lummis. He wrote in his diary that in December, a few weeks after he arrived, the alguacil, or pueblo sheriff, told him point-blank that he could not stay. But the alguacil clearly did not speak for everyone. Lummis's landlord was Juan Rey Abeita, the patriarch of one of the most prominent families in town.[4]

Lummis's ticket past the guardians of pueblo privacy may well have been his knowledge of the sheep business. His first contacts with Isleta in 1888 came during the spring when he was researching and writing about sheep. In his newspaper stories he included long passages about the fabulous prices that could be obtained by using the railroads to connect directly with the booming California market for sheep and wool. He met on several occasions that summer with Archibald Rea, a surly Englishman who had operated a trading post in Isleta for three years. At Rea's store, sheepskins were as good as cash. The village women traded them for ten or fifteen cents apiece, depending on their weight, in exchange for sugar, flour, lard, candles, calicoes, chocolates, and sundry other manufactured wares.[5] Rea, whom Lummis later described as "a rather brainy Englishman—but hopelessly English," also served as a broker for consignments of sheep by the train-car load and wool by the ton from owners of the largest herds in the valley, including the Abeitas, the family that rented a room to Lummis. They had thousands of head of sheep and had made a small fortune selling entire flocks to the U.S. Army in the 1850s.

Rea and the Abeitas may have regarded Lummis as their key to the California market. But if Lummis did finagle his way into Isleta by portraying himself as a well-connected wheeler-dealer from Los Angeles, the Isletans were quickly disabused of such thoughts after he dragged his crippled frame into town and made himself at home.

Lummis was the strangest gringo the Isletans had ever seen. He was poorer than they were. When his physical condition worsened, as it did periodically, he seemed helpless. He had several recurrences of severe paralysis and on one occasion ended up in a convent hospital in Santa Fe for a period of recuperation. During another relapse, his neighbors found him using his good arm to drag himself on his belly over the hard, dusty ground. He was determined to make it to the post office under his own power to check on his mail. Over his protests, they plopped him into a wheelbarrow and gave him a ride the rest of the way. The checks he got by mail in those days were often just five or ten dollars for a ditty or humorous line of prose for *Life*, *Puck*, or *Judge*. The proceeds barely covered the cost of postage on his large volume of outgoing mail. In fact, he sometimes had to borrow money from his poor Indian neighbors to pay for stamps.

Hobbling around town with his left arm hanging uselessly at his side, he frightened the more superstitious townsfolk. Heeding an old

Pueblo folktale, they believed that if they touched a person who was paralyzed or had another serious physical disability, they would come down with the same malady. So they gave Lummis a wide berth. Others, however, wondered whether there was some mystical kinship between Lummis and Isleta's own paralyzed cacique, a sentiment that left them more favorably disposed toward the odd American.

Despite their fears of him and their innate suspicion of all outsiders, the Isletans slowly warmed up to the gregarious Lummis, with his infectious joie de vivre that belied his sorry physical state. Amado Chaves, who paid him a visit in January, less than month after he moved in, found that he had settled in comfortably. He had a "nice clean room" on the outskirts of the pueblo on the main lane leading into the church courtyard, and the Indians "liked him very much," Chaves reported.[6]

Their nicknames for him reveal that the chief sentiments toward the strange new villager were sympathy and amused affection. One Tigua name that they gave Lummis meant One Whom We Worry About. Others called him Kha-tay-deh, which means Withered Branch. But the nickname that stuck was Por Todos—For Everyone. It was a reflection of his chronic generosity. He never returned from a trip to Albuquerque without a handful of candy for all the children. And he gladly shared his tobacco with the men of the village, as long as they didn't mind him sticking around for a smoke and plying them with questions.

Indeed, one of the many things that set Lummis apart from almost every other gringo that the Pueblos had ever met was his intense interest in pueblo life. He wanted to be in the middle of everything. In one story that illustrates the point, Lummis, still a newcomer in Isleta, showed up for a festival featuring a footrace between the married and unmarried men. To the surprise of everyone, he hobbled up to the starting line with the married cohort, gamely completing one lap of the village before collapsing on his face in the dust. Lummis also took on a tutor in Tigua named Henry Kendall, a troubled young man who was one of the ostensible academic stars of the village, a graduate of the famous Indian School in Carlisle, Pennsylvania. Lummis paid him twenty-five or fifty cents a session depending on how long he stayed, if he showed up.

Lummis's income was slowly but surely creeping up along with the number of publications that ran his dispatches. He continued to contribute to a string of newspapers across the country. He also began to break into many of the leading literary and political magazines of the day, including the *Cosmopolitan, Scribner's Monthly, Harper's Illustrated Weekly, New West,* the *Atlantic Monthly, Munsey's Weekly, Drake's, Punch, Puck, Bric-a-Brac,* and *St. Nicholas, an Illustrated Magazine for Young Folk.* In 1888 he earned $218 from his freelance writing. His diary for 1889 has been lost, but in 1890 his earnings were up to $1,044.90.

Lummis was able to subsist on those earnings, but barely. His diet consisted of wild fruits that he foraged, ducks and geese that he shot on the Rio Grande, and cheap provisions purchased at Isleta's weekly market. "Those were the days when even a poor man could feast," he recalled in his memoir. "You could get four pounds of beef tenderloin for 24 cents, a big leg of mountain mutton or a six-pound hen for the same price or a beef tongue for 20 cents. Juan Rey Abeita cared for and corn-fed my horse, Alazan, for $2.50 a month—the same price I paid for rent." Still, he struggled to keep pace with expenses for his indulgences: tobacco, candy for the children of Isleta, photo supplies, postage for all the letters he wrote, and a growing collection of Indian pottery, jewelry, and Navajo blankets.

Lummis wrote about his life in Isleta as if he were practically one of the Indians. No doubt he was perfectly comfortable surrounded by Pueblos. But still there was nothing quite like an evening with the Rea family to make him feel at home. Besides Archibald Rea, the family included his gentle and kind-hearted wife Alice, their two-year-old son, Louis, and two of Alice's younger sisters, Flossie and Eva Douglas.

The Douglas girls were three of a family of nine who were born and raised in Lime Rock, Connecticut. Their mother had died in 1875. Alice, the oldest, moved to New Mexico five years later to marry Archibald, a well-educated young Englishman who had ended up in the Rio Grande valley of New Mexico with a wagonload of merchandise and enough capital to open a store. A few years after Alice settled in, Flossie and Eva—who was more often called Eve—joined her in New Mexico. Flossie was seventeen when Lummis arrived in Isleta. She worked in the store and helped Alice care for the baby. Eve, who was nineteen, had just an eighth-grade education, but she was smart enough to get the job of teacher at the Catholic day school. One of the most widely adored residents of Isleta, she was engaged to be married to M. C. Williams, the U.S. Indian agent for the Pueblo tribe, who was stationed in Santa Fe but regularly visited Isleta.

To Alice, Lummis was like an overgrown son. To the younger girls he was like a big brother. He often dropped by for dinner toting a brace of ducks or a fat goose. After dinner they played whist or other games or sang songs. On carefree afternoons they took their horses on rides up out of the river's floodplain and across the prairie, shooting at rabbits. Lummis got all three Douglas sisters started on personal scrapbooks, like the ones he was keeping for himself at the time—collages of news clippings, mementos, and his own blueprint photographs—spending hours with them on the volumes.

One of Lummis's photographs of himself with the Rea family seated in their living room captures some of the mood of those evenings when Lummis dropped by for a visit. The photo shows a cozy room with a stone fireplace and adobe walls decorated with a pair of deer antlers and framed portraits, a glass case filled with knick-knacks, a wooden bench, and several chairs. Archibald, with a long beard, is sitting in a straight-backed chair playing his fiddle. Alice is knitting. Flossie is cradling a cat in her lap. Eve has her nephew Louis on her knee. Lummis himself is in the corner of the picture holding the bulb that triggered the shutter. He has a slight smile on his face as he gazes slightly off center from the lens. Eve's warm gaze is fixed firmly on him.

By early 1889, more than a year had passed since his stroke and Lummis still hadn't regained use of his left arm. But in most other respects 1888, as bleak as it had looked at the start, had turned out to be a banner year for Lummis. Rudely ejected from the world of the *Los Angeles Times* in which he had been immersed, he had already begun to make an exciting and very full new life for himself in New Mexico.

For Dolly, on the other hand, 1888 had been a dreadful year. If ever there was a chance for her to kick Charlie out of her life for good and sever her self-destructive attachment to him, this was it. But she couldn't bring herself to do it. If he had taken the initiative to terminate the relationship, she could have gotten on with a life without Charlie. But he had no reason to cut her off, not yet anyway. Lummis wasn't ever going to be a husband in the traditional sense of the word, even though he sometimes insisted he was committed to staying married. But he cherished Dolly as an intellectual soulmate and confidante, telling her everything in long letters that he wrote several times a week. Dolly also

filled another important role in Lummis's life: she was a willing sex partner every several months during their stormy reunions on her trips to
New Mexico or on his trips to Los Angeles. Those visits were wonderful for a day or two but always ended badly, with both convinced the
marriage was doomed.

Lummis's relationship with his wife during his first year away from
Los Angeles was complicated by his infatuation with the daughter of
Ygnacio and Ysabel del Valle. Close friends of the Chaves family, the
del Valles were of the same old Spanish stock, and they too lived in an
enchanting hacienda, on a large pastoral estate called Camulos in the
Santa Paula Valley north of Los Angeles. Lummis had paid his first visit
to Camulos soon after reaching Los Angeles and had fallen in love with
the place. The del Valles became lifelong friends.

In the summer of 1888, Lummis began to delude himself into believing that there were romantic possibilities between himself and teenaged Susie del Valle. A gangly adolescent when Lummis first visited
Camulos in 1885, she had matured into a seductive young woman three
years later. The pen pal friendship that Susie and Lummis had maintained over the years had slowly evolved into a more mature and intimate sharing of hopes and dreams.

In August 1888, during his first return visit to Southern California
after his move to New Mexico, Lummis's fantasy took flight. He was in
much better shape than when he had left Los Angeles six months earlier, though his arm was still useless, and he and Dolly spent four satisfactory days together. But on his fifth day back, he left his wife behind
in Los Angeles to spend a week in Camulos, arriving on Sunday, August
19. Nestled against the brown coastal hills in a grove of massive walnut
trees, it was a heavenly place. Susie may not have had any inkling of his
intentions, but a line in his diary on the day he arrived hints that he was
confident he would not be disappointed. "Susie meets me and she gets
to know me," he wrote.

By Friday he was swinging in a hammock with Susie and her older
sister Rosa, "kissing" his "little sisters," chatting and singing all afternoon. That evening Lummis and Susie and Rosa went for a walk, and
Lummis and Susie were so enraptured by each other, he wrote, that
they didn't even notice the fog blowing in until it had enveloped them.
At that moment "I knew that my Susie loves me," he recorded. His last

day with the del Valles, Sunday the twenty-sixth, was a "precious day." He spent the afternoon swinging in the hammock, alone with Susie this time. "Very affectionate," he noted in his diary.

Back in Los Angeles that evening, Dolly met him at the train station. Lummis never hid anything from her, but this time he waited until the next day to break the news. That made for a restless night. "Big pain in my head," he noted in his diary. He couldn't decide how to tell Dolly. He hadn't slept a wink. The next morning, he simply "told Dolly everything." He must have known by then how she would react to the news that he was in love with Susie and was going to marry her. But he expressed amazement anyway. "What an angel!" Lummis marveled in his diary. "She will sacrifice herself to make me free."

Lummis dashed off a letter to Susie indicating that he would have "very good news to tell her Xmas." He and Dolly had "decided to say adios."

For the rest of the spring and summer in his travels through New Mexico, Lummis couldn't stop thinking about Susie. He wrote her long letters almost every day. Apparently she didn't write back nearly as often, but he wasn't discouraged. He bought her gifts, such as an opal ring from his favorite jeweler in Acoma. And he wrote and published poems about her, conjuring up his romantic fantasies about the relationship, changing only the names.

It didn't work out in real life quite like in the poems. That fall, Lummis noted in his diary, he exchanged letters with Ysabel del Valle. Lummis doesn't indicate what Susie's mother had to say to him. But it's probably no coincidence that his ardor for Susie began to wane, judging from the page count of his outgoing letters that he tallied in his diary. By October, Dolly was once again the recipient of his longest, most frequent missives.

Lummis returned to Camulos, by prior invitation, that Christmas. He arrived December 23, and by the next day he still hadn't had a word with Susie. He didn't see her for the first time until Christmas Eve dinner. He had undoubtedly been officially informed by then that though the del Valles were honored to count Lummis as one of their closest friends, they weren't about to permit their teenaged daughter to marry a man who already had a wife. Nor would their Catholic faith allow a marriage after a divorce. Lummis apparently didn't have any time alone with Susie until December 28, when they spent a few hours at an activity clearly designed to put their relationship back in its proper place.

She helped him correct some of the mistakes he was making with Spanish in his letters.

Lummis returned to Los Angeles on December 30. Dolly wasn't there to meet him, but he went directly from the station to her house. It was a pleasant reunion. The next evening, New Year's Eve, they attended a play together. Afterward, Lummis noted in his diary, "Dolly me la cielo"—which, roughly translated from Lummis's fractured Spanish, means "Dolly and I went to heaven." From the months and years of diary entries that followed that notation of December 31, 1889, it is clear that the phrase, later reduced to just the one word "cielo," meant that Lummis had had sexual relations with his wife that day. Reflecting his obsession with the subject, he entered the word in his diary presumably every time he had marital relations for the rest of his life and in some years recorded an annual total of "cielo" entries at the end of the volume.

If Charles and Dorothea shared a glimmer of hope that they might yet salvage their marriage, there was no time to test that hope. The next day he was on a train headed back to Isleta alone.

Dolly's on-again, off-again union with Lummis was sheer torture for her. Her pain smolders in the letters she wrote to him. During the final years of their marriage, they were resigned to the fact that she could not have children, a major source of her sense of inadequacy as a wife. But she never got over the feeling that they were perfect soulmates.

While they were still married but living apart, he occasionally wrote her from New Mexico to say that the marriage was over. In other letters he would plead with her to join him in New Mexico. She vacillated as well. Sometimes she refused his summonses, but on other occasions she agreed to travel to New Mexico to check on his health and cheer him up. The visits were never as pleasant as Dolly and Charles, in the more steamy moments of their correspondence, hoped they might be. As Dolly put it in a letter declining his suggestion that she move to New Mexico, "Don't think me unkind, but don't you remember how you abominated me on our brief trips there. . . . And now you actually suggest a steady thing of it," she wrote. "Ah no! my boy, I want you to get well, and I'm not conducive to that. I don't at least put you into cold or hot and always injurious rages when I'm 500 miles off.

"I assure you, Carl, I'm not half so good as I was then," she added. "Not half so tender, so unexacting, so contented, so anything a wife ought to be as I was then." And yet Dolly ended that very letter speculating about what it might be like if she actually did come to live with him in New Mexico. She wondered where they could live and what she could do during the long, cold winters, "for I might really do it in one of my insane moments." Her spark for Charlie couldn't be extinguished. "Yes! things are hollow, awfully hollow, and I know I'm old, but I'd give every drop of my blood to have you young and happy and contented—only I know that my blood would be of no use."[7]

In some of his letters Lummis apparently professed that he was lonely for her. But as Lummis settled into his new life in Isleta, at the end of 1888, he was writing to others that he was having a swell time. "Baching it suits me down to the ground," he wrote.

Not long after midnight on Valentine's Day 1889, Lummis's promising new life in Isleta nearly came to an abrupt, dramatic end. He had spent the evening at the Reas' and then returned to his adobe to write, as usual, into the early morning hours. It was a cold night. But it was toasty where he had been sitting, close to his stove. So he wasn't wearing his coat or his holster when he took a break from his writing and stepped through his front door to stretch and admire the moon. His right arm was raised high above his head and his mouth was opened wide in a yawn at the instant two blasts from a double-barreled shotgun shattered the quiet of the night in Isleta. Most of the two loads of lead shot slammed into the wooden door behind Lummis, but some of the pellets found their mark. One hit his fingertip. Two furrowed his scalp. One that could have killed him stopped in a bundle of papers in the pocket of his shirt over his heart. Another that could have inflicted devastating damage passed through his cheek as he yawned, missing his teeth and jaw and lodging in his neck, coming within an inch of smashing into his spine at the base of his skull.

A competent marksman at close range with a double-barreled shotgun should have been able to reduce Lummis to a pile of bloody meat. But Lummis survived the blast still on his feet and with enough presence of mind to spot the silhouette of his assailant twenty yards away behind the low brick wall of his neighbor's pigpen. The man had distinctively sloped shoulders that Lummis swore he never would forget. It was the unmistakable profile of Tiburcio, the thug from Mexico hired by Baca the previous fall to kill Lummis. Blood was flowing freely from his wounds as he dashed inside to grab his gun and charged back out the door toward the wall where the gunman had been. Lummis made it several blocks, searching futilely for the would-be assassin with his gun drawn, before he either collapsed in the street and was carried by the Indians to the Rea household or, by another account, staggered there under his own power, falling into a heap at their front door.

The Reas stopped the bleeding with the ice they made on cold nights by placing basins of water outside. Lummis rested on the Reas' couch for an hour or so. Declining their suggestion that he should head immediately to the hospital in Albuquerque, or at least that he should let them summon a doctor, he insisted on returning to his room for the rest of the night, where he stayed awake until dawn, his rifle in his hands, his door wide open, hoping his attacker would return. The next morning, when Alice went to check on Lummis, he was delirious, unable to talk, and so weak from the loss of blood that he was barely able to stand. He apparently didn't resist when Alice called over some of his Indian neighbors to carry him to the Rea household. Alice was clearly worried. Whether Lummis wanted a doctor or not, she took it upon herself to send a telegram to Dorothea. Her husband had been shot, Alice informed Dorothea, and she should come to Isleta immediately. Dolly boarded the eastbound train that afternoon.

Accounts of the shooting of Charles Lummis, still nationally renowned for his nervy transcontinental tramp, appeared in dozens of newspapers coast to coast. But accurate details about the incident were hard to come by in the first several days. A number of journalists and editors headed for Isleta to get the story at the scene of the shooting, but it took them days to arrive.[8]

The first published account of the shooting appeared in the *Los Angeles Times* on February 16. Rolling off the presses just twenty-four hours after the shots had struck Lummis, it was a seventy-five-word dispatch based largely on Alice's cryptic telegram to Dolly, supplemented with the *Times* staff's suppositions about who was behind the attack. Charles Lummis had been "bushwacked at midnight last night by Mexicans," and though he had survived, he was seriously wounded, the story said. An editorial in the same issue named the culprits: "The Bacas have raised the blood of a Gringo who will make their existence anything but a pleasure."

The *Albuquerque Morning Democrat* sent its own reporter by train to Isleta on the second day after the shooting. He was able to dig up more details, but the fearful telegraph operator in the pueblo refused to transmit the story, so the reporter had to borrow a horse and rush back to Albuquerque to file. The *Democrat* too harbored no doubt that the attack on Lummis was the latest in the string of shootings that had taken the lives of Kusz, Barrett, and Provencher. "Who is next is the question asked by people who live in the vicinity of these crimes and are terrorized to such an extent that even the telegraph operator dared not send the particulars which were obtained by special messenger sent by the *Democrat* and which are reliable."

Other early newspaper reports got the facts all wrong. The *Albuquerque Citizen* reported that Lummis was shot at a train station somewhere south of Albuquerque in revenge for his unflattering reports about the Penitentes and certain Valencia County politicians. Badly wounded, he boarded the next train and tried to make it to the hospital in Albuquerque but had to disembark in Isleta on the verge of death from loss of blood.

The most bizarre account appeared in the *Prescott (Arizona) Hoof & Horn*. The story was so far off base that it may well have originated with the Bacas themselves to sow confusion. After Lummis was ambushed by an unknown assailant, the *Hoof & Horn* reported, he "was taken on a train back to Grants where he is being kindly cared for by Don Roman Baca at his residence where he has been a guest for several months." While enjoying the hospitality of the Bacas on that earlier visit, as the *Hoof & Horn* told it, the *Los Angeles Times* correspondent had written "a series of fascinating articles touching on Mexican usages and traditions and historical sketches of the Navajo and Pueblo Indians."

Colonel Webb, formerly of the *Golden Retort* and now editor of the *Albuquerque Democrat*, rode down to Isleta to see Lummis for himself three days after the shooting. He published his account February 19, in which he sought to dispel one line of rumor spawned by Lummis's behavior immediately after the shooting. "Ridiculous stories got around that he wanted to die and would have no doctor," Webb wrote. Some papers had suggested that Lummis was more concerned about damage to his "much cared for corduroy coat" than for the threat to his life. But the truth was that Lummis was simply waiting for his wife, the highly regarded Dr. Dorothea Lummis of Los Angeles, who was expected to arrive tomorrow, Webb said. He conceded that "Lummis's bravery has in it a dash of recklessness that in so great a genius is a misfortune." But he concluded, with a large measure of wishful thinking, that Lummis, though "obstinate to a fault," might be a bit more prudent from now on. "The world has not enough such men as Charles F. Lummis that he can court the death that we fear is coming all too soon."

The shooting was, needless to say, treated as momentous news by the *Chillicothe Leader*. By press time for the issue of February 19, Carrigan surely would have seen the latest wire reports indicating that Lummis was out of mortal danger. But he hadn't yet received any word from Lummis himself. So he decided to wring some extra drama out of the Valentine's Day shooting in Isleta. "Alas, Poor Lum!" the *Leader's* first story on the incident began. "There are strong grounds for belief that . . . the indomitable and irrepressible 'Lum' . . . has met his death at the hands of an assassin."

The sad news was subtly hedged. Carrigan undoubtedly was already planning the next week's installment in the continuing saga of Chillicothe's favorite son, the one about Lum's miraculous escape from the jaws of death, a story that hopefully would be told by the intrepid correspondent himself, if a letter arrived in time. Sure enough, the day before the next issue went to press, the much anticipated report from Lummis arrived. The readers of the *Leader* awoke February 26 to the amazing news that Lum, as the headline in the paper proclaimed, was "Still on Deck." The headline continued:

THE *LEADER* AT LAST RECEIVES EVIDENCE THAT 'LUM' IS ALL RIGHT

Though Shot in the Neck He Is Still Able to Vent His Anathema Upon the Greasers

He Is Pulling Himself Together Fast, and Is Now Loaded for Bear.

The headline in the *Leader* touched on a theme that other papers around the country picked up and ran with. The attempted murder of Lummis was treated as yet another act of infamy by the evil Greasers who dominated New Mexico. "Mexicans" was the standard term, though "Spanish Americans" or "Hispanics" or "Hispanos" would have been a more accurate label. Whatever they were called, they formed the vast majority of the population of the territory. In the 1880s Hispanos accounted

129

for about 125,000 of the 175,000 people in New Mexico. The 30,000 Indians were a distant second-largest ethnic group, and the 20,000 Anglos were the smallest minority. The attempted assassination of Charles Lummis came at a time when many in the Hispano leadership of New Mexico had begun to mount a new push for admission to the Union. That goal had been frustrated for decades, in large part because of concern in the rest of the nation that a territory filled with dark-skinned, non-English-speaking Catholics was incompatible with the other states. The opponents of New Mexico statehood now had another case in point.

The *New York World* certainly made good use of the Lummis shooting to denigrate the territory. In an April 14 story, the paper recounted Lummis's tramp and his years in Los Angeles and then noted that since moving to New Mexico a year earlier, he had stirred up ill will by exposing the "orgies" and "hideous rites" of the Penitentes. Lummis's dispatch to the *Los Angeles Times* about the Provencher murder made the bosses who rule New Mexico even angrier, the *World* reported. The story concluded with a virtual call to arms against a region that could give sanctuary to the perpetrators of such a deed. "The need of something which can control, exterminate or humanize a certain element in New Mexico is becoming more and more apparent as one outrage after another is perpetrated."

In New Mexico, home to a lively Hispano press, some papers took offense at the haste with which most commentators assigned blame for the attack on Lummis. As the bilingual *Santa Fe Sun* put it, "Whenever an unsolved crime occurs in the southern states a Negro gets the blame. When similar crimes occur in this territory, a certain class of papers at once jump to the conclusion that a Mexican is the guilty party." The paper noted that Lummis had been a guest of "Mexicans" in San Mateo for many months. "Let us be just if we cannot be generous, and try to give all nationalities and kindred decent treatment," the *Sun* concluded.

Lummis was uncomfortable being at the center of a controversy that was ultimately a racial conflict pitting "Mexicans" against "Americans." Some of the newspaper pieces he wrote later that year clearly were an effort on his part to set the record straight concerning his own views about who was to blame and what that meant for New Mexico.

One observation that he made in several pieces would evolve into a recurring theme in his writing for the rest of his life. While easterners liked to think their New England ancestors were the first Europeans to colonize North America, they were conveniently forgetting, as Lummis pointed out, that the Spanish pre-dated them by more than a century. Anglo-American easterners also believed their kind conquered the West. But Lummis noted, "If it weren't for the Mexicans half the southwest would be wilderness today."

The Territorial Legislature's determination to protect the Valencia County killers was enough to turn Lummis against statehood, at least for the time being. But he made it clear that he didn't share with other opponents of statehood a fear of the territory's unwashed, brown-skinned masses. "The trouble with New Mexico isn't the common paisanos," he wrote in an article for the *Times* in November. "Its curse is the educated, wealthy, and unscrupulous amos or bosses and the scrub Americans who fawn to them and keep them in power . . . The assumption that the Mexicans are a dangerous population is erroneous and ignorant. They are good people, good neighbors, good citizens."

To prove that he had no fear of ordinary New Mexicans, Lummis made a point of traveling widely as soon as he was back on his feet. The *Democrat* reported that he passed through Albuquerque, casually visiting friends less than two weeks after he was peppered with buckshot, and marveled that he had nothing to show for the ordeal but a small hole in his right cheek just about exactly where a dimple might be. Lummis had already resumed his career as a "freelance poet and brilliant journalist," the *Democrat* noted. "Charles F. Lummis may be a queer fellow to 'bury himself at Isleta,' but his is a brain that is making a place in the history and literature of the new world."

A week later Lummis defied warnings from friends that perhaps he should stay away from San Mateo for awhile. He hopped the train to Grants, borrowed a horse from Sol Bibo, and rode into town, jauntily making the rounds of every house, offering his greetings and joking that if there was going to be another shooting and they wanted it done right, they had better include him.

Twelve days after the shooting, Lummis ran into the Bacas on the platform at the Isleta train depot. Don Roman and Liberato were waiting for the same train to Albuquerque as he was. "You never saw faces turn so many colors ending in a deathly pallor," Lummis recalled.

According to the story, they stammered, "We were shocked and sorry to hear of your accident."

131

"No doubt," Lummis snapped. "Next time send a better marksman. Or come yourself."

Lummis wasn't so rash that he would have wished it upon himself, but the shooting hadn't hurt his reputation as a courageous crusader, a force to be reckoned with in the Southwest. In Isleta, the shooting earned Lummis a new nickname that was more to his liking than the pitying ones: El Cabezudo, the Headstrong.

After the shooting, Lummis grew even closer to the Reas. Alice paid more attention to him, making sure he was taking care of himself and eating right. She often dropped off food at his adobe on those nights when he didn't eat with them. He reciprocated with a steady stream of ducks and geese, or an occasional batch of rabbits, and in the fall dozens of quarts of jam—wild plum, peach, greengage, crabapple and blackberry—that he spent days at a time putting up.

In early 1890, in a sharp escalation of an occasional past practice, Lummis started to mention food in his diary practically every day. His menu included tongue, tamales, roast pork, pie, pickled pig's feet, fried potatoes, sausages, pickled tripe, frijoles, mustard, sardines, a variety of puddings, Neufchatel cheese, canned lobster, and coffee—of which he never drank fewer than nine cups a day, Amado once said—in addition to the rabbits, waterfowl, and muskrats that he shot, and the jam and doughnuts he made.

No food item got more space in his diary than doughnuts. He made his first batch January 23, successfully recreating his grandmother's recipe. Before long he was supplying his entire neighborhood with doughnuts, judging from the daily tally he kept in his diary. On one day that March, he turned out sixty-six. He also devoted a disproportionate amount of space in his diary and his correspondence to what was at the time perhaps his most important source of sustenance: ducks.

Lummis was proud enough of the spread he could lay on that he occasionally had members of the Rea family for dinner at his adobe, a one-room combination living quarters and photo lab, decorated with guns, bows and arrows, Indian pottery, Navajo blankets, stuffed skins, antlers, jars of photographic chemicals, mixing pans, and measuring vials, not to mention the shelves groaning with books and the stacks of newspapers and magazines on the floor. These dinners afforded

Lummis the opportunity to spend additional time with a member of the Rea family who would change his life, the serene and beautiful Eve.

Despite her lack of any formal schooling beyond eighth grade, Eve was intelligent and well read and had a yearning to expand her intellect. Within a few years of her arrival in Isleta, she was fluent in Spanish and proficient in Tigua. Though she was an Episcopalian, in 1888 the village's Catholic priest recruited her to teach at the day school in Isleta, one of eight that the New Mexico archdiocese opened in the pueblos that year to stem the influence of a string of Presbyterian day schools opened a year earlier.

Eve was the Indian agent Williams's betrothed when Lummis arrived in Isleta. But Williams was soon out of the picture, thanks to a croquet match in the fall of 1889. "I had admiration but no sentimental interest whatever in the Indian Agent's lovely young fiancee," Lummis explained in his memoir. "But when one day they tolled me into a [croquet] game in the rough adobe patio and he mocked my one-armed plight, I Saw Clear—and shot a game that would have beaten an expert. He so thoroughly lost his temper that his lady broke with him at once. Then for the first time it occurred to me that I might have a chance with Eve."

According to his diary, there were actually three croquet matches with Williams that fall. The first took place on October 4. Lummis didn't indicate who won. In the second, on December 13, Lummis "walloped" Williams. The climactic match took place on Christmas Day 1889. One-armed Lummis trounced Williams once again. As Lummis's diary entry summed up what happened next, "He lost his temper, she dumped him."

Flossie and Alice were delighted to see Williams go. Eve, too, must have been relieved. She yearned for more excitement and a greater intellectual challenge than she was likely to find as the wife of a junior functionary in the Indian Bureau of the U.S. Department of the Interior. A life with Lummis offered infinitely more exciting prospects.

Lummis and Eve didn't rush into a relationship. Lummis, after all, was still married, and though it was obviously a tenuous union, he and Dolly continued to pay visits to each other's home. In the spring of 1890, Charlie and Dorothea spent several weeks traveling through Lummis's favorite haunts in the western pueblos, a journey chronicled in another series of "Lum and Doc" stories for the *Times*.

But that summer on Bosque Peak, a romance between Charlie and Eve blossomed. The dark silhouette of the 9,600-foot-high mountain dominates the eastern skyline from the Rio Grande valley near Isleta. Grumpy Archibald Rea had suddenly decided earlier that year that he would leave his Isleta trading post in the hands of Alice and her sisters and move his main residence to a sheep camp in a clearing that he chopped out of the forest just beneath the peak thirteen miles by horseback from Isleta. Lummis agreed to join the members of the Rea household at the clearing for a few weeks that June and help them set up the camp. During that first trip to the peak, Lummis contributed three weeks of hard labor building a cabin for Rea—chopping down trees, hewing the trunks into logs, building the walls and roof and chinking the spaces between the logs with mud. Lummis had never before built a log cabin from the ground up. The finished product was far from perfect, as a photograph he took attests. The structure apparently leaked, judging from the canvas patches held down by rocks over portions of the roof. But it was serviceable enough for a mountain man, which is what Rea evidently intended to become.

There is no mention in Lummis's diary of any remuneration for his work. Perhaps his labor was repayment for multiple favors the Reas had done for him in his first year in Isleta. If he was simply being neighborly, the proximity to Eve for an extended period of time would have been compensation enough.

He fell asleep each night to the sound of Eve breathing just a few feet away in the darkness of the cramped cabin. During occasional respites from the hard, dirty work, Charlie and Eve and Flossie would ride through the meadows shooting at targets and making wagers on their marksmanship. But Lummis didn't mention any overtly romantic encounters until June 24 when something clicked. "Eve muy angel"— what an angel—he wrote in his diary that day. The next day he repeated that phrase, adding a new detail, "She woke me up with a kiss." His diary entry for that day concluded, "It was a very good day for me."

Lummis may have proposed to Eve, or at least he may have suggested that he might soon be in a position to properly propose, on Bosque Peak. In any event, a few weeks later Lummis paid a visit to a lawyer in Santa Fe to discuss how to go about getting a divorce from Dolly. He talked to the lawyer again in October. In November Lummis told the famous archaeologist Adolph Bandelier, with whom he was spending increasing amounts of time, about his plan to marry Eve and Bandelier was very pleased for him.

As for Dolly, they had talked about divorce on and off for years. She knew by then, courtesy of Lummis's long letters to her from Bosque Peak, that he now had a new true love. So the news that divorce was soon going to become a reality was received by Dolly with a mixture of grief and probably a certain measure of relief, as well, but not with shock.

In August, between trips to Rea's cabin, which had to be finished before winter set in, Lummis squeezed in a quick trip to California to file for a divorce. It must have been a bittersweet reunion with Dolly— their first meeting during which it was a certainty that their eight-year marriage was coming to an end. Even then there was still a spark of sexual passion left. An entry in his diary for August 17 tells the tale: "Cielo dos veces." While making love with Dolly twice that day, his thoughts must have been high on Bosque Peak with Eve. Three days later, he filed the divorce papers with the Los Angeles County Court.

Dolly reacted with characteristic anguished resignation. As she put it in one of her letters to Charlie in response to his reports about his new love, "If it means that once more can dwell in your heart all the delightful pains, the miserable joys of a fresh passion, I am glad—yes I am glad, though to think of it seems to make my heart tear its way up into my throat and the very daylight turn to darkness."

Apparently she had just one request before she would accede to a divorce. She wanted to meet Eve. In fact, it seems, she insisted that Eve come to Los Angeles and live with her for a while. That, at least, is an inference that can be drawn from what happened next in the curious relationship between Charlie and Dolly and Eve.

Lummis returned to Isleta in early September. He rejoined Eve and the rest of the Rea household on Bosque Peak in October, where he set to work helping Archibald clear more land, make bricks, and shore up the cabin in preparation for the fast approaching winter. During that October sojourn to the mountains, Lummis broke the news to Eve about the need for both of them to travel to Los Angeles. She was not at all happy at the thought of meeting her fiancé's wife. She cried, Lummis noted in his diary. But her anxiety was relieved to a certain extent when she and Charlie returned to Isleta on November 2 and found two letters from Dolly inviting them to come to Los Angeles. One was addressed to Eve personally. The reaction of her sisters and brother-in-law to the news also helped Eve on her way. They were dismayed and angry, and told her that if their home wasn't good enough for her, she should get out now. So with that hostile farewell, Charles and Eve boarded the westbound train on November 19, Eve's twenty-first birthday, reaching Los Angeles two days later.

Whether it was Charlie's idea or Dolly's isn't clear, nor is it clear exactly what the two women expected from the peculiar arrangement. But whatever the case, they all got along remarkably well. Dolly was waiting for them at the train station in Los Angeles and greeted them both with genuine warmth and affection. The three spent lots of time together, and one evening Dolly took Eve to a play. Lummis took some photographs of the two women—his soon-to-be ex-wife and his wife-to-be—together. Then on December 1, Lummis returned to Isleta, leaving Eve ensconced in Dolly's home in Los Angeles.

Later, when Lummis's many critics were looking for a way to discredit him, they seized on this episode in his life, among others, to question his morals. His diary entries are uncharacteristically short on many of the ten days that they were in Los Angeles together. But if he adhered on those days to his lifelong practice of tallying his sexual encounters, the three were chaste. Still, it was a highly unconventional arrangement, to say the least.

From New Mexico, Charlie sent long letters to Dorothea and Eve several times a week—one long missive to both women addressed to "My Dear Two," and spicier, private notes to Eve.[9] In one of her responses in January, Eve hinted at a lingering reluctance about proceeding with a marriage. She was especially frightened about facing the pain of childbirth, she said. Lummis had quite a response for that. "You know nothing yet, my little virgin wife, of the dearest physical joys in life—joys so unearthly sweet that half the world becomes a criminal for their sake—and it is a great happiness that I am to teach you and I will teach you so lovingly, so tenderly." When Eve told him he sounded like a man who "wants my body, but who seems to give me only a little room in his heart," he replied, "You will be not only my bedfellow which is the extent of some marriages and a very sweet and lovely and pure thing when love is pure but my little chum & companera and confidant and helper. Not my slave or my housekeeper but my wife."

All the while, Eve was developing a genuine affection—and sympathy—for Dorothea. In one letter she suggested that perhaps they should wait a year to get married for her sake. Eve was also worried about the hearing in a divorce court that they still faced. "It will not amount to much, my appearance in February," he reassured her. "I shall really have to say nothing against her, so it will not be so bad—only disagreeable of course."

In February, for a period of several weeks, Lummis stopped receiving a letter from Eve every other day. He expected, indeed demanded, a letter from her on every other daily mail train and was not pleased, to put it mildly, about the unexplained break in that routine. The letters that followed from him should have given Eve additional cause to be wary about proceeding with the marriage to Charles Lummis. But by then she was hopelessly in his thrall.

"I want to know what it means that I am six days without getting a letter and I want to know might quick," he snapped, suggesting that Dolly was to blame for the lapse. "If she had put you up to any idiocy, God have mercy on both of you and if you are doing it yourself you will find it a poor bargain."

The letters got even meaner. He gushed with love for her when he received a letter after a four-day break, but then five more days passed without a word from Eve and he was livid again. "One letter in nine days is too damned thin," he wrote. "The mails are running with perfect regularity so I know it's not their fault. . . . This week is your last chance. . . . If you can't send your letters regularly every other day and at the right time of day you can find someone that is better worth writing to."

A week after that note, the decree of divorce was issued. Dorothea had demanded that Eve and Charlie wait six weeks from that point to transact their marriage, a pause that Dolly hoped would help her save face. In the end, a five-week wait apparently sufficed. On March 27, 1891, Charlie and Eve were married in San Bernardino, California. It was a civil ceremony at the courthouse with no fanfare. Shortly after the deed was done, they were on an eastbound train headed back to Isleta.

Charlie and Eve apparently had a private berth for the two-day journey to New Mexico. So Lummis was able to log a "cielo" in his diary on that day and the next, as well as on the twenty-ninth, the day they arrived in Isleta to begin their new life as husband and wife.

Lummis had spent all winter fixing up the relatively spacious two-room adobe he had rented in December—cutting out and framing a pair of large windows, putting on fly screens, installing a sink, inserting floor-to-ceiling shelving along one wall, building a large oak bureau, and helping two Indian women lay down a sleek new ox-blood-and-adobe floor. Eve was delighted with the result. "La gusta mucho a Eve," he proudly noted in his diary. Two days later he wrote, "Estoy enteramente feliz por la primera vez"—I am entirely happy for the first time.

Lummis had big plans for a honeymoon. But the excursion he had mapped out would have to wait several months. His writing career had taken an important new turn. He had graduated from writing articles for newspapers and magazines to working on books. He was close to finishing his first, *A New Mexico David*, a compilation of extended versions of twenty-two of his dispatches from his first two years in New Mexico. And he had at least four other books in the works.

His postnuptial pace was no less hectic than before. He averaged a thousand words of new material a day, not including revisions of previously written stories that he regularly repackaged for sale to other publications, a practice that sometimes irritated editors who had been led to believe they would get entirely original material. Nor did it include his heavy load of daily correspondence. Less than three months after he had returned to Isleta with his bride, he had shipped his first book off to the publisher and had piled up a stack of chapters of other books in progress, with bits and pieces of each shipped off to a dozen magazine and newspaper editors.

By June, Lummis finally felt caught up enough on his many projects for the honeymoon to begin. They set off toward the west on June 20 for a planned thousand-mile circumnavigation of the Southwest on horseback. But the first leg of the journey, from Isleta to Laguna forty-five miles away, may have been enough to induce Lummis to scale back his plan. Eve was a very hardy traveler, having proved her mettle on the many rough thirteen-mile rides by horseback between Isleta and Rea's cabin on Bosque Peak. But that first day's ride up out of the Rio Grande valley and over dry, treeless, wind-whipped West Mesa to the land of the western Pueblos was harder than either had anticipated. In fact, it was nearly catastrophic. Eve, perhaps out of concern over the effect of riding astride a horse on a woman's childbearing capabilities, had chosen to use a dainty Mexican sidesaddle on her rented Indian pony. The silly saddle was an "instrument of torture," in Lummis's estimation. In her contorted position on the back of an unfamiliar horse, she was in pain from the outset. Then, fifteen miles out of Isleta, as they were crossing the deceptive sandy shallows of the Rio Puerco river bottom, Eve and her pony nearly perished in quicksand. With much effort, Lummis and his trusty Alazan managed to haul them both out. But Eve was so exhausted that a few miles farther up the grade, she fainted in her saddle and Lummis caught her just before she hit the ground. For the remaining ten miles to Laguna, she rode in Lummis's big saddle on Alazan while Lummis walked alongside.

They spent a couple of days at the Chaves hacienda. Lummis helped the Chaves ranch hands corral a band of a couple dozen wild horses, and he singled out one for Eve, commencing the process of breaking it that day. Since its new lot in life was to become "Eve's beast," Lummis named it Adan, Spanish for Adam.

Lummis sent a letter to the *Leader* from San Mateo telling of the adventurous honeymoon ride so far, giving the paper another thrilling story to tell its readers. In an editor's note accompanying the letter from "our dear Lum," Carrigan noted: "Isn't that Lum clear through! Mrs. Lummis number 2 must be a genuine mountain girl indeed to undertake a thousand mile jaunt while her husband assists in rounding up a herd of wild horses and capturing and breaking one for her to ride. . . . That Lum is thoroughly happy and contented now no one who knows him will for a moment doubt."

In fact, Charlie and Eve returned to Isleta less than two weeks after they set out, having traveled fewer than two hundred miles. But they had their share of adventure. Adan, slow to accept this new assignment, regularly tried to return to life on the range. Every morning saddling up, "we had a terrific fight, saved only by the fact that a plucky and powerful young woman was on the end of his stakerope," Lummis recalled in his memoir. The horse was still too wild for Eve, so she rode Alazan while Lummis struggled with Adan all the way back to Isleta.

The most exhilarating moment of the summer came a few weeks after the honeymoon. Charlie and Eve were in Bernalillo, thirty miles upriver from Isleta, for a gathering of the Chaves clan at the home of one of Amado's sisters. As Lummis told it, he was sitting in a chair half asleep, while Eve sat on the floor at his feet, leaning back against the left arm of the chair, reading a book. Lummis was idly combing his fingers through her thick, dark hair when it dawned on him. He was using his left hand to caress his wife—the hand that hadn't so much as twitched in three years and seven months.

He, Eve, and the Chaveses could hardly believe it at first, but as the hours passed and his dexterity didn't leave him as quickly as it had returned, they were overcome with emotion, celebrating the miracle with several extra bottles of wine at dinner that night. Lummis described this dramatic new development in his next letter to the *Leader*. "Please don't refer to me anymore as a cripple," he matter-of-factly asked.[10]

Chapter 8

Taking On the Albuquerque Indian School

The years 1891 and 1892 were possibly the happiest of Lummis's life. The paralysis he had accepted as permanent had vanished. Dorothea had bowed out graciously, or so it seemed. She had warmly embraced Eve—insisting she couldn't be happier that Eve and Charlie had found each other—while retaining her role as one of her ex-husband's closest confidantes. For her part, Eve didn't seem to mind that Lummis and Dolly continued to exchange frequent long letters.

His miraculous recovery gave him a sense that he was starting life anew. He certainly had a new attitude toward marriage. He was content with the institution for a change. Not that he didn't get away often. But his forays into the wilds of New Mexico, sometimes to survey Indian ruins with Adolph Bandelier, seldom lasted longer than a week. He was always happy to return to Isleta and settle down for weeks at time, catching up on his writing and correspondence, making blueprints by the hundreds, and ensuring that he could maintain a respectable monthly tally of "cielo" entries in his diary.

His status in Isleta had improved markedly since his marriage to the universally adored former day-school teacher. Lummis as a bachelor had dodged eviction orders from the alguacil for two years, eventually taking the part-time job of U.S. postmaster to strengthen his claim on a right to reside in the pueblo. But once Eve moved in with him, there were no more references in his diary to efforts by the pueblo sheriff to kick him out of town.

Best of all, his writing career was taking off. His standing as a minor literary sensation was confirmed the previous March by the *Cosmopolitan*. The magazine had published more than a dozen articles and poems by Lummis. But that issue carried a short article *about* him, along with a half-page illustration with Lummis in a corduroy jacket and sombrero smoking a hand-rolled cigarette. The article recounted the highlights of his career as a newspaperman and noted that he had now turned to more enduring literary pursuits with books and poetry. His best work, the magazine noted, was reminiscent of Bret Harte.

By 1891 the curt rejection notices were outnumbered by acceptance letters from the best political and literary periodicals of the day. The reviews of *A New Mexico David* that began to reach him that fall were reasonably good, and the book was a modest commercial success. It sold well enough that the next year the Century Company gave a green light to a second collection of Lummis's New Mexico dispatches entitled *Some Strange Corners of Our Country*. The editors at Charles Scribner's Sons, agreeing with Lummis that there was a market for a retelling of the story of his 1884 cross-country trek, accepted yet another of his works in progress, *A Tramp Across the Continent*. Meanwhile, *The Land of Poco Tiempo* was just beginning to take shape, so Lummis hadn't begun to pitch it to publishers. Only *Spanish Pioneers* was foundering, piling up rejection slips.

A New Mexico David generated a helpful trickle of royalties. Coupled with his freelance fees from newspapers and magazines, and the small stipend he received as postmaster, the royalties meant that for the first time in two years he was making more than enough for himself and a wife to live on. It was a simple life. Monthly expenses for food and shelter for Lummis and Eve, Alazan and Adan, amounted to less than the proceeds from a couple of poems sold at ten or fifteen dollars apiece to *St. Nicholas* or *Puck*. Rent for the relatively spacious two-room adobe was $2.50 a month—the same that Lummis had paid for his one-room dwelling—and feed and shelter for the two horses came to $5 a month. The ducks and geese that Lummis shot on the Rio Grande practically every evening, along with his special-recipe doughnuts and homemade jam, made up a large part of the household diet. So they needed only a few dollars a week for store-bought food.

Their travel costs were also minimal, thanks to the policy of many western railroads in those days, which gave free passage to journalists, hoping their stories would drum up interest in the region. Lummis succeeded in persuading railroad officials that Eve, as an invaluable assistant in his journalistic endeavors, needed a railway pass as well. Lummis had enough clout to win the coveted privilege of hitching rides in the caboose of freight trains. They ran during the day and were more convenient than the passenger trains, which traversed Lummis's oft-traveled New Mexico routes—north to Santa Fe and west to Grants—during the wee hours of the night.

Their simple lifestyle was perfectly satisfactory to both, at least for the time being. But they had bigger dreams—to have a family, for example, and to buy a home. And Lummis had ambitious plans to travel. Since his earliest days in the Southwest, Mexico and South America had beckoned. So he was always on the lookout for ways to make more money.

A new opportunity, one that Lummis had been seeking from his first months of residence in New Mexico, began to materialize in September of 1891. Wilbur Campbell, a prominent Los Angeles–based dealer in pioneer curios, dropped by Isleta to visit the famous correspondent. The two had met previously when Lummis, on one of his trips to Los Angeles, had stopped in at Campbell's store to show him prints of some of the Indian blankets, pots, and other artifacts that Lummis said he could procure. It turned out that Campell was as interested in the blueprints as he was in the artifacts. So Lummis showed him a selection of his best shots of the scenery and denizens of Indian country.

As photographic compositions they were amateurish. But the subject matter was exotic and the prints, remarkably crisp, rendered in varying shades of blue, had a haunting quality. On his visit to Isleta, Campbell checked out the crude but effective photographic production line that Lummis had rigged in his adobe and in the courtyard in front. Over time, Campbell would buy thousands of the postcard-sized prints of the pueblos, the Penitente crucifixion ritual, and other Southwestern scenes, which Charlie and especially Eve produced for a small profit. In April 1892, Lummis noted in his diary that he and Eve had made 19,526 blueprints in New Mexico to date. Campell and others in Los Angeles also bought Indian handicrafts from Lummis. In one week of October in a swing through the western pueblos with Eve, Lummis paid Bibo

$2.90 for thirteen water jars from Acoma and bought two Navajo blankets in Zuni for $6 and $22. A few months later, in Los Angeles, the Navajo blankets brought $75 each and he also sold the jars with a similarly handsome markup.

While Lummis never made more than just enough to get by, that was more than could be said for Adolph Bandelier. When the two met in 1888, Bandelier was still reeling from a business catastrophe that had devastated his family a few years earlier, the first of a succession of financial crises that dogged him throughout his life. One of the things he found intriguing about Lummis was the younger man's ingenuity and modest success at making money.

Adolph Bandelier was born in Switzerland in 1840.[1] He and his mother immigrated eight years later to Highland, Illinois, to join his father, who had arrived ahead of them to set up a homestead in the bustling German community twenty-five miles east of St. Louis. The Bandelier family prospered—until 1885, when an economic downturn sank the family-owned bank. The Bandeliers lost everything in the collapse, their home was vandalized, Adolph's despondent father abandoned his family, and Adolph himself was arrested on fraud charges, though he was quickly cleared of any wrongdoing. His involvement in the family business had been minimal. He had already made a name for himself in archaeology as a protégé of the legendary Lewis Henry Morgan, who died in 1881. But the bank failure was a devastating psychological blow. And it wiped out all the family assets that Adolph could have fallen back on later. For the rest of his life, he was entirely dependent on whatever funding he could coax out of organizations and wealthy patrons willing to sponsor his archaeological work.

Bandelier first came to New Mexico in the summer of 1880 on a contract with the year-old Archaeological Institute of America to study the Pueblo cultures of the Rio Grande valley on a salary of $500 a year with $1,000 for expenses. The AIA supported him in the Southwest and on trips to Mexico for the next four years. In 1888, when Lummis met him, Bandelier was relatively prosperous, working on a salary of $116 per month as historiographer for the Hemenway Southwestern Expedition, funded by Boston philanthropist Mary Hemenway and headed by Smithsonian anthropologist-turned-Zuni-war-chief Frank Cushing. But it was becoming apparent at about that time that the expedition had been badly mismanaged. In the spring of 1889, its budget was slashed and the position of historiographer was eliminated. Bandelier was kept on in a different capacity, but at the end of that year he received "sickening news," as he put it in his journal. Cushing had been "unveiled." The "whole troupe" had been exposed as a "band of adventurers who have simply abused Mrs. Hemenway's kindness. Wine cellars found at Zuni, etc. It is abominable." Bandelier hadn't engaged in any unprofessional escapades. But with the complete collapse of the expedition, he was facing destitution once again by 1890.

Bandelier, who had been joined in Santa Fe in 1882 by his wife, Josephine, known as Joe, dabbled in a number of different money-making schemes to make ends meet. He tried his hand at teaching Spanish and selling paintings. He started studying law but didn't like it and dropped out. He brought in some income selling articles to the same publications as Lummis, including the *St. Louis Globe-Democrat* and the *New York World*. Then in 1890 Dodd, Mead and Company published his novel *The Delight Makers*, about the Pueblo Indians of New Mexico before the Europeans arrived. It won acclaim among anthropologists and archaeologists but didn't catch the fancy of the book-buying public.

Making enough money to live on was always a struggle for Adolph and Joe Bandelier, and in his journal he was often on the verge of despair. On top of his financial woes, he was often sick, afflicted at one time or another with everything from diarrhea to smallpox. Bandelier was, in short, miserable when he and Lummis first started spending time together. His gloomy outlook actually suited him in an odd way. Bandelier, who had converted to Catholicism in 1881, always harbored a secret fear that if he were to be seen having too much fun, God would strike him down to keep his ego in check.

Exuberant, fun-loving Lummis was clearly a poor fit for Bandelier as far as their personalities went. And there were other basic differences. While Bandelier was a meticulous, cautious scientist, Lummis was a shoot-from-the-hip journalist for whom drama was as important as impeccable attention to facts. Bandelier never could get over the suspicion that Lummis was out to steal his glory. But they had the same intellectual interests and were in the same general line of work. So it wasn't such a stretch that they ended up as partners in exploration and interpretation of the history of the Southwest. Both were indefatigable in their pursuit of new insights and wouldn't hesitate to trek on foot for days through barely passable terrain to reach an interesting archaeo-logical site. Bandelier didn't match his younger sidekick in athleticism but, Lummis marveled, he "could walk after he was physically dead!"

Soon after moving to New Mexico, Bandelier, like Lummis, lived in a pueblo for a while. In Cochiti he had to overcome the same wary resist-ance that Lummis faced in Isleta. He did so by employing some of the same personal skills as Lummis. "He could find common ground with *anyone*," from peons to presidents, Lummis explained in an introduction to an edition of *The Delight Makers*. He met with "extraordinary success in learning the inner heart of the Indians."

Lummis felt a special kinship with Bandelier from the moment they met. As Lummis described it, he was in a solitary campsite holed up in his tent during a fierce sandstorm when the crunch of footsteps alerted him to the presence of someone outside. Opening the tent flap, he beheld a tall, trim, sun-bronzed European gentlemen looking for shel-ter, "dusty but unweary after his 60 mile tramp from Zuni." It was the famous anthropologist himself. "Within the afternoon I knew that here was the most extraordinary mind I had met," Lummis later recalled of that first chance encounter. "There and then began an uncommon friendship which lasted till his death, a quarter of a century later; and a love and admiration which will be among my dearest memories so long as I shall live."

They visited each other from time to time in their respective homes in Isleta and Santa Fe, and Lummis began to tag along with Bandelier on some of his excavating and surveying trips to ruins scattered through-out the backcountry of New Mexico. Their trips into the wilderness were usually on foot since, Lummis said, Bandelier didn't like to ride a horse. With Lummis weighed down by his heavy camera equipment and Bandelier hauling his bulky surveying gear, they couldn't even carry bedrolls or a tent. So they slept on the ground wrapped in their coats, pressed up against the base of a cliff for protection from the wind, if they couldn't find a cozy cave dwelling to shelter them. "Thousands of miles of wilderness and desert we trudged side by side—camped, starved, shivered, learned and were Glad together," Lummis wrote.

In his favorite story about Bandelier, Lummis overstated his involve-ment somewhat. He claimed that in October 1890 he and Bandelier were the first Europeans to explore the extensive system of cave dwellings and other ruins at Tyuonyi in Frijoles Canyon, now the centerpiece of Bandelier National Monument twenty miles northwest of Santa Fe. And he was the first to photograph the place, Lummis said. In fact, Bandelier had visited the site a decade earlier with a photographer.

Lummis would have considered the discrepancy immaterial. His references to his role in discovering the site weren't necessarily meant to be taken literally, as he explained in his memoir. "A Discoverer is one who not merely finds something, but Makes it Part of the World," he wrote. "In this sense, I have 'discovered' a good many things bringing the wonders of nature and wonders of human nature from unknowness to the light of national day. Among such discoverings I place the Tyuonyi."

Bandelier's suspicions of his partner weren't necessarily allayed by semantic explanations. Bandelier was forever concerned that Lummis, even if he didn't openly steal credit, would reap most of the rewards of his work. In fact, Lummis never stopped singing the praises of a man he always considered one of his dearest friends and an unsung national treasure. He had no pretensions to being in the same league as Bandelier, Lummis always took pains to explain. But Lummis had a knack for selling stories, something Bandelier envied and admired. It was an assessment of Lummis that rubbed off on Bandelier's widow. Several years after he died, she gave Dodd, Mead permission to publish a new edition of *The Delight Makers* with a preface by Lummis, because it might help sell books out west, but only if Frederick Hodge of the Smithsonian Institution agreed to supply a second, more scholarly introduction.[2]

In 1891 the two men realized they might be able to help each other achieve a long-standing mutual dream to travel into the southern reaches of Spanish America. Bandelier had tried and failed to raise funds for an archaeological expedition to South America. He recognized that Lummis, with his high profile as a writer, might be able to loosen someone's purse strings.

Lummis and Bandelier mulled over the idea every time they crossed paths that summer and fall. Late at night on November 19 in Isleta they settled on a plan. "After long discussions Bandelier and I shake hands in a solemn pledge to get up a scientific expedition to Peru," Lummis wrote in his diary. "I make a Tom and Jerry in celebration; and give B my beautiful .32 Smith & Wesson revolver."[3]

In his memoir Lummis recalled his discussion with Bandelier about what he thought he could contribute to the venture. "I said to him:

'What you need, what the science of man needs now, is not so much more students, nor more scientific societies run by Latin professors nor even more devoted souls toiling and starving to investigate—but an audience.' . . . It was my thought then (a hundredfold proved now) that if we could give back to that perennial story the humanness that belongs to it, a million Americans would understand where one understands now, and the epoch-making research now buried in sacrosanct reports for a few Bostonians would become not merely history but part of the consciousness of America."

In short, Bandelier would make the scientific discoveries and Lummis would disseminate them to the public. It sounded like a fine plan to Lummis. Bandelier was somewhat less convinced. But they could iron out that difference later. First, they would need to line up financial support for the trip. They agreed to make a joint fund-raising excursion to New York early in the new year.

Lummis obtained railway passes that would get them as far as Chicago. They had a few hundred dollars between them to live on beyond that point. But they were in high spirits as their train trip began after midnight on January 14. The next day they passed through Denver and turned east. With the snow-covered wall of the Rockies receding behind them, they celebrated with a sumptuous lunch. Lummis had brought along an eighteen-pound Canada goose that had fortuitously flapped within shotgun range on the Rio Grande a couple of weeks earlier. He had frozen it to save for the trip and Alice Rea had roasted it in a Pueblo oven the day before their departure. The goose was accompanied by bread and plum jam, and two bottles of Marcelina Abeita's fine red wine.

They were in the Hudson Valley as dawn broke on January 18, and rolled into New York City at 8 A.M. It was Lummis's first return to the eastern seaboard in nearly a decade. They checked into the Hotel Metropole on Forty-second Street and Broadway, bathed, and immediately went their separate ways on their respective missions to drum up publicity and commitments of hard cash for the great exploration of Peru that they hoped to commence later that year.

Lummis was well received by his editors and publishers, many of whom he had been corresponding with for years but had never met. Success seemed to be in reach already on January 22 when Lummis told his wife in a letter, "Another flattering day and a very delightful one, made better just now by Bandelier, who reports most encouraging progress in the very highest circles. . . . He has some of the biggest powers in New York actively at work in the good cause."

Lummis made the rounds of New York dressed in the outfit that was rapidly becoming his trademark: an ostentatious sombrero, a worn suit of green corduroy, a red squaw belt, and silver and turquoise Indian jewelry. The editors, no doubt expecting nothing less from Lum, were more charmed than put off by his peculiarity. They were all "very lovely to me," Lummis noted in his diary. He wasn't averse to taking full advantage of their hospitality. S. S. McClure, editor of the *New York Tribune*, took him to dinner and Lummis "broke his heart by ordering lobster" while McClure pointedly supped on a ten-cent plate of mush. W. F. Clark, the editor of *St. Nicholas*, the illustrated monthly for children, paid Lummis a very welcome hundred dollars for stories recently accepted for future issues of the magazine, and later went with him to see the newly opened Tiffany's, where Lummis held in his hand a 125-carat diamond worth $100,000 and commented that it would look nice on Alazan's bridle.

Lummis titillated the ladies in the lingerie department of a store where he picked up something for Eve. And he created a stir at the Authors' Club, where he spent several long evenings playing poker and hobnobbing with the literati. He upstaged everyone, even the more famous Rudyard Kipling. Having dined with Kipling one evening at the club, Lummis pronounced him "shy and not at all interesting."

In his flamboyant choice of attire, Lummis may have been taking a cue from Frank Cushing. In fact, his garb was almost understated compared with the getup that Cushing had donned back in 1882 when he had toured the East in the persona of Medicine Flower. He had held the large crowd spellbound in the Hemenway Gymnasium where Lummis first saw him, and the publicity he had generated on that trip had paid big dividends four years later after he lost his job with the Smithsonian. He won the backing of Mrs. Mary Hemenway herself, who agreed to underwrite the massive Hemenway Southwestern Expedition to the tune of a staggering $25,000 a year.

Bandelier, it turned out, wasn't as close to winning financial support for his expedition as he had thought. As their weeks in New York passed and their funds began to run low, the two would-be Peruvian explorers might have begun to consider Cushing's fund-raising coup a cruel joke. For a while it looked as if none of the possibilities would pan out. Lummis spent many hours every day feverishly working on the *Spanish Pioneers* manuscript, hoping to find a publisher for it. With sheafs of manuscripts and poems to present to the editors he was visiting, he made a number of small sales, but they merely assured that he wouldn't run out of spending money. Bandelier's funds did run out. So Lummis had to loan him ten or fifteen dollars every several days, buy him an overcoat, and cover his hotel bill.

In a letter to Eve in February, Lummis dropped a hint that he and Bandelier weren't seeing eye to eye. Out of courtesy to his scholarly companion, he had shown Bandelier a chapter from his *Spanish Pioneers* manuscript about the explorer Cabeza de Vaca. A shorter version had already been published in *St. Nicholas* and Lummis was proud of it. But in looking it over, Bandelier "didn't leave a shred of it" untouched, Lummis complained to Eve. "So I shall have the whole thing to write over tomorrow." In his journal at about that time, Bandelier was open about his growing antipathy for Lummis. He "is extremely ambitious, vain, and begins to be very conceited," Bandelier wrote.

A week or two later, Lummis's luck began to turn. He wasn't able to sell *Spanish Pioneers*, but the *Tribune* agreed to serialize five chapters from it. While he was in New York, he also landed contracts for two other books, *A Tramp Across the Continent* and *Strange Corners of Our Country*. And Lummis and Bandelier got a much needed psychological lift when *Scribner's Monthly* made a commitment to buy four articles from Peru for four hundred dollars each.

Success was harder to come by for Bandelier. He "had neither the front nor the gall to be a promoter," Lummis later recalled. Bandelier's frustration steadily grew, approaching a state of quiet panic. But finally, one day in March, he scored a breakthrough. Bandelier returned to the hotel "with the almost unbelievable news that he had won a promise of $7,500 a year from Henry Villard, builder of the Northern Pacific Railroad." It wasn't an overly lavish sum, but it was more than enough. "Bandelier and I had a hugging match that day!" Lummis said.

Bandelier had a slightly different reaction. "Oh, how I felt!!" he wrote in his journal for March 12. "God knows that I have suffered long and terribly and waited patiently withal. Now there is at least hope before me, for Joe and for myself. Also for Lummis, if he is careful and not too conceited."

*   *   *

Lummis and Bandelier made their triumphant return to New Mexico at the end of March. They had been gone longer than expected—two and a half months. "But we brought home the bacon," Lummis recorded in his diary.

With financial support for their Peruvian expedition assured, Bandelier, back home in Santa Fe, turned to planning the details of the trip that he hoped would commence by early summer. Back in Isleta, Lummis had a number of loose ends to tie up before he would be ready to leave. The project at the top of his list was the Pueblo folklore book for Scribner's. He already had more than a book's worth of stories in hand, some completed and already published in magazines, others in rough notes. But he continued to collect more and to check and recheck those he had already transcribed. He had promised the publisher a book that would be popular with a general audience but one that scholars would also appreciate as the first thorough and accurate published account of the creation myths and folktales of one of the most advanced Indian tribes in North America. Ultimately, while *Scribner's Illustrated Weekly* published many of the stories, the Century Company would publish the book in 1894, entitled *The Man Who Married the Moon*.

Lummis began many of the folktales with a dramatic prelude in which he himself was a character, a beloved resident of Isleta called Don Carlos. He was an honored guest in the innermost sanctums of the Old Ones, the village elders who were the living repositories of tribal traditions. On the long evenings in winter when the fields and irrigation ditches didn't needed tending, he would join the multiple generations of boys and men for long storytelling sessions. They sat on blankets unrolled on the floor or on benches around the edge of the room, eating roasted ears of corn, waiting for ancient Lorenso to speak. "He pauses only to make a cigarette from the material in my pouch (they call me Por todos, because I have tobacco 'for all'), explains for my benefit that this is a story of the beginning of Isleta, pats the head of the chubby boy at his knee, and begins again," Lummis wrote.

Whether or not this sort of encounter was fabricated, as some critics have suggested, Lummis undoubtedly did have extraordinary access to a society that had been notoriously secretive for centuries.[4] Fiercely protecting their privacy was a survival response to the repression that the tribes of the Rio Grande valley had endured for most of the three

151

centuries since the flag of Spain was first planted on the banks of the river. Indians who participated in breaches of the tribe's privacy were routinely punished with banishment or worse. Indeed, when *The Man Who Married the Moon* was published in 1894, two years after he left Isleta, some of his sources and suspected sources were called before the pueblo council to defend their actions. But when he was in their midst, with his gregarious nature, disarming eccentricities, and sheer persistence, Lummis succeeded in breaking down many of the barriers that had kept out most other outsiders. His friends weren't deterred by fear of the consequences of obliging Lummis's insatiable curiosity.

The large and powerful Abeita clan, for one, formed a deep, lifelong bond with Lummis and his family. Charlie and Eve were practically members of the Abeita clan themselves, and the family clearly let down its guard in their presence, yielding to Charlie's persistent questions and inviting the couple to witness some ceremonies, such as wedding rituals, that had seldom been seen by outsiders.

Lummis's most important source in Isleta, however, was his Tigua tutor, Henry Kendall. His real name was Domingo Jiron, but he had received the new name and a new identity at the famous Carlisle Indian School in Pennsylvania. He had spent four years at Carlisle, never once returning to Isleta during that time, in keeping with the policy of the school. The only way to civilize Indians, insisted the school's founder, Captain Richard Henry Pratt, was to completely cut them off from their families and their culture for long enough to enable a new way of thinking to take root.

Kendall, who was in his early twenties and had returned from Carlisle several years before Lummis moved to Isleta, was widely cited by approving white people as proof that the strategy worked. While he was still in school, he had sent a letter to Pedro Sanchez, the U.S. Indian agent for the Pueblos, endorsing Pratt's educational policy of forcibly removing children from the influence of village elders. The letter was published in the *Santa Fe New Mexican* on November 24, 1884, the day before Lummis arrived in Santa Fe on his tramp. Kendall was "A Fair Specimen of the Educated Indian Boy," a headline on the letter proclaimed. The letter itself was proof that the Carlisle School approach was "no longer an experiment but a true solution of the Indian problem."

More than four years after Kendall wrote this letter, Lummis first met him in Isleta. Kendall was having great difficulty fitting back in, and he wasn't alone. By the mid-1880s, the first several classes of graduates of four- and five-year stints at Carlisle and its sister school at the Hampton Institute in Virginia had begun to return to their homelands. Most were at least initially charged with a desire to lift their people out of squalor. But many of the returning graduates—dressed awkwardly in their western-style clothes, with a fading facility in their native tongue and with much ballyhooed skills that were useless on the reservation— became laughingstocks or pariahs.

Kendall was caught halfway between two worlds when Lummis met him. He was living in Isleta but still professing embarrassment at the backwardness of his people. In the references to Kendall in his diary, Lummis often calls him the "renegade" or the "apostate" Indian. But he had retained enough information about his culture to be of great use to Lummis.

Lummis clearly got more out of the tutoring sessions, which began in March of 1890 at the generous rate of twenty-five cents an hour, than language instruction. Speaking nearly perfect English, and with his grasp of Tigua not completely erased, Kendall was invaluable in helping Lummis transcribe and translate many folktales. "Kendall gives me the story of Red Scalp," Lummis noted in his diary one day. And on another day, "Renegade Indian Kendall gives me precious medicine song." The information "requires careful checking, for he has lost much of the advantage of the aboriginal feeling in his Eastern school," Lummis noted, but Bandelier, who had other sources for some of the stories that Kendall told, was a big help. On a number of Bandelier's visits to Isleta, he and Lummis would "cross-examine Kendall on many points" in sessions that lasted for hours.

Kendall didn't know it, but Lummis had an ulterior motive in collecting and publishing the Pueblo folktales. The same purpose infused virtually everything he wrote about Pueblo culture during his years in Isleta. He had become convinced that the philosophy of Indian education embodied in Captain Pratt's Carlisle Indian School, which had recently spread to dozens of other schools around the country, was a cruel, inexcusable travesty of justice. The pieces he wrote from Isleta were intended to counterbalance the widespread view at the heart of the Carlisle philosophy that Indian villages were hives of depravity.

This opinion of government Indian schools represented a change of heart for Lummis. During his transcontinental tramp in 1884, he had visited two schools that were experimenting with Pratt's approach to Indian education—in Lawrence, Kansas, and in Santa Fe—and he had been very impressed. Pratt was a progressive by the standards of the day. He fervently believed Indians were capable of being civilized, which contrasted with the more prevalent view that Indians could never adapt to—or even coexist with—modern Western civilization and were destined for extinction. After fighting for the Union in the Civil War, Pratt had enlisted in the regular army and fought Indians in the West. His ideas about education evolved out of an assignment overseeing the confinement of seventy-two captive warriors. He developed a rapport with them and eventually won permission to send them to the Hampton Institute in Virginia, a school founded by the American Missionary Association for freed slaves. Impressed with their rapid progress, he decided to expand that experiment, and in 1879 he got permission to use abandoned army barracks outside Carlisle, Pennsylvania, to set up a school modeled after Hampton specifically for Indians.

Many adherents to Pratt's approach were genuinely concerned with improving the Indians' position in the new society that had overwhelmed their way of life. In Santa Fe, for example, the Indian agent Sanchez, who met Lummis during his tramp, was a good-hearted man who was convinced that mandatory education at some distance from the home was the best way to help Indians. When Lummis visited with him in 1884, Sanchez showed him letters from Indian children, most likely including the one he had just received from Kendall, to prove that the approach worked. At the time, Lummis accepted Pratt's arguments, but he soon began having second thoughts. His initial observations about Pueblo family life at the San Ildefonso pueblo where he spent a night just before he reached Santa Fe didn't jibe at all with the view of Indian depravity promulgated by Pratt. His travels among the pueblos since then, and particularly his affection for his neighbors in Isleta, completed the transformation of his outlook.

The first newspaper article he wrote about Indian education policy ran in the *Los Angeles Times* in April of 1890. It was entitled "Poor Pedro, the Fate of the Indian Who Was Educated," and it began with an anecdote written in the style of a folktale about an Isleta boy who had gone off to a government school for years and had returned to lead a tragic life as an outcast among his own people. The "Pedro" in the story was obviously Kendall, whom Lummis had met a month earlier. The damage they did to the students was just part of the problem with the government Indian schools, Lummis asserted. "Of course the fundamental objection is the very same one that we or any other decent people would have if a superior race (self-asserted) were to come from Mars, overrun the land and force us to send our children away from home to be rid of our silly superstitions, religion and customs, and instructed in the better ways of the people of Mars," he wrote.

Over the next two years, Lummis got steadily more entangled in the issue. The heart-wrenching situation that his landlord, Juan Rey Abeita, found himself in was the catalyst that pushed Lummis into action. Abeita understood the value of an education, and had gladly enrolled three of his sons in the Albuquerque Indian School. But he hadn't been able to get them out since, even during summer breaks. The school had recently begun to model itself after the Carlisle institution and, in keeping with that approach, the administrators were doing their best to push the parents out of their children's lives. Other Isleta parents had the same problem and were getting increasingly desperate. In the summer of 1891 the pueblo council approached Lummis for help in getting their children back. He leapt enthusiastically into their fight.[5]

By casting his lot with the Isleta parents against the Albuquerque Indian School, Lummis was also taking a position in a religious conflict pitting Protestants against Catholics. As the son of a Methodist minister, Lummis was a Protestant by upbringing if not by practice and still harbored plenty of his Anglo Yankee prejudices against the Church of Rome. But in the battle over Indian education policy, he wound up squarely in the Catholic camp.[6]

The Catholics had centuries of experience in the Southwest, not always on friendly terms with the natives. Indeed, for the first hundred years of Spanish rule in the Rio Grande valley, Catholics had played a central role in the brutal suppression of the Pueblos. But that era had begun to fade more than two hundred years earlier with the Pueblo Rebellion of 1680. After the Spanish Reconquest twelve years later, the Catholic Church had gradually settled into an accommodation with Pueblo culture. As long as the Indians went through the motions of paying obeisance to Catholicism, they were free to quietly maintain their own traditions. Catholic schools therefore were relatively tolerant of Indian customs and languages. Most important, they were usually located on or near Indian reservations so the families of the students maintained regular contact with their children. The students were welcome to spend their vacations at home.

In light of that long history of Catholic involvement with the Indians, the Protestant reformers who emerged on the Indian policy scene in an organized way in the late 1870s viewed the Catholic Church as an accomplice in the perpetuation of pagan traditions. The most influential of the Protestant reform groups, the Indian Rights Association, was established in 1882 by Herbert Welsh, the scion of a wealthy Philadelphia family. The IRA and other groups created a national platform for their views at an annual meeting at a resort hotel in the Adirondack Mountains of New York, called the Lake Mohonk Conference of Friends of the Indian, the first of which was held in 1883. Catholics weren't expressly excluded from the Mohonk Conferences, but they wouldn't have felt welcome. A major theme of the first meetings was the need to curb "Romanist influence" in the management of Indian affairs.

On the heels of the narrow election victory of the Republican candidate, Benjamin Harrison, in the presidential election of 1888, IRA allies filtered into Indian policymaking positions in the federal government. In the summer of 1889 a pair of Mohonk Conference organizers were awarded the top two Indian policy posts. Daniel Dorchester, a Presbyterian minister from Massachusetts, took over as superintendent of Indian schools in May. General Thomas Jefferson Morgan, a Civil War veteran who had commanded black troops in the Union army, was appointed commissioner of Indian affairs a month later.

Morgan and Dorchester were just the sort of characters that Lummis loved to despise. Reminiscing years later about what he thought of them when they first took office, Lummis wrote that they were "two men I believed at the time to be honest bigots, but have had opportunity to know better." Neither seemed to have had any prior experience in the West or for that matter much firsthand exposure to Indians. But that didn't deter them from handing down sweeping pronouncements about exactly what needed to be done to solve the "Indian problem" in the West. Morgan wasted no time in staking out a hard line. "The Indians must conform to 'the white man's ways,' peaceably if they will, forcibly if they must," he declared in his first annual report to the U.S. secretary of the interior, issued in September three months after he assumed his post. "This civilization may not be the best possible, but it is the best the Indians can get. They cannot escape it, and must either conform to it or be crushed by it."[7]

Morgan took his first two-month whirlwind tour of western Indian reservations later that fall, passing through New Mexico in November. According to a notation in his diary, Lummis intercepted the commissioner in Laguna on November 9. The most prosperous of the pueblos, and the only one where Protestant missionaries had made significant inroads, it was a favorite showcase for Protestant officials on their visits to New Mexico. But it was often at odds with the other pueblos. Indeed, two years before Lummis moved to New Mexico, the schism got so bad that several hundred Catholics left Laguna, took their sheep with them, and settled near Isleta. Lummis had a "little chat" with Morgan about the Albuquerque Indian School and its superintendent, William Creager. But he didn't establish any rapport with Morgan. The November 9 diary entry about the commissioner ended with Lummis's favorite epithet for those he loathed: "Tenderfoot."

Lummis's relationship with Morgan would get steadily worse. But it was nothing like the bitter and highly personal rancor that would well up between Lummis and Superintendent of Indian Schools Dorchester. There was no evidence that the two ever met during the years that they clashed over Indian education. But they had crossed paths years earlier. Dorchester had known Lummis's father from ecumenical conferences of ministers in New England and may have even visited at the Lummis home when Charlie was a young boy. But if Dorchester was ever under the impression that the family connection would keep Charlie, now a noted young writer, in his camp, he would soon be disabused of that thought. Charlie Lummis turned out to be a major thorn in Dorchester's side.

Dorchester was a fervent advocate of educating Indian children at distant boarding schools. There wasn't much of a humanitarian tint to his expressions of support for the policy. Indian children should be taught that the United States, "not some paltry reservation," is their home, Dorchester contended. "Education should seek the disintegration of the tribes, and not their segregation. They should be educated, not as Indians, but as Americans. In short, the public school should do for them what it is so successfully doing for all the other races in this country, assimilating them." Dorchester wasn't troubled in the least at the thought of breaking up Indian families. For Indian children, "blind loyalty to family and clan" was a sign of backwardness. Indian parents, after all, considered their children to be tribal property. They didn't have the same sort of attachment to their offspring as Christian parents, he believed.

At the start of his stint in government service Dorchester, along with many other Protestant reformers, seemed to think the Indians could be persuaded to accept their educational program willingly. But it wasn't long before they were faced with the question of what to do if the Indians refused to honor the compulsory education law. By law, Indian parents didn't have any choice in the matter. Administrative rulings from the Bureau of Indian Affairs established that since Indians weren't citizens but were wards of the U.S. government, Indian children could be taken from their homes and shipped to distant boarding schools against their will. But the first line of law enforcers on most Indian reservations, the Indian Police, weren't getting that job done, complained Indian agents throughout the West.

S. G. Fisher, the Indian agent in Ross Fork, Idaho, described his solution to the problem in his 1892 annual report. "I have gone in person and taken quite a number of school children by force, which required considerable force as I have been pounced upon on more than one occasion," he wrote. One time "it became necessary for me to choke a so-called chief into subjection. We, however, placed his children in school." Fisher and other agents with the same problem pleaded with Morgan for armed reinforcements. The commissioner replied that he would prefer the Indian agents to continue to handle it on their own. He didn't want to send out U.S. Army troops to round up kids to send to school, though he wouldn't hesitate to do that if he had to.

Morgan's and Dorchester's sanctimonious pronouncements about what the Indians needed to do to lift themselves up out of wretchedness didn't sit well with Lummis. Practically everything he wrote about the Pueblos during his last three years in Isleta carried a barbed message for them and other misguided Indian-policy reformers. The theme of much of what he wrote was that the Pueblos were superb parents and they raised perfect children, unquestionably an exaggeration. But he must have been seething with anger in those days at the way people whom he was proud to have as friends and neighbors were being treated by government bureaucrats. The pieces he was writing for popular magazines were one way to hit back.[8]

"A Pueblo town is the children's paradise," Lummis asserted in an article for *Harper's Young People*, a version of which was published half a dozen more times in other magazines and in one of his books. "The parents are fairly ideal in their relations to their children. They are uniformly gentle, yet never foolishly indulgent. A Pueblo child is almost never punished, and almost never needs to be. Obedience and respect to age are born in these brown young Americans and are never forgotten by them." The children are "all my very good amigos," Lummis wrote, marveling at their "good breeding and perennial content."

Isleta's youngsters had "none of the countless appliances to which our youth look for amusement," Lummis noted in a story for another childrens' magazine, *Munsey's Weekly*. They didn't have any of the baseball bats and storybooks and other fancy toys that cluttered the lives of American children. "And yet I never saw anywhere in the east such endlessly happy young people as my aboriginal neighbors. I have known the Pueblos for six years and I have lived with them for two and never saw a fight or a quarrel or a sulk."

Between 1889 and 1892 Lummis published dozens of articles projecting a flattering view of Pueblo life. Dorchester tried to ignore Lummis, refusing to give him the honor of responding directly to anything he wrote and pointedly refraining from using his name. But by the end of that three-year stretch, it became apparent that Lummis had gotten under Dorchester's skin, which explains why, out of more than twenty-five major tribal groupings that the school superintendent had charge of, Dorchester became obsessed with the Pueblos. They were arguably the most prosperous and best adjusted of all of the Indian tribes in the West. Yet Dorchester devoted fully half of his twenty-thousand-word report for 1892 to what he insisted was the terrible state of the pueblos on the lower Rio Grande.

Dorchester introduced his discussion of the Pueblos by establishing his own credentials for speaking about the tribe. He noted that in his three years as superintendent he had visited all eighteen of the Rio Grande pueblos and had carefully studied all of the most authoritative scholarship on the region, a category of writings that most certainly didn't include the "poetic figments" of a certain unnamed "magazine writer." "Notwithstanding the verdicts of some superficial observers," Dorchester explained, he had come to the conclusion after his exhaustive investigation of the Pueblos that there was hardly a tribe in America that was as utterly depraved.

Lummis had written about how modest and chaste Pueblo youth were taught to be. "Pueblo etiquette as to the acquaintance of young people is extremely strict," he asserted. "No youth and maiden must walk or talk together; and as for a visit or a private conversation, both the offenders—no matter how mature—would be soundly whipped by their parents." But Dorchester begged to differ, combing the extensive literature on the Pueblos in search of the most lurid passages he could find to cobble together a strikingly different portrait.[9]

The pueblos were rife with witch killings, incest, thievery, and every vice and perversion imaginable, according to Dorchester. One first-hand observer had witnessed a ceremony in which "filthy brutes drank heartily" of a "strange and abominable refreshment": the urine and excrement of men and dogs. Dorchester quoted another authority who reported that in one of the pueblos "men are allowed to wear women's costume, and work with the women in the house." The very religion of the tribe fostered such depravity, Dorchester maintained. Pueblo children were taught to steal from outsiders and even from each other, and to revel in promiscuity, bastardy, and other forms of perversion. They are "brought up in utter disregard of modesty or chastity," Dorchester added. "There is great carelessness in the training of children; and the promiscuous life of these communities, as well as some of their heathenish dances, tends to great licentiousness." Yet another observer quoted by Dorchester claimed, "I have seen an Indian man and woman, in open daylight, go through the whole operation of copulation in the open plaza. The heathen dances at midnight are even worse ofttimes."

The Pueblo Indians, Dorchester concluded, tipping every sentence with a barb that seemed to be aimed squarely at Charles Lummis, were "an exceedingly ignorant and stultified people" held back by pagan beliefs and grotesque displays of fetishism. "They are dwarfed mentally, the result of centuries of indifference to the outside world. Not one in five hundred can read at all, and those very little. . . . Their close, ill-ventilated homes, and a system of existence which allows of no ventilation of ideas, has stifled life and thought. Moreover, their social habits

160

have sapped physical strength and mental energy, and made them a small, obtuse people."

While Lummis had written often about the prosperous farms and neat, clean homes in Isleta, Dorchester described unkempt fields with paltry crops and dirty villages filled with decrepit dwellings: "Dynamite would perform a benevolent work if applied under these old pueblos, unless our antiquarians and ethnologists too strongly insist upon preserving and setting apart some of them, as curious relics and reminders of the olden times."

Dorchester's grossly overblown assault on Lummis's beloved Pueblos betrayed the bitter frustration he clearly felt as he sat down in the late summer of 1892 to write that annual report, his fourth since becoming superintendent of Indian schools. Despite all his hard work and thousands of miles of rough travel, many of the schools under his charge were still half empty. And he had a much bigger worry. A month before the August 16 date of his report, the Bureau of Indian Affairs' compulsory education policy for Indian schools had suffered a devastating setback in a courtroom in Albuquerque. The mastermind behind the litigation strategy was none other than Charlie Lummis.

The immediate target of Lummis's legal attack was William Creager, the superintendent of the Albuquerque Indian School.[10] Creager took charge of the school at the same time that the Morgan-Dorchester regime was installed in Washington, and he wasted no time in overturning policies that had been in place since the school was founded five years earlier. The first superintendent, William Bryan, wrote in his 1885 annual report about the need to "guard against the formation of a wide gulf between parent and child and to prevent the child from acquiring notions inconsistent with the proper filial respect and duty." Bryan encouraged students to spend their vacations at home. Even though he was a Presbyterian, he endorsed a bid by the archbishop of the Santa Fe archdiocese, John Baptist Salpointe, for funding to open up more day schools in the pueblos. One of the first changes made by Creager, a follower of Pratt's approach to Indian education, was to let the contract for the day schools expire, forcing them to close down—and putting Eve out of a job. Trying to educate Indian children without removing them from their backward environment was a waste of time, as Creager saw it. Besides, Pueblo parents had used the day schools as an excuse not to send their children to the Albuquerque Indian School, which as a result had suffered a chronic shortage of students since its inception.

It may have troubled Creager that so many children were missing out on the educational opportunity that his school could provide. But he was certainly concerned that he was missing out on government funding. The amount of money the school received was based in part on the number of students on its rolls.

There were perhaps 1,000 school-age children among the 8,000 or so residents of the eighteen Rio Grande pueblos ostensibly served by AIS. The school had a relatively modest goal of enrolling 200 of them in 1886. But attendance that year reached only 156, and some of those were Apache children shipped in from reservations far to the west to help give the school a semblance of being close to fully utilized. AIS administrators even brought in Mexican children from south of the border after getting their parents to sign affidavits that they were Indian. Many Pueblo parents valued an education for their children, but not at AIS. In 1888 only ten of the eighteen pueblos sent any children at all to the school, and by far the largest number came from the one Protestant-dominated pueblo, Laguna.

Creager continued to rely on imported Apache and Mexican children to fill empty seats in the school. But thanks to the closure of the day schools and aggressive recruiting on his part, he did better than any of his predecessors in boosting Pueblo enrollment. In 1889 the pueblos sent 130 pupils to the school, including 36 from Isleta.

Olive and Wallace Hite, the publishers of the *Albuquerque Times*, were close friends of the Lummises'. But they apparently had no idea about the case against Creager that Lummis had been building for more than a year. They joined the rest of the Albuquerque press in lavishing praise on Creager for his success in civilizing his young charges. His handiwork was on public display in an evening of entertainment provided by some of Creager's students at Grant's Opera House on June 30. The show featured precision twirling by the AIS wand team and a program of marches, quicksteps, waltzes, and gallops "played not only with precision but expression" by a twenty-seven-piece band made up of children who four months earlier had never seen an instrument. The

Albuquerque Indian School was a "monument to the wisdom of the government," the *Times* exclaimed in its review of the show.

The Hites and the rest of Albuquerque first learned of a more sinister side to Creager just a week after the variety show at Grant's Opera House. The parents of the students from Isleta, with the help of Lummis and an Albuquerque attorney that he had hired, scored a stunning victory against the superintendent, who quickly settled a sensational case filed against him.

According to Lummis, who had a stack of sworn affidavits to back up his allegations, many of the students at AIS were being held at the school against their will. Some had even been kidnapped from their villages and hauled off to Albuquerque by Indian School agents. Juan Rey Abeita had eagerly enrolled two of his sons in the school, but the third and youngest had been grabbed and carried off to AIS more than three years earlier when Creager had been especially desperate to get enrollment numbers up. Abeita had been barred from seeing his children ever since.

On one occasion, Juan Rey had gone to Albuquerque to try to check up on his children, not even knowing if they were alive. "He was thrown off the grounds by the professional 'bouncers,' with threats of prison if he came back," as Lummis told it. A mild-mannered man who had never raised his voice during the years that Lummis knew him, Juan Rey returned to Isleta with badly bruised arms, mementos of the rude reception that he received at AIS. Children who tried to run away were treated much worse, Lummis contended.

The legal action against Creager and the Indian School had evolved out of a series of meetings of Isleta's Congress of Elders beginning the previous summer. After the farmers had finished their work in the fields, the elders had gathered on consecutive nights talking for hours about what to do for the "little cautivos" or captives, as they called the thirty-six Isleta children at AIS. The parents had been "half wild with anxiety" for more than a year but were powerless to intervene, Lummis said. So they turned to the man they called Por Todos for advice.

In the summer of 1891 Lummis had sent letters to Morgan and Dorchester on their behalf seeking permission for their children to come home during the summer vacation. But Creager, having made great efforts to fill his school with students, didn't want to go to the trouble of rounding them up again. So that summer he allowed only three Isleta children to return, and even then he let them go one at a time, holding the others hostage pending the return of the one who was temporarily freed.

The next summer the Isleta parents' appeal for permission to bring their children home for vacation was flatly rejected. The parents were given the "comforting assurance" that their children would remain in school for nine more years, Lummis said. "When they begged me for help there was only one thing to do."

Lummis suggested that the parents initiate legal proceedings against Creager. The pueblo congress agreed, and so Lummis paid forty-five dollars out of his own pocket to retain a Catholic attorney in Albuquerque, Joseph Marron of the law firm Collier & Marron. He filed a writ of habeas corpus, the procedure that allows anyone who believes they have been wrongly imprisoned to appeal to a judge for their freedom. A hearing on the writ was scheduled for July 6.

According to Lummis, Creager resorted to strong-arm tactics in an attempt to sabotage the legal proceeding. On the night before the hearing, Creager and two henchmen came to Isleta and tried to waylay Lummis and Juan Rey Abeita, the key witness, on their way to the depot to catch the train to Albuquerque. Lummis never explained exactly what happened, but one of the men accompanying the superintendent was the "apostate" Indian, Lummis's Tigua tutor, Henry Kendall. They failed to stop Lummis and Abeita from making it to the city.

The next morning, Lummis and Abeita were at Marron's law office in last-minute preparations for the hearing when a courier arrived with a message from Creager. He had agreed to release the Isleta children. By 11 A.M. the Isleta boys were turned over to Lummis, who loaded them into a wagon and set out for the pueblo that afternoon. The girls had been sent away to summer camp in the mountains, so they weren't released for another week. Lummis had to make several other trips to confront Creager in Albuquerque before all of the Isleta children were freed. But the villagers were jubilant that evening over the return of the first group of boys. All 1,100 residents of the pueblo turned out for a celebration in the plaza in front of the church. "There wasn't a dry eye in the crowd as the little cautivos returned," Lummis wrote.

There were more tears at the Abeita household, where Luis was getting reacquainted with the parents he hardly knew. He had forgotten

164

every last word of Tigua and could no longer talk to his mother. Eve had to translate. "And Pita—as fine and motherly a woman as I ever knew—cried; and Luis cried; and so I think did we all," Lummis wrote. "For we were sentimental enough to think a baby and his mother should not be divided thus, and that any man who put this gulf between them to get himself a salary was, no matter how virtuous he fooled himself into feeling, a devilish scoundrel."

Creager and AIS, of course, were still in business, with a couple hundred other Indian children still under their control. But by then the local press was on to the story. Even the *Democrat* ran some critical commentary about the folly of keeping Pueblo children in school against their will. In the *Times* the Hites, after interviewing former students who corroborated Lummis's allegations, launched a withering attack on Creager starting with a story published on July 19. They kept up a barrage against the school and its principal for much of the next year.

The first story, written by a reporter who days earlier had extolled the wisdom of Creager, portrayed the superintendent as a sadistic monster. The story told of a homesick Pima boy who had escaped from the school and tried to make his way home. Creager personally chased him down in a wagon, hauled him back to Albuquerque, and threw him in the school's "dungeon," chaining him up in a manner that he apparently used regularly on those students who crossed him. He "hangs his pupils up by their hand-cuffed wrists till the weight of the body rests on the ball of the foot and the arm sockets and then shuts the cell door and leaves his poor victim alone with his agony and tears," the story asserted. After stringing up the homesick Pima child in this manner, Creager retired to "his comfortable chair—paid for by the government—smiling a sweet smile of satisfaction while he stroked his patriarchal beard and listened to the pitiful moans and cries from the tortured boy in the nearby jail."

In another case a young Pueblo boy, who worked as a personal servant in Creager's home, had a quarrel with Creager's young son, prompting Creager to thrash the Indian boy with a buggy whip. When the boy ran away, the superintendent chased him as far as Isleta, chained him to the back of a wagon, and forced him to run behind the wagon all the way back to Albuquerque. "Was the Apache ever more bloodthirsty than this man who can coolly whip till the raw, quivering flesh flies open at every cut of the bloody lash?" the *Times* asked. "Who

can drag children at the cart's tail and teach them to sing—in public—
'Hurrah for Creager and Morgan'?" Right-thinking citizens of Albuquerque should rise up and denounce the slave-driving principal, the
story concluded. "We want no . . . Legrees to scourge the backs of our
brown skinned neighbors' children."

In a long three-part series of articles for the *Boston Evening Transcript*
that August, Lummis exulted in the legal victory and offered an eloquent denunciation of the astonishing arrogance behind the Indian
Bureau's brutal education policy. "Are the thoughtful of us so absolutely
secure of the success of our civilization as to force it upon the unwilling?" Lummis asked. "Are we so modestly all conscious of our superiority
that we must needs drag them toward our own dubious achievement,
careless if it serves no other end than to make them wretched?"

Lummis went on to describe the miserable fate that awaited Indian
children who were sent to the schools, where they were summarily
stripped of their identity, their name, even their appearance. "Extorted
from home and arrived at school the Pueblo child is at once treated to
the distinguished consideration invented by civilization for convicts
and wards. The magnificent flowing black hair—always carefully
tended at home—is cropped Sing-Sing fashion. Furthermore, a hat is
imposed. The superior race having proudly achieved baldheadness,
steps must of course be taken to make its wards bald. Nature having
impudently given the pupil a better chest, neck, back and head of hair
than the instructor, Nature shall be rebuked and her work undone as
speedily as possible."

The "industrial training" they received in the process was at best a
"cheap godsend to the farmer or mechanic," Lummis wrote. Indian boys
"who have been detained five to seven years in a government school are
then turned loose to practice shoemaking, watchmaking, tin-roofing,
plumbing or typography among their nomad fathers." No wonder they
eventually rejected what they learned. "I cannot too sharply remind
you that this is no relapse into barbarism. The Pueblo customs are very
far from perfection, but they will, at least, compare favorably with
ours." The only argument for the compulsory education of Indians that
Lummis found convincing was that it would give them a better chance
of fending off greedy whites. "[W]ithout it [they] will fall prey to
the . . . licentious and the earth-hungry of the superior race."

Their legal victory over Creager had been an exhilarating educational experience for the people of Isleta. Creager lost his aura of invincibility. "A cowed bully cannot hope to hide his status from Indian eyes; and it was delicious to see, even in their self-contained faces, their appreciation of the change from the times when he had browbeaten them and threatened handcuffs," Lummis noted in the *Evening Transcript*. "The parents now understand their legal and human rights, and intend to stand by them," Lummis added in a letter to the editor of the *Albuquerque Times* published in August. "They mostly favor education; but slavery they will no longer submit to—and I shall endeavor to help them." He concluded the letter to the editor with a challenge. "If Creager wants to carry on this particular battle, he knows where to find me."

In fact, Morgan and Dorchester, though badly stung by the fiasco in Albuquerque, weren't prepared to give up. Morgan continued to insist that Indian parents don't have "any right to forcibly keep their children out of school to grow up like themselves—a race of barbarians and semi-savages." Dorchester traveled to Albuquerque that fall, stayed for two weeks to investigate the accusations of brutality by Creager, and offered a ringing defense of the schoolmaster. "A more causeless and baseless libel upon any institution and its officials I have never met in my life," Dorchester maintained, taking a shot at Lummis, though as always not deigning to use his name. "This accuser is one of those prolific authors who can write more glibly without a basis of facts than with one. Evidently his sphere is the invention of fiction, but I protest against the adoption of such fiction by the American people as bona fide facts."[11]

Lummis, to his considerable regret, was no longer in New Mexico when Dorchester arrived. Two watershed events were in the process of changing his life. The first was mentioned in an editor's note in the *Chillicothe Leader* accompanying the latest letter from Lummis about the Indian education battle. "Charley Lummis sends us some strong matter on the Indian question in the w. & w. West," Carrigan wrote. "He is, however, helping to settle it—the question—by populating New Mexico with a little Lummis, which is fat and sassy. If congratulations are in order, here they are!" As the story intimated, on June 8 Charlie and Eve had become parents of a daughter. The baby's godmother, Marcelina Abeita, chose her name, Turbesé, meaning Sun Halo.

The other big event was the fast-approaching trip to Peru. When Lummis and Bandelier were planning the expedition the previous fall, Lummis had hoped that Eve could come along. But about then she had become pregnant, ruling out that possibility. And his own status as a member of the expedition was shakier than he realized. Bandelier, who was departing for Peru in June ahead of Lummis, was having serious second thoughts about whether he wanted Lummis to join him after all. Dorothea warned Eve about Bandelier's concerns in a letter written May 29 and marked "private but not incendiary." She had just met Adolph and Josephine in Los Angeles a few days before they sailed. Bandelier had talked frankly with her about his concerns that Lummis was unwilling to be controlled and that the two might end up in a constant fight. "I don't think we must get puzzled over our C.'s odd ways," Dorothea told Eve. "B. says 'he is all heart without the proper balance of judgment.' And he is right and that explains much about him: his irresponsibility, his impulsiveness, his lovableness, even his vanity." She added that Eve shouldn't worry Charlie with the news, not yet anyway. Bandelier "seems settled upon giving him a chance at least. I had feared even for that." She signed off with a word of congratulations for the baby that was due at any time. "I kiss you and the child and love you 'ere to the edge of doom'," Dorothea wrote.[12]

By September, Bandelier had been in Peru for a couple of months and no letter had arrived telling Lummis not to bother coming. So Charlie and Eve packed up their belongings and on October 2 left Isleta, their beloved home for so many years, with their baby daughter and a Pueblo nanny, Maria, to begin a new life in Los Angeles. Lummis would have several weeks to help his family settle in before he was scheduled to sail from San Francisco in late October.

Lummis was still in Los Angeles on October 15 when he received a telegram from Olive Hite about Dorchester's activities in Albuquerque. The telegram was enough to make Lummis seriously consider returning to Albuquerque, if only for a few days. Dorchester, it seems, had passed a tip on to the U.S. Secret Service alleging that while Lummis was living in Isleta, the freelance writer had actually been counterfeiting currency. Dorchester had learned of this shocking crime from someone who had seen the counterfeiting operation himself, Henry Kendall. Lummis and his wife, Kendall said, frequently shut themselves up in a room for hours at a time, sternly warning that no one should open the door while they were at work inside. They produced thousands of small rectangles of tinted paper, which they bundled up and mailed to various addresses back East, receiving checks in return, Kendall reported.

Thomas Hughes, editor of the *Albuquerque Citizen*, who had become Creager's leading apologist in the press after the court debacle, ran a story about the allegations against Lummis. A Secret Service agent traveled to Albuquerque to investigate, but it didn't take him long to get to the truth of the matter. The so-called counterfeit bills were the Lummises' famous blueprints.

The Hites assured Lummis that there was no need for him to return to Albuquerque to defend himself against such a ridiculous accusation. Lummis had to content himself with flaying Dorchester from afar. The day after he received Hite's telegram, he fired off a 2,500-word open letter to the *Times*, addressed to his accuser, "roasting Dorchester alive." "There could be no sharper commentary on the utter desperation of your cause than that you have made a charge so idiotic," Lummis wrote. "By the way, too, I would like to see your next meeting with my father— who was for years your associate in the New England Methodist conference. I would like to see you cower before that old man's honest eyes when you know that he knows what you have done."

The controversy simmered in the Albuquerque papers for months. Hughes, of the *Citizen*, continued to pick at the evidence that Lummis had gathered against Creager and that had found its way into the *Times*. Some of the evidence in fact proved to be overblown. The child who had supposedly died from treatment received in Creager's dungeon, for example, had indeed run away from the school and was pursued, caught, and hauled back in a wagon. But Hughes said there was never any evidence he had been injured in that incident, the boy's alleged deathbed affidavit to the contrary. He had died twenty-two months later from a totally unrelated illness.

In the early months of 1893 Hughes continued to rail against "the gross absurdities" in Lummis's attack on Creager and the "specious manner" in which he had persuaded Mrs. Hite to take up his crusade. He professed his confidence that the unfairly sullied superintendent would be vindicated in the end. "The howling of the diseased female mind on the *Times* will not accomplish its nefarious designs," Hughes declared.

Whether the allegations against Creager were true in all their gory detail or not, there was no denying that the writ of habeas corpus had struck a major blow against the government's policy of forcibly removing Indian children from their homes. Later that year Congress approved a bill ending the practice of sending children away from their reservation without the consent of the parents. They could still be compelled to attend government schools on the reservation, a policy that would lead to more Indian education battles down the road. But the Carlisle model of Indian education could no longer be implemented with the help of the legal—and military—might of the state. In the course of congressional debate on the bill, a senator on the Indian Affairs Committee reportedly denounced Morgan on the floor of the Senate as a narrow-minded bigot. A broken man, Morgan resigned his post on March 1, followed out the door by Dorchester several months later.

Morgan's replacement, D. M. Browning, began slowly to move the Indian-policy bureaucracy toward a somewhat more tolerant outlook on Indians. In his first annual report, delivered in August 1893, Browning offered a grudging concession that neither Morgan nor Dorchester would have ever allowed to escape their pen or lips. "Even ignorant and superstitious parents have rights, and their parental feelings are entitled to consideration," Browning acknowledged.

Creager, Lummis's chief opponent in the Albuquerque Indian School battle, lasted longer than either of his two superiors. But Lummis was determined not to let him off the hook. For several years after leaving Isleta, Lummis continued to gather evidence and write articles and letters to editors accusing Creager of pressuring female teachers at his school for sexual favors. At first, Dorchester's replacement, R. V. Belt, summarily dismissed the allegations. But when a former teacher produced corroborative evidence, Belt called for an investigation.

A BIA inspector spent a week in Albuquerque looking into the accusation. He concluded that while the totality of the evidence tended to exonerate Creager, the longtime principal's continued presence at the school would be an embarrassment to the government. So under pressure from his superiors, Creager resigned on March 31, 1894.

Even then Lummis wasn't finished with Creager. Nearly a decade later, on July 21, 1903, Lummis received a letter from James Foshay, superintendent of Los Angeles city schools, asking for his opinion about an applicant for a teaching position in the city.[13] Foshay was

170

aware that Lummis had lived in New Mexico and therefore thought that perhaps he might know something about an applicant named W. B. Creager. As a matter of fact, Lummis did know something about the man. He noted in his diary that he responded with a letter to Foshay that would guarantee Creager wouldn't be resuming his career as an educator in Los Angeles.

Chapter 9

The Lion of Out West

Lummis had a few tasks to finish up in Los Angeles before leaving for Peru. He raised some last-minute cash by selling $232 worth of Navajo blankets and serapes to his old curio-dealing contact Wilbur Campbell, who had recently "risen to some importance as a trader." He also took out a ten-thousand-dollar insurance policy on his life.

Then there was a personal matter to attend to. He and Dorothea and Eve had continued to get along famously, but outsiders had poked their noses into the arrangement. Just four days before he was set to leave Los Angeles, Dorothea sent a note to Eve and Charlie saying that people were whispering nasty things about their threesome, and so she couldn't see them anymore. Lummis wouldn't stand for that. It wouldn't do to have people ostracizing his "dear two" when he was half a world away in Peru. So Lummis moved immediately to squash that scandal before it could spread. "I trot double quick to J. D. Hooker, millionaire pipe man and pig, who neglects a lovely wife, Dolly's best friend, and has no redeeming feature but love for astronomy," Lummis wrote in his journal that day.[1] "Face him down and bluff him stiff as to his scandalous suggestions to Dolly." Lummis's intervention apparently worked. Dolly dropped by for an hour and a quarter on the evening of the twenty-first. Lummis left the next day for San Francisco. On October 25 he embarked on the steamer *San Jose* for the long trip to Lima, arriving November 21.

The Villard Expedition was supposed to keep Lummis gainfully employed for two or three years at an annual salary of three thousand dollars. He hoped to relocate Eve and Turbesé to Peru at some point during that time, and although he would miss them terribly until then, he couldn't turn down money like that. The salary could set them on a secure footing at last. He planned to get by on as little as possible, leaving enough money to buy a home for his family in Los Angeles. As it turned out, Lummis ended up spending less than ten months in South America. And he learned on arrival in Lima that Bandelier had decided, without telling Lummis, to slash his assistant's salary in half.

In the book they wrote about their father, Lummis's children Keith and Turbesé described the South American adventure as one of the most uplifting and enriching experiences of his life. "Perhaps there was never a time when he could not still feel the Andean gusts in his face," they wrote. "At a word or even an odor its recollections would rush to his mind: Indians of the Bolivian uplands winding along the brick-red trail playing their Pan's pipes and flutes as they drove their flocks of burros and llamas before them . . . the windswept crudity of Peruvian tambos where he had sought shelter at night, the awful glory of the cordilleras." The experience certainly left its mark, as Turbesé was acutely aware since her father forced her to spend a good deal of her youth in a queer peaked Peruvian cap with long, floppy earflaps. But despite his own rave recollections of the trip, Lummis experienced far more misery than pleasure while it was under way. His dear friend Bandelier was largely to blame.

Bandelier had had several good months of excavating the pre-Inca ruins at Chanchan before Lummis reached Peru, so he was in a relatively good frame of mind that summer and fall. Still, the excessively ebullient letters that Lummis was sending grated on the older, far more serious scientist. Decades later, writing his memoir, Lummis still gushed about what he thought he and his mentor could accomplish together to disseminate Bandelier's scientific findings. Lummis said he explained to Bandelier, "With your leave, I am going to make it my part of this to say to the world: 'Lookee! Don't be scared! All these Greek words are harmless! All these Ologies are only the story of man—the story of you and me . . . and carried back five or ten thousand years. And it's fun!'" Bandelier recorded his reaction to his partner's suggestion in his journal: the "fellow must be laboring in craziness."[2]

Peru, in short, brought the long-suppressed personality contrast between the two men to the surface. As Bandelier once described his own attitude toward life, "It is good to be a Catholic. I was cut out for one after all. But it's not proper to be buoyant. At any time HE may send us sore trials and we may prove wanting after all." It was cause for great anguish to Bandelier in Peru, after the first few fruitful months of the expedition, that a grossly disproportionate share of the sore trials fell on his head instead of Lummis's. Indeed, the troubles he faced were on a par with the tribulations of Job.

The medical problems that had plagued Bandelier in Mexico years earlier returned with a vengeance, including writer's cramp and severe diarrhea. He had an eye infection and lost some teeth. He had chills and fevers that he attributed to malaria. He had such severe eczema that he had to stay out of the sun for days at a time. Then he developed a bad ear infection that wouldn't go away, so he allowed a quack doctor in Lima to treat it with carbolic acid, which didn't cure the infection but instead caused a horrific burn. It too got infected, and he lost all hearing in that ear for a while.

In early December, less than two weeks after Lummis reached Lima, Joe got sick. Her condition quickly worsened. To help Adolph care for her, Henrietta Ritter, a Swiss woman with three grown daughters who had befriended the Bandeliers, took Joe into her home, but it did little to ease the excruciating pain from a condition diagnosed as a blockage of the intestines. A series of doctors including a Chinese healer could do nothing for her either. Adolph got virtually no sleep for a week until December 11 when his beloved wife died.

The release from her agony was a great relief to Bandelier, whom Lummis pronounced "very affectionate" after the funeral the next day. His spirits were also relatively bright on Christmas Day when—after consulting in spirit with Joe, who became something of a guardian angel to him for the next several years—he proposed to twenty-two-year-old Fanny Ritter. Lummis was the first person Bandelier told about his plan to remarry, explaining in his journal that he confided in his partner because he "is so faithful and so attached."

It was a rare kind word for Lummis in Bandelier's journal in those days. His woes were by no means over, as his own medical problems were just beginning. And he had serious difficulties with Peruvian government authorities who were especially nervous because of an ongoing political crisis. When he and Lummis were in Lima together, they spent an hour or so every day in conversation, according to Lummis's diary. But they spent virtually no time together exploring ruins. In fact, for most of Lummis's ten months in South America, they had no contact at all with each other. Judging from his treatment of Lummis, it was as if Bandelier, having lost faith that God would step in and do His duty, took it upon himself to knock some humility into his sickeningly cheerful sidekick.

Lummis tried to make the best of his months in South America. But he didn't even get out of gloomy Lima until December 23, after having spent most of his first month in the country carefully packing dozens of crates of artifacts that Bandelier had collected during the summer. He made occasional solitary excursions out of Lima, over the cordillera of the Andes on a brand new railroad, up to Bolivia, across Lake Titicaca by steamer. And he poked around for about a week in the ruins of Pachamac, where he got to see mummies that had just been unearthed from ancient graves.

But mostly Lummis spent hour after hour for days on end sitting around in Lima pining for Eve. He wrote long letters to her every day, keeping in his diary a running count of the number of words. The total came to 56,700 words mailed in nineteen different packages in February and 58,800 words mailed in sixteen packages in March. He also wrote long letters to "my dear poet," Dorothea. The letters to Eve were primarily about how much he desperately missed her but were fairly upbeat about his experiences in Peru, where, he said, "every day and every hour brings me some new wonder, some new beauty."

He was more truthful in his letters to Dolly. "I expected this year to be hard—but certainly not as hard as it has been," Lummis wrote. Bandelier "has done nothing to soften it—except with money. . . . He hasn't made the loneliness any less," abruptly cutting off any talk of family, leaving Lummis "without any touch of human companionship nearer than 5,000 miles." In that letter of March 20, Charlie told Dolly that he was going to level with Bandelier. "He's got to hear the remarks I have to offer, even if it shall be necessary to spike his ears to the wall."

Four days later Lummis told Bandelier that he couldn't stand being without his wife and child a day longer. Surprisingly, Bandelier was "very understanding and fair," granting him a leave of absence from the expedition. Lummis was so excited, he stayed up until 2:30 in the morning packing his bags, though his ship didn't leave for another week. He arrived back in Los Angeles April 22 after a six-month absence, hugged Eve for a full twenty minutes, marveled at how large his baby girl had gotten, and logged two "cielos" in his diary that day.

Over the next several months, Lummis worked feverishly on magazine and newspaper articles, signed a deal with Scribner's to publish *The Land of Poco Tiempo*, made a triumphant return visit to Isleta and Albuquerque with Eve and Turbesé, and, in the most momentous development of all, bought a house at 14 Forester Avenue in Los Angeles. He spent most days in June from sunrise to sunset fixing up the house, building a chicken coop and a rabbit hutch, planting grapevines and more than a dozen types of fruit trees from peaches to cherimoyas. On June 23 he saw Turbesé take her first step. The next day, he somewhat reluctantly departed once again for Peru.

Back in Lima, his relationship with Bandelier worse than ever, Lummis resumed his obsessive letter writing. During his 279 days in Peru, he wrote a grand total of 416,600 words to Eve. By fall the predominant theme of his letters was his homesickness. As he wrote on September 1, "Thank heaven a new month has begun and the old one is behind us instead of between. A day is a very small thing, but at least it is something off the total that separates me from my darling." The fact that he had installed his family in a home before he left helped his mood immensely. "It comforts me the last thing before I am asleep and first when I awaken," he wrote. "Before it used to be just your faces but now it is your faces set with the dear and beloved little home that is ours. I don't think you have ever dreamed what a desperate hunger I had for a home of our own . . . and it seemed so absolutely hopeless."

As for the glorious archaeological expedition with the famous Adolph Bandelier, by October Lummis was no longer disguising his disdain for his mentor, at least not in his diary. After weeks waiting in Lima for a word from Bandelier that never came, Lummis wrote in November, "Damn his dirty face." What little charms Lima had ever offered had disappeared in the gloom that Lummis measured by way of diary entries recording the amount of sunlight each day: ten minutes one day, a rare spell of three hours of sunshine the day after that, and a more typical thirty minutes the next.

By the end of November, Lummis had had enough and so, it seemed, had Bandelier. Officially, it was with a deep sense of mutual regret that Lummis and Bandelier parted company. Bandelier was "all tenderness and understanding," to hear Lummis tell it in his diary, as he gave his faithful assistant the final installment of his salary and bid him adieu. But Bandelier offered a sharply contrasting account of the parting in his own journal. "I took the draft for Lummis for $350—a poorly earned salary indeed," he wrote. Lummis "did nothing for three months fully. And yet, he will, in all probability, derive all the public benefit from the whole enterprise." Lummis was on his way home "I hope and pray NEVER to RETURN. . . . He is an over-ambitious, greedy, reckless, and grasping spirit." He has "not the slightest scientific capacity." He is "not even a conscientious photographer."

Bandelier's remarks reflected one of the sources of tension in the relationship, his paranoia that the glib and prolific freelance journalist would steal all the credit. His concern ultimately scuttled their big plans to jointly publish their Peruvian findings, along with the fact that there really hadn't been any discoveries that Lummis had participated in. So the four articles that Lummis was going to write for *Century* magazine at four hundred dollars each never panned out.

That financial loss paled in comparison to another setback that smacked hard-luck Bandelier at the end of that year. He got word that Henry Villard had been implicated in a "gigantic swindle" of the stockholders of the Northern Pacific Railroad. The financier's contributions to Bandelier's Peruvian expedition soon ended. Adolph and Fanny, who had married that December just past the one-year anniversary of Joe's death, would remain marooned in Peru for the next ten years, doing lots of significant archaeological work but living a hand-to-mouth existence.

As for the rancor between the two in 1892–93, Bandelier's biographers came to Lummis's defense, arguing that Lummis did little to deserve the neglect and the bitter outbursts, other than being his usual eccentric self. They suggest that Joe's death "created deep mental disturbances in Adolph," magnifying a paranoia that had always been a submerged part of his mental makeup. In any event, the hard feelings didn't last long. Within a few years, Lummis once again was a "dear good boy" in Bandelier's journal and correspondence. A decade later Lummis, to whom Bandelier occasionally wrote despairing letters pleading for help, played a key role in raising funds that enabled the esteemed archaeologist to return to the United States. And he was a fiercely loyal friend to Adolph and Fanny for the rest of their lives.

* * *

After his troubled sojourn in Peru, Lummis was especially happy to be back in Los Angeles. The trees he had planted in June had taken root, leafed out, and started to bear fruit. The flowers of the southern California winter were in full bloom. The chicken coop and rabbit hutch were squirming with animal life. Turbesé was toddling everywhere, romping with the family dog, mussing up her father's hair. For the first time in his life, Charlie had a family and a home of his own.

To be sure, all was not perfect. Despite the head-over-heels love poured out in all those letters from Peru, on December 26 Charlie and Eve got into a "peleo tremendo." Lummis didn't explain in his diary what the big fight was all about; they made up two days later. But a good guess is that it was about money.

Many of Eve's letters to Charlie in Peru had been about her financial woes, which were compounded by the fact that Sis Lund, their friend from Bernalillo, New Mexico, had come out to Los Angeles with her new baby to keep Eve company. Unaccountably, she turned out to be broke and was dependent on Eve for everything, even streetcar fare around town and milk for her baby. Charlie had requested that most of his Villard Expedition paychecks be sent directly to Eve, but they didn't go far in an increasingly expensive city. And now, that source of income had been abruptly shut off. Charlie had spent every last bit of cash on Peruvian curios, including an old gold and steel flintlock musket signed by Juan de Soto (great-grandson of the discoverer of the Mississippi River), a 1723 edition of a two-volume history of Peru by the Peruvian Indian writer Garcilaso de la Vega, other rare books, and a steamer ticket back from Peru. He returned broke and out of work to a penniless home.

Lummis immediately cranked up the same sorts of moneymaking schemes that had sustained him in Isleta. He sold off some of his curio collection to Wilbur D. Campbell and private collectors. He set up another blueprint production line. On days when it was running, Eve, with some help from Charlie, started cranking out anywhere from 350 to as many as 850 prints a day. To capture more of the profits of the photo sales for himself, he revived a publishing venture that he had launched when he was on the staff of the *Times* called Chas. F. Lummis & Co. He ran a few ads in newspapers and magazines offering a booklet of photographs illustrating *Ramona*, Helen Hunt Jackson's best-selling novel about the Mission Indians, for $1.50 each, and another booklet of photographs of the Spanish missions in California for 75 cents. He had little to say about that venture, so it probably didn't amount to much.

Lummis resumed a frenetic pace of writing and sending out freelance submissions, concentrating on some of the so-far-unpublished Pueblo folktales and the first of his stories from Peru. A number of disappointing rejection slips came back from editors, but Lummis also made his share of sales. He also landed several more book contracts. His Peruvian stories were gathered together into *The Gold Fish of Gran Chimu*, published in London in 1895 and in the United States the next year. That was his seventh book, not counting *Birch Bark Poems*. *The Spanish Pioneers* had finally found a publisher and, along with *The Land of Poco Tiempo*, it had come out in 1893. And his first book of Pueblo folktales was published as *The Man Who Married the Moon* in 1894. Together with *A New Mexico David, A Tramp Across the Continent,* and *Some Strange Corners of Our Country*, they produced a respectable stream of royalties.

But all together it didn't amount to a career. Now that he had the family and home he had always wanted, he was no longer free to rove widely in search of new travel stories. He needed a decent regular salary. Los Angeles, after all, wasn't Isleta. With a population of 85,000 people in 1895, it had become the nation's thirty-second largest city, vaulting from fifty-seventh place in the previous five years. There were wide paved boulevards, an electric streetcar network, modern office blocks that scraped the sky at six stories. It was not the sort of place, in other words, where he had the option of feeding a family on wild plum jam and ducks shot on the Rio Grande. He was running out of ideas about what to do next.

One possibility had been dangled in front of him ever since he got back from Peru. Charles Dwight Willard, who had recently left a career in journalism to become secretary of the Los Angeles Chamber of Commerce, had urged Lummis to accept a job as editor of a magazine called the *Land of Sunshine*. Launched that June, its chief function was to tout the virtues of Southern California as a place to live and do business. Not coincidentally, its purpose dovetailed nicely with the mission of the Los Angeles Chamber of Commerce, which was the main source of support for the magazine through bulk purchases of copies sent to libraries in the East.

A confirmed enthusiast of Southern California with the national profile of a Charles Lummis would be perfect for the job. But Lummis didn't want to become a mouthpiece for the Chamber of Commerce. He accepted the offer in November only after learning that Willard, who had worked for the *Times* in the days when Lummis was contributing to the paper from New Mexico, owned a one-third interest in the company that published the magazine. Willard needed to keep his interest in the magazine quiet to avoid the appearance of a conflict of interest in his job with the publication's chief benefactor, the Chamber. But Willard was in a position to give Lummis the reassurance he needed that he would have unfettered editorial control.

The pay wasn't going to bail Lummis out of his financial difficulties. Willard offered Lummis a salary of $50 a month with an additional $25 payable in a lien on Land of Sunshine Publishing Company stock, plus a one-third ownership interest in the business. But the editorship was a platform that could boost Lummis's books as well as his career as a contributor to many of the nation's leading magazines. By early December he was fully immersed in planning his first issue, which appeared in January 1895.

Willard was well aware that Lummis was, to say the least, unconventional. But he was delighted with his catch. "He has certain oddities but you soon forget them," Willard noted in a letter to his father shortly after Lummis took the job, adding that he was a "tireless worker and is throwing his whole soul into the undertaking."

Lummis made it clear from the outset that he intended to make the magazine more than a superficial booster for the region's business interests. He wasn't going to be a "hireling 'promoter'," he asserted in an editor's note in the first issue. But there was plenty of content in the magazine that served the Chamber of Commerce's interests. One of Lummis's favorite themes, in particular, undoubtedly pleased the region's real estate developers, resort operators, and hotel keepers. He extolled the virtues of the Southern California climate with religious zeal in editorials, feature articles, and photographic layouts. Every January or February he ran photos of cherubic children in the buff surrounded by flowers enjoying the balmy delights of a Los Angeles winter. Some of the early feature articles in the magazine under his tenure—such as "Los Angeles: The Metropolis of the Southwest,"[3] unsigned but almost certainly written by Lummis, and "Memories of Our Italy," by Elizabeth Bacon Custer, the general's widow—gushed with adulation for the Southern Californian paradise.

Lummis was careful to avoid leaving the impression that sunshine was the only thing Los Angeles had to offer. The phenomenal growth of agriculture and industry in recent years had silenced the sneer once widely repeated by eastern visitors that Los Angeles is "founded on nothing but climate." But the climate was an essential part of Southern California's appeal, in Lummis's view, for reasons that ran far deeper than personal comfort. While conventional notions of manifest destiny held that the Anglo-Saxon race was the rightful conqueror of the West, Lummis hoped the American West might achieve a different sort of conquest of the white race. Lummis admired the entrepreneurial spirit of his New England forebears and believed Anglo-Saxons could teach other races something about achievement. But they were equally in need of a few lessons from other cultures about enjoying life. Moving to a more benevolent climate could start the process of racial transformation. "I'm a great believer in environment," Lummis wrote. "[T]he transplantation of the Saxon oak, which has known only stingy soil, to a country where the sky is not a menace and the climate is friendly. . . . should revolutionize the race."

Lummis wasn't alone in espousing such theories. Charles Dudley Warner, the *Harper's Magazine* editor and coauthor with Mark Twain of *The Gilded Age*, expounded on the theme in an early 1896 article for the *Land of Sunshine* entitled "Race and Climate." According to conventional wisdom, Anglo-Saxons were best suited for harsher, northern climes, Warner noted. But seconding Lummis's hopes, he suggested that the whites moving to Southern California might evolve into a "new sort of humanity." He hoped their Anglo-Saxon energy and intensity would "have added to them something of the charm of a less anxious and more contented spirit."

During his tenure as editor of the magazine, Lummis published plenty of pieces about the pleasures of life in Southern California. But Lummis didn't waste any time in signaling that he would also publish more provocative fare. His major contribution to the first issue was an essay entitled "The Spanish American Face." It was one of dozens of articles he would write for the magazine over the years as part of his lifelong crusade to promote awareness of and an appreciation for Southern California's Spanish heritage.[4] But beyond that, the article was a thinly disguised sermon on the virtues of miscegenation. Race mixing was against the law in many states at the time, and it was not a topic of open conversation in polite society. Moreover, anti-immigrant furor was reaching a fever pitch, driven in part by a fear that dark-skinned newcomers would pollute the white race. But that didn't deter Lummis from offering his theory about why Spanish colonization was more humane than the Anglo-Saxon conquest of North America. Anglo settlers generally exterminated the native inhabitants of the regions they colonized. But the Spaniards intermarried with them, Lummis explained.

"It is a curious fact that no other nation in history has ever legitimately produced crosses with so many aboriginal bloods as has the Spaniard." Indeed, the "seal of Spain is written in the faces and in the racial makeup of all the people of Spanish America." As for the Anglo-Saxon colonist, Lummis wrote, "Something of his face goes to the half-breed he begets but will not father; but even this physical impress is much less marked than in the case of his Latin predecessor."

Lummis leapt from that observation into an extended, quirky disquisition on the relative merits of the various types of dark-skinned beauties of Spanish America that it had been his privilege to size up firsthand. Quoting a line from a poem that asserted "brown maids are my passion," he conceded that such a suggestion amounted to rank heresy to the fair-skinned. So be it. "The perfect moreno is the most perfect skin in the world," Lummis maintained. "That perfect brown is so transparent, so fine, so soft, so richly warmed with the very dawn of a flush, as no other cheek that is worn of woman."

The most conspicuous platform for Lummis's commentary in the magazine was a column that he inaugurated in the June 1895 issue. In the same issue, he changed the cover art, replacing a pastoral collage of an orange grove, palm trees, and snow-capped mountains with a more virile image of a mountain lion and a radiant sun. Playing off that theme, he titled his column "In the Lion's Den," calling himself the Lion and his office the Den. It was a collection of items of personal commentary that often filled ten pages in the magazine on topics that ranged from reflections on modern life to denunciations of U.S. foreign policy.

Lummis also made his mark in "That Which Is Written," a book review section that he wrote almost single-handedly for five years. His reviews quickly earned Lummis a reputation as an eagle-eyed and sometimes merciless critic. Nothing provoked his ire more than writers who dared to write about the Southwest while evincing ignorance of the region.

Tales of the Sun-land, a collection of short stories ostensibly about the Southwest, was written in a "sub-hysteric style," he snapped in one review. The stories were so off target in their depiction of the region that they were "dangerously near to deserving the blunt epithet fake." Another book set in Los Angeles "has no more to do with California than with the mountains of the moon." Even authors he admired came in for some cajoling when they slipped up. The esteemed anthropologist and *Land of Sunshine* contributor Dr. Washington Matthews was to be commended for his latest book, *Navaho Legends,* Lummis remarked. But it was regrettable that he had capitulated to "politician meddlers" in his spelling of Navajo.

The pool of contributors to the magazine was thin at first. Lummis produced so much of the copy himself that he disguised some of his contributions with the pseudonyms C. Arloz and C. R. Lohs, plays on the Don Carlos moniker that he had picked up in Isleta. J. D. Willard, who filled in as fiction editor in the early years, was sometimes pressed into service to crank out a quick short story. His "The Century Plant" was conceived, written, and prepared for the printer in four hours, he told his father in a letter a few months after Lummis took charge of the magazine. "Such is editorship in the far west," he remarked.[5]

It may have been cobbled together haphazardly at first, but under Lummis's leadership the magazine quickly attracted attention. The *Los Angeles Times* observed, "Mr. Lummis belongs not to Los Angeles alone, for already his name has become a household word throughout the land." Indeed, across the continent, the *New York Daily Dispatch* reported that the "bright and famous young American author, Mr. Charles F. Lummis" had taken charge of the *Land of Sunshine,* and asserted that success was the foregone conclusion of "every effort made by this indefatigable intellectual athlete." The 5,000-copy pressrun for his first issue sold out in three days, prompting the publishers to order a second pressrun. The two leading newsstands in the city sold 527 copies of Lummis's first issue, compared with 385 copies of *Harper's, Century, Scribner's, McClure's, Cosmopolitan,* and the *Overland Monthly* combined, Lummis proudly reported in his second issue.

Lummis immediately began soliciting contributions from the best writers in the West, including veterans of California's pioneer literary era such as Joaquin Miller and Ina Coolbrith and newer luminaries including John Muir and Jack London. Muir, for one, wrote back right away in June of 1895 with an encouraging note. "I have read your little plucky magazine and I like it," he said. "It has the ring and look of true literary metal. So has your letter to me. I doubt not you will be successful."[6]

Lummis couldn't afford to pay more than a token ten or fifteen dollars per story, but he managed to coax contributions out of some of the notable writers he courted. Muir, who gained a large following for his conservationist views with the 1894 publication of *The Mountains of California,* ended up forming a close friendship with Lummis and writing occasionally for his magazine. London hadn't yet achieved much success when he wrote a couple of short stories for *Land of Sunshine.* In 1902 he griped about an associate editor's delay in responding to a submission, begging forgiveness "for bothering you in this, my everlasting chase of the glimmering dollar." In another letter he complained that he was paid fifteen dollars for his first story in *Land of Sunshine* but only ten for the second. The next year, London became a national sensation with the success of *Call of the Wild*—and never wrote for *Land of Sunshine* again.[7]

Lummis's most dependable contributors were several writers who were just getting started when he discovered them. Sharlot Hall, the future poet laureate of Arizona, wrote more than forty pieces for Lummis's magazine and eventually became an associate editor. Mary Austin, who won fame as a novelist, playwright, and essayist on topics ranging from mysticism to Native American culture, and the cowboy storyteller Eugene Manlove Rhodes also made names for themselves in the *Land of Sunshine,* which Lummis renamed *Out West* in 1902. In all, more than six hundred individuals contributed to the magazine during the eleven years that Lummis was in charge, though none came close to matching Lummis's output. He wrote more than 250 pieces for the magazine.[8]

* * *

Beyond whatever literary merit it attained on its limited budget, the magazine was an important publicity outlet for three civic movements that Lummis sought to foster, seeking populist irrigation reforms, the preservation of California's old Spanish missions, and better treatment of Indians.[9]

Lummis had been interested in irrigation ever since he first tramped through the dry fields surrounding Santa Fe and speculated about the Eden it could become with help from a few artesian wells. But he was happy to hand off coverage of water policy in his magazine to William Smythe, a former newspaper reporter with an admittedly religious fervor for an egalitarian irrigation policy and cooperative planning.

Lummis had a far deeper personal attachment to the crusade to save California's Spanish missions. Tessa Kelso, the city librarian in Los Angeles, had started an organization in 1892 to raise funds for restoration projects, but not long after Lummis returned from Peru, she was offered a job in the East. Before she left town, she handed the reins, along with a ninety-dollar bank account, to Lummis. It was the first real test of his organizational skills, and Lummis would display flashes of genius at marshaling people and money to get things done. But above all he demonstrated the boundless zeal of an indefatigable crusader. In 1895 Lummis incorporated the Landmarks Club after recruiting a number of big-name civic leaders, including *Times* publisher Harrison Gray Otis and Richard Egan, a prominent civil engineer and a director of the Santa Fe Railroad lines in Southern California, to serve on an advisory board.

Individuals could join for just a dollar a year, or twenty-five dollars for a life membership. Lummis coaxed bigger contributions out of wealthy benefactors. Over the next twenty years, the Landmarks Club raised more than eight thousand dollars. It was a relatively modest sum, but Lummis claimed that more than ninety percent of that income went directly into mission repairs, and through shrewd bargaining the club was able to get thirty percent more value out of each dollar spent. The Landmarks Club ultimately succeeded in reversing the deterioration of more than half a dozen missions.

Built in the late 1700s by Indian laborers working under the direction of Franciscan friars, the historic structures "were falling to ruin with frightful rapidity, their roofs being breached or gone, the adobe walls melting away under the winter rains," Lummis wrote. Amidst the rampant anti-Catholic sentiment at the time, fueled by a secretive hate group called the American Protective Association, few Californians seemed to care. But with his characteristic enthusiasm, Lummis tirelessly promoted the cause of mission restoration in public appearances and in the pages of his magazine, and he slowly helped turn the tide of apathy and outright hostility. The loss of the link to California's past would be a tragedy of incalculable proportions, he argued. "Those mighty piles belong not to the Catholic church but to you and to me, and to our children and the world. They are monuments and beacons of Heroism and Faith and Zeal and Art. Let us save them—not for the Church but for Humanity," he proclaimed.

In the name of the club, Lummis also fought a running battle against efforts to erase or bastardize Spanish street and place names in California. But perhaps the club's most remarkable achievement, Lummis later said, was its role in helping to bridge the deep divide between Protestants and Catholics. "It is hard to realize today what that meant then," he wrote in his memoir. But at the first public meeting of the Landmarks Club, "the audience (nearly all Protestants) actually gasped when [Episcopal] Bishop [Joseph] Johnson walked into the room and up to the stage, shook hands with [Catholic] Bishop [George] Montgomery and took the seat I proffered him at Montgomery's side. That one evening and the far reverberations it made in society did more to break down the brutal fences of intolerance than any other single thing could have done."[10]

A third cause championed by the *Land of Sunshine* and later *Out West* was by far the most important to Lummis. During his tenure as editor, he created a new vehicle for his lifelong crusade to win land security, civil rights, and basic respect for the "First Americans."

There was plenty of material in the magazine that, as one critic put it, winter tourists would have found comforting. But Lummis's Indian rights crusade was one of several recurring topics that gave the magazine a harder edge. Just beneath the magazine's cheerful surface, Lummis kept up a steady drumbeat against racial violence, ethnocentrism, discrimination against women, and intolerance of all sorts. He was careful not to overwhelm the upbeat tone of much of the copy in the magazine, but Lummis wasn't averse to making his readers squirm. "This little magazine tries to be 'popular' enough to live and substantial enough to deserve to live," he explained in an 1897 letter to W. J. McGee, of the Smithsonian's Bureau of American Ethnology. "We believe it a magazine's duty to teach as well as to tickle."[11]

In his fourth issue Lummis laid down one of the ground rules he intended to follow. It concerned a common term that he himself had casually used on occasion in his early days in the Southwest. But not anymore. "Greaser is a word used in carelessness or ignorance by many people who ought to know better. . . . It is precisely on a par with the word 'nigger,' as offensive per se, and as sure a brand of the breeding of the user," Lummis declared. "It is high time this indecency of thoughtless speech be abandoned."

In his column Lummis regularly inveighed against lynchings, sometimes in very graphic terms. In a column in 1899 he described how a mob in Georgia grabbed a black man, accused him of a crime with no evidence whatsoever, "cut off his ears, fingers and other projections one by one," and burned him alive. Then the murderers "carved their human barbecue and fought over the morsels, and peddled slices of a man's liver at two bits each." The participants and the so-called "innocent bystanders" alike had no right to call themselves Americans, Lummis exclaimed in another column. "They are not even dogs! Neither in morals nor in brains. For what they think they do to the Negro individual, they are in fact doing to themselves, and to their own children, and to their children's children," Lummis wrote, making an often-repeated prediction that the nation would be paying for its history of racial oppression for generations to come.

Lummis also used his magazine to attack anti-Chinese prejudice. He regularly ran articles about California's Chinese-American heritage and he published short stories by Sui Sin Far, the pen name of Eurasian writer Edith Maude Eaton, that explored anti-Chinese discrimination. Eaton was one of an impressive number of strong women writers who found a forum for their work in Lummis's magazine. There were few if any strident calls for women's suffrage in what they wrote. But in a quiet yet convincing way, many of their contributions to the magazine made an eloquent case for equal rights. In 1904 Lummis published Charmian Kittredge's article "Cross Saddle Riding for Women," which asserted that riding schools continued to steer women into posture-contorting sidesaddles for the self-serving reason that women would need extensive training to master the awkward technique. For reasons of health, safety, and just plain common sense, women should ride horses just like men sitting astride a saddle, Kittredge argued. It wasn't a particularly radical suggestion in the West by that time. But sidesaddles were still considered the proper mode of riding for genteel women. The article was risqué enough that the *St. Louis Christian Advocate* was moved to denounce it. "Next to our God we honor womanhood and necessarily we dislike anything which is calculated to lower her in character or position," the magazine declared. Though riding astride a horse might indeed be safer for a woman, "there are some things we would even prefer to her safety."

Lummis was quick with a retort. Was the *Christian Advocate* suggesting, he wondered, "that women should move by hopping, as though they had but one foot, instead of taking steps, which inevitably predicates the 'unclean' fact that they have two?"

By the late 1890s Lummis had begun to ask pointed questions about the expansionist foreign policy of President William McKinley, a Republican whom Lummis had been proud to introduce at a party meeting in Chillicothe years earlier. Defenders of the nation's adventures abroad, from Panama to Cuba to the Philippines, argued that America was lifting up backward nations. But in light of the nation's many shortcomings in extending basic civil rights to its own citizens, Lummis couldn't help recognizing the hypocrisy in that stance.

"People who ought to know better . . . are talking a great deal nowadays about our moral obligation to take Filipinos and other half-civilized peoples 'under our protection'," he wrote in 1898 in the immediate aftermath of the wildly popular Spanish-American War. "Hm! A moral obligation, no doubt, to treat them as philanthropically as we have treated our Indians—whom we rob and oppress until they turn, and then kill off for their rebellion. As philanthropically as we treat the Chinese—proscribed, disenfranchised, and occasionally mobbed. As philanthropically as we have treated our Southern Negroes—deprived (in the teeth of the Constitution and our laws) of their right of suffrage, herded apart as if they were pariahs, and lynched every week in the calendar."

Hardly a month went by in the years after the Spanish-American War without another broadside against U.S. imperialism fired from "In the Lion's Den." But in the eleven years that Lummis was in charge of the magazine, no civil rights issue got more attention than his crusade for fair treatment of those he called the First Americans.

The magazine provided extensive and respectful coverage of Indian music, crafts, and other cultural traditions, treating them not as quaint relics of the past or even as dying arts but as practices that still had considerable merit and deserved to survive.[12] Lummis also kept up a running critique of the U.S. government's Indian policies. He had an opportunity to revisit the issue of Indian education in the summer of 1899 when a national convention of Indian educators met in Los Angeles. He attended the meeting and afterward commenced a seven-part series entitled "My Brother's Keeper." One encouraging presentation that Lummis heard was made by Estelle Reel, the new superintendent of Indian schools. In a remarkable sign of how times had changed in less than a decade, Reel responded to his warm words about her in his magazine with a fawning letter, concluding with a remark he couldn't have imagined coming from the office previously occupied by Dorchester. "If at any time you find that I am making mistakes, I will appreciate your advice and be very grateful indeed, Mr. Lummis," she wrote, enclosing one dollar for an annual subscription to the *Land of Sunshine*.

But the mindset that Lummis had battled from Isleta was still alive and well, represented by the dominant figure at the convention, his old nemesis Richard Pratt of the Carlisle Indian School. As a whole, the Indian Service was much improved from a decade earlier, Lummis acknowledged, owing in large part to the fact that in 1896 employees of the service were placed under the jurisdiction of the Civil Service. Pratt had been one of the most vehement opponents of the reform, arguing that he would get stuck with "scum" if he were unable to select his own employees. But a succession of scandals involving patronage appointees to the Indian Service doomed the spoils system. "There are fewer thievish agents, fewer vile school-principals, fewer tangible scoundrels and visible ignoramuses," Lummis wrote. "But the task is only begun. As much injustice is done the Indian as ever; but now under the name and fetish of civilization."

In the series in his magazine, Lummis proceeded to lambaste Pratt for continuing to insist that the only way to educate Indian children was to separate them from their families and tribes. Pratt had been around Indians for thirty years but only as a "patronizing boss," Lummis wrote. In all those years, he had not yet "learned that the Indian has a soul; that he loves his parents and his children, and even the birthplace that we have stolen from him."

Pratt later returned fire in the Carlisle School newspaper, the *Red Man*, calling Lummis a "fantastic litterateur" and the *Land of Sunshine* "a thin little magazine." And he ridiculed Lummis for constantly invoking the sanctity of the Indian family, a fixation that reflected Lummis's "superstitious regard for the mere tie of blood." In response, Lummis asked in his series why Pratt saved his wisdom for Indians. Why shouldn't all Americans send their children "to be taught the Higher Wisdom of contempt for the womb that warmed them?" Lummis argued that America would pay a dear price for generations to come for its oppression of the Indians. "With whatever measure we mete it shall be meted to us at last," he wrote. "Not by lightning strokes nor by the rain of brimstone, but by the political and social decay that comes soon or late to any people that fail to deal justly."

Lummis took a final shot at Pratt five years later in a frank obituary. The Lion simply wasn't one to be a "polite liar" and say something nice about the man just because he was dead, he told his readers. "It is not an easy thing to say about a man whose honor has never been called into question." But "while his official life is without official stain, his official death is the greatest good fortune that every befell the cause to which he thought he was devoted. God absolve Pratt for what he did, and credit him only with what he meant to do."

The job at the magazine, coupled with his book projects, gave Lummis something he hadn't had in years: a modicum of financial stability. But when he took over as editor, he still didn't have something else he had always wanted: a place that he could call a permanent family home.

With just two bedrooms, the Forester Avenue house was too small for all the children Lummis wanted. Nor could it accommodate the constant stream of visitors he liked to entertain. He had used up every square foot of the property with his carefully mapped out orchard, chicken coop, rabbit hutch, dovecote, and other improvements. He needed more space to absorb the overabundant energy he wanted to expend on a home.

Within weeks of his return from Peru, Lummis started looking for a new homesite. The task took on a sense of urgency in April of 1894 when Eve announced that she was pregnant with their second child.

He scouted out a number of locations, but the area where he focused his search was a natural for Lummis: the rugged Arroyo Seco, a rocky watercourse extending for more than ten miles from downtown Los Angeles to Pasadena. The leafy defile, which had a stream carrying a trickle of water for most of the year with occasional deluges after winter rains, was filled with the scattered homesteads of artists, writers, and assorted self-styled bohemian intellectuals. Lummis would fit right in. In May he found a two-and-a-half-acre lot six miles north of downtown Los Angeles going for $650. He bought it with $100 down.

The lot had several features that Lummis liked, including a towering grove of old sycamore trees and a seemingly limitless quantity of large water-worn boulders out of which he intended to build a castle for the ages in the shade of the sycamores. He had been mulling over his dream home for a decade, storing up ideas during his travels to pueblos, missions, forts, and homes throughout the Southwest. On September 15 he drove stakes marking the corners of the home he had in mind. Three months later, on November 14, 1894, Eve gave birth to their firstborn son. In honor of the two friends he admired most, Lummis named him Amado Bandelier Lummis.

At about the same time Lummis came up with a name for his hacienda-to-be. The dominant natural feature on the property was the largest of the sycamores, a huge old tree with four main branches more or less aligned with the points of the compass. He had decided that it would be the centerpiece of the patio in the middle of the cluster of buildings he was planning, and so using an old California-Spanish word for a sycamore grove, he christened his home El Alisal.[13]

Lummis wasn't able to move his family to the property until the fall of 1896 when he finished building a four-room redwood shack that would serve as temporary living quarters. Once Eve and the children were settled in, construction on the new home began in earnest and the outlines of a castle began to take shape.

Practically every day that he was in town for the next fourteen years, Lummis spent at least a few hours at hard labor hauling rocks and mortar, hewing the ceiling beams and floorboards, building windows and doors and furnishings for the house. He often had one or two teenagers from Isleta to help with the work in exchange for a modest monthly stipend, free room and board at El Alisal, and what Lummis promised would be a priceless education that they would absorb at such an intellectually

191

vibrant place. One Pueblo boy who spent two years with Charlie and Eve was Tuyo Abeita, the son of their Isleta landlord and one of the cautivos Lummis had liberated from the Albuquerque Indian School.

By working for twenty or more hours a day, Lummis managed to write for and edit the growing magazine, move several other books through the pipeline, and launch the Landmarks Club, all while building El Alisal. By January of 1899, when Lummis finished the large main room of the house, the twenty-eight-by-sixteen-foot Museo, his family had already moved in. He added a couple of rooms each year for the next five years before the bulk of the construction was complete. The Lummises led a fishbowl existence as a constant stream of visitors dropped by to have a look at the remarkable work in progress and marvel at the energy and genius of its creator. Lummis often received callers without stopping his work, sometimes asking his guests to grab a bucket of mason's cement and carry it up the ramp to the top of the wall where he was perched placing another row of stones.

Lummis believed everyone should build his own dwelling. Anything less hardly deserved to be called a home. "A man's home should be part of himself. . . . Something of the owner's individuality should inform it," he once wrote. "Everyone knows that the thing he has made is more genuinely his than the thing he has bought. The creative thrill is so fine and keen, it is pitiful for a man to get a home off the bargain counter, and miss all the joy he might just as well have had in building it."

It was the sort of remark that grated on some of those around him, burnishing his image as an egotist. But no one could deny the brilliance of his achievement. By the time ill health forced him to put away his hammer, saw, adz, and trowel, Lummis's stone castle and an adjacent guest house had thirteen rooms, not counting four attics, two concrete cellars, and the foundation and outer walls for four more rooms. The building was "of construction to last 1,000 years unimpaired," Lummis declared.[14]

Every component was custom built. The beams were charred and rubbed to display the grain and impart a satiny finish. Each door and window was unique, many inspired by famous landmarks he had visited or, as in the case of one door, a Diego Velasquez painting. Each of the fireplaces had its own inscription: "A casual savage struck two stones together—now man is warmed against the weather," read one. In the master bedroom occupied by Eve, the inscription over the fireplace read, "Love and a Fire, they're easy lit; but to keep either—wood to it!" In the living room the legend over the fireplace read "Gather about me! Who can weld iron—or friends—without me?" Practical considerations also went into the design. The entire ground floor, made of cement, was carefully graded so that it could be cleaned with a garden hose.

Years of Lummis's life went into the home, but it was time well spent, as far as he was concerned. The busier he became, the happier and more productive he got, and when construction was at its peak, he was busy virtually around the clock. He didn't mind. "I would rather take pleasure in putting in 2,600 tons of masonry than in two million strokes with a golf club—because it leaves a mark," he once said. When asked on another occasion when he expected to finish the house, he replied, "Why, never, I hope. It is my gymnasium."

Long before he scaled back on construction, Lummis began filling El Alisal with the retinue that in its heyday made it a lively, tumultuous place. There almost always seemed to be at least half a dozen house-guests in residence. His Indian helpers lived on the premises, while a procession of musicians, artists, and writers in need of temporary accommodation passed through El Alisal. Then there were the secretaries and stenographers, two of whom Lummis seemed to need in his employ at any given time, once the magazine got up to full speed and the Landmarks Club began to generate a steady stream of correspondence, bookkeeping, and other paperwork. They would often work tag-team fashion, with one quitting work for the day just as the other began, assuring the availability of clerical help late into the night. At least one secretary was usually living at El Alisal, in some cases with a child of her own. And hardly a week went by without an old friend or colleague passing through and staying for a day or two.

Pets added to the carnival atmosphere. There was Horn Pout, the fish, which came to the surface of the small pond in the courtyard every time Lummis whistled, as well as a mammoth African frog and Methu-salem, a turtle said to be 135 years old. The family had a succession of dogs, and some members of the household had cats, though Lummis detested the creatures.

Lummis was unmistakably the master of the premises. But many visitors to El Alisal found Eve equally memorable. She was adored by many of the artists and writers who flocked around her husband, and she also had a social circle of her own, including a group of Arroyo artists who enrolled in a Spanish class she taught at El Alisal.

Edith Maude Eaton, who struggled against prejudice all her life, found a refuge with both Lummises. They warmly welcomed her into their home, she wrote in an autobiographical essay, "Leaves from the Mental Portfolio of an Eurasian." "They are broad-minded people whose interest in me is sincere and intelligent, not affected and vulgar." Mary Austin, another writer at odds with the world, also found a safe haven at El Alisal and benefited from the mentoring of both Lummises. She dedicated her first book, *The Land of Little Rain*, "To Eve, comfortess of unsuccess."[15]

By the first years of the new century, Lummis's home had become one of the best known gathering spots for artists, writers, and intellectuals in Los Angeles. Lummis didn't need much of an excuse to have a party of some sort, featuring a shifting selection of people from a large circle of friends. They ranged from leaders of the Los Angeles establishment such as the prominent lawyers Henry O'Melveny and Isidore Dockweiler to scientists, conservationists, and avant-garde bohemian intellectuals. There were grizzled veterans of various crusades such as Horatio Nelson Rust, who had raised funds for John Brown's abortive slave revolt before the Civil War, and dreamers such as Madame Helena Modjeska, a famous actress in her native Poland before she came to California in 1875 in a failed attempt to create a utopian commune near the German village of Anaheim.

Over the years, the parties at El Alisal became increasingly elaborate. Lummis had a different type of party—and a different outfit—for various occasions. Besides his standard Spanish-style corduroy suit, he had a set of "party buckskins" and a charro suit, a soft suede riding costume from Jalisco, Mexico, with bellbottom trousers that were so tight his children wondered how he managed to get them on.

The most intricately choreographed of the gatherings was called a Court of El Alcalde Mayor, named after the majestic sycamore tree in the center of El Alisal's courtyard where the events were held. They were usually convened to welcome a dignitary visiting from out of town. Invited guests received an elaborately printed summons a few weeks prior to the event, naming the defendant—the visiting dignitary—who stood accused of "the High Misdemeanor of 'Not Knowing an Old California Good Time When You See It'." The plaintiff in the case was "The Good Old Days."[16]

When all the guests were seated at the massive banquet table, Lummis would solemnly lay a sixteen-inch double-barreled shotgun pistol on the table at his right hand and a fourteen-inch Bowie knife at his left hand while his son Quimu would serve as constable, a rank symbolized by the huge star pinned to his chest and the enormous machete strapped to his waist. While the wine flowed, a prosecuting attorney would present the charges against the accused and a "defender of the poor" would speak up for the defendant before introducing his client. The defendant was then expected to make a speech absolving him or herself of the crime of not knowing an Old California Good Time. Lummis would pronounce the verdict, "Not Guilty, Come Again." Then the dinner would begin and afterward one of the resident troubadours at El Alisal, or perhaps a famous musician passing through town, would strike up a tune and everybody would join in as best they could, with Lummis lustily leading the way. Dozens of notables faced trial in a Court of El Alcalde Mayor at Charles Lummis's house over the years, including John Muir, Joaquin Miller, John Burroughs, Ernest Thompson Seton, William Lloyd Garrison, John Philip Sousa, and Frederic Remington.

Lummis held another big bash each March in honor of all of those who like himself were born in that month. He called those assemblages annual meetings of the Order of the Mad March Hares. On the occasion, Lummis served hasenpfeffer to as many as sixty guests, who would all join in various festivities including singing the "March Hare Hymn."

Lummis had another set of peculiar rituals for Christmas, beginning on Christmas Eve when he hauled in a giant Brazilian pepper tree, a species that thrived in Los Angeles, in lieu of a traditional conifer that didn't belong in the local climate. And when Lummis couldn't think of a reason for a special event, he would hold a party and call it a "noise." Food, music, singing, and lively discussions were the hallmark of the gatherings. "No one invited ever failed to come," the singer Edith Pla reminisced years later. "And there were people who wanted to come for years but were never invited."[17]

During the festivities, Lummis would turn to a new page in the El Alisal House Book that sat in the entry hall and ask his guests to sign their names. Hundreds of clever inscriptions in the book bear testimony to the diverse range of guests who attended dinners and parties in Lummis's home, from Will Rogers, Clarence Darrow, and Muir to Marguerite Zitkala Noni, one of the few Sioux survivors of the 1890 massacre at Wounded Knee. Prominent artists including Ed Borein, Maynard Dixon, and Remington contributed sketches or watercolors. Sousa, who first came to El Alisal on the recommendation of friends to listen to Lummis's collection of phonographs of Indian songs, signed his name beneath a few measures of music. Garrison, the elderly former publisher of the famous pre–Civil War abolitionist paper the *Liberator,* weighed in with a poem:

> A tenderfoot on the Pacific Coast
> Concedes, reluctant, California's toast;
> Its wondrous air and climate stand confessed
> And Boston bows in homage to "Out West."

In her entry in the House Book, the Scottish short story writer Lorna Moon reflected the adoration many visitors to El Alisal felt for their eccentric host: "Dear Minstrel and Bard: Of the white silk hair and the clay-red eagle face . . . stay long with us to warm us in your glow. For writers there be by the thousands, and singers are as the sands of the seashore, but a radiant soul is to be held preciously upon the palm like an opal."

Amidst the constant procession of outsiders circulating through El Alisal, members of Lummis's own family began to feel like an afterthought. For his part, Lummis could never imagine that anyone with the privilege of living in a home as exciting as El Alisal wouldn't be completely enchanted with the place.

But Eve would come to resent her husband's constant, almost frenetic socializing. The brunt of the work of running the gatherings fell on her, as did the responsibility of buying all of the provisions on a very limited budget. Some of the wealthy regulars would sometimes quietly pass a hat among themselves to help cover the costs. But there was never enough money to pay the bills. The children recalled that their father would often reduce Eve to tears with his sharp questioning about the grocery budget at the end of every month. But she had to put on a happy face as the crowds arrived. It was Eve's job to welcome the guests—who invariably included fawning young women—and make sure their needs were met. Lummis was the center of attention, the star attraction, once the parties began.

Despite the tensions in their relationship, which usually stayed beneath the surface, life was good for Charlie and Eve at the start of the new millennium. Charlie had a stable job and income that, while not sufficient to accommodate his open-handed hospitality, was enough to assure that there was food on the table and a steadily expanding roof over their heads. The magazine was on an even keel and gaining more critical acclaim by the month. The Lummises had a home that would last for the ages and a growing circle of devoted friends. On January 19, 1900, they had third child, a boy their Indian friends named Quimu but who was officially christened Jordan, after Lummis's close friend, Stanford University president David Starr Jordan.

With their growing flock of children, Charlie and Eve would have been looking forward to an especially joyous Christmas in 1900. But as the holiday season began that year, disaster struck. By early December both Amado, who was six, and eleven-month-old Jordan were seriously ill with pneumonia. The cryptic entries in Lummis's diary for the week leading up to Christmas Day only hint at the agony that he and Eve experienced trying to comfort two small children seriously ill in the days before antibiotics. Amado, a beautiful child with golden hair that Lummis never cut, letting it reach all the way to the small of his back, was "critical," Lummis noted one day after he had been up all night with the sick children. Another day that week, Eve was "exhausted," and the next day she collapsed under the "grueling strain." Fourteen-year-old Tuyo Abeita, who was living with them at the time, was left to run the house alone, even preparing the Christmas turkey by himself. A nurse stayed for one night to give Eve a break. A doctor came on another day and declared that Amado was somewhat better. But there was no hope for much joy at El Alisal that Christmas. Lummis tried to salvage some of the spirit of the season by hauling in a giant pepper tree and decorating it on Christmas Eve. But nothing could stop the tragedy that followed.

On Christmas Day, the entry in Lummis's diary reads, "My lovely boy Amado dies at 8:30 P.M. and we lay him out. One thankfulness—his wonderful golden hair is unspoiled. Now I take off the beautiful curls to save." Charlie and Eve's firstborn son was cremated two days later.

Lummis shared his grief with readers of "In the Lion's Den" in January. "The Den is dim this month. It is at best but a room for the Lion's passing thought; and today his thought paces up and down a narrow bound. He has just closed the eyes of one he hoped should one day do that office for him. He has just surrendered to the incorporating flames the fair husk of what had been his tawny-maned cub, . . . the lad who was a Man at six and an old-fashioned gentle fearless little knight whose first thought was always for others; whose last words in the agony for breath were 'Yes, please.' . . . [O]ne noted that his undefiant eye never fell before any eye . . . that he never lied nor dodged nor shirked his fault nor sulked from its consequences. Love we are born into, but to win respect is victory for a lifetime, long or short. It is well with the boy. But the Lion had not cubs to spare."

Lummis, as always, had plenty of work to lose himself in. The magazine had doubled in number of pages since he took it over, and in addition to his usual complement of pieces for his own magazine, he continued to write for other leading national publications.

In one major freelance project over the course of several years in the mid-1890s, Lummis made several trips into Mexico, where he befriended that nation's new president, Porfirio Díaz, and wrote a series of articles for *Harper's Magazine*. He intended to expand on those pieces in a more comprehensive book but ran out of time. So in 1898 his magazine pieces were bundled mostly verbatim into a book entitled *The Awakening of a Nation: Mexico of Today*. Lummis included an apologetic introductory note for not having had the time to do additional research for the book, explaining that "more exigent duties already stretch my work-hours to twenty in every twenty-four." But if the book "may help another American to more neighborly feeling for a nation we have every reason not to despise . . . my recompense will be ample for all the work I would like to have done."

By the end of the decade, *Harper's* had commissioned Lummis to write another lengthy series of articles, this one about California's first half century as a state and what that had meant for the Union. *Harper's* published the first installment in January 1900. But it was filled with so many typographical errors, which badly muddled several key passages, that Lummis broke ties with the magazine in an exchange of angry letters with the editor. He continued to publish the series in the *Land of Sunshine*.

The magazine by then had a national audience and a loftier reputation than ever to maintain. "Courage has a permanent berth in the
office of the *Land of Sunshine*," the venerable New York weekly the *Nation*
editorialized. The *Dial*, published in Chicago, praised the "brave little
magazine" and the "sober and fearless words" of the editor who "keeps
up a running fire of comment on the literary and political happenings
of the day." In recognition of his literary accomplishments as a writer
and editor, the University of Santa Clara awarded Lummis an hono-
rary Doctor of Letters degree in 1903. His national stature was such
that three years later even Harvard, on the occasion of the twenty-fifth
reunion of the class of 1881, awarded him a degree—the Bachelor
of Arts that he had fallen two final exams in math short of earning
outright.

Around the turn of the century, when Lummis realized he could no
longer continue to turn the magazine out each month almost entirely
by himself, an able assistant materialized just in time. Charles Amadon
Moody, an appreciative reader of the magazine from back east, moved
to town at the end of 1899, hoping to get a job on the staff. A native of
Binghamton, New York, Moody had worked as a newspaper editor for
several years after graduating from the University of Rochester in 1881.
But a bout of poor health prompted him to go west to Denver in 1888.
There he recuperated and also prospered financially in mining and real
estate before his business went bust in the Panic of 1891. He returned
to New York, where his health deteriorated once again, and floundered
in various attempts at business. So he headed back to the West, this
time deciding to give California a try. To be close to the headquarters
of the magazine he had read and admired, Moody, who was thirty-six
at the time, settled in Pasadena, just a few miles from Lummis's home. In
January 1900, shortly after arriving, he got his first job on the staff, with
responsibility for circulation. Moody also began writing book reviews
and did so well with them that Lummis gradually shifted full responsibility for that section to his new man. In February 1903, Moody's name
appeared on the masthead as assistant editor, the first person in the
eight years since Lummis took over the magazine to get that billing.

There was a far more conspicuous change on the cover effective with
the January issue in 1902. That was when Lummis unveiled the new
name, *Out West*. "The title which fitted its beginnings is now out-
grown, and the time for a re-christening has come," he had explained in

his column the previous October. The more expansive geographical scope implicit in the name was even more apparent in a new motto on the cover, "A magazine of the old Pacific and the new."

Out West "will mean to be the magazine not only of the West— its freedom and its strength and its culture—but of the new world-movement . . . now in actual process of realization—the opening and control of the Pacific," Lummis wrote. "It will be the standard-bearer of what it believes to be the right solution for the most tremendous problems this half of the United States has ever faced; and it will appeal to a much larger constituency. . . . For the world's greatest ocean is to be the world's greatest highway; and the Pacific Coast is the American door to it."

Long before Lummis explicitly stated that the scope of his magazine might extend overseas, he had begun to use his column to criticize U.S. foreign policy. As early as February 1896, barely a year after he took charge of the Los Angeles Chamber of Commerce's relentlessly upbeat *Land of Sunshine,* he complained that the United States was acting like an "ignorant or quarrelsome schoolboy" in its treatment of Venezuela. A couple of months later he decried the "ghastly stupidity and indecency" of the Cuba affair, in which the United States recognized a motley band of rebels in Cuba who were attempting to foment a revolt against Spain. The next year, when the new McKinley administration replaced a capable bilingual ambassador to Mexico with one who couldn't speak a word of Spanish, Lummis worried that the United States was presenting itself as "an asylum of imbeciles instead of the smartest nation in the world."

Ignorance about Latin America and Spain was fueling the fever for war, Lummis maintained. One of the most popular misconceptions was that Spaniards were extraordinarily cruel and that they had exhibited an abnormal lust for blood in historical episodes from the Inquisition to the conquest of Mexico and Peru. Lummis offered a different perspective in his magazine. "All war is cruel; Spanish wars no more, no less, than others," he wrote. "When Sherman marched to the seas his men were not fed from Washington restaurants. They ate the country—and what they could not eat they burned. That was not pleasant, but it was war. In our Indian wars more 'squaws' and papooses have been killed than warriors; and . . . two Indian scalps have been taken by whites for every white scalp taken by Indians. That may not be altogether war, but it is truth."

Lummis continued to speak out against a war with Spain right up until the fighting began. At that point, his deep sense of patriotism trumped his concerns that the war was unwarranted and unjust. The outbreak of war "shuts all doors but one," he wrote in the June 1898 issue, the first to go to press after the U.S. declaration of war against Spain in late April. "It is not necessary to be glad of the war, nor to deem that it was inevitable; those matters will be settled by history. The only thing now is to 'fight for all that's out'."

Lummis remained steadfast in his support of American troops while the war was under way. But his attack on what he decried as the imperialistic underpinnings of U.S. foreign policy did not abate. It didn't surprise Lummis that no sooner had the United States ousted the Spanish from Cuba and the Philippines than it found itself embroiled in a war with Filipinos who wanted independence. Didn't the Filipinos know that "liberty meant a swapping of masters?" Lummis sarcastically asked. Scoffing at the claim that U.S. policies were designed to bring civilization to oppressed nations, Lummis observed that there were three saloons in Manila before the Americans arrived to liberate the country from the evil Spanish; afterward there were three hundred. When rumors circulated that American soldiers were committing atrocities in the Philippines, he called for an aggressive investigation. Most American soldiers were honorable men, Lummis said, though he insisted there was nothing traitorous about tracking down and punishing the few "brutes who have shamed us."

His carefully worded criticisms didn't stop many readers from calling Lummis a traitor. Bolstered by many other readers who supported him, Lummis stood his ground. "To some people patriotism means love of country. To some it means blind obedience to politicians," he wrote in July 1899. But eventually his constant drumbeat against U.S. imperialism started to pinch those who bankrolled his magazine. W. C. Patterson, president of the Los Angeles National Bank and also president of the Land of Sunshine Company, became a lightning rod for criticism of Lummis. In a letter published in the February 1900 issue, he said he would stand by Lummis's right to express his opinions even though he didn't share them.

Behind the scenes, Patterson's support for Lummis was shakier. After an exchange of heated letters in which Lummis asserted that if pushed he would take a better-paying job with a weekly publication, Patterson invited him to leave for the greener pastures. "I believe in 'discussions' and in 'opposition' but it pains me to see how wildly intolerant you are toward those who venture to take issue . . . with your own rabid, but conscientious notions," Patterson wrote in August. "If you sincerely believe that the country needs the kind of matter which lately has predominated in the 'Lion's Den,' it is your duty to leave the narrow monthly field, and enter the larger weekly domain, where as you say, you can have ten times as large an audience at double the length, and at twice as much money per week as you now get per month."[18]

The willingness of Patterson and other Chamber of Commerce types to continue to subsidize the magazine appears to have ended at about that point. By 1902 the magazine was in dire need of an infusion of cash. Ultimately *Out West* was saved by a loan from someone who had been a leading benefactor of the Landmarks Club, Phoebe Apperson Hearst, the mother of newspaper publisher William Randolph Hearst and the matriarch of a family that had made a fortune in the Gold Rush.

Willie Hearst's newspapers, ironically, had been among the leading outlets for exaggerated tales of Spanish atrocities that had provided justification for the war. With Phoebe Hearst's backing, Lummis's blasts against imperialism continued unabated. Publicly, Lummis took all the criticism in stride. "When most people shall agree with everything the Lion says, he will cease to say anything," Lummis observed at one point. But he appreciated the readers who agreed with everything he wrote. One such admirer was Caroline Severance, one of the leading women's suffrage advocates in Los Angeles. "You are amazing!" she wrote in one letter at the height of the tumult over his opposition to the Spanish-American and Philippine wars. "Pray God your courage never wavers and your strokes cut to the bone as they must in high places." And in another note she exclaimed, "Poor Teddy! How your scathing criticism must cut him."[19]

The Teddy that Caroline Severance mentioned was of course Theodore Roosevelt. As it happened, Roosevelt was one of three people whom Lummis knew personally and admired greatly who were integrally involved in the prosecution of the foreign policies that he so persistently lambasted. Colonel Harrison Gray Otis, itching for a taste of battle once again more than thirty years after he had last worn a uniform, had volunteered for military service when the Spanish-American War broke out. He was promoted to the rank of brigadier general and commanded U.S. troops in the Philippines for several months. Leonard Wood, the army surgeon whom Lummis had befriended during his stint covering the Apache War from Fort Bowie in 1886, had moved up rapidly through the ranks of the army. During the Spanish-American War he commanded the Rough Riders in Cuba, was promoted to brigadier general, and was appointed U.S. military governor of the island.

And then of course there was Theodore Roosevelt himself. Since he and Lummis had crossed paths at Harvard, Roosevelt had gone west to manage a cattle ranch in the Dakotas in the early 1880s, returning to the East after several years to begin a political career. But his experiences out west, during which he became an avid big-game hunter and had firsthand encounters with both hostile Indians and villainous frontier whites, were enough to make him a confirmed westerner in Lummis's eyes.[20]

Over the years, Lummis and Roosevelt had occasionally exchanged letters. Roosevelt had given a copy of *Birch Bark Poems* to his sister, and he had read Lummis's books on the Pueblos, considering him an expert on the Indians of New Mexico on a par with Frank Cushing. While Roosevelt was working on his four-part magnum opus *The Winning of the West* in the early 1890s, he occasionally turned to Lummis for help confirming obscure facts about Western history. In one exchange of letters, he sought Lummis's help with the derivation of the word "hoss-wrangler." As Lummis recounted the episode in his memoir, "Piqued by the problem, I trailed the word back to the Spanish caballerango—in Mexico, the vaquero who tends the herd of spare riding-ponies. Every Texas cowboy knows that caballo means 'hoss.' And not knowing what the termination meant, they adapted it to a familiar English word—and there you were—'hoss wrangler'." When Lummis passed that suggestion on, Roosevelt was greatly impressed. "My dear Mr. Lummis," he replied. "O, Lord, I wish I had a head into which things like that would occasionally 'pop'! . . . I wish you would sometime write out, and put in permanent form, an article on all these Spanish terms."

"I think this one etymology did more to pull us together than any volume of ordinary words," Lummis remarked.

By then Roosevelt was a subscriber to, and apparently a regular reader of, the *Land of Sunshine*. He remained one of Lummis's admirers, recognizing in the California editor the same pugnacious spirit and penchant for straight talk that he was known for, despite their starkly contrasting views of America's role in the world. Roosevelt regarded the principle of manifest destiny as God-given marching orders for white domination of the North American continent. Lummis called manifest destiny "manifest thievery."

The rhetorical skill with which Lummis managed to oppose the war while still closing ranks with the American soldiers who were fighting it undoubtedly helped Lummis avoid alienating Otis, Wood, Roosevelt, and other supporters of the war. As Lummis stated his position in one editorial while the fighting in Cuba was under way, "For these fine men who bear the brunt of battle the Lion has nothing but honor and pride. But he would be a little better satisfied if the yellow newspapers, the speculators in Cuban bonds and the hysterical congressmen could be set in the forefront of the battle they have sent their betters to fight. Somebody is likely to get hurt before the war is over; and it will not be the people we could best spare."

Roosevelt emerged from the war in Cuba as a national hero. Just four months after leading the famous charge up San Juan Hill as second in command of the Rough Riders, he was elected governor of New York. He had served in that post for less than two years when he was drafted by the Republican Party to serve as McKinley's running mate in the president's bid for a second term. Roosevelt had no great desire to trade his position as governor of the most important state in the Union for the historically dead-end job of vice president, but he succumbed to pressure from the party's power brokers. Lummis, though still a staunch Republican, despised McKinley. Roosevelt, of course, supported U.S. policies in Cuba and the Philippines, but McKinley was the chief architect of those policies, the president who was willing "to sell our national birthright for a mess of Imperial pottage." When the more reasonable Roosevelt agreed to join the McKinley ticket, Lummis was appalled. "Our Teddy is Dead," he wrote in *Out West*. "Shame, Gov. Roosevelt!" For the first time ever in a presidential election, Lummis voted for the Democratic candidate, William Jennings Bryan, that fall.

The one consolation that Lummis found in McKinley's victory was that at least he had a vice president who was amenable to common sense. As it turned out, Roosevelt didn't remain vice president for long. On September 6, 1901, McKinley was shot by an anarchist in Buffalo, New York, and died a week later. The next day, September 14, Theodore Roosevelt, then aged forty-two, was sworn in as president, becoming the youngest commander in chief in the nation's history.

Though Lummis detested McKinley, he was sobered by his violent death. McKinley was the third U.S. president to fall to an assassin's bullet in just thirty-six years, Lummis noted. That fact should be taken as a sobering warning for a nation that spent so much time loudly proclaiming its moral superiority, a claim that was akin to that of "a boy floating on a bladder in the ocean boasting that he can swim," as Lummis put it. "The ocean is old and deep and has dealt with boys and bladders before—and shall again."

His distress over the assassination was tempered by excitement about the man who had been vaulted into the presidency. "It is a sheer Godsend that for once in our modern history we did not pick a nonentity for the 'tail of the ticket'," he wrote. Roosevelt was capable of becoming the best president in the nation's history, Lummis believed. On October 8, Lummis sent a letter to Roosevelt expressing his condolences, offering his support, and criticizing U.S. policy in the Philippines. He couldn't be sure that the busy new president would ever see his note. But just a week later, Roosevelt wrote back. "I thank you very much for your letter," Roosevelt said. "Can't you get on to Washington? I should like to see you."

Lummis would have hopped on a train for Washington the next day. But he was too tied down with obligations to the magazine and the Landmarks Club to leave right away. He replied to the president that he would be along in a month or so. Then he settled down to get ahead on his work and prepare for the big trip.[21]

Lummis consulted with a number of people about how he should best use his time with the president. Ultimately he decided to address three issues. The first two were relatively peripheral concerns that he would mention briefly: he would urge Roosevelt to implement a national irrigation policy for the West, and he would seek the president's help in winning compensation for Jessie Benton Fremont, the widow of the great western explorer John Charles Fremont, who in Lummis's view had been unfairly evicted from her home on a military base. The third issue was by far the most important of the matters he intended to take up with the president: Indian rights. In general, he planned to urge Roosevelt to help forge a new policy toward Indians, a policy that would treat the tribes as allies, not enemies. But he also wanted the president's help in a specific situation that was coming to the forefront in Southern California. A group of so-called Mission Indians were threatened with eviction from their homeland on a ranch in the barren mountains southeast of Los Angeles. They had recently lost the final round in a long court battle to keep the property, called Warner's Ranch. Lummis wanted Roosevelt to appoint him to a commission to find the tribe a new home.

Scattered among several dozen barren parcels of land in the dry, rocky mountains of Southern California, just a few thousand Mission Indians survived, descendants of perhaps seventy thousand Indians who had occupied the southern coastal region of California when the Spanish began settling the area in the eighteenth century. They had been forcibly converted to Christianity and "civilized" by the Franciscans who were in the forefront of Spain's colonization of California. Lummis's own account of that era was, true to the pattern of his reporting on the Spanish conquest of North America, highly sanitized, almost entirely devoid of any mention of the brutal methods that were used to force the natives of the region to submit to the authority of the missions.[22] But his purpose was clearly to counterbalance the widely held perception that Anglo-American settlers were magnanimous in comparison with the brutal reign of the cruel Spaniards. In fact, the opposite was the case. As ruthless as the Spanish had been, their treatment of the Indians didn't begin to compare to the genocidal conduct of the prospectors and settlers who flooded into California during the Gold Rush in the second half of the nineteenth century. In Spanish mission society, the Indians had official status and sacrosanct legal rights, but under American rule, the Indians had no status at all. As the population of California surged from 92,000 in 1850 shortly after the discovery of gold to 380,000 just ten years later, Indians who got in the way were simply exterminated. As James Wilson observed in *The Earth Shall Weep: A History of Native America*, "More Indians probably died as a result of deliberate, cold-blooded genocide in California than anywhere else in North America."

Horace Bell, a curmudgeonly Los Angeles journalist who founded a weekly newspaper called the *Porcupine* in 1882, actually boasted about the stark difference in the way Indians were treated under American rule in California. "We will let those rascally redskins know that they have no longer to deal with the Spaniard or the Mexican, but with the invincible race of American backwoodsmen, which has driven the savage from Plymouth Rock to the Rocky Mountains, and has headed him off here on the Western shore . . . and will drive him back to meet his kindred fleeing westward, all to be drowned in the Great Salt Lake," Bell wrote.[23] By the turn of the century, the Mission Indians hadn't been driven back quite as far as the Great Salt Lake. But they were barely hanging on to the rockiest, most inhospitable parcels of land in the backcountry of Southern California. Their plight had periodically been a cause célèbre among humanitarian-minded citizens of Los Angeles since Lummis first walked into town.

By the early twentieth century, however, their situation was more precarious than ever. They had been isolated on scattered parcels of land that were inhospitable to begin with. Now the best pieces of those barren reservations were being taken. The predicament of the Warner's Ranch Indians was a case in point.

A band of about two hundred Indians were left on the property in an unassuming little village alongside a hot spring called Agua Caliente in northern San Diego County. It was hardly a prime piece of land, though the spring was a convenience to the Indians, who used the strong flow of hot water to wash their clothes and soften the plant fibers that they wove into baskets and textiles. The springs also generated a small but important stream of revenue from the rental of bathing facilities to white health seekers. The Indians had occupied that spot for several hundred years. Generations of their ancestors filled the graveyard near the village. Their impending eviction from the site was the latest travesty in the "pitiful chapter of oppression and cowardly wrong" that had been inflicted on the Mission Indians, Lummis declared in his magazine, which had begun to rally support for their cause in 1899.[24]

The situation that led to their imminent eviction was a long and tangled one. Lawyers for the Indians argued that their title to the land stemmed from an old Mexican land grant that should have been fully honored under the terms of the Treaty of Guadalupe Hidalgo. But an American rancher named Harvey Downey claimed that the title he had acquired dated back to an 1844 grant by Mexico to Juan J. Warner, which made no provision for the Indians on the property. In mid-century, when the newly admitted state of California created a board of land commissioners to resolve just such uncertainties, the Indians had failed to present their claim for confirmation. For that reason, a series of courts had ruled that they had forfeited any right they might have had to the land.

The Indian Rights Association and religious groups in Southern California raised funds for an appeal bond and for legal counsel, enabling the Indians to take their case to the California Supreme Court, where they lost in October 1899, and from there to the U.S. Supreme Court. But they lost there, as well, in a May 1901 ruling. Lummis and others pleaded with Harvey to sell the portion of his land that the Indians occupied, but he refused, agreeing only to give the government time to find them a new home before forcibly evicting them from their village near the hot spring.

The Supreme Court ruling led to a resurgence of concern for the Mission Indians in general and the Warner's Ranch group in particular. Lummis spoke at several public meetings in Los Angeles and San Diego in the spring and summer of 1901 and was encouraged by the fervor of the large crowds. In the fall a permanent association would be formed to advance the cause of the Mission Indians, Lummis declared. "And God pity the vulgar oppressor then! For his name shall be made a stench in the nostrils of the decent."

After Lummis received his summons from Roosevelt inviting him to come to Washington for a chat, he accelerated the plan he had announced in the summer to create a new Indian rights organization. He held an organizational meeting at El Alisal on November 22. An influential crowd of more than a hundred people turned out for the event. The ecumenical coalition that Lummis had pulled together under the banner of the Landmarks Club pitched in on this crusade as well. The Episcopal bishop Johnson and the Catholic bishop Montgomery came to the meeting. Lummis's Arroyo neighbor Horatio Rust, who had previously served as an agent to the Mission Indians, and distinguished Pasadena photographer Adam Clark Vroman were there. Charles Cassat

Davis, a prominent local attorney, was one of several members of the Los Angeles legal establishment on hand to lend their support. California senator Thomas Bard was expected but had to cancel at the last minute because of a scheduling conflict. Lummis himself almost didn't make it. He had spent the previous two days in the Pala Valley in a remote corner of northern San Diego County on Landmarks Club business. He had succeeded in enlisting residents of the valley to help in the restoration of an old Spanish mission chapel, and got back to El Alisal just in time for the meeting.

Not much progress was made that evening in launching the new association. Drawing up a constitution, and for that matter settling on a name, would have to wait. But those in attendance did manage to draft a memorial for Lummis to present to the president and the Bureau of Indian Affairs. It called on the bureau to appoint a commission that could relieve the plight of the Warner's Ranch Indians who were facing imminent eviction. The petition would serve as a wedge that Lummis could use in his upcoming meetings in Washington to insert himself into the policy-making apparatus that he had been fighting from the outside for years.[25]

Lummis left for Washington on November 29, the day after Thanksgiving, and arrived at noon on Thursday, December 5. His friend Dr. Frederick W. Hodge of the Smithsonian Institution was at the train station to meet him. Dressed in his well-worn corduroys and stained sombrero, Lummis was smelly and unkempt after the cross-country trip, according to Hamlin Garland, one of the people who greeted him as he passed through Chicago. But when Lummis called the White House to explain the situation, Roosevelt, no stranger to sweat and dust, insisted that he should come as he was for a luncheon that was just getting under way.

On arrival at the White House, he was ushered directly into the presidential dining room where Roosevelt was already seated with his other guests. There were six others—a pair of generals, a couple of industrialists, a senator, and a St. Louis journalist—in addition to the president's young son. The president introduced Lummis and then made a comment that Lummis recorded in his diary verbatim in English, departing from his usual practice of filling the cramped pages of the pocket-sized book with cryptic notes in Spanish. He clearly wanted to capture the triumphant moment for posterity exactly as it had happened. "You

must know I always read the *Land of Sunshine*, though it's the only magazine I have time to read now," Roosevelt said. "I read even the anti-
Imperialist editorials. And I am tremendously in sympathy with so
many of the things it is working for."

With the president's permission Lummis printed that endorsement
on *Out West* stationery just below the name of the magazine. A White
House aide later tried to get Lummis to remove the quote, but Roosevelt interceded and let him continue to use it.

At lunch Lummis mentioned that the magazine would soon have the
new name, and passed around a copy of the new cover. Everyone
heartily approved of the change. After lunch Lummis and Roosevelt
had a short time alone, the first of four private meetings that Lummis
would have with the president during his week in Washington. Lummis
was able to mention briefly his three concerns before Roosevelt's next
appointment. Lummis left the White House at 3 P.M. with an invitation
from the president to return and continue the discussion the next day.

During the week, Lummis squeezed in several dozen other meetings
around town. He visited with many of the leading Indian experts at the
Smithsonian. He had several meetings with Senator Bard and after
repeated attempts finally caught up with another senator, Boies Penrose
of Pennsylvania, his old partner in pranks at Harvard. Lummis was
delighted to learn that his Fort Bowie compadre Leonard Wood was in
town, on leave from his assignment as military governor of Cuba.
Wood took Lummis for a spin around Washington in an automobile.

Lummis also had important meetings with government officials who
would play key roles in finding a new home for the Warner's Ranch
Indians. On the president's recommendation, he met Secretary of the
Interior Ethan Allen Hitchcock, who was "buried under senators" when
Lummis dropped by at the appointed hour, but spared time for a long
talk the next day. Lummis also had a couple of fine long talks with
Commissioner of Indians Affairs William Jones. In one of the most
important accomplishments of the entire trip, Lummis convinced Jones
of the need of a careful search for a suitable home for the Warner's
Ranch Indians. Jones "promises commission" and "gets me to name it,"
Lummis noted in his diary.

When Lummis wasn't dining at the White House, he usually opted
for steamed oysters at Harvey's with the Hodges. Each night, he stayed
up until well past midnight in his room at the Savoy Hotel, writing long

letters to Eve and Turbesé and many others, and working on the statements he wanted to leave with the president. Lummis told everyone he met in Washington about the new organization that was just getting started, and got commitments of help from many. The most important offer of support came from the president himself.

In his memoir Lummis recalled his conversation with Roosevelt about the new organization and its big plans to transform Indian policy, and about how difficult that task would be. "Mr. President, it is absolutely hopeless to attempt any of these things unless there is someone in the White House in sympathy," Lummis said he told the president. "This has been burning in me for more than a dozen years, but I knew it was hopeless to start anything. But you understand the West. We would not bother you with trivialities, nor with old-wives' complaints; but if the ideas I have outlined appeal to you as right, I will start the ball rolling, if I could be sure that in a pinch, you would stand behind us."

" 'To the last gun!' he half-shouted, clicking his teeth and bringing his fist down on the table; and that he meant it was to be proved several times in the next few years—and sometimes very dramatically," Lummis wrote.

Lummis's last visit to the White House came on his last morning in Washington. He arrived at the White House at 10 A.M. and was ushered into a large reception room where he joined nearly eighty people—senators, governors, and other VIPs—all waiting for a chance to see the president. Lummis, as usual, was in full southwestern regalia. By one account he passed the time ostentatiously rolling cigarettes and lighting them with the flint and steel he always carried in one of his many pockets.[26] After a while Roosevelt entered and started working his way through the crowd. He gripped each supplicant in a firm handshake, had a quick word, "and without loosing his handshake, shoved the man onward like a catapult" so that he could move on quickly to the next. "Nobody but a powerful wrestler could have resisted that push," Lummis said. In that manner, the president expeditiously "mowed down" a room full of dignitaries. When he was finished, the president called out, "Is Lummis here?" When Lummis stepped forward, Roosevelt pulled him to the side of the room for a private conversation that went on for a full eight minutes while the rest of the envious throng could only watch from afar.

That afternoon Lummis returned to his hotel to write a final flurry of letters from Washington, squeezed in one last round of appointments, had a late lunch of steamed oysters at Harvey's, and boarded the westbound train at 6:20 P.M., working late into the night on more letters. He got back to Los Angeles five days later, exultant about what he had managed to accomplish. Most important of all, Roosevelt had promised to back him up in his effort to help the Mission Indians, and the bureaucrats in the Department of the Interior knew it. Lummis, who had been a detested outsider for more than a decade, had succeeded during his week in Washington in becoming a force to be reckoned with in national Indian policy.

Chapter *10*

Showdown at Warner's Ranch

When Theodore Roosevelt became president, there were 270,000 Indians in the United States submerged in a national population of 76 million. Scattered among 300 tribes on 160 reservations, they were administered by a bureaucracy with 6,000 employees. The last flicker of armed resistance had been extinguished a decade earlier. The First Americans had become wards of the U.S. government; the Indian menace had become the Indian problem. At the start of the twentieth century, government officials, educators, and social scientists were in the midst of a reevaluation of the Indian policies that had been followed for the previous several decades, and many were uncertain what to do next.

The first round of treaties with the Plains Indians that had taken effect in the 1860s typically envisioned thirty-year transition periods. The special governmental protections and assistance promised under the treaties would end after that, by which time it was assumed the Indians would be self-sufficient and integrated into the larger society. But at the start of the new millennium most Indians were more destitute, dislocated, vulnerable, and dependent on government assistance than ever.

In the field of education, Captain Pratt and his Carlisle School approach to educating Indians by removing them from their tribes for years on end had lost its luster. The first generation of students to pass through Pratt's regimen had become adults and yet they hadn't blended seamlessly into white society as hoped. And off-reservation boarding schools couldn't accommodate more than a fraction of school-aged Indian children anyway.

The social science theories that had undergirded Indian policy were also in a state of flux at the start of the new century. Lewis Henry Morgan's optimistic theory of social evolution—which suggested that Indians, when given the chance, could quickly step up from savagery to civilization—was falling out of favor. A much more pessimistic consensus was emerging that the Indians wouldn't be ready to assimilate into American society for generations, if ever.

As for Roosevelt's views on Indian policy, he is best known for some of his more strident pronouncements glorifying the white conquest of the continent. He was scornful of any suggestion that there was anything to be ashamed of in that heroic episode in the nation's history. "This continent had to be won," he declared in a lecture in Boston in 1898 shortly after he was elected governor of New York. "We need not waste our time in dealing with any sentimentalist who believes that, on account of any abstract principle, it would have been right to leave this continent to the domain, the hunting ground of squalid savages. It had to be taken by the white race. . . . The man who puts the soil to use must of right dispossess the man who does not, or the world will come to a standstill." The Indians would have to conform to the reality imposed by the new rulers of the continent. Roosevelt insisted that coddling them with a comfortable level of rations and special protections would do them more harm than good. Setting aside reservations was a transitional strategy that he believed would have to be phased out soon. As he explained in an address on Indian policy at the Mohonk Conference in 1892, "We must cut them loose, hardening our hearts to the fact that many will sink, exactly as many will swim."

As unsympathetic as he sounded, Roosevelt had a greater interest in the American Indian than any president since William Henry Harrison. In 1892 he spent two weeks thoroughly exploring six reservations in the West by horseback and wagon and went out of his way to visit with a number of Indians in their homes. Later he displayed an appreciation for aspects of Indian culture, from pottery to architecture to dancing, that was foreign to many Indian policy makers. And he had enormous respect for some of the individual Indians he got to know, including several dozen of his Rough Riders. At the same time, he despised the unscrupulous whites who flocked around reservations like buzzards, siphoning off government aid and otherwise preying on vulnerable Indians.

While he loathed "sentimentalists," Roosevelt was highly amenable to the entreaties of a tougher breed of Indian rights advocate, men who could speak from hard experience in the West. He often heeded the advice of men like Lummis, Garland, and George Bird Grinnell, an authority on the Plains Indians and editor of *Forest and Stream* magazine, who were part of a group of informal advisors on Western affairs known as the Cowboy Cabinet.[1] The three men were also allied in another group, the Indians rights organization that Lummis created soon after Roosevelt became president. Thanks in large part to the influence of these advisors, Roosevelt's actions on Indian matters regularly belied his sometimes belligerent rhetoric.

After his series of meetings with Roosevelt and other policy makers in late 1901, Lummis could sense that Indian rights advocates had an unparalleled opportunity to seize the initiative. On his last afternoon in Washington, one of the people he wrote before boarding the train to return to Los Angeles was Grinnell. Lummis could hardly contain his excitement.

"The psychological moment has come, my dear Grinnell," Lummis wrote. "The President seriously desires a better policy. The Interior and the Indian Bureau are more than willing. The sentiment of fair-play has grown in the public. . . . You and I have ached for years—and now, I believe with all my heart, our hour has struck. Let's pile in; soberly, patiently, tactfully, but like good Out-Door men who know about what we want, and together can devise how to get it. I'm not a visionary; but I believe thoroughly that I can see a Way Out."[2]

Lummis was never one to spend time fretting about the theoretical underpinnings of Indian policy. His own views, as he liked to boast, were based on plain common sense. The simple truth at the heart of his approach to Indian affairs was that Native Americans should be able to decide for themselves what they wanted to do with their lives—within the limits, to be sure, that had been imposed on them by a continent rapidly filling up with white settlers. To adjust, American Indians would have to learn new skills in fields ranging from farming and ranching to law and politics. But there was no reason why many aspects of their culture couldn't survive. Their way of life was far from perfect, but Lummis recognized that contemporary white society had its own serious short-comings, so he was skeptical of most of the proposals being batted around in the debate about how to improve the Indian. No complicated theory about social evolution nor any regimented educational program was necessary. Government policy makers could make better Indians simply by treating them better. That thought became the motto of Lummis's new organization, which finally got a name several weeks after Lummis returned from Washington: the Sequoya League.

Lummis didn't want the group to be dominated by professional Indian policy types. Though he would certainly need some of them on board, it was just as important to have unreconstructed straight thinkers with experience in the West. He decided that while half of the twenty-five-member advisory board should be experts on Indians, the other half should be prominent people from other fields.

The high-powered list of names Lummis was able to assemble was a testament to the breadth of the contacts he had made and to the respect he had won over the years. The executive committee included Grinnell and C. Hart Merriam, head of the U.S. Biological Survey, both of whom would prove to be invaluable members because they were even closer to President Roosevelt than Lummis was. Lummis's good friend David Starr Jordan, the president of Stanford University, also served, along with Richard Egan, the San Juan Capistrano civil engineer who was a leading force in the Landmarks Club.

For the advisory board, Lummis recruited Senator Bard and Phoebe Hearst. Major John Wesley Powell, explorer of the Grand Canyon and head of the Bureau of American Ethnology, and Professor W. J. McGee, second in command at the bureau, also agreed to join, though Powell did not last long, dying in 1902. Two anthropologists Lummis greatly admired, Alice Fletcher, a fellow at Harvard's Peabody Museum, and his good friend Frederick Hodge of the Smithsonian Institution, gave their profession prominent representation in the league. Estelle Reel, the superintendent of Indian education, and Hamlin Garland rounded out the high-powered list of advisors.

This diverse group held a variety of views on Indian policy, some of which Lummis would have vehemently rejected. But Lummis never intended to run his association as if it were a democracy. The league would operate as a "despotism," Lummis had told Roosevelt and Hitchcock. "All agreed that it was the only way to keep the movement headed right," he told Grinnell.

Of all the people on the advisory board, McGee held views that were furthest from Lummis's. He was a leading purveyor of the notion that while social evolution might elevate the Indians, their racial inferiority would drastically impede the transformation. "The savage stands strikingly close to sub-human species in every aspect of mentality," McGee explained in an address to the Anthropological Society of Washington in 1901. In fact, he said, the lowest Indian cultures have more in common with the higher animals than with the "engine-using inventor" type of peoples of Northern Europe and the United States.

Other members of the league's advisory board had a more sympathetic but essentially no less condescending view of the prospects for American Indians in the new century. Hamlin Garland, for example, had grown up on frontier farms in the upper Midwest in the 1860s and 1870s but headed to Boston in 1884 at the age of twenty-four after failing in an attempt to carve out a homestead in the Dakotas.[3] He didn't become deeply interested in Indians until the 1890s, when he made several extended trips through the West. Garland admired many aspects of the culture of the Indians he met, but he thought it would take many generations for them to become fully civilized. Until then, he believed, they would have to exist in a childlike state of dependence on magnanimous whites.

Grinnell was much more Lummis's type. Lummis and Grinnell both shared a disdain for eastern sentimentalists. Each had gained an intimate familiarity with the Indians of the Far West by living in their midst. In fact, Grinnell's own experiences in the West would have made even Lummis envious.

Grinnell was born in the East to a wealthy family, graduated from Yale in 1870, and went west for the first time that summer on a fossil-collecting trip that ranged from Kansas to Utah. He befriended several Pawnee scouts who were on the expedition, leading to a lifelong connection with the tribe. One summer Grinnell joined a group of Pawnees on a buffalo hunt and had the thrill of engaging in a skirmish with legendary Plains warriors when raiders from another tribe attacked his hunting party. In 1874 Grinnell made another western excursion as a naturalist accompanying Lieutenant Colonel George Armstrong Custer's

Black Hills expedition. Two years later Custer invited him to join the Seventh Cavalry on the ill-fated expedition that ended on the Little Bighorn, but Grinnell had to decline because a Harvard professor he was assisting at the Peabody Museum refused to grant him leave.

A few years later, when the buffalo were all gone and the Plains tribes faced starvation on the inadequate government rations that made it through the gauntlet of swindlers, Grinnell pulled strings in Washington to get extra supplies for the Indians. In gratitude, a family of Northern Cheyenne whom he had befriended adopted him as their son, and the Blackfeet named him Fisher Hat after an esteemed leader of the tribe then deceased.

Grinnell wrote a number of books about the Plains tribes, and was a regular contributor to *Forest and Stream*, becoming editor of the magazine after his father bought it. He organized the first Audubon Society, and along with Theodore Roosevelt was a founding member of the Boone & Crockett Club, a wildlife conservation and hunting group. As president, Roosevelt occasionally enlisted Grinnell's help in sorting out controversies over Indian lands. While he didn't hesitate to defy the Bureau of Indian Affairs, Grinnell could be equally hard on "Indian cranks" who made excessive demands on the government and resisted taking steps to become self-sufficient. Grinnell was, in short, sympathetic toward the Indians but no sentimentalist, just the sort to wield considerable influence in the Roosevelt White House—and to help Lummis set the Sequoya League on a sensible course.

One of the first orders of business was to rein in Garland. When Lummis was slow to settle on a name for the group, Garland wasted no time in pushing his own idea—the Teepee, or Tipi, League. "It symbolizes much of the charm of the old life and lends itself to camp-fire meetings, to ornamental letter heads, etc. It could be taken as a trademark on goods manufactured and so on," Garland wrote Lummis on December 24, explaining that he had pitched his idea to Grinnell and Ernest Thompson Seton, a writer, conservationist, founder of the Boy Scouts of America, and visitor to El Alisal. They both liked it, he said. The image of Indians in teepees and buckskins would help maintain public sympathy and support for the cause, he went on to say, concluding by informing Lummis that he and Grinnell were going to get to work on a proposed constitution for the new group.

Lummis sent a curt reply. "We must save our Indians first," he told Garland. "Afterwards we can decide about their tailoring." In another letter to Garland, Lummis added: "I am glad to have your vigorous manhood harnessed to our car, but please don't run away with the horse."[4]

In a letter in early January, Lummis enlisted Grinnell's help in curbing Garland's "impetuosity." "We are not quite ready to formulate a constitution and platform, nor must we have a mushroom growth of all sorts of eager things all over the country diverting knowledge and confusing the field. The very first thing that is needed in a movement of this sort is infinite patience," he wrote. As for Garland's suggestion of a name for the group, Lummis told Grinnell, "It will hardly do for two reasons. One is that the League is not intended to bring Indians up in tipis." Moreover, a name that made the venture look too "artistic" would scare off Congress and the Department of the Interior. "They can stand a little romance, a little symbolism, but they have got to be convinced that the backbone of the thing is just plain horse sense."[5]

By then Lummis had come up with a name he liked: the Sequoya League. It had the advantage of being a familiar word. There was of course some danger the league might be mistaken for a conservation group, since the name was associated with the majestic big trees of California. But the name also referred to the Cherokee Indian leader who had developed a written form for his tribe's language. Lummis liked the implications of that: the idea that progress didn't have to come at the expense of native culture but instead could be a vehicle for preserving the old ways. Sequoya League it was.

The next task was to settle on a constitution. Lummis, Grinnell, Garland, and others traded drafts back and forth in the early weeks of 1902. The document that the executive committee ultimately adopted was published in *Out West* in March.[6] It established in subtle but significant ways that the Sequoya League would be far more respectful of native traditions and interests than government policies of the past and earlier reform movements alike. The league would work with the government to implement common-sense Indian policies, and in doing so would seek the "consent and cooperation of the Indians" in formulating those policies. The league would help Indians achieve "security in those rights of home, of individuality and of family which must be the basis of successful dealing by statecraft with any race." The league would encourage Indians to acquire education that would be useful to them, and in that process "the family and the tribe must be made allies, instead of being treated as enemies." Finally, the league would help tribes develop industries that suited their abilities and local markets, whenever possible helping to revitalize aboriginal crafts that could be made profitable.

That last provision reflected a long-standing personal interest of Lummis's. He knew from his experience in the curio trade that many native handicrafts could command handsome sums in the modern American marketplace. While proponents of Carlisle School–style industrial training contended that such an approach would keep Indians in a state of picturesque backwardness, Lummis believed that supporting those ancient industries offered a far more promising route to prosperity for many Indians.

The Bureau of Indian Affairs had been a staunch proponent of the policies that the league was implicitly and explicitly criticizing. But Lummis had reason to hope that the Roosevelt administration would be receptive to a new approach. Encouraged by his cordial visits with Hitchcock and Jones, Lummis believed the league could have a constructive relationship with the bureau. As he explained in his December 12 letter to Grinnell, "Instead of fighting the Bureau and getting in such bad odor that it hates to see us coming—as the Indian Rights Association has done, we must make ourselves so useful that the Bureau will find our way the line of least resistance," he wrote.

For anyone inclined to think the league would be too friendly, Lummis had a warning in his column in the April issue of *Out West*. "If there are people who think they are foxy enough to fool this organization, let them try. But if they will take a fool's advice they will save money and credit by accepting the inevitable. . . . People who really knew better have maltreated the Indians just because it was no one's organized business to stop them; but now it is someone's business."

The Warner's Ranch Commission would be a "good introduction and appetizer" for the bigger things that the Sequoya League would go on to accomplish, Lummis said in a letter to Grinnell. But not long after he returned from Washington, it became apparent that the bureau had other ideas. Jones and Hitchcock had professed their support for a commission, and Jones had gone so far as to promise that Lummis would be allowed to pick the members. But early in the new year, the bureau dispatched one of its most experienced Indian inspectors, James McLaughlin, to California to select a new home for the Warner's Ranch Indians, obviously hoping they could quickly resolve the matter without the need for Lummis's commission.

There was no shortage of ranches for sale in Southern California at the time. An ongoing drought had driven many farmers out of business. Dozens of beleaguered landowners were eager to unload their property on the government. McLaughlin paid quick visits to ten parcels before filing a report with the department recommending purchase of the Monserrate Ranch in northern San Diego County. McLaughlin knew just enough about Southern California to know that access to water was critical. He was impressed by the fact that the Monserrate Ranch included a mile of frontage on the San Luis Rey River. And the asking price of $70,000 seemed acceptable.

Lummis, however, saw through the bureau's gambit. He made a quick one-week wagon trip of his own to the Monserrate Ranch and surrounding areas, did some research on the property, and concluded that McLaughlin's assessment had been far too superficial to support a decision to move the Warner's Ranch Indians there. The site had been used in the past in a failed attempt at stock raising, and had been sold at foreclosure for $25,000, Lummis had learned. It is a "beautiful piece of scenery," he reported in *Out West*. "But the consensus of opinion among experienced Californians who are familiar with it is that it would be a mistake—and many use a stronger word—to put the Indians there." A "far more thorough" search for a home was needed, he said. "Far from removing the need of a commission, this merely emphasizes it." Lummis used stronger words in a letter to Roosevelt. "The ranch is a white elephant with a history of transfers so peculiar that it would figure admirably in a novel," he wrote.[7]

Lummis's lobbying succeeded in fending off that threat to his proposal for a commission, though it took several more months for Senator Bard to succeed in getting authorizing legislation through Congress. In the meantime, Lummis had begun his search for commissioners as soon as he got back to Los Angeles.

It was no easy task to find people with the expertise and dedication for the job, which would be unpaid and would entail a lengthy inspection tour of dozens of ranches in the rugged backcountry of Southern California. He eventually found two men for the job, Charles Partridge and Russell Allen, who had experience with California ranch land and Indians. Combined with Lummis's eighteen years in Los Angeles, the three had a cumulative forty-four years of residency in Southern California. Allen brought another asset to the group. He had been a classmate of Roosevelt's. Lummis realized that the commission might need all the leverage with the president that it could get.

Two other men with useful expertise, Richard Egan and William Collier, offered to join the tour. Egan, the Landmarks Club veteran and Sequoya League executive committee member, had thirty-four years of experience in appraising land and measuring water flows. He would assure that the commission wouldn't be fooled by exaggerated claims that many landowners desperate to sell were making about their property. Collier, a special attorney for the Mission Indians who had been involved with Southern California's tribes for eighteen years, was an expert in land titles. To record the voluminous notes that Lummis planned to collect along the way, Miss Mary Haskins volunteered her services as a stenographer. Two members of the Agua Caliente band of Indians, Ambrosio Ortega and Salvador Nolasquez, agreed to accompany the expedition as observers. Two others rounded out the entourage, Lummis's daughter, Turbesé, who would turn ten on the trip, and Lanier Bartlett, a reporter for the *Times*.

It took until May 27 for Congress to approve the bill authorizing formation of a commission "to aid in selection of a suitable tract of land" for the Warner's Ranch Indians. The bill included an appropriation of $100,000, of which $70,000 could be spent on land, leaving $30,000 to cover relocation costs. Lummis got word about the congressional action in a telegram from Secretary Hitchcock on May 28. Three days later, the Warner's Ranch Commission set out from Palm Springs in a convoy of wagons fully outfitted for a month-long expedition. The Department of the Interior had agreed to cover the commission's expenses, but Lummis had no intention of waiting around for an advance. He had arranged for a thousand-dollar line of credit from the Los Angeles National Bank, with Senator Bard and *Los Angeles Times* executives Harry Chandler and Albert McFarland serving as guarantors.

Lummis could hardly spare the time for a lengthy wagon trip through the backcountry of Southern California. *Out West* was bigger than ever. Moody was taking on an increasing share of the workload, but Lummis still had more than a full-time job as editor, reading dozens of submissions each week, editing stories, and writing thousands of words a month. As the Warner's Ranch Commission set out on its expedition, a deadline was looming for a major freelance project—a ten-thousand-word treatise on California for the *Encyclopedia Americana*. And the summer construction season was in full swing, both at several Landmarks Club restorations that Lummis had to monitor and at El Alisal, which continued to absorb many hours a day of his time. But he enthusiastically poured all of the energy he could muster into the task that confronted the commission. The trip lasted until June 23.

In the midst of the drought and a local farming depression, the commission had been flooded with offers of property. Lummis realized that might compound his problems. "The Indians, poor folk, will blame us for the removal we are trying to make less cruel; and every man who doesn't sell his ranch through us will have a grudge. But I think we can mitigate a bad affair," Lummis wrote in a letter to Phoebe Hearst the night before the commission departed.[8]

No one had a better reason to hold a grudge against the Warner's Ranch Commission than the owners of the Monserrate Ranch. The sale of the ranch for $70,000 had looked like a done deal until Lummis and other advocates for the Indians raised objections. Lummis promised to give the Monserrate Ranch as fair a hearing as every other piece of property he intended to consider. The owners of the ranch, however, didn't bother to wait for Lummis's verdict before lashing out.

After the commission's visit to the property, the manager of the ranch sent a letter to the editor of the *Los Angeles Times* ridiculing the inspection. "The commission came through like a circus, on horseback and in big wagons drawn by four horses with cook and commissary wagon and a box on top to which Mr. Lummis held the key," the letter asserted. Lummis and his stenographer came along a bit later in another wagon. They ambled around the property, Lummis took photographs, and with great seriousness for such a silly exercise, they filled a tin can with water from the stream, the manager wrote. Picking up on some of the same themes, the *San Diego Tribune* ran a story lampooning the commission as a "traveling circus" out on a joyride through the picturesque countryside of northern San Diego County. The newspaper offered an additional titillating detail about the locked box in the cook wagon. It held a supply of liquor, access to which was controlled by the chairman.

In one of the photographs that Lummis took, the entourage did indeed look a bit like a circus caravan. Leading the procession astride a horse was ten-year-old Turbesé in a checked tam-o-shanter. In a line behind her were a large prairie-schooner-style chuck wagon, a wagon with a large umbrella for a canopy, and a smaller wagon that carried the two Indian observers bringing up the rear. But the critical reports were the exception to the rule. Most papers that wrote about the inspection tour acknowledged the extraordinary effort that the unpaid commission was making on behalf of a small band of Indians who were about to lose their homes. The *San Francisco Chronicle* complimented the work of the commission and its chairman in an editorial published June 7. Lummis "feels deep sympathy with [the Indians] and is absolutely honest in all his dealings and his promises," the paper noted.

The days were long and hard. Upon arrival at each ranch they inspected, the members of the group set up camp. Then they walked the breadth and length of the property, measured the degree of the slope in the fields, took soil samples, assessed the quality of any crops, checked the fallow fields for infestations of weeds, and surveyed the timber. Lummis hauled his tripod and camera around the property and took photographs from different vantage points. Egan built a weir dam to impound any streams, and then carefully measured the flow at different times of day.

At the end of every day after dinner, Lummis unlocked the box that critics of the procession had noticed. It did, indeed, contain a modest supply of wine, whisky, and cigars, which Lummis doled out to members of the party, who enjoyed a short spell of relaxation. Then they would get back to work recording their findings that day. Lummis and the stenographer would stay up until midnight while he dictated and she took down notes. The group would be up again at five the next morning.

"It was no picnic jaunt but an uncommonly arduous journey," Lummis noted in his report to the Department of the Interior.[9] The commission traveled several hundred miles by wagon on that three-week expedition. By the time its work was done, Lummis figured, the members and advisors had traveled a cumulative total of 6,823 miles by rail and 7,049 miles by wagon, and had contributed 276 eighteen-hour days of labor. They collected hundreds of pages of stenographic notes and 200 photographs. As the *Times* summed up the effort, "Sending out this unique commission was one of the most interesting experiments of the government in the history of Indian affairs."

The great care with which the commission went about its work was a dramatic departure from past practice. Finding reservation lands for Indians had usually been an afterthought. The consensus around the turn of the century, which even many self-proclaimed friends of the Indians shared, was that reservations shouldn't be particularly inviting places. If Indians settled in too comfortably, they would never progress. The quicker their homelands disintegrated, the better off they would be.

The Warner's Ranch Commission's objective contrasted sharply with that attitude. Lummis was determined to find a new homeland for the Warner's Ranch Indians where they would be secure from further encroachments by white society, free to maintain their traditions and decide for themselves how to live their lives. Of course, they would have to adapt to the new reality of life in Southern California, whether they liked it or not. To begin with, they would have to accept the verdict of the U.S. Supreme Court, as unjust as it was, and vacate their home beside the hot springs. And they would have to develop a new source of income, most likely farming, even though they had never farmed before. It wasn't an easy task. But the commission's report was a masterpiece in making the best of a bad situation.

Lummis completed a preliminary draft of the 136-page report, got Allen and Partridge to sign off on it, and delivered it to the Department of the Interior on July 23, just a month after the commission completed its grueling trip. Illustrated with several dozen blueprints of photographs that Lummis had taken and Eve had printed, it began with a description of the tribe's present home next to the Agua Caliente spring and a brief history of the land dispute that led to their impending eviction. Photographs showed their humble village in a rocky ravine and examples of the baskets and rugs they made from yucca fibers softened in the hot water. Other photographs showed some of the sites the commission had inspected.

The commission concluded that it had found a new home that was far better than the site they would have to abandon in every respect but one: it didn't satisfy their determination to stay put. Lummis stated, for the record, that finding a way for the Indians to remain in the "ancient home to which they are so pathetically attached" was still the commission's first preference. "Their irrevocable choice of their old home should outweigh the choice of other and wiser people for them, if it were possible," he wrote. The commission made a last-ditch plea for a resolution that government lawyers had already rejected: condemnation proceedings to strip Harvey Downey of the spring and five thousand surrounding acres. The compensation Downey would get in such a proceeding would far exceed the revenue from the cattle he planned to run on the property. "This suggestion has already been fully brought to your attention, however, and the matter is at your discretion," Lummis noted.

The report proceeded to discuss the alternative sites that the commission had inspected—106 in all. Most had been summarily ruled out because they were too small or had no water. But the report included a painstaking analysis of twenty-eight of the best sites. To objectively assess them and compare them with each other, Lummis had devised a complex point system, rating each parcel on nineteen different criteria ranked in order of importance. Out of a maximum possible score of 400 points, the factor that the commission deemed most important, the amount of available "gravity water," was worth up to 100 points. Other criteria included safety from encroachment, and the supply of wild foods and basket-making materials, down to the factor deemed least important—"favored by the Indians"—which was worth at most 5 points.

A number of the sites that the commission visited had considerable merit, but the point system demonstrated that they weren't suitable for an Indian reservation. Etcheverry's Santa Maria Rancho, with its shallow, weak soil, "would make a fair sheep ranch but is out of the question for Indians." The Agua Tibia Rancho on the flank of Mount Palomar, with a spectacular bird's eye view of a cordon of mountains, was the most "artistic" of the lot. "As a site for a Granadan or Florentine palace, your commission has never seen a more ideal location," Lummis wrote. But the "irksome approaches" on a steep trail would be a serious drawback for farmers trying to get produce to a market.

As for the Monserrate Ranch, which the Indian Bureau had continued to insist was its top choice, Lummis's commission agreed that it was better than some. "As a landscape the Monserrate is an exceptionally beautiful area, and might well fascinate a stranger to California," Lummis wrote, taking a not too subtle shot at McLaughlin. But the commission spent two nights and three days there and found that the property

226

had serious drawbacks. The soil was alkaline. Potato fields on the ranch were overrun with weeds. And despite McLaughlin's claim that the land was an excellent choice because of its abundant water, Lummis's commission found to the contrary that most of the water couldn't be put to use by Indians without an expensive network of pipes and pumps. Finally there was the issue of the $70,000 asking price, which was "excessive to state it mildly."

The best site by far for the Warner's Ranch Indians, in the well-reasoned opinion of the commission, was a 3,428-acre parcel in the Pala Valley on the west flank of Mount Palomar near Temecula. The site had practically everything going for it—timber, native foods and basket materials, 316 acres of prime irrigated farmland, and five hundred times more gravity water than the Monserrate Ranch. Tucked into a picturesque valley, it was protected on all sides from unscrupulous intruders. The price was another big selling point. Lummis had arranged with the landowner to buy the spectacular site for $46,230. Setting aside the $30,000 that had been earmarked for relocation costs, the commission would have $23,770 left of the amount that Congress had appropriated and the department had been prepared to spend on the Monserrate Ranch.

Going beyond the call of duty, Lummis came up with an impressive list of ideas for how to use the savings to relieve the misery of other Mission Indians. There were nearly three dozen other reservations in Southern California that were home to about two thousand Mission Indians, Lummis noted in a supplement to the Warner's Ranch Commission report. With just a modest expenditure to buy a few hundred acres here, a few hundred there, Lummis had shrewdly made preliminary arrangements to significantly improve the precarious lot of hundreds of other Indians. "There is one case where the addition of 100 acres of adjacent land would probably double the farming capacity of a reservation of 29,000 acres! This simple fact perhaps gives the clearest idea of present conditions," he wrote.

Lummis had devised seven similar deals. But the ideas for spending the savings were a bonus. On its own merits, the Pala Valley was the clear winner. No other ranch came close to matching Pala's score of 372 out of the possible 400 points.

On July 25, two days after Lummis finished the report, Commissioner of Indian Affairs Jones and his wife dropped by El Alisal for a friendly visit. Lummis gave him a copy, and Jones looked it over, said he was impressed, and wired Washington that it had met with his approval. Lummis had no reason to doubt that the Department of the Interior would be delighted.

Halfway through August, however, he still hadn't received word from Washington that the report had been officially approved. Though Lummis preferred to make entreaties to the president sparingly, he sent Roosevelt a letter explaining that time was of the essence. The letter did the trick. Hitchcock promptly gave the report his imprimatur. All that was needed to complete the work of the commission was quick action to acquire the land before speculators could get their hands on it and drive up the price. With the commissioner of Indian affairs, the secretary of the interior, and the president of the United States all on board, Lummis assumed prompt action by the government was a foregone conclusion. Winning the Indians' assent would be another matter.

Lummis thought he had a reasonably good rapport with the Warner's Ranch Indians. He had visited their village near the hot spring on several occasions and had been cordially received. But he also knew that some of the old-timers hadn't budged from their position: they wouldn't leave under any circumstance.

One Indian in particular spelled trouble. His name was Cecilio Blacktooth and, as luck would have it, he had just been elected captain of the tribe. With a reputation as a troublemaker, he wasn't especially popular with the others. But given the sad fate that awaited them, no one else wanted the job. No one was more bitterly opposed to a move than Blacktooth.

As months rolled by with no action from Washington to complete the purchase of the Pala tract, Lummis grew increasingly alarmed, all the more so upon learning that Blacktooth had acquired some unscrupulous allies. He had used tribal funds to hire a part-Indian lawyer from San Bernardino named John Brown, who was insisting that there was still hope to stave off an eviction. A shady freelance journalist named George Lawson was also counseling the Indians to stay put.

As time passed, other potential troublemakers came out of the woodwork. Mrs. Josephine Babbitt, a dedicated and much-loved teacher in the government school at Agua Caliente, was telling the Indians that Lummis was lying about them. In boasting about the work of his com-

Lummis spent more than a decade building El Alisal, his stone castle in Los Angeles. Amado stands in the foreground. *Photo N13716*

The main room of El Alisal, called the Museo, held many of the artifacts, rare books, and other treasures that Lummis collected during his travels through the Southwest, Mexico, and South America. *Photo N42976*

Dressed for heavy lifting at
El Alisal, Lummis shocked
some visitors to the construction
site with his "immodest" attire.
Photo N13690

Lummis's illegitimate daughter
Bertha, left, with his wife Eve.
Lummis's doting attention to his
"firstborn" after her unexpected
appearance in late 1904 caused
great tension in his marriage to
Eve. *Photo N21267*

Lummis, here with his daughter, Turbesé, and his son Jordan, also known as Quimu, took up the guitar in 1903, often enjoining his family to sing with him. *Photo N42938*

Francisco Amate, El Alisal's resident troubadour and groundskeeper, killed another member of the household staff in a fight three weeks before Lummis took this photograph. *Photo N42942*

John Muir, an occasional contributor to *Out West*, was in the middle of a four-day visit to El Alisal when Lummis took this photograph of the famous conservationist. *Photo N18976*

NOV. 21, 1909

Eve was justifiably suspicious of her husband's relationship with Marie Aspiroz, pictured here with his son Quimu, but Lummis refused to evict his "friend" from El Alisal. *Photo N42959*

Lummis and Theodore Roosevelt at Occidental College in Los Angeles in 1911.
Roosevelt conferred regularly with the eccentric California editor on Indian and
western affairs. *Photo N20093*

Lummis, in 1926, proudly wearing the medallion that he received from King Alfonso XIII of Spain in recognition of his lifelong work in drawing attention to the Spanish heritage of the Americas. *Photo N42943*

In 1927, Lummis was together with all of his surviving children for his last Christmas. *Back row, left to right,* Keith, Jordan (Quimu), Betty (Quimu's wife) with baby, Lummis. *Front row, left to right,* Turbese, Quimu's toddler Patricia, and Bertha. *Photo N21253*

Lummis in 1928, in one of the last photographs taken of him. Photo N24517

mission, Lummis had told officials in the Department of Interior that Pala was the tribe's second choice for a home. In fact, she pointed out, they had never said any such thing. They had only one wish, and that was to stay at Agua Caliente. The most disturbing thing about Babbitt's campaign to damage his reputation with the Indians was that she was citing his private communications with the Department of the Interior to prove her point. Clearly someone within the department was out to do him in.

By then, if not earlier, Lummis realized he had been naïve to think his brilliant plan to help the Mission Indians would win quick approval. The Indian policy bureaucracy was filled with old-timers who had long memories, men who had been lying in wait for Charles Lummis since the days of his vendetta against the Albuquerque Indian School. The way he had embarrassed the department's star inspector McLaughlin had revived those bitter memories and made new enemies. The delays his proposal had encountered were clearly their handiwork.

By early January, Lummis decided it was time to deploy the heavy artillery. He sent a letter to President Roosevelt on January 8. "I hate to bother you; but the whole work of the Warner's Ranch Indian Commission will be strangled unless this Red Tape is loosed mighty quick," he wrote. "You were good enough to 'Stir 'em up' in August on our report—and your rattling among the dry bones was effective; the Department instantly examined our report, and on examination approved it." Now Lummis needed immediate approval of the abstract of title that had been stuck in the bowels of the Department of the Interior for more than two months.

Roosevelt came through for Lummis once again. In February, in short order the title was approved, the money was disbursed, and the Pala property was purchased. Lummis still hadn't received an official response to his idea about how to utilize the money he had saved. But if necessary, that could wait. At least the more immediate issue of moving the Agua Caliente Indians to a new home could proceed to its conclusion.

Having sidestepped his foes in Washington, Lummis turned his attention to obstructionists closer to home, starting with the writer Lawson. Lummis had done some research on the reporter, who was working as a stringer for the *Los Angeles Express* but had bigger plans for his writing career. Lawson had pitched a story about the Warner's Ranch Indians to the prestigious *Collier's Weekly* the previous fall. Editors at the magazine had informed him they weren't interested in the story "unless the matter took on sensational aspects," as Lummis explained in a letter to Senator Bard in April. "He has been trying to make the story sensational and he has succeeded."[10]

In Lawson's most incendiary gambit, he had persuaded the Indians to cover his expenses to check out the Pala Valley on their behalf. He had traveled to San Diego to look at the title to the property but never actually made it to the valley. He nevertheless wrote a lurid story about it for the *Express*. The paper ran the story on its front page on April 4. The reporter's investigation had revealed "that another injustice to the Indian is about to be added to the long list of outrages perpetrated in the name of the United States," the story declared. Lawson wrote that he had traveled up a precipitous grade from Temecula and was aghast at his first sight of the property onto which Lummis proposed to drive the poor Indians, at gunpoint if necessary. "There is a glimpse of a valley abounding in huge boulders surrounded by sand as deep and as unproductive as that on the great Sahara desert," Lawson reported. A few patches of arable soil here and there were an "enchanting deception." The sad fact of the matter, according to Lawson, was that farmland in the desolate valley wouldn't hold more than a six-row bean crop.

In the course of his research, Lawson wrote, he had discovered the real reason for Lummis's fixation on Pala. It concerned a feature of the site that Lummis hadn't bothered to mention, but that his critics were quick to point out. Nestled in the center of the property was the hundred-year-old mission chapel that Lummis's Landmarks Club was renovating. "To restore the mission for an unoccupied landmark hardly could be expected to be the ultimate object for which Mr. Lummis and his architect have given so much time in the past few years," Lawson wrote. "The backdrop of the mission must be picturesque and in that particular feature of the plan, the Indians would be serviceable, whereas the white families would be useless. . . . To establish a renaissance of mission rule was the motive that determined the selection of Pala for the new home of the Warner Ranch Indians."

It was quite a scoop. But any glee that the editors of the *Express* enjoyed didn't last long, since anybody who had actually been to Pala would have known immediately that Lawson's description of a barren desert was far off the mark. The *Express* admitted as much two days later in a story headlined "the Beauty of the Pala Valley," in which the editor decried "malicious reports" about Pala that had been circulated by people who wanted to sell their property to the commission. Those stories had proved to be unfounded, the *Express* said.

Lummis published his own biting rebuttal in the *Times* on April 8. Lawson was an "ignoramus and a prevaricator," Lummis wrote. The chapel at Pala was an "incidental advantage" that wasn't even considered by the commission. "The Landmarks Club has spent far more money at Capistrano, likewise at San Fernando, but has not found it necessary to colonize either with Indians," he insisted.

Lawson's "Valley of Boulders" hoax ended his career as a stringer for Los Angeles papers. But it apparently didn't hurt his reputation with the Indians. He remained at Agua Caliente, still in a position to stir up big trouble. And he wasn't the only reporter drawn to the story. The looming eviction, which was by all accounts a grand tragedy in the making, had attracted the attention of the national press.

Lummis wasn't supposed to have any part in the actual eviction and removal. His official role in the matter of the Warner's Ranch Indians had ended the previous August when the report of his commission was received and approved. He should have welcomed the opportunity to make a graceful exit at that point, avoiding the thankless task of helping to evict the Indians from their beloved home. The fact that in this conflict he was cast as the heartless government agent riding roughshod over the Indians' rights should have given him pause about staying around until the bitter end. But it simply wasn't in Lummis to avoid a fight.

On April 16 he traveled to Agua Caliente with the U.S. agent for the Mission Indians, the lawyer who had represented them in their long court fight, and a priest, to make a last-ditch plea for a peaceful departure from the hot spring. More than a year had passed since Harvey Downey had said he would give the government time to find a new home for the Indians, but his patience had run out. In just a few weeks, he would exercise his right to call in the sheriff to kick out the trespassers.

The Indians greeted the delegation with hostile stares. Lummis knew that he was in for deep trouble when Ambrosio, who had joined the commission on its fact-finding tour and gotten along well with Lummis in the past, refused to shake his hand. Still, the meeting started on a positive note. Captain Blacktooth, the only Indian who spoke, said through an interpreter, "We thank you for coming here to talk to us in a way we can understand. It is the first time anyone has done so." But he proceeded to make it clear that the Indians would not budge from their position. "You see that graveyard over there?" he said. "There are our fathers and our grandfathers. You see that Eagle-Nest Mountain and that Rabbit-Hole Mountain? When God made them, He gave us this place. We have always been here. We do not care for any other place."[11]

Speaking in Spanish, Lummis asked the members of the tribe to consider what they would do if the government couldn't buy Agua Caliente. What place would they like next best?

"If the government can't buy this place, we will go into mountains like quail and die there," Blacktooth said.

Lummis replied that if they moved to Pala, in five years they would be the envy of all the Mission Indians. But Blacktooth retorted, "We never asked for Pala, but if it is bought, it must be bought for you to use."

He said the Indians were prepared to meet their fate at Agua Caliente. "No matter if they kill us with the big cannon or tear down our houses, we will be well and die and somebody will publish that the Indians were killed for being thieves and murderers," he said. That was the treatment they had come to expect from the white man. They didn't care anymore.

The meeting deteriorated from that point. Lummis scolded the Indians for taking advice from "vagabond liars." Blacktooth accused Lummis of calling the Indians liars. Lummis apologized for having given that impression. Unassuaged, Blacktooth said Lummis had promised to help the Indians get what they wanted. Then he had proceeded to buy the property in Pala that only he wanted.

"What I said in the first place was that I thought it could not be accomplished but that I would do everything that was possible to find a way for you to keep your old homes. That was the word I gave," Lummis replied. "Like a man who has a good dog to follow a track," he had pursued every possibility that might allow them to remain at Agua Caliente. But the Supreme Court had spoken, and even the president of the United States has to obey the Supreme Court, Lummis said.

Nothing Lummis could have said would have made any difference. Blacktooth signaled to his people that the meeting was over. They all rose and walked out together.

Lummis knew then that the Indians would have to be marched out at gunpoint. They would hate him for it, and he didn't blame them. "It is not at all strange that their greatest anger is directed against me," Lummis remarked in a letter to Senator Bard a few days later. "I have told them from the first that there was no reasonable possibility in the world of their keeping their old home after the Supreme Court decision," yet "everyone else has hemmed and hawed . . . and assured them that if they only hung on everything would come out all right."

Lummis was seriously worried that the eviction could turn into a bloodbath. The best way to prevent that from happening was to call in the U.S. Army, Lummis believed. He made his case for a detachment of federal troops in several letters to Jones. The hopeless impasse at the meeting on the sixteenth confirmed his worst fear. "There are going to be some of the old people, particularly the old women—and there are some mighty stiff necked ones among them—that will at the very least sit down on the ground and refuse to move. When the evicting officers pick them up or touch them the crisis will come. . . . Gentle as they are these people can fight," Lummis warned.[12]

Deputy sheriffs wouldn't be able to handle that situation, nor would the Indians give them any respect, Lummis said. "If we send irresponsible and random Americans in overalls or hand-me-down clothes to do this office even if they were all good men, the outcome I am afraid is certain to be bloody. On the other hand, if we have twenty U.S. Regulars who wear their credentials in the blue on their backs, who need no papers, who are used to guns and to keeping their fingers off the trigger until it has to be, I believe we can still perform this difficult task without any incident which will go down into history as a sorrow and disgrace," Lummis wrote.

Lummis took pains to stress the importance of keeping the possible use of U.S. soldiers secret. Lummis told Jones that if word got out, the Indians would surely take to the mountains "and the yellow journals will have something to harp on." Lummis had already warned Jones that there was a leak in his office. "Mrs. Babbitt, who no doubt is an extraordinary liar, says she has copies of my letters to you," he wrote. "She brags of confidential connections in the Department."

233

If Lummis thought that would suffice to plug the leak, he would soon know otherwise. Before long it was common knowledge that Charles Lummis, erstwhile defender of downtrodden Indians, was advocating use of the U.S. Army to drive the Warner's Ranch tribe from their ancestral home. That would be thrown in his face for years to come.

The Los Angeles papers reported the surprising development even before Lummis had returned to Los Angeles from the disastrous trip to Agua Caliente. The *Evening Herald* ran one story April 18 which reported that the Indians, as the headline put it, would "Resist Removal to the Last." The headline of a second story in the same issue read "Lummis Threatens Force."

When Lummis got back to El Alisal the next day, three reporters were waiting for him. He declined to talk at length, explaining that he was under a tight deadline to complete his treatise on California for the *Encyclopedia Americana*. However, he did talk long enough to explain why reporters and members of the general public should butt out. "The actual removal of the Indians will be no more a place for strangers and the curious than a funeral would be." If interlopers steered clear of Agua Caliente, "every possible chance of friction, force, or hardship to the Indians will be eliminated," Lummis said.

The *Herald* took him at his word. The headline in the next day's issue read, "Expect No Trouble: Warner Indians to Be Moved Quietly." The *Evening Examiner* offered a sympathetic take on Lummis's predicament. "There is no better authority on the Mission Indians than Mr. Lummis, and there is none who has their best interests more sincerely at heart," the paper declared in an editorial. "He should have the moral support of the people of Southern California in carrying out the onerous task that lies before him."

Jones and Hitchcock weren't inclined to go out of their way to give Lummis any support. Hitchcock responded to Lummis's request for U.S. troops with a telegram that said, "I will not call on army until I have exhausted every other resource." At about the same time, Hitchcock also rebuked Lummis for continuing to refer to himself in correspondence as "Chairman of the Advisory Commission." The Warner's Ranch Commission, he pointed out, had long since ceased to exist. In his instructions to James Jenkins, the experienced U.S. Indian agent whom he had selected to supervise the removal of the Indians from

Warner's Ranch, Hitchcock said, "It is not presumed necessary for you to confer with Mr. Lummis."

Despite his public displays of friendliness toward Lummis, Jones was even more disdainful. In fact, Jones himself was the most likely source of the damaging leaks. In a letter about the Warner's Ranch situation to Herbert Welsh, head of the Indian Rights Association, Jones had written a year earlier, "While the President means well and will do what he thinks proper, I am afraid he is entirely under the influence of a man in that country by the name of Lummis."

The scornful sentiment was mutual. In a 1903 letter to Merriam, Lummis wrote: "So far as Indians go, Jones is more kinds of a damned fool than almost anyone within three doors of his official inner office, but I myself still believe that he is in business honest."[13] In 1902, prompted by rumors that Jones might be leaving office, Lummis dropped a hint in a letter to Roosevelt that either Grinnell or Merriam would make an excellent Commissioner of Indian Affairs, if the post were by chance to become vacant due to "resignation, removal or death."[14] The rumors of Jones's departure proved to be premature. He stayed in office until 1905.

In early May of 1903, with the eviction days away, Lummis took a trip that helped him forget his Warner's Ranch troubles for a while. He left Los Angeles on May 3 aboard the 7 P.M. train bound for Williams, Arizona, just east of Flagstaff. After a night in Williams, he took another train north for the short ride to the rim of the Grand Canyon. Lummis planned to rendezvous at the canyon with President Roosevelt, who was traveling with a large entourage on an extended trip through the West. Roosevelt had spent a week in Yellowstone, where he had enjoyed a mountain lion hunt, had camped in Yosemite for three nights with John Muir, and then headed for the Grand Canyon, where his train was scheduled to arrive May 6.

Lummis had exchanged letters with his friend Muir a few weeks earlier about their respective plans with the president. Lummis advised Muir to make sure he didn't let Roosevelt get him on a horse, to avoid a mishap like the one that befell their mutual friend John Burroughs, who fell off his mount while trying to keep up with the president in Yellowstone a few weeks earlier. The president evidently reveled in demonstrating his western grit by outriding any man who dared try to keep up. So Muir should "keep him afoot and guessing," and maintain a relentless pace, Lummis advised. He added that he'd like to be a "fly on a redwood stump as the procession goes by."[15]

When Roosevelt was planning his trip, Lummis had offered to show him around the pueblos of Isleta and Acoma, believing that exposure to the ancient civilization of the noble Pueblos was essential to the education of the president. Even if Roosevelt didn't have time to get off the train, Lummis wrote the president's secretary, William Loeb, "I could show him, in the quiet 400 miles from Albuquerque westward to the cañon, a good many things he would enjoy seeing even from the car window and that no one else is likely to point out." Loeb replied that regrettably there would be no room on the presidential train for Lummis on the New Mexico leg of the train ride. But the president would be pleased to have him along for the ride from the canyon back to Los Angeles.[16]

Lummis drew up an ambitious agenda for the occasion. He planned to bring Roosevelt up to date on the Warner's Ranch matter and see if he could persuade the president to overrule Hitchcock's decision not to deploy U.S. troops. He intended to discuss another Indian controversy, this one involving an agent named Charles E. Burton at the Hopi Agency in Keams Canyon, Arizona, that was heating up. Lummis also wanted to talk to the president about Jones. He had failed the previous spring to persuade the president to replace the commissioner, but he would try again. As Lummis summed up his plans in a letter to Merriam written May 2, "I am just off for the Grand Cañon loaded with bear shot for the President on the commissionership matter, Burton and the Warner's Ranch case—in which latter the Secretary of the Interior is playing tenderfoot very hard."[17]

Many of those on the eastbound train from Los Angeles were, like Lummis, headed to see the president. Among the passengers were a number of Roosevelt's Rough Riders, who tended to dog his every appearance, hoping to get a chance to shake hands with their old commander and perhaps get him to intercede in a personal matter on their behalf. Williams was filled with Rough Riders, Arizona politicians, and ordinary citizens on their way to the canyon. The throng arrived at the south rim an hour before sunset on May 5. Lummis slept in a tent that night. The next morning at nine the presidential train arrived. Roosevelt "received me with great enthusiasm," Lummis noted in his diary, written in Spanish as usual, though he lapsed into a rare English phrase: "Tells me he had eye on me."

Later that day, with Lummis standing just a few feet away, Roosevelt delivered his famous speech on the rim of the canyon. "Here is your country. Do not let anyone take it or its glory away from you!" the president thundered. "Cherish these natural wonders, cherish the natural resources, cherish the history and the romance as a sacred heritage, for your children and your children's children. Do not let selfish men or greedy interests skin your country of its beauty, its riches or its romance. The world and the future and your very children shall judge you according as you deal with this sacred trust.

"I want to ask you to do one thing in your own interest, and in the interest of the country," Roosevelt concluded. "Leave the canyon as it is! You cannot improve on it—not a bit."

It was the sort of speech that sent chills up Lummis's spine. It was credited with stopping a push to allow unfettered commercial development up to the brink of the canyon and leading to designation of the area as a national park. The sentiment embodied in the speech also suggests why Roosevelt had such a high degree of tolerance for Lummis. The eccentric editor could be annoying, but in everything he did he was putting up a good fight for the West they both loved.

Roosevelt's train left the canyon at six that evening with Lummis aboard. He rode in the presidential dining car, talking, smoking, drinking brandy, chatting with Roosevelt and a select group of dignitaries, as the train clattered across the Coconino Plateau while the sun sank into the west and stars filled the night sky. The next morning, Lummis was again invited to join the president for breakfast. Later in the day, as Lummis recalled the episode in his memoir, Roosevelt desperately wanted to ride in the locomotive, a gigantic new oil-burning model. But Secret Service agents, alarmed at the thought of the president sitting a few feet from the raging furnace and seething boiler, vetoed the idea. Roosevelt was the first president to be constantly surrounded by the Secret Service, a response to the McKinley assassination less than two years earlier, and he didn't like it a bit. Lummis helped him devise a plan to elude his protectors for a while.

At one point in the middle of the desert when the train was idling on a siding, Lummis and Roosevelt stepped outside for a breath of fresh air and eased up the track toward the front. In an instant when the agents were looking the other way, the two conspirators bolted for the loco-motive, hopped aboard, and told the conductor, who was in on the trick, to give the engine full steam. "Frantic Cabinet officers and detec-tives were running yelling for the president. But the conductor was an old-timer and bundled them aboard saying, 'Don't worry about the Old Man—he is all safe. If you don't get on you'll be left here in the desert'," Lummis recalled in his memoir. For the next leg of the trip, Roosevelt was at the controls of the locomotive. Lummis was sitting on the fire seat right behind.

The next day they reached Southern California. As the president's train entered the populated coastal region, large crowds were waiting at each stop. Stages decorated with red, white, and blue bunting had been built beside the depots at Palm Springs, San Bernardino, Riverside, Pomona, and Pasadena. At each stop Roosevelt alighted from the train, greeted the local dignitaries, shook hands with many in the crowd, and while Lummis stood nearby exhorted his audience about all of the won-drous things he had seen out west and the glorious future that he could envision for the region.

When the train reached the end of the track in Pasadena, Lummis hurried home with exciting news for Eve and Turbesé: the president had invited the whole family to join him for dinner. That evening Roo-sevelt told Eve, as Lummis noted in his diary, "I can't tell you how much I've enjoyed having your husband with me. As they say in Arkansas, I've been reading after him for years."

On the train trip with Roosevelt, Lummis had been able to forget his troubles for a few days. He hadn't noticed from his position on the stage next to Roosevelt, but far back in the crowd at the whistle stop in San Bernardino stood three sad men, reminders of the biggest con-troversy Lummis faced: Juan Maria Cibimoat, Ambrosio Ortega, and Captain Cecilio Blacktooth from Agua Caliente. When they learned that Roosevelt would stop at San Bernardino, they traveled to the train depot to request a personal meeting with the president in which they hoped they could persuade him to call off their eviction. They were "goaded by lawyers too ignorant to be aware of the fact that even the president cannot set aside the decision of the Supreme Court," Lummis later wrote. But they didn't get close to Roosevelt. The *San Diego Union* reported that they were rudely "jostled away from the president's car-riage by the crowd."

* * *

Lummis didn't intend to be anywhere near Agua Caliente on the day the removal was to take place. But he had arranged for Grant Wallace, a friendly reporter from the *San Francisco Bulletin,* and a photographer for the *Los Angeles Herald Examiner* to get through the cordon that he hoped would keep the rest of the press out. They would cover the event for *Out West.* As it turned out, the removal went far more smoothly than Lummis had feared, even though deputy sheriffs were overseeing the move.

According to Wallace, who arrived on the scene a week before the eviction, sounds of wailing filled the air every night leading up to the day of departure. On May 12 the Indians visited the graveyard of their ancestors one last time and prayed in the chapel. Later that day Wallace encountered a woman tossing textbooks from the village school into a fire. She explained that "now they hated the white people and their religion and their books," Wallace wrote. The next day twenty-five families quietly left the village headed for Pala in light wagons, going ahead of the heavy wagon train that would carry the rest of the tribe and their belongings.

During their first night on the trail to Pala, the Indians refused rations. They had never taken handouts from the government before and didn't want to start now. On their second night, however, they relented and accepted a steer, which they slaughtered, cooked, and ate. Upon arrival in Pala, the valley was "a house of tears," Wallace wrote. On their first Sunday in the valley, the Indians refused to worship at the newly restored chapel. "What kind of God is this you ask us to worship who deserts us when we need him most?" one of the Indians asked the priest. The next morning, however, "dusky children, who will compare favorably in intelligence with average white youngsters," showed up for school. In a particularly poignant and ironic moment, Wallace noted, they began the day by standing at attention before the Stars and Stripes and singing "America—Sweet Land of Liberty."[18]

It was sheer luck that soldiers hadn't been needed, Lummis wrote in his postmortem on the removal. But he was especially disturbed that the worst agitators, Brown and Lawson, had played a key role that day, and now were getting credit for the peaceful transfer. Having reassessed their situation, Brown and Lawson had apparently decided at the last minute that if the removal was going to happen, they had better be involved in it. Agent Jenkins had recognized that they held sway over the Indians and asked them to intercede on his behalf. They had instructed the Indians to go peacefully. Now Lawson and Brown were ensconced in Pala.

In a May 30 letter to Jones, Lummis said he did not mean to denigrate Jenkins's success by criticizing his use of Lawson and Brown. But "many people feel that it was rather undignified business for the Government to lean on these discredited persons." He was even more troubled about "these two scoundrels being allowed to remain at Pala." Lummis learned that Lawson had become a "squaw man," marrying a woman in the tribe to gain membership and permanent residency among the Indians, and was now "trying to get appointed Special Agent over these people." Brown and Lawson could still make plenty of mischief.[19]

That unfortunate postscript aside, Lummis always regarded the entire Warner's Ranch affair as a major success story. He maintained that the removal to Pala was the "first time in United States history when Indians were moved to better lands and more lands than they had before."

That might be true, but the Agua Caliente Indians themselves never saw it that way. The early years in Pala were especially hard on them. There were many nagging little problems as the Indians tried to adjust to a radically different style of life from that they had enjoyed around the hot spring, and they weren't in a frame of mind to tolerate the problems. It didn't help that Brown and Lawson had remained in their midst, rallying the Indians behind one attempt at redress after another.

A couple of decades later, the 1925 edition of the Rider's guide to California suggested that the episode had taken a decidedly less flattering place in the state's history than Lummis had hoped. In a passage about the Pala Valley, the travel guide for motorists observed of the removal of the Indians to the reservation, "more than one rider has stigmatized it as the 'crowning crime against the California Indians'."

Another half century later, a reporter for the *San Diego Tribune* went to Pala to interview eighty-five-year-old Roscinda Nolasquez, the last surviving member of the tribe who remembered that dark day of May 13, 1902, when the Indians were forced to leave their old home. Lummis's name still brought back bitter memories, the reporter found. A young child at the time of the removal, Nolasquez didn't have a clear picture of the man himself. But she recalled that her sister had named a bull calf

Charles Lummis. The impression she left with the reporter was that it hadn't been a cherished family pet.

Lummis never did blame the Indians for hating him. They had good reason not to trust any white man, he said. But Lummis received a much more bitter pill to swallow from that difficult episode in his career: the utter lack of credit and respect from the Department of Interior and Bureau of Indian Affairs for what he had accomplished.

The bureaucracy in Washington demonstrated its disdain for Lummis in several ways. A couple of months after the Warner's Ranch Commission completed its wagon trip in search of a new home for the Indians, Lummis was notified that a Treasury Department auditor had rejected a few items on his expense report. Lummis regarded that as an insult, given that the commission had worked free of charge and its expense total of $1,107.96 was exceedingly modest. The officials in the Department of the Interior undoubtedly had a different perspective. They would have seen the minor furor that ensued as yet another indication that Lummis was a major nuisance. He easily could have lumped the rejected items into a category called "miscellaneous supplies" or "provisions." But Lummis insisted on identifying the items on his expense report as exactly what they were: 1 case of Germain Wine Co. wine, 1 gallon of whisky, 2 gallons McKin & Chambers claret, 1 gallon zinfandel, 200 Barman Bros. cigars, and another 100 miscellaneous cigars. The total cost of these items came to $22.70.

Lummis wasn't about to accept the government's refusal to reimburse him without a fight. The modest amount at stake wasn't exactly small change for Lummis. But it was the principle of the matter more than the sum involved that led him to pursue the issue with the same determination that had characterized his search for a new home for the Indians. Lummis pleaded his case in a series of long letters to officials in Washington. A few gallons of alcoholic refreshment and three hundred cigars were hardly extravagant for a commission that had worked so hard for no recompense, he insisted in a letter to Senator Bard in December 1902. "Considering that this was a party of twelve persons for a month's trip away from stores and supplies, working very hard and very long hours, I felt we had reason to be proud of our moderation," he insisted. "I think it would have required a much larger amount of stimulants to keep a treasury clerk up to the work we did for a week."[20]

241

Three months later, the bill still unpaid, Lummis had elaborated on this line of argument. "In a strenuous trip of this sort not only are stimulants needful to be taken along—as an economic measure they save the government three times their cost, at least as 'lubricants' in dealing with the large number of people of many classes with whom we had to do business," he argued in a letter to Jones in March 1903. They were "no Havana cigars but decent little '5-centers'; no imported wines, nor even the fine California vintages, but just modest, good table wines for the menu of overworked men in the desert."[21]

In June Lummis still hadn't been reimbursed and he was paying interest on the $22.70 to the bank that had advanced him the money. But he hadn't given up. He had one last card to play. In a long letter to President Roosevelt dated June 3, a few weeks after the train ride from the Grand Canyon, Lummis thanked the president for the hospitality and for his kindness to Eve and Turbesé, recapped the remarkable accomplishments of the Warner's Ranch Commission, and ended with a plea for help with the unpaid liquor and cigar bill. The president had plenty of other things on his mind at the time, such as an increasingly tense situation in Panama and Colombia. But his personal assistant responded promptly that the president would do what he could to fulfill Lummis's wishes. Two weeks later, the Treasury Department notified Lummis that his expense report would be honored after all.

That left just one issue unsettled, the matter of Lummis's suggestion about how to spend the amount of the congressional appropriation that the commission had saved in its shrewd purchase of the Pala property. The eight modest parcels of land that Lummis had identified and that could be purchased for the $23,770 in savings were still available. But given the passage of time, the deals might have to be renegotiated. Lummis volunteered his time and energy once again to handle all the details himself. All he said he needed was a formal designation from the Department of the Interior giving him official status, which he would need to cut through any red tape that might block his path.

He made a pitch for a new commission in his June 3 letter to Roosevelt. "I want no feathers nor titles . . . just fair tools to work with. I can take a jack knife and a cobble stone and do more work and better work than some people with a full kit of tools; but I don't want to be robbed of my jack knife and I would like a hammer and a saw," Lummis said. The president passed that suggestion over to the Department of the

Interior, where it is safe to say there was no enthusiasm whatsoever for the idea. But it is a testament to the clout that Lummis still wielded with the commander in chief that Jones, in a June 23 letter to the president, was exceedingly careful about voicing his objections.

The Warner's Ranch Commission "deserves a great deal of credit," he began. But as for Lummis's request to be appointed as an unpaid commissioner on behalf of the Mission Indians, Jones noted, "there is not a position now vacant that I can recall to which he can be appointed." Jones concluded, "I would be very glad, personally, to see Mr. Lummis recognized, but at present I do not see how this can be done officially."[22]

Lummis's hopes of becoming a volunteer roving commissioner for the Mission Indians died. As for his request to spend the money saved on other land purchases, word eventually came to Lummis through bureaucratic channels that the department's lawyers had rejected the idea. The appropriation from Congress specified that the funds were for the sole purpose of finding a new home for the Agua Caliente Indians.

As if to add insult to injury, the Department of the Interior went on to inform Lummis that there was no longer any surplus left. It had been used up by the department for the costs it had incurred in overseeing the work of the Warner's Ranch Commission. Lummis fired off a few angry letters demanding a congressional investigation, but he got no response and, having a number of other problems on his hands by that point, let it drop.

Chapter *11*

The Tyrant of Keams Canyon

When Lummis was in the thick of the Warner's Ranch fray, he had so many other projects under way that it was inevitable he would make errors of judgment and careless mistakes. He admitted as much in a correction in the March 1903 issue of *Out West*. In the previous month's edition, the magazine had identified a certain Sanskrit scholar as a professor at Yale and a certain geologist as a professor at Harvard, getting the schools reversed. "This stumble perhaps shows the danger of a not very long-legged mind trying to ride at once, or in the same day, such an unmatched span as Sanskrit and Geology going in opposite directions," Lummis remarked.

If he had been capable of heeding such a warning and had started cutting back on his commitments and slowing his frenetic pace, he could have spared himself some grief later on. The little mistakes were relatively harmless, but the reckless tactical blunders he would commit did heavier damage. The next Indian rights fight that Lummis plunged into under the auspices of the Sequoya League was a case in point.

The seeds of the controversy were sown in the first weeks of the Sequoya League's existence, in January 1902, with an unsigned directive from the Department of the Interior's Bureau of Indian Affairs that was mailed to all Indian agents in the United States. The order on Indian Bureau stationery was signed "commissioner," which presumably meant it had come from Jones himself.[1] Though there would later be some equivocation about what it meant, it seemed perfectly clear at the time.

"This office desires to call your attention to a few customs among the Indians which, it is believed, should be modified or discontinued," the order stated. "The wearing of long hair by the male population of your agency is not in keeping with the advancement they are making, or will soon be expected to make, in civilization. The wearing of short hair by the males will be a great step in advance and will surely hasten their progress toward civilization. . . . You are therefore directed to induce your male Indians to cut their hair and both sexes to stop painting."

The ban on face painting was necessary because when Indians perspired, the order explained, the paint ran into their eyes and caused eye disease. Indian costumes, blankets, Indian dances, and "so-called Indian feasts" that were really subterfuges to disguise immoral revelry also had to end. In the bureau's view, it was especially objectionable that "returned" Indians, who had come back to their reservations after lengthy and costly training at boarding schools, often reverted to disgusting habits that their "education in our industrial schools has tried to eradicate." Their training couldn't be faulted, the order observed. It was the licentious reservation environment that was to blame. So that environment had to be changed.

Some Indians were likely to comply readily with the order, the document from the Indian Bureau asserted. For others, coercion might be necessary. "The returned students who do not comply voluntarily should be dealt with summarily," the order stated. "Employment, supplies, etc., should be withdrawn until they do comply and if they become obstreperous about the matter a short confinement in the guard-house at hard labor, with shorn locks, should furnish a cure." The statement concluded by instructing Indian agents to submit a progress report by June 30.

For many Indian agents, frustrated that their charges still looked and acted so uncivilized, which made them seem all the more ungrateful for the U.S. government aid they were getting, the order was a welcome green light to take action. They eagerly started rounding up every Indian man they could find, at gunpoint if necessary, and hacking off their locks if the men refused to do the deed themselves.

The order drew howls of derision from most of the nation's press. Lummis was in the forefront of the attack. At first he was inclined to believe that the order was a hoax. He had enjoyed several fine visits with Jones and Hitchcock just a couple of months earlier on his trip to

245

Washington. And though they didn't pretend to know much about Indians, they had seemed fair-minded. Maybe an ignorant underling in the Indian Bureau had issued the order, he thought. When he learned that in fact it had come from the top, he unsheathed his acid pen and commenced his attack. If the Indian Bureau was serious about enforcing the order, then first the U.S. government would have to bring back the 60,000 troops who were then tied down in a nasty guerrilla war in the Philippines, he asserted. "We have not enough soldiers in the United States now to kill off all the Indians who object to being 'civilized' by spitting in their faces," Lummis explained. "What would you think of a law compelling every voter to shave his face smooth every day? Or to have his hair clipped once a month. Or to wear cutaway coats and creased trousers? If there were such a law passed, you and I, who wear our hair short, would be first to rebel against it."

To be sure, the bureau had its defenders. *Leslie's Weekly* of New York ran an editorial praising not only the haircut order but a parallel campaign by the bureau to "abolish the uncouth and grotesque names which Indians are wont to attach to themselves." But overall, the outcry against the order was so widespread and vehement that the bureau was forced to retreat, at least a half step. A new letter was sent to all Indian agents insisting that the order had been willfully misconstrued by the critics and that it was "simply a declaration of the policy of this Office" meant to be implemented gradually, "using tact, judgment and perseverance." But the new missive concluded on a defiant note: "This letter does not constitute a withdrawal or revocation" of the original order.

That clarification didn't mollify Lummis. By the end of 1902, while a resolution of the Warner's Ranch affair was still up in the air, the Sequoya League launched its second initiative, a campaign against the haircut order and several agents who had brutally implemented it.

At the time, Lummis had a number of other daunting responsibilities.

The Landmarks Club was in the middle of its most ambitious project yet, the reconstruction of the tile roof at the San Juan Capistrano Mission. To raise additional funding for the restorations, Lummis had compiled a book of Spanish American recipes called *The Landmarks Club Cookbook*, which went on sale that summer for $1.50 a copy. Lummis contributed forty-three recipes of the several hundred in the book, including ones for Peruvian stuffed peppers, stewed jackrabbit, fried bananas, and "drunken pigeons," a concoction of pigeon, toasted tomatoes, citron, and raisins. He also wrote an idiosyncratic essay about the necessity of eating foods suited to the local climate, a lesson he had learned in his rambles through Spanish America. "It is a stupid traveler who mocks the ancient wisdom of the country as to what in that country should be eaten," Lummis asserted. Potatoes, corn, chocolate, cocoa, tapioca, lima beans, and peanuts were some of the indigenous foods of Spanish America that a prudent resident of that region could safely eat. But one ingredient above all others was a necessity: chiles. "Most Americans do not at first flush like dishes in which it predominates; but it is an easily acquired taste—and once learned, there is nothing of which one becomes fonder than a good concoction of chiles," said Lummis, speaking from personal experience. "It is one of the most healthful condiments in the world, and almost a hygienic necessity in California and other non-humid lands."

In 1903 Lummis launched yet another civic association that would absorb an increasing share of his time and energy in the years to come. The impetus was a visit to El Alisal in September by Professor Martin D'ooge, a University of Michigan archaeologist and officer of the Archaeological Institute of America. He suggested that Lummis should start a Los Angeles chapter of the AIA. The Boston-based institute had tried to launch western chapters in the past but had never succeeded. Lummis didn't need any more encouragement than that. In his second issue of the *Land of Sunshine* he had remarked that Los Angeles needed a museum to commemorate the region's ancient cultural heritage. A local chapter of the AIA would be the perfect sponsor for such an institution. Within a couple of months, he had rounded up an impressive list of prominent, wealthy civic leaders who had agreed to serve as founding members of a group that would be called the Southwest Society. The group was granted a charter as an official chapter of the AIA, and within two years, plans for the Southwest Museum were well under way.

Back at El Alisal, construction on new rooms to add to those that had already been completed was in full swing. Lummis spent hours each day setting boulders into place, pouring cement, and hewing beams and planks for floors, ceilings, doors, and window frames, in addition to his eight or ten or twelve hours spent on magazine and association work. As if his schedule wasn't full enough, he had started to learn the guitar and spent anywhere from thirty minutes to a couple of hours a day practicing, carefully logging in his diary the time spent. After dinner every night, Lummis set aside another small block of time for "toco y canto"—playing and singing.

He thought these sessions would promote family togetherness of a sort that he had experienced with the Chaveses in San Mateo and the del Valles in Camulos. But the members of his own family had a different perspective on life at El Alisal. "He had forgotten that the del Valles and the Chaveses sang because they were happy," Turbesé observed in the book she and her brother Keith wrote. "There we sat like members of a chain gang, contributing only a grudging mumble, waiting to be set free. . . . It is painful to remember now how we begrudged him even the short half hour of companionship with us he had to spare before the night work took him."

As for Eve, there were indications in 1902 that her patience with her husband of eleven years was wearing thin. She spent Christmas that year with Phoebe Hearst in Berkeley, explaining in a letter in early December that she had no intention of being anywhere near the festivities at El Alisal. "I do not grudge you your relaxation," she wrote. But she added, referring to Amado's death two years earlier, "I do not like to celebrate that terrible anniversary with a noisy crowd." She had put up with his obsessive socializing for years, but had had enough of it. "I do not know of any other woman who would so continuously surround you with women you care for, working hard herself to do it, and getting for herself very little courteous attention," she wrote. "I have not the strength to cook for the crowd."

Eve had also begun to lose patience with her husband's string of secretaries. One in particular, Gertrude Redit, a young Englishwoman who started working for Lummis in 1903, was a thorn in Eve's side almost from the start, treating Eve like a nonentity in her own home. It is probably no coincidence, therefore, that in the summer of 1903, when Redit began spending many hours every day with Lummis, the "cielo" entries in his diary became fewer and farther between. By the end of the year, his diary each day often ended with the forlorn notation "Duermo con Eve sin nada"—I went to bed with Eve but nothing.

At about that time, Lummis began keeping a detailed tally in his diary of something else that was becoming an obsession. "Juisque," he would write, using an old Spanish term for whisky, or "muchisimo juisque," a lot of whisky. The care with which he began to record what he drank, how much, and at what time of day suggests that he realized it could become a problem, or perhaps already was. But the drinking, which usually began after eight or nine at night, obviously gave him a second wind. His workday often wouldn't end until 4 or 5 A.M.

It never occurred to him that it might be the staggering workload he imposed on himself that was driving him to drink. He never let up the pace of work; if anything, he was always looking for more to do. In his office, his antidote for the workload that overwhelmed one desk was to install a second one facing the first, with a swivel chair in between, which allowed him to switch from one project to the other with a quick half turn of the chair. Physical infirmities were the only thing that ever slowed him down.

He had a variety of well-developed rationalizations for his workaholism. The hours of hard manual labor were therapeutic. Having so many different projects going at any one time was also helpful, he insisted. If he began to bog down on one, he would switch to another, working deliberately, not frantically, but never letting up. "It is tension not work that tires," he explained. "I learned in the hard school of paralysis to go slow; not to hurry and not to worry. Indeed, I have made it my gospel, so much so that even though I kept presses waiting, and the wolves of the office were howling, I would never allow myself to be rushed or to feel that I was being pursued."

Nor did he ever allow himself to take a break and do nothing at all. "No labor union would ever admit me," he once proudly asserted. "They would have nothing to do with a man who is willing and glad to work twenty hours a day."

The Indian Bureau's haircut order landed on Lummis's agenda while he was still mired in the Warner's Ranch matter, not to mention his many other projects. But he couldn't ignore the story he heard first from Adam Clark Vroman, the Pasadena photographer who lived a few miles from El Alisal. Vroman had friends on the Hopi reservation near Keams Canyon, Arizona, where he had spent time in 1901 photographing the ancient pueblos perched on rocky bluffs high above a vast plain. They passed on word that Charles E. Burton, head of the Navajo and Hopi agency based in Keams Canyon, had been exceedingly zealous in carrying out the order.[2] Within days of receiving the directive from

Washington to rid Indian men of their long locks, Burton and his employees had swung into action. Before long, they were using whips, guns, and sheep shears to get the job done.

In June of 1902, Lummis persuaded the executive committee of the Sequoya League to authorize an investigation of the situation at Keams Canyon. The league would need to gather solid facts before it could press for Burton's ouster, and Lummis knew someone who would soon be perfectly situated for that task. She was Gertrude Lewis Gates, wife of Peter Goddard Gates, one of the nation's leading lumber barons— until he had retired a couple of years earlier at the age of forty-five to become a philanthropist and to dabble in archaeology. The Gateses lived for most of the year in Pasadena. But they had spent the summers of 1900 and 1901 camping in the clear, dry air of Keams Canyon, where he did some excavating and she sought relief from respiratory ailments. She planned to return in July of 1902 by herself. She hoped to benefit once again from the climate, but this time she also had another mission. Gertrude Gates had developed an interest in the Hopis, and as she informed Burton by mail, she looked forward to "studying the domestic life of the Indians."

The Gateses had enjoyed cordial relations with Burton in the past, so he wrote to welcome her back. Since she would be returning without her husband, he offered to send someone to meet her at the railway depot in Holbrook sixty miles away and escort her to the reservation. Lummis got to her shortly before she left Los Angeles. He told her what he had learned about Burton and persuaded her to accept an assignment as a special agent of the Sequoya League to gather information about the Indian agent's reign over the Hopis.

Gertrude Gates wasn't completely comfortable with the element of deception in her return to Keams Canyon. Burton thought Gates was there for her health, and secondarily to study Indian family life. He wouldn't learn until sometime later that she was also on a mission to investigate him. Her sister sought to assuage her guilt by pointing out in a letter that since the satisfaction she would gain from helping oppressed Indians would be good for her health, she was arguably still acting within the scope of the stated purpose of her trip.[3] In any event, she ardently carried out her assignment for the league.

Gates reached the Hopi reservation on July 5. Burton and agency officials greeted her warmly. They must have wondered about her behavior, but they didn't stop her from setting up her camp on the promontory called Third Mesa just a hundred yards from the edge of Oraibi, an ancient pueblo that had been continuously occupied for more than eight hundred years and at the time was home to nearly two thousand Hopi Indians. Gates lived there in a tent for the next five months. When she returned to Los Angeles in November, she had an explosive story to tell the Sequoya League. She presented her findings to the league on December 3 in a twenty-four-page report backed up with seventy-one pages of supplements and affidavits.

Opinions of Burton himself were mixed, Gates reported. He was "not altogether bad," but his "weakness of character and limited mentality have worked to his moral undoing," she wrote. His worst fault was his failure to curb the unredeemably evil conduct of several sadistic employees. The most damning evidence that Gates collected concerned a teacher at the Oraibi day school named Herman Kampmeier. Both he and Burton "act upon the assumption that 'all Indians are liars', 'are unreliable', and 'should be made to do what we think best for them'," she wrote. But Kampmeier went far beyond that. Even the "progressive" faction among the Hopis, a group known in the Indian Service parlance as the Friendlies, agreed with the traditionalists, known as the Hostiles, that Kampmeier had to go.

He regularly patrolled the village in search of truants and children wearing native dress, which Kampmeier and Burton condemned even when the students were at home. "This is his fourth year as Teacher there, and he is still 'hunting' 'scared rabbits' (children) with armed policemen, having habitually hunted them himself with pistol or gun, and so intimidated the entire village that men, women and children run trembling at his approach, some of the children screaming in terror," Gates wrote. "He has battered in doors and destroyed property, and terrified the people by abusive language, kicks, blows, and pistol and gun shots, frequently going at night to make his attacks, all in the name of Progress!"

Corporal punishment at Indian schools had been officially banned by an Indian Service regulation adopted a few years earlier. But Gates documented numerous instances in which Kampmeier and other teachers, and even Burton himself, had beaten children and their parents with leather straps and the butts of guns. In Oraibi several children were lame from the punishment meted out by Kampmeier, and one child had died of injuries and fright inflicted by the sadistic teacher, Gates reported. He showed no mercy when parents complained. On one occasion, when Kampmeier was dragging a child away kicking and screaming, the child's father tried to intervene but was overpowered by the teacher, who tied the father's hands with baling wire and had his hair hacked off close to the head.

The supplements to Gates's report included thirteen pages detailing instances of whippings, with dates, names of witnesses, and the exact circumstances of each case. A twenty-seven-page supplement described exactly how Burton had implemented the haircut order. And a thirty-one-page appendix entitled "Indians' Accounts of Herman Kampmeier's Acts" contained affidavits and letters from many of his victims.

Gates was a regular visitor to El Alisal in the months after she presented her report to the Sequoya League, as she and Lummis and others plotted their next step. Meanwhile Lummis sent out letters to many of the people he knew in ethnology and anthropology circles seeking further information on Burton. The effort produced a few mildly interesting leads. McGee, of the Bureau of American Ethnology and a Sequoya League advisory committee member, wrote back to say that he knew of two researchers who had "had trouble with him" and considered him "not merely arbitrary but hypocritical, if not worse."[4]

Lummis also began writing in *Out West* about the scandalous situation at Keams Canyon as disclosed by the Sequoya League's in-depth investigation. The publicity helped stir up more evidence against Burton and his employees. A former teacher at the agency named Belle Axtell Kolp, for one, sent an affidavit to the Sequoya League explaining that she had resigned to protest the cruel methods employed on Hopi children by another official at the agency, John Ballinger.

Burton had learned that Gates was up to no good while she was still encamped at Oraibi. He initiated a campaign to discredit her even before she completed her report about him. In a letter to her shortly before she returned to Los Angeles, he accused her of interfering with his effort to civilize the Hopis. He charged that she had encouraged them to skip work at the agency in order to attend pagan ceremonies. He had received shocking reports that she had actually joined in some of the dances, Burton added. Gates replied that in fact she had encouraged the Indians to avoid dancing on Sundays, except in the rare instance when the sun's position in the sky on a particular Sunday compelled them to hold a ceremony. But she wasn't ashamed to admit that she had participated in rehearsals for the Wu-ha-co-fo-licht dance. It was "a decorously conducted and perfectly innocent ceremony, partly social, partly religious in nature," she said.[5]

Several weeks before Gates filed her report with the Sequoya League, Burton received reassurance that the charges, whatever they might be, wouldn't stick. "I will protect you to the fullest extent of my ability," Jones told Burton in November. "I do not have much fear that the league or any one else will succeed in doing you any harm."[6]

Jones immediately realized that Gertrude Gates was the least of Burton's worries. He knew the bureau would soon find itself in yet another battle with Charles Fletcher Lummis. In late 1902 he began sending out feelers in all directions in a search for damaging information about Lummis. He had heard rumors that Lummis had committed sexual indiscretions while he was living in Isleta. He sent discreet inquiries to a number of people, including the incumbent superintendent of the Albuquerque Indian School, to find out more. All he learned was that indeed there had been rumors to that effect.

Samuel Brosius, an official of the Indian Rights Association, with which Lummis had maintained an uneasy alliance through the years, wrote Jones the following June to say that he, too, had heard about Lummis's "unenviable record" at Isleta. Brosius also passed on another salacious tidbit that Jones undoubtedly had already heard from others. In the course of divorcing his first wife and marrying his second, Lummis and the two women had engaged in "a sort of free-love affair," Brosius said. Referring to the Warner's Ranch eviction that had taken place a few weeks before he wrote, Brosius added that he intended to spread word far and wide that Lummis had called for the U.S. Army to evict the Indians by force. "This will come out against him, and show that he is a fake and his paper not to be relied upon," Brosius remarked.

Lummis and the Sequoya League formally launched their attack on Burton in early 1903 by calling for an official investigation of the charges in Gates's report. The Indian Bureau obliged, looked into Gates's allegation, and found that Kampmeier had been guilty of improper conduct. But he had been properly reprimanded by Burton, who was cleared of all of the charges leveled against him.

The exoneration of Burton in the bureau's internal investigation didn't deter Lummis. In the June 1903 issue of *Out West* he unleashed his first barrage, a lengthy article illustrated with sixteen of Vroman's stunning photographs. It was entitled "Bullying the 'Quaker Indians'." The first in a series of articles, it recounted the history of the tribe—more commonly but incorrectly called the Moquis in those days—from the time of the first contact with Europeans. They were among the most peaceful Indians on the continent, Lummis wrote, hence his name for them in the title of the article. Even the supposedly ruthless Spaniards of the seventeenth century had treated them with greater kindness and respect than had the Americans in the twentieth century, Lummis asserted. He cited a decree issued by the king of Spain in 1621 to prove his point. In it, the king rebuked Spanish colonial officials who had ordered the Indians of the Southwest to cut their hair, which "is for them the greatest insult possible" and must be stopped, the king declared. "It was not until 280 years later that anyone foolish enough to think to barber people forcibly as a Means of Grace had authority upon any portion of the North American continent," Lummis wrote. The hair-cutting order was the latest in a long line of "brutal and stupid laws," "doddering policies," and other assorted "indignities and oppressions" that had been inflicted on the Hopis by Burton and other U.S. government officials.

Lummis's articles in *Out West* were a powerful card to play in his campaign against Burton. But the ace up Lummis's sleeve was President Roosevelt. A few weeks before the June issue of the magazine, carrying the first "Bullying the 'Quaker Indians'" story, went to press, Lummis met the president at the Grand Canyon. On the train ride back to Los Angeles, he gave Roosevelt an earful about Burton, and an advance copy of the article.

Roosevelt passed it on to Hitchcock on May 9, the day after Lummis had disembarked from the presidential train in Pasadena. "Please take this up at once and go over it with me Wednesday or Thursday," Roosevelt instructed the secretary of the interior. "I think Burton should be removed immediately."[7]

Lummis unleashed his second salvo in the July *Out West.* Part two of the series zeroed in on the recent conduct of "pin-head" Burton himself. The article featured the lengthy affidavit from the former teacher Belle Kolp about the cruel tactics used by Burton and Ballinger to enforce attendance at the government schools on the reservation. The Sequoya League had far more where that came from, having amassed "overwhelming evidence" against Burton and his employees. "It is a 'dead open-and-shut case,' and the league will press it until it finds the remedy," Lummis declared.

Despite the president's own preliminary concurrence in Lummis's verdict, Burton got a reprieve. In lieu of firing the agent outright, the Department of the Interior consented to giving the Sequoya League a government mandate to conduct its own investigation of the agent. Given that the department had already cleared Burton of any wrongdoing, it was an extraordinary concession to the league, and a sign of its clout. As much as Hitchcock and Jones had come to loathe Lummis, they had to grit their teeth and let him have his way that summer.

A two-man commission would travel to the Hopi reservation in August to look once again into the charges that had been leveled against Burton and his employees in Mrs. Gates's reports. The department would select one member of the commission from among the ranks of U.S. Indian inspectors but would give the Sequoya League the right to veto the choice. The second person on the commission would be a member of the league itself.

The league readily concurred in the department's selection of Jenkins, who had successfully supervised the removal of the Agua Caliente Indians to Pala a couple of months earlier. Jenkins was familiar with the Sequoya League and the work done under league auspices to resolve the Warner's Ranch matter. Lummis had praised the agent's handling of the removal in his recent communications with the government. So he had good reason to assume Jenkins would give the league's charges against Burton a fair hearing.

Lummis had a harder time recruiting a league representative to participate in the investigation. Both Grinnell and Merriam turned down his plea for one of them to take the assignment. They couldn't spare the time to travel from the East Coast all the way out to Arizona. Several other veterans of western Indian rights battles also declined the job. Lummis himself never considered going, perhaps realizing that his strident attacks on Burton in print would call his objectivity into question. Lummis ultimately had no choice but to send Charles Moody, the assistant editor of *Out West*. He had never tangled with the Indian Bureau before, but the case against Burton was so overwhelming that Lummis wasn't worried about the outcome. On July 23 Lummis had a long talk with Moody about the charges against Burton. Moody left for Arizona the next day.

In Los Angeles, Lummis was back to running the magazine single-handed while Moody was away. He was also preoccupied with some major construction and maintenance projects at El Alisal, including expending the better part of a couple of days trying to fix a malfunctioning septic tank. He spent hours every day that July working with his new secretary, Gertrude Redit, on his card catalog, a massive collection of facts about Spain's role in the New World that he hoped one day to publish as his magnum opus, a multivolume encyclopedia of Spanish America. Then there was the usual whirl of social engagements. On July 27, his old Camulos flame Susie del Valle came by El Alisal with her aunt, an occasion for a big Spanish dinner and a longer stint of "toco y canto" than usual. The next night, Lummis joined Susie and her aunt at the aunt's house for more of the same. During those busy days, Lummis found time to take his guitar downtown to a music shop where he traded his eighteen-dollar model for a better thirty-dollar instrument. He had so many other things to think about that he gave only passing consideration on July 31 to Moody's first letter from Keams Canyon.

It might have behooved him to pay closer attention to the tone of the letter. Moody remarked that Jenkins was a fine man whom he greatly respected and that Burton, too, had seemed nice enough. He had greeted the two investigators cordially when they reached the reservation, assuring the two men that they would have unfettered access to every part of the reservation without any interference from him. Moody had been impressed and was even more amazed by how happy the Indians seemed.

Moody and Jenkins planned to spend a day or two in each of the three villages on the three mesas before returning to Keams Canyon for a final set of hearings in which they would get Burton's official response to their findings. The ancient-looking adobe villages perched on rocky bluffs were the most exotic sights Moody had ever seen.

In the hearings that Moody and Jenkins convened, a few of the witnesses mentioned several instances of questionable conduct by agency officials and infractions of a few rules. But almost everyone who testified insisted that they were very happy on the reservation. They liked the government schools and were fond of Burton. Moody didn't detect any hint of the "reign of terror" that his own magazine had so vividly described. While *Out West* had asserted that the Hopis cringed in fear when Burton showed up, Moody had observed Indians running to greet him. The series of hearings had barely begun before Moody started apologizing for the harsh and obviously false charges that his magazine had published. He was utterly embarrassed, he repeatedly stated. He couldn't get over how his magazine had gotten the story so wrong.

He wasn't attempting to absolve himself entirely of blame for the fiasco. But it was clear where he thought most of the responsibility lay: with Mrs. Gates. *Out West* and the Sequoya League had been very poorly served by her, he concluded. He was confident, he said in the hearings at Keams Canyon, that his magazine would retract what it had said about Burton and would publish an effusive apology.

Before Moody and Jenkins parted company at Keams Canyon, Jenkins drafted a report on their findings criticizing Kampmeier for a single incident in which he had used unduly harsh corporal punishment. The draft report also gently chastised Burton for being well-meaning but a bit overzealous in implementing the haircut order. Otherwise, the report fully exonerated the agent of all of the Sequoya League's charges. "Instead of a 'reign of terror,' we found a most quiet, peaceable, harmonious, happy 'reign of contentment'," he wrote. The entire controversy, Jenkins implied, had sprung from the overheated imagination of Mrs. Gates, "a no-doubt well-meaning woman of a sentimental turn of mind" whose "methods of procedure were peculiar, to say the least." She had no complaints about Burton, Jenkins observed, "until she got to participating in objectionable Indian dances and was prevented from further dancing by an order from Mr. Burton." Burton could not be faulted for that. As the Sequoya League's own representative had agreed, Jenkins wrote, the dances "are not of proper character for a woman to take part in."

Moody told Lummis about the collapse of the Sequoya League's case against Burton in a second letter dated August 4.[8] It reached Los Angeles three days later, at about the same time that the August issue of *Out West* hit the streets. Moody couldn't have known what Lummis had written in his Lion's Den column, since Lummis didn't finish the issue until after Moody left for Arizona. So he had no idea that he had put his boss in an exceedingly awkward spot.

In the August issue Lummis noted that as the magazine's readers received their copies, the investigation of Burton was under way. Lummis wrote, "The League has tried to be gentle to Burton, believing him to be a man who meant well, but who had a great deal of fault to find with his Creator for his mental equipment." Lummis scoffed at Burton's explanation that he had never forced all the Hopis to cut their hair, but had merely asked those who had jobs with the agency to adopt a hairstyle like that of the white employees. "White employees can wear their hair anyhow they Blooming Please," Lummis noted. In general, he concluded, Burton had shown himself to be, as the *New York Sun* had recently observed, "an unbaked barbarian."

Considering the weight of evidence that the Sequoya League had amassed over the course of a year and the competence of the members of the investigating team, "there is no reasonable doubt of the outcome," Lummis proclaimed.

Effectively announcing the results of the investigation in the August issue of *Out West* before the investigation was completed was a blunder from which it would take Lummis years to recover. Even those bureaucrats who had tolerated Lummis, and lent him grudging support, now had good cause to write him off. Besides being too quick on the trigger, Lummis also erred by carelessly distorting the case that Gates had carefully made in her report. She had been very careful to assign all of the blame for the most serious acts of violence against the Hopis to Kampmeier. Burton was guilty of poor oversight and had owned up to meting out an occasional whipping on an unruly student. But Gates hadn't placed him anywhere near Oraibi when Kampmeier had inflicted his sadistic punishments on the people. On the other hand, in Lummis's magazine articles, ostensibly based on Gates's report, Burton was fully engaged in almost every facet of the "reign of terror" on the reservation.

Moody, of course, also shared a large part of the blame for botching the Keams Canyon investigation. It apparently never crossed his mind while he was on the reservation that if the Indians really were terrorized, they wouldn't have said so in a public forum to an investigator who would be gone in a few days. Lummis surely was tempted to unleash his wrath on Moody when he returned to Los Angeles. But his diary doesn't offer any hint of a harsh exchange with the assistant editor who had put him in such an embarrassing spot. Not unlike Burton, he may have surmised that it would be more productive to use gentle suasion.

Back in Los Angeles on August 11, Moody came directly to El Alisal. Lummis's housekeeper Alice made a Spanish dinner for the occasion. Lummis and Moody held extensive discussions about Burton over the next several days. By August 19, when Moody came by El Alisal to drop off a copy of his final report on his investigation for Lummis to edit, he had a dramatically different point of view from the one he had publicly expressed during the hearings at Keams Canyon.

Jenkins, whom Moody had so admired, was the first person to whom he wrote about his change of heart. "It makes me actually sick at the stomach to think of the feelings of Burton and his wife," who believed the matter had been happily settled, Moody said.[9] But he had concluded upon further reflection that Burton wasn't entirely free of blame, and that the Sequoya League's charges, while overblown in a number of minor respects, weren't completely groundless, after all. The harmony he had observed among Burton's employees, their obvious loyalty to their boss, and the charm and courtesy with which Burton had treated him "combined to blind me to deeper facts and to conditions much more vital to this case." He felt nothing but "humiliation at such blundering on my part." But he insisted he was recanting his exoneration of Burton entirely of his own volition, without any pressure from anyone.

The fact is, Moody said, Burton was guilty as charged on all of the most serious allegations leveled in Gates's report to the Sequoya League. The rule on corporal punishment flatly states, "In no case shall school employees resort to . . . corporal punishment." And yet Burton had actually shown the two investigators his rawhide whip, explaining that he had instructed that it should be used only "across the shoulders" of students. Burton admitted that the device had been used in that manner from time to time. Unless "in no case" actually means "not very often," Burton had clearly violated the rule against corporal punishment.

Kampmeier had regularly used illegal violence against students, Moody added. While Burton claimed he didn't know about it, oddly enough he claimed to have known exactly what Mrs. Gates had done at Oraibi. So his plea of ignorance about his own employee's conduct lacked credibility. Burton also said he used "constructive force" to implement the haircut order. But he had exceeded his authority when

he told his employees that the order from Washington was an invio-
lable mandate, which it clearly wasn't, Moody said. Concerning one of
the raids on Oraibi, Burton had admitted that some children were
wrested from the arms of their parents by armed white men on a morning when the temperature was zero degrees and that some parents who
put up a struggle were "tapped on the head" with the butts of revolvers.
Again, he was guilty as charged.

In short, he had succeeded in proving the main thrust of the Sequoya
League's charge against the agent "out of Burton's mouth," Moody concluded. "That I should have done exactly that thing and yet failed to see
it at the moment is a rueful mystery," he lamented.[10]

Mrs. Gates was livid over Moody's blunder. She sought to salvage
her reputation with a follow-up report to the Sequoya League in which
she blasted him for his gullibility and incompetence. "Entertaining a
high regard for Mr. Moody's ability and integrity of purpose it dis-
tresses me to recall my endorsement of his course as being thorough,
which I think I wrote you, before seeing his report," she wrote Lummis.
In fact, his investigation had been laughable, particularly his failure to
recognize the obvious fact that Indians testifying in a public forum
about a man they mortally feared, a man who had complete control
over their lives, wouldn't be the most reliable witnesses.[11]

Lummis was easier on his assistant. As he wrote in a letter to Merriam
a few weeks later, Moody's handling of the affair "was simply an illustration of what Balzac calls the Danger of Being Innocent. Moody is as
smart as steel but it was the first time he had seen Indians Raw, or
bumped up against the Service."[12] In his letter to Merriam, Lummis
conceded some errors on his part. "As a matter of fact, a lot—in fact a
damned lot—of the glittering generalities fell down when it came to
examination under oath; but it was only the nonessentials in which we
failed." When all the dust settles, the Burton regime will be pretty much
at its end, Lummis concluded. "His teeth are pulled for as long as he
stays there," Lummis said.

Indeed, in a September 5 letter to Burton announcing the secretary
of the interior's conclusion, Jones announced that Burton had been
"fully exonerated from all of the personal charges against your administration of the Moqui School and agency preferred by the Sequoya
League."[13] But in fact Burton hadn't escaped entirely unscathed. Kampmeier was fired from the Indian Service. Ballinger, the other school offi-

cial cited in one of the league's affidavits, was transferred and reprimanded for failing to discipline two teachers. Burton himself was also
reprimanded for failing to take action against two teachers. Jones also
told Burton that Hitchcock had concluded "the methods employed by
you in carrying out the so-called 'hair-cutting order' were ill-advised
and improper, and that you should be told explicitly that neither threat
nor force of any kind should be employed in reference to hair cutting,
but that you must trust entirely to persuasion and example."

So some of the league's charges had stuck. But Hitchcock was in no
mood to offer any congratulations when he wrote Lummis on September 10. "Permit me to further remark," Hitchcock snapped, "that your
willingness to make in advance, and the fact that you did make prior to
the investigation, serious charges couched in excited and unwarranted
language correspondingly diminishes the value of your representation
to the Department." Moody's retraction after he returned to Los Angeles
"in which he admits his absolute change of mind on his part, when not a
new fact had been produced, renders his opinion neither creditable nor
valuable," he added. Hitchcock concluded his letter with a demand that
Lummis publish an apology in the next issue of his magazine.

Word of the demand for an apology had Lummis watchers on the
edge of their seats awaiting the editor's response. As the *Los Angeles
Express* put it, "If Secretary of the Interior Hitchcock has really asked
Editor Charles F. Lummis of '*Out West*' to apologize for what he wrote
about the Moqui Indian agent, Charles E. Burton, the apology that He-
of-the-Corduroy-Clothes-and-Sombrero will write in his magazine will
be a beaut! It will be almost worth going as far as to the snake and antelope dances to see."

Indeed Lummis's response, doled out in several issues of the magazine that fall, was a clever mixture of defiance and humility leading
eventually to a qualified apology but no semblance of a retraction. If
anyone owed an apology, it was the department, he declared in the
September issue. The next month, he presented a long list of the
charges that had been "absolutely proved" in the investigation. "But
now comes an unexpected humor in the case," he added, proceeding to
describe how Jenkins and Moody "could not find the forest, there were
so many trees" when they were in the midst of the hearings. Toward
the end of his lengthy recounting of the whole story, Lummis did manage to say that while the Sequoya League was as confident as ever that

Burton was unfit for his job, it "has never attacked Mr. Burton's private character." In the next issue Lummis, perhaps sensing belatedly that any further bluster would hurt him in his future relations with Indian policy bureaucrats, finally apologized. "To Mr. Burton, the League frankly tenders its direct apology for whatever injustices have been done him personally." But the league had gotten what it wanted for the Hopis. "They don't have to cut their hair until . . . a respect for their short-haired instructors shall lead them to desire to resemble the latter." Nor will government officials smash their furniture, cut up their blankets, kick their children, or bully their women again. "The Hopi will be no more insulted nor maltreated by any one. And that is what the League was after."

The whole affair elicited a giddy reaction within the network of Lummis haters, who considered it a thumping defeat, whatever he might say about it. Moreover, Roosevelt was not at all pleased with how the whole matter in which he had initially sided with Lummis had turned out. In late August the president sent Hitchcock a letter that undoubtedly touched off celebrations in the department. He agreed that Lummis should make a full retraction. "If they are willing in advance to make reckless charges and are determined upon insisting . . . as to their truthfulness, then their usefulness in co-operating with the Department is at an end," Roosevelt concluded.[14]

Two weeks later Roosevelt wrote Lummis directly. "My dear Mr. Lummis," the letter began. He was appalled that Lummis had put so much weight on the testimony of a lightweight, sentimental, tenderfoot woman, who seems to have instigated the whole controversy. "I went through the testimony of Mrs. Yates, who was said to be a representative of the Sequoya League, and, upon my word, I think the Sequoya League should sever all connection with her," Roosevelt said, getting Mrs. Gates's name wrong. "Her testimony shows her utter unfitness to go into such work at all."

Lummis had a thick skin, but one line in particular in the letter would have made him wince. "Why, my dear fellow," Roosevelt told Lummis, "we would not hang a dog on such evidence!"

Chapter 12

Tumult in the Last Home of Old California

For a full year after the Hopi haircut fiasco had blown over, there were no new furors in Lummis's life. Then on November 22, 1904, he received a letter from Bertha Page, of Goshen, New Hampshire. It was "a womanly but rather startling letter" that conveyed "an extraordinary story," as Lummis put it in the response he immediately sent. The twenty-year-old Miss Page had informed Lummis that she believed he was her father.

"I am not aware of any daughters back East, and you are somewhat indefinite. What was your mother's name?" Lummis asked. "[U]nriddle this riddle as best you can."

That was the first of what would become hundreds of letters that he would write to Bertha over the years.[1] She was indeed his daughter.

The year and month of her birth, March of 1881, and the name of her birth mother, Emma Nourse, were proof enough. Lummis had had a fleeting, passionate romance with teenaged Emma in the summer of 1880. They were both on the staff of the Profile House, where he had begun to produce his *Birch Bark Poems* book.

Emma had been forced to give the baby up for adoption at six months. The child had been taken in by a simple New Hampshire farmer and his wife, Mr. and Mrs. Orrison Page, who had a small farm near Goshen. Musically gifted, Bertha had studied with some of the best music teachers in Boston and had graduated from the Moody Institute, a music school in Northfield, Massachusetts. The humble couple who had raised her as their own had recently purchased a four-hundred-dollar piano for her when she started corresponding with Charles Lummis. She was as ambitious as she realistically could be in the narrow confines of the world in which she had been raised. When she made contact with her biological father, she was enrolled at Miss Wheelock's Kindergarten Training School, studying to become a kindergarten teacher.

The story of how she had come into the world had been kept from her. But she had recently heard the gossip that had long circulated in Goshen, and when she asked her parents about it, they told her the truth. She had located her mother, and Emma had told her that her father was the famous writer, Charles Lummis of Los Angeles. Bertha sent him that first letter with considerable trepidation. She had learned that he had a family of his own. She had no idea how he, or they, would take to the news that he had another grown daughter.

His reaction was in some ways even more discomfiting than a rebuff. It took him no time at all to warm up to Bertha once he determined that she was his long-lost firstborn daughter. Within a few weeks of the initial contact, he began sending Bertha lengthy, ardent letters two or three or even four times every week.

When she wrote him that first letter, it is possible that she had just seen an item in a local newspaper reporting that he was soon due in Boston to give a lecture. A week after receiving Bertha's letter, he was on his way to the East Coast for a month-long tour to give lectures at all of the local chapters of the Archaeological Institute of America. His speaking tour was scheduled to culminate in a presentation at the association's annual meeting in Boston in late December.

He was busier than ever prior to the start of his long trip. For the first time after 114 consecutive issues of the magazine, the December issue went to press without an "In the Lion's Den." In November he spent a couple of weeks traveling through the desert to check on the condition of the Mission Indians and many more days preparing the lectures he would deliver in the East, and in the process he "simply left no hours whatever for writing 'the Den'," he reported in a note to his readers. The startling letter he had just received may have been the last straw that knocked him off kilter, but he didn't mention anything about that to anybody.

Lummis met his daughter for the first time on December 31 in Boston after the AIA meetings were finished. They visited from 11:30 A.M. until 8:30 P.M., and dined at the Brunswick Hotel. He had picked out an Indian name for her, Ti-Ta-uan, which meant I Have Found Her.

He thought she looked very much like her mother, but he immediately recognized himself in her, as well. Like him, Bertha was smaller than average. She was not feeling well when they met. She was pale and had the sniffles, looked frail and perhaps a bit bewildered, which tore at Lummis's heart, bringing up memories of his own childhood bereft of a parent. That sentiment, converging with his own need to be surrounded by people who fawned over him, expressed itself in a line of argument that he broached at that first meeting and pursued in dozens of letters for months to come: she must leave the East as soon as possible and come to Los Angeles to take her rightful place as the firstborn child in her father's home.

Bertha showed some true Lummis pluck in resisting her father. She wasn't as frail as he seemed to think, she told him. She insisted on finishing the remaining semester at school, and giving her "Papa and Mamma" time to get used to the thought of her moving away. And then there was the small matter of his wife. "I know she is a dear lovable woman and one who is keenly sensitive," Bertha wrote. "I feel positive that she would be kind and generous in her treatment of me, but at the same time, she *would* be hurt to the quick, and she will suffer. You men are so inconsiderate of a woman's feelings! You know you are happy in doing what you believe to be right, but you don't and can't realize what the women in the question feel and suffer. . . . Don't you think she ought to have a little while to get accustomed to it?"

Lummis wouldn't take no for an answer. "I do know something of what women are—there's some mother in my own heart, and some girl; and it isn't all Greek to me." As for Eve, "she will love you first for my sake, and when she gets to know you for your own."

"Don't put off things," he said in another letter. "I will never have an easy day till I get that fragile little physique away from the New England winter." He was "keenly disappointed, of course" that she wasn't coming right away, he said in yet another letter. It was a "hard disappointment" that he was "trying to swallow cheerfully." To wait longer than summer would be unbearable. "I can hardly think of anything else at all," he wrote. "But I don't want to crowd or force your mind. . . . We must both compromise—I by being more patient, you by being a little more adventurous."

Lummis returned to Los Angeles on February 1 after a nine-week absence. He waited until the third to break the news to Eve about Bertha. "She takes it quietly but without pleasure," he noted in his diary. There were no other repercussions, at least not yet.

Lummis was immediately sucked back into the swirl of his various civic, professional, and personal activities. Moody had handled the magazine competently, putting out two entire issues in Lummis's absence. The Lion had sent columns for those two issues from the East, and he continued to fill that space in the magazine. But after ten years as editor, Lummis had begun to phase himself out of that job.

The Landmarks Club was still going strong, having branched out from saving crumbling missions to trying to resurrect El Camino Real, the King's Highway that had supposedly linked the Spanish missions. Lummis's own quixotic crusade under Landmarks Club auspices in those days was to get Californians to pronounce Los Angeles properly—not Loss Angie-lees, as it was "miserably and shamelessly" mispronounced by most, but Loce Ang-el-ess. He wrote a poem, scholarly treatises, and numerous letters to the editor about it over the years, all to no avail.

The Sequoya League was still licking its wounds from the Burton fiasco, even though Lummis proved to be quite correct in his initial postmortem that the league had won on the merits. By the end of 1903, Roosevelt officially canceled the infamous haircut order. But the way Lummis had handled the campaign clearly burned some bridges.

Though Roosevelt had expected a full apology from Lummis that never came, he probably admired the feisty editor's refusal to back down. Lummis stayed in touch with the president as if nothing had happened. On October 3, 1903, less than two months after the stinging rebuke, he was rewarded with a gracious note from the White House. "The investigation has been productive of real and great good, and of course you and the Sequoya League are responsible," Roosevelt wrote.[2] The next year, during Lummis's AIA lecture tour, Roosevelt invited him back to the White House. On December 19 Lummis dropped by with Turbesé to give the president a portrait of John Muir and was asked to return the next day. "Lunch alone with Prest. Roosevelt nearly

1 hr. & most perfect talk I've ever had with him," Lummis proclaimed in his diary for December 20.

Now that there was an East Coast chapter, the Los Angeles Council of the Sequoya League, as the original group officially rechristened itself, was free to concentrate all its energies on local issues. And in 1904–5 the big Indian rights story in Southern California once again was the plight of the Mission Indians. The severe deficiencies of the scattered, barren reservation lands on which they were supposed to subsist had still not been addressed. And as winter approached, many Indians were in dire straits. Lummis, another league member, and a government Indian agent spent a week in November just prior to Lummis's departure for the AIA lecture tour traveling two hundred miles by wagon through the backcountry of Southern California to investigate conditions on five reservations.

In a report on the trip that ran in the December issue of *Out West*, Lummis wrote: "It is safe to say that there is actual starvation on these five reservations. . . . The three investigators did not find one sack of flour, one peck of beans, one peck of potatoes, nor one pound of rice— nor, in fact, any other article of food on these five reservations, except wild acorns—and some of the big American ranchmen grudge the Indians even the acorns, because these would fatten marketable hogs and steers!"

That article prompted an outpouring of donations from hundreds of people. Several thousand ordinary citizens packed Simpson Tabernacle, one of largest auditoriums in Los Angeles, for a mass meeting on the issue. Two young brothers pooled their pennies and sent in a nickel. Reporters at the *Los Angeles Times* contributed a crate of apples. More than $650 was raised for an emergency relief fund for food and blankets that helped the Indians get through that winter.

But this was only a temporary solution, as Lummis pointed out in the April 1905 *Out West*. "There is only one permanent remedy, and that is to give them lands upon which, by hard work and sharp economy, they can make a poor living," he wrote. Referring to the unsuitability of the reservations for raising food, Lummis noted that the government "has known for forty years of this wicked blunder." Yet the Indian Office had "foolishly and illegally squandered" the $23,770 in funds that the Warner's Ranch Commission had saved from the last congressional appropriation that might have helped solve the problem.

Lummis's continued harping on the issue eventually paid off. In 1906 the Indian Bureau appointed a San Jose lawyer and Sequoya League member, C. E. Kelsey, as special agent for the California Indians. With the help of sympathetic senators, he succeeded that year in getting a new appropriation of $100,000 through Congress to buy additional reservation lands.

In the meantime, the Sequoya League had launched a novel venture to help the Indians earn a living for themselves. The league sold baskets made by Indian artisans. Besides generating much-needed cash, the basket sales could help revive an ancient handicraft, Lummis believed, and so he encouraged the artisans to use traditional patterns and natural dyes and discouraged buyers' requests for "freak baskets" that didn't conform to a traditional design.

Eve and other women in the league handled all of the work of packing and shipping baskets. Lummis took care of league publicity, correspondence, and the nagging administrative work that the vexatious basket sales necessitated. His secretaries helped out, but they tended to change so often, throwing his affairs into chaos, that the administrative burden often ended up back in his lap.

By 1905 another of Lummis's civic associations, the Southwest Society, was rapidly moving to the top of his list of priorities. Planning for a Southwest Museum was gaining momentum. Several of the wealthy industrialists that Lummis had brought into the society at the outset had largely taken over the role of raising funds for the monumental project. But Lummis did his part to keep the society growing.

Indeed, Bertha wasn't the only one on whom Lummis was turning the screws by mail that spring. He tried valiantly to cajole Jack London into joining the society.[3] London turned him down in a letter of March 20, saying he was "compelled to decline the honor—not because of lack of interest in your cause, but because of too great interest in my own Cause, which is the socialist revolution." Lummis replied two days later, "We can hardly compare the relative importance of causes; but the work of the Southwest Society has this peculiarity; unless this work is done right away, it can never be done." As for the socialist revolution, on the other hand, "Whatever is right in this movement is coming in time." London wrote back, "You can get capitalists to contribute to your fight, but I'm damned if we can get capitalists to contribute to my fight." Characteristically undeterred, Lummis replied on April 6 that capitalists were indeed contributing to the society. "Still, I would a great deal sooner have people like you. . . . I always wonder that people don't follow my example and be pliable. . . . Power to your elbow for it is only a question of time when we shall have you with us."

Plenty of others were flocking to the Southwest Society's cause. In the monthly newsletter for the society, Lummis kept up a running boast about how rapidly the AIA's Los Angeles outpost was growing, surpassing one by one all the other, older chapters. The group that had started with twelve members in the fall of 1903 had grown more than tenfold by the time of the first annual meeting a year later. The gala event held at El Alisal on November 19, 1904, just four days after Lummis had returned from his inspection tour of the Mission Indian reservations and ten days before he left for the East, featured thirty-four old paintings from Spanish missions that had recently been acquired for the future museum, Spanish songs played on a phonograph, and an elaborate Spanish dinner. It drew 150 people, including many of the most prominent civic leaders in Los Angeles.

By the next July the number of members had grown to 296, Lummis boasted in *Out West*. "It will do no harm to remark again that only four other societies among the fifteen of the Institute *have* as many members today as the Southwest Society has *gained* since March 1, 1905." By August the number of members hit 309, "which is a gain in five months of more than a third as many members as the twenty-five-year-old Boston society has in all," Lummis wrote.

Through the spring and into early summer, Lummis hadn't let up in his campaign to get Bertha out to Los Angeles. But he changed tactics, cutting back on the heavy-handed demands, trying instead to pique her interest in the excitement of life at El Alisal. He went on for pages day after day about the whirl of important activities and fascinating people that filled his home.

"A wire tonight from John Muir says he will be down Sunday," he observed in his May 31 letter. Three days later he wrote, "I got a nice letter today from Prest. Roosevelt consenting to become a life member of the Southwest Society." Two days after that, John Muir arrived, drawing a flock of "awestruck neighbors" who dropped by "to bump their heads on the floor at his feet." In Muir's honor, he had invited to dinner a select group of local activists and literati, and they were all serenaded by Rosendo, a blind Mexican one-string harp player who regularly graced gatherings at El Alisal with his peculiar music. Lummis and Muir "chewed the rag" until late at night, and when Muir retired, Lummis "got busy and did some work" until 4 A.M.

The next day, as Lummis told his daughter, he had to lead Muir on the six-mile streetcar ride into town because the famous mountaineer who could find his way through trackless wilderness tended to get hopelessly lost in cities. Muir returned to El Alisal that evening in an automobile, which Lummis suspected was the first time he had ridden in one.

That same day Lummis was surprised to get a letter from "an Indian agent that I kicked out of the service," Herman Kampmeier. He wanted to drop by to visit the "person who fought him so successfully but unjustly" and promised not to bring a Gatling gun. "I did not think it worthwhile to remark that he could bring all the gatling guns he liked. I feel that a man who kicks women and children would not be dangerous if he had all the guns he could haul on a freight train." A shipment of eighteen Indian baskets also arrived that day, which meant half a day's work to get them ready to sell. Lummis worked until 4 A.M. again, and awoke at 6:15 for a trip with Muir to San Juan Capistrano for a Knights of Columbus barbecue at the first mission that the Landmarks Club saved.

A crowd of 2,500 was on hand for the event, which was the largest group of Americans devoid of "untaught hogs that want to smash things or steal relics" that Lummis had ever seen at an historic site. The bishop who addressed the crowd paid Lummis a noble compliment and blessed him. Later Lummis and Muir strolled the grounds as Lummis introduced his guest to many of his innumerable friends who were present, including Count Bozenta, the husband of Madame Modjeska, the Polish actress who had come to Southern California to establish a colony in the German village of Anaheim, and Anita Newcomb McGee, daughter of the famous astrologer Simon Newcomb.

A couple of days later Muir's two daughters, one of whom was a railroad engineer, joined their father at El Alisal. "I told Muir about you this morning," Lummis wrote to Bertha, "and he and Helen and Nanda are ready to fall in love with you—in fact, they've fallen already, from your picture and what I told them about you." But, alas, she wasn't yet on her way to Los Angeles. "I'm tired and sad tonight, dear little one," he wrote on June 10. "Your letter has come saying that I'm not to see you even in July—and it is a hard blow to me."

Bertha had recently graduated from Miss Wheelock's Kindergarten Training School, so that was no longer an excuse. She might have been wondering whether her famous and extraordinarily busy father would have any time at all for her, if she came to El Alisal. He reassured her that she would be treated like a queen. In fact, he was building a new tower in his stone castle just for her, he said. "I am going to be proud of my little girl; and I am going to give her such a Chance as not one girl in a million ever has. And you will appreciate and enjoy it. You will be among the company that Leads; and you can play the part," he wrote. The only thing that had kept him from being overwhelmed by "merciless overwork" was knowing that she would be coming soon, he added. "I think I should have broken down with overwork last month, if it hadn't been for that. You can't realize it, but you surely will believe it when I tell you that my life is pinned to you. . . . God bless my Baby! God give her to me, and soon, that I may give her her birthright! There is nothing, I believe that I have not carefully thought out. I believe I know what is best for you and for all. Let me do it! With all love, Your old Father."

There was just one thing he hadn't thought out. It hadn't yet occurred to Lummis as he wrote that letter in June that the summer of 1905 wouldn't be the best of times for an illegitimate daughter of his to suddenly appear on the scene in Los Angeles. He would realize it shortly. A long-running brouhaha in the Los Angeles Public Library was coming to a head. The incumbent city librarian, Mary Letitia Jones, was on her way out, and the board was moving toward a decision to appoint in her place Charles Fletcher Lummis.

It was a controversial decision, to say the least. Lummis had no training in library science. The job had traditionally been held by a woman, and he was an alarmingly unusual man: irrepressibly eccentric, iconoclastic to the bone. People wondered whether he had ever worn a normal set of clothes. Critics of the appointment said he'd mock the job by showing up at the office in moccasins and a dirty sombrero, though they were a bit more discreet about his other peculiar ways: the scandalous manner in which he had glided seamlessly from his first wife to his second; the unusual lifestyle at El Alisal; and his well-known fondness for the bottle. Bertha would give his critics all the ammunition they would need to finish off his bid for the job. And Lummis wanted the job.

271

Head librarian in Los Angeles wasn't as improbable a position for him as it might have seemed at first. Lummis had always been interested in books. He had an impressive collection of his own at El Alisal, featuring many fine, rare Spanish volumes. He had occasionally commented on library affairs in his "Lion's Den" column. And he had big ideas and boundless enthusiasm for the position. He also needed the job. Not only was he tiring of magazine work after more than ten years, *Out West* was in financial trouble. Phoebe Hearst had kept it afloat with thirty thousand dollars in loans two years earlier, but the magazine was still running at a loss. Moody was capable of editing it himself, so it was a good time for Lummis to bow out. Besides, the position of head librarian paid $250 a month. That just might be enough to put an end to the monthly struggle, which often erupted into an angry confrontation with Eve, to cover the costs of maintaining as manically hospitable a household as El Alisal.

And so, in a dramatic change of tune, Lummis wrote Bertha on August 8, "It's a bad time for both of us, just now. . . . It won't do for you to come out yet." Jones's many defenders on the library staff were fighting tooth and nail to keep her in her job and Lummis out, he explained. "Some of these hen women are as venomous as snakes. I'm winning but it is a slow job [and] you shouldn't come out until the storm blows over."

In a four-to-one vote of the library board—which was headed by a Lummis ally and frequent visitor to El Alisal, prominent lawyer Isidore Dockweiler—Lummis got the job. He demonstrated just how serious he was about it by wearing, at least for a while, a set of conventional clothes. The newspapers had great fun with that. "Librarian Lummis Sheds Corduroy; Keeps Old Hat. Picturesque Garb He Used to Wear Gives Place to Store Clothes and Stiff Collar With Tie," read the headline in the *Los Angeles Examiner* over a story that included a photograph. It showed Lummis standing stiffly in profile in a dark suit and his trusty old sombrero, with a sly smirk on his face. The *San Francisco Newsletter* offered the biting comment that Lummis, the "embodiment of vulgar vanity, egotism and bombast," would no longer clothe his "strutting frame" in corduroy now that he was librarian.

Lummis was unruffled by his critics as he bid farewell to the readers of *Out West* in his "Lion's Den" for the August issue, announcing that he was taking the new job. Lummis would continue to be listed as coeditor until 1909, and he continued to write fairly regularly for *Out West*, but he sharply curtailed the time he devoted to the magazine after taking the library job. "In undertaking this new public duty, the Lion has no apologies to make. . . . He is going to do his duty as he sees it, no matter what anyone else does. He isn't a 'trained librarian'—and is glad. There are about fifty already in the library. That ought to be enough." Alluding to the controversy that attended his appointment to the post, he added that only fifty out of the 200,000 people in the city were protesting his selection. All fifty critics, he might have added, were members of his staff.

It was a big responsibility. Los Angeles by 1905 was the twentieth largest city in the nation. Its library was the sixteenth largest public library in the United States, with 120,000 books. His years as head librarian proved to be "the most controversial period of my father's controversial life," Turbesé wrote, but he slowly and with considerable struggle won the grudging admiration of many for the zeal and creativity he brought to the job.

By the end of the year, the situation at the library had settled to the extent that it was finally safe for Bertha to come. Lummis met her train in Arizona and escorted her the rest of the way to Los Angeles. She arrived on Christmas Day. Apparently he had told few if any of his friends about Bertha. A small crowd had gathered at El Alisal for the usual gala Christmas dinner when Lummis entered with his daughter. By the account that appeared in one paper, he broke the news about her by announcing to his guests, "I want to introduce you to my Christmas present."

Not everyone was quite that nonchalant. The people of Los Angeles assumed that Lummis's life had already had "its share of romance" and were dismayed by the revelation that there was more to it than they had realized, the *Portland Oregonian* observed. With the sudden appearance of an illegitimate daughter on top of the earlier tale of the "discarded" first wife, "Lummis' matrimonial affairs resemble those of Ruskin," the paper noted.

Although the reference to the nineteenth-century British writer and critic was somewhat off target—Ruskin, who suffered periodic bouts of insanity, was divorced by his wife on grounds that after five years their marriage was still unconsummated—the two writers were alike in that the lurid details of their personal lives provided endless fodder for the press. Lummis's clipping service sent him stories about Bertha's arrival from newspapers across the country. He proudly pasted them in a scrapbook.

El Alisal was in its heyday when Bertha arrived. Hardly a week went by without a gala party of some sort. The house was packed to the rafters with residents. In the summer of 1904, Eve had given birth to a son, whom they named Keith, after the artist William Keith. So he was a year and half. Jordan, or Quimu, was six. Turbesé was going on fourteen. In addition to Lummis's four children, counting Bertha, Procopio, a teenaged Pueblo boy, was the resident helper from Isleta at the time. Maria, a Mexican woman who also served as house help and cook, had a room on the premises. Lummis almost always had one of his secretaries in residence, accepting room and board as part of her pay. And for six years beginning in 1904, El Alisal also had a resident groundskeeper/musician, an Andalusian troubadour named Francisco "Pancho" Amate. But there was always room for congenial additions to the household, Lummis thought, and so a constant parade of visitors continued to stream through, some of them, usually impecunious writers or artists, to stay for weeks or months.

Lummis described his philosophy of household hospitality in an essay about Amate's arrival at El Alisal that was published in his last book, *Flowers of Our Lost Romance*. As Lummis explained, by the start of the twentieth century, all of the old Spanish families in California had been "gringoized." They didn't bother to cook in the Spanish style any longer. In fact, many of them had Japanese cooks. Many of the surviving haciendas were museums overrun with American tourists. But not El Alisal. It was "the last ditch of the old California patriarchal days." The home was "hog proof (if barbed wire, a bull-dog and certain 'company manners' of my own could make it so), but with its latch-string out for Love and Humanity." It was in the spirit of the old Spanish hospitality, which he had enjoyed years earlier at San Mateo and Camulos, that Lummis opened his heart and his home to the troubadour.

Amate arrived at El Alisal one day tagging along with Rosendo, the blind Mexican virtuoso of the one-string harp who frequently provided musical entertainment for Lummis's parties. The event that night was a Court of El Alcalde Mayor. After a meal of baron of beef, Rosendo played the guitar and sang, then he played a violin, and finally his

Rosendolin, the one-string harp that he had invented. He "played such poignant music that not an eye there but leaked." But the highlight was yet to come.

Rosendo handed his guitar to Pancho, his friend of several days who had arrived in Los Angeles from his native Andalusia, Spain, just a few weeks earlier. "Pancho swept the strings thrice," Lummis recalled. "I shall never forget the little rattle of forks laid down, and then the dead hush. Just that question of his fingers to the chords stopped everything else. . . . He was a weazened, grizzled, shaven man of 58, and about 95 pounds. . . . He could barely write his name; and a dozen words would have covered his English. . . . But in the space of a minute, and for the space of two hours, he was Master."[4]

Amate returned to El Alisal to entertain at festivities on the next two Sundays. After the third, he waited until the company had left before approaching Lummis with a bold request. "I not like your country—it is cold in the heart," he said. "But I like this! You are like Home. Would your excellency mind if I came to live with you?"

"I looked him up and down. It was too good to be true! Get the Last Minstrel for my own," Lummis recalled. He told Amate: "It is your house. Come, and God be with you."

"For six years he was the most interesting person in this house—or in this region," Lummis declared.

The trouble was, Eve didn't think so. From her point of view, Amate was one of a growing number of irritants, all the more so after an incident in the summer of 1907 when the troubadour got into a fight over a garden hose with one of her household favorites, the Indian boy Procopio, and shot him to death. By Lummis's account, as he related it to coroner's office investigators a few days later and years later in print, Procopio was the aggressor.[5] He was nineteen at the time, a "stalwart Indian youth" and "a big powerful Pueblo farmer" who rudely snatched the hose out of the hands of the frail troubadour. When Amate held on and sprayed Procopio with water, the Indian "ran amuck" and chased Amate with a three-pound rock, yelling, "I'll kill you." Amate ran into his room and shut the door, but Procopio smashed it open with the rock, and that's when Amate shot him.

Procopio lingered for three days, and all the while, Amate sat or knelt by his bed, "their arms entwined, and brushed away the flies, and was jealous of the doctors."

"God forgive me, little son! I was afraid," Amate said.

"You had reason," Procopio replied over and over.

Lummis was disturbingly cavalier about it in his journal written at the time. "Not much doing to-day except that since 8 A.M. I have been nursing a gentleman who has a .38 caliber bullet somewhere in his intestines," Lummis wrote the day after the shooting. "Strange to relate he doesn't seem to enjoy it—nor to intend that I shall." Lummis was sorry about Procopio, "though he deserved what he got." Lummis knew how painful a bullet wound could be the day after getting shot, having experienced it himself more than once. But he had been sensible enough to lie still while the wound healed, Lummis noted. Procopio, being rather neurotic, had squirmed too much and so "his troubles are over," Lummis wrote the next day.

Lummis had no comment on what his wife thought of the incident, but she apparently considered it murder. She was probably even more disturbed by her husband's attitude. However, the coroner's jury believed Lummis and Amate and declared the killing a justifiable homicide on grounds of self-defense.

Lummis said Amate never got over his grief. In fact, Lummis believed, his distress was one of the causes of the cancer that afflicted him soon after the shooting. Doctors eventually had to remove his stomach. But that didn't diminish the brave troubadour's love of life. In fact, just six months after the operation, he asked for Lummis's permission to marry a forty-two-year-old Mexican maid named Elena. She "was not unsightly, for her age and birth," Lummis observed. "But the more she smiled, the less one could forget the absence of one front upper tooth." Amate filled the gap with a false tooth that he carved from an ivory toothbrush handle. "They made a wonderful difference in the house—and were as great a joy to our friends."

Again, Eve didn't think so. But none of the motley throng of hangers-on at El Alisal gave Eve more grief than the endless procession of secretaries and stenographers. The more assertive of the secretaries sized up the pecking order at El Alisal, realized the wife was well down in the pack, and let her know it. As Turbesé observed of her mother, "As her husband gained importance, he relegated her to an inferior position in the household. Always there were at least two secretaries inclined to treat her as a prudish and backward country girl."

Many of them happened to be pretty young women who doted on her husband and were willing to stay up late at night with him up in his Den on the second floor of El Alisal to take dictation or help him with his paperwork. Eve had reason to be suspicious that some of the secretarial relationships went farther than that. Some of the young female artists, poets, and writers who had found shelter at El Alisal were questionable as well.

For many years Eve had also had serious concerns about her husband's unconventional views on child rearing. He insisted that the children go barefoot as much as possible, not cut their hair, and sleep outdoors, or at least with all the windows opened. Though she had mostly kept the painful conjecture to herself, she feared it was his faith in the tonic effects of the Southern California winter air that had given little Amado the pneumonia that killed him.

In 1907 Eve, with the help of several respected family friends, finally won a battle to get the kids registered in a school for the first time. Lummis had insisted that living at El Alisal was better than any classroom training they would get. Yet the children didn't enjoy a free-spirited atmosphere at home. Lummis was a stern, uncompromising disciplinarian.

While he had always been so proudly individualistic in his choice of clothing, it never seemed to occur to him that his own children should have that same choice to dress as they pleased. "Lummis wore exactly what he pleased, and his children wore exactly what pleased Lummis," Turbesé wrote. His children sometimes suffered for it. Turbesé was teased about her name, called a Moqui, and ridiculed for the outfits her father selected for her. She recalled a time when she was left in charge of the family baggage—consisting of a large collection of suitcases, two guitars, a typewriter, and a horn phonograph—on a train station platform in Kansas City. "Wearing the gaudy Peruvian cap with ear flaps that he had selected as my headgear, I felt as gloomily conspicuous as a fly speck on a wedding cake," she wrote. "A woman completed my falling apart by stepping up and asking, 'Are you traveling with a circus?' I say it with affection: we Lummises were indeed traveling with a circus."

Eve gamely put up with it for years, sustained in the marriage by the respect she had for the work that her husband was doing, which she believed was having an impact that would last for generations. But eventually she had had enough. Eve shared her concerns and frustrations about her marriage with Charles Moody. Lummis also used Moody as a go-between to help mediate marital disputes, but Moody's sympathies rested largely with Eve.

In 1909 Moody did some undercover work on Eve's behalf. He was able to get access to a detailed archive of information about her husband that was off limits to everyone else—the diaries he had been keeping for years. Moody helped her pore over the volumes one by one. For the first time Eve learned that her husband had been keeping a detailed record of their sex life. She was less than pleased. Someone, presumably Eve, went through a number of the volumes kept since their relationship began and tried to blot out many of the "cielos." She and Moody noticed something else—short words sprinkled here and there through the volumes covering the previous half decade or so that were written in the Greek alphabet. Moody helped Eve decipher those entries. It turned out that they were a record of Lummis's sexual relations with other women. Eve couldn't figure out exactly how many there had been, but in the divorce proceedings that soon followed, her lawyers suggested that the indefatigable Charles Lummis had engaged in extramarital sexual relations with somewhere between twenty and fifty other women. Eve kept two of the volumes as evidence, replacing the rest in their place in a cabinet in his Den.

The press coverage of the breakup of the marriage of Charles and Eve Lummis was more sensational that anything that had been written about Lummis before. In fact, Turbesé, who was seventeen when the story broke and was ready to start college, was denied admission to at least one eastern school on the grounds that the articles about her parents that had appeared in the papers were just too scandalous.

Lummis was shameless about virtually every other personal scandal and attack on his character that had happened so far in his life. With the help of his clipping service, he collected practically everything that had been written about him, pasting many of the clippings in scrapbooks. But the stories about his divorce from Eve comprise one set of clippings that Lummis did not keep. A clue to his thinking about the subject lies amidst the avalanche of charges and countercharges that poured back and forth between the two.[6] While he was all too happy to wage a public war over any other accusation, he explained, he wasn't going to refute the "scandalous, false and absurd libels" that she had circulated for years about his alleged sexual indiscretions. To be sure, he had the "absolute ability to disprove" the charges with "overwhelming" evidence. But as long as he didn't contest the allegations, they would remain mere rumors that would soon disappear from the record and from memory. If, on the other hand, he took the bait and offered a rebuttal, the issue would become "a matter of public record bound up in the archives of every library."

It was a clever tactic. He essentially dared Eve to make the next move concerning her charges about his sex life. To do so could cause considerable embarrassment not only for him but for his partners. And as one of his lawyers pointed out in a letter to one of hers, the more than fifty women with whom he had allegedly engaged in illicit relations included "no lewd women but many prominent and faultless ladies who consulted him as an authority in literature, history and science."

The tactic also enabled Lummis to remain in denial about one of the most unsavory aspects of his character, his obsession with sex, a compulsion that caused him grief for much of the rest of his life. He never did come to terms with it, or even admit it to himself. The issue would certainly have been at the center of any divorce proceeding in court. And so Lummis spent hundreds of hours scheming to make sure that if Eve knew what was good for her, she would keep the matter from getting to that point.

Eve left El Alisal for the last time in the summer of 1909, taking seventeen-year-old Turbesé and five-year-old Keith with her to San Francisco, where they were put up by Phoebe Hearst. Eight-year-old Quimu stayed in Los Angeles with his father. Both seemed to realize when she left that, unless there was a dramatic change by either one or both, their marriage was over. But she said she would return after a few weeks to discuss the terms of a marital settlement. By December, however, it was clear that she wasn't coming back to Los Angeles. Mrs. Hearst, the founding patron of the department of anthropology at Berkeley, was going to help her get a position at the university. Despite her own limited schooling, Eve had become a highly regarded translator of Spanish literature by then, sought after by the best publishers in the country, and so perhaps there would be some position for her in the linguistics department. In any event, Eve planned to stay in the San Francisco Bay Area, she wanted custody of the three children, and she had damaging evidence that her husband was unfit to keep them.

Lummis had offered her a "generous monetary settlement" to be funded by a sale of property, and joint custody of the children. But if those terms were unacceptable, and if she wanted a fight, he would give her one, he warned in a December 29 letter. "I have my ammunition—never having thought until lately to secure it; and it isn't gossip nor jealous suspicions but legal evidence."

He also had two of the most prominent lawyers in Los Angeles on his side, Isidore Dockweiler and Henry O'Melveny. They helped him shield the one asset he had that Eve might go after in a divorce proceeding—El Alisal itself and the many valuable artifacts and rare books that filled it to the rafters. In a preemptive strike against any such move, on February 28 he bequeathed the house and his entire collection of southwestern artifacts to the future Southwest Museum then still on the drawing boards but getting closer to reality. The only condition attached to the transfer was that his children be allowed to live in the house for as long as they chose. The director of the museum foundation hailed the prospective bequest as "the most important donation ever made to a Western museum, or to this community." But the tone of the last will and testament in which Lummis offered the donation made it clear that his motive was more vindictive than magnanimous. "I pray that God may pity any so base, so ignorant, or so selfish as to set aside my wishes for jealous, selfish, venal or other unworthy motives," he stated.

Eve objected to the way he had decided by himself how to dispose of the family home. But that was far from her main concern. She was willing to reconcile and try to make the marriage work, but there would have to be some major changes at El Alisal. Her lawyer conveyed her list of demands to Lummis in a letter dated March 11.

First, she would agree to donate the house to the museum when their youngest son, Keith, reached twenty-one, if the children agreed. But until then El Alisal would have to be conveyed to her for the use of the children. More important, two women who had been living at the house, Gonda Brown and Marie Aspiroz, would have to leave immediately, taking their possessions with them. And Brown would have to give up her position as secretary, with her salary going to Eve. Amate and his wife would also have to move out. They could return during the day to work, and Amate could play his guitar for guests in the evening, but they couldn't stay overnight. "The other persons mentioned can never return to the house at all," the letter stated.

"Eva will have absolute management and control of the house and the children who are to wear shoes, have their hair cut, go to school and Sunday school," the letter continued. "Bertha Lummis is to be kindly treated, but not to be recognized as the oldest daughter, nor to live in the common house." Eve would consent to her living in a house to be built on part of the property across the street from El Alisal, and if they wished, Amate and his wife could live there with Bertha, the letter said, going on to list several other conditions.

"If all these demands are complied with, she will 'forget the past, laying aside all rancor, return early next week and devote my life to his interests and happiness. I will in every way be to him an affectionate, loving, faithful and devoted wife, helping him and serving his interests in all ways'," the letter concluded. On the other hand, if her demands were not met, divorce papers that had already been drawn up would be filed in court on Monday, March 21. Hinting at what that filing would include, the letter noted that Eve had "in her possession diaries showing illicit relations with many women."

Lummis wasn't easily rattled. But he quite possibly had never been more mortified in his life than he was about the prospect of getting hauled into open court to defend himself against the lurid allegations about his extramarital affairs. With his high-powered legal team, he knew he would fare well enough in the legal arena. But in the court of public opinion, he was staring at a disaster in the making. Rumors about what might come out in the divorce had already cost him dearly: earlier that spring the library board had told him that he must go.

Lummis portrayed his impending departure from the library job as an enormous relief. He was proud of what he had accomplished. Among the more startling innovations he had implemented was a program to brand books, which had helped cut down on theft; to criticism that it amounted to vandalism, he replied that surely a book was as valuable as a head of cattle. He had ordered his staff to paste labels on books written by those he deemed "pseudo experts," directing readers to other volumes that offered "later and more scientific treatment on this subject." He had opened a Roof Garden reading room where smoking was permitted. On a more mundane note, he introduced competitive bidding to library procurement, and sharply increased pay for the staff. At the national level, he made a big splash by showing up at the annual meetings of the American Library Association in his corduroys, moccasins, squaw belt, and Stetson sombrero and forming a caucus of like-minded free spirits that he dubbed the Bibliosmiles, a Rally of Librarians Who Are Nevertheless Human.

During his stormy tenure as city librarian, Lummis was credited with a number of commonsense changes, but in the end, he had gained more enemies than admirers. In his final years, the criticism focused on his habit of doing most of his library work at El Alisal. The tally he kept in his diary indicated that he put in twelve, fourteen, sixteen or more hours a day, often seven days a week, on library work. But his overseers downtown didn't believe it. One of his critics on the Library Board reported that he had been entirely absent from the library for seventy-eight days in 1907 and seventy-five days in 1908, and while he had been away, discipline had "gone to the dogs." Lummis was probably eased out for that reason. But he was convinced it was rumors about his scandalous sex life spread by Eve that did him in.

A message to the staff in March 1910 portrayed the departure as something he had chosen in order to free himself at last from the constant political struggle. But in fact Lummis was devastated over the loss of the job, primarily because he would need the money more than ever. *Out West*, in which he had remained a stockholder up until the previous November, was on the verge of financial collapse. He was legally liable for at least some of the forty-thousand-dollar debt that the magazine still owed Phoebe Hearst, who now harbored his estranged wife. He had sent her a letter in December explaining that he never could have known Moody would be such an irresponsible manager, and that though the magazine's near collapse wasn't his fault, Lummis realized he owed her money. "I am writing to you simply to find out how much you hold me responsible so that I may try to adjust my work henceforth to discharge an obligation which I shall never forget," he wrote. Apparently, Hearst never tried to collect the debt from Lummis. But even if he was free of that obligation, the divorce would cost him dearly. In his "old age," as he had begun to put it in letters to friends, he was losing confidence in his ability to make it again as a hard-driving freelance writer. A scandalous divorce splashed all over the papers would finish him off.

A few days before Eve's March 21 deadline for either complying with her demands or facing the consequences of her divorce complaint filed in court, Lummis mailed his response. Months of work had gone into it, and though he was still nervous about her threat, he was fairly sure she would back off. "Have not been able to sleep much in the last few days and haven't strength to wrestle with a grasshopper, but my mind is very much relieved now that I have decided never to be blackmailed again, even by my own family," he wrote in his journal on Saturday, March 19. "I feel better for having got off my hands my own very mild statement as to the hell I have been through for the last nineteen years, and now I can sit back and wait for results."

Then Monday came and went. He wrote in his journal that evening, "Great pity, but no earthquake came today as predicted; and no suits were filed. I think mebbe the fear of God is beginning to leak through the frozen north." Fear of God, indeed. Lummis's "mild statement" about what he intended to haul into a divorce court if Eve chose to make a fight of it would have convinced Attila the Hun and his horde that they had met their match. His response to her demands was written in the form of a cross-complaint that he intended to file in court, if she made good on her threat to file her complaint.

He had agreed to a few of her demands, but with conditions of his own. She could cut the children's hair and dress them as she liked. But the parents would take equal responsibility for controlling them. As for Bertha, neither he nor she cared "whether she is called the first or fortieth daughter." He would agree to discharge Francisco and Elena Amate, but only if Eve could find another man and wife to do the cooking, washing, clearing, and irrigating, cultivating, and caretaking of the three-acre grounds at El Alisal for the sum of twelve dollars a month plus room and board. He would also discharge Gonda Brown and give her salary to Eve, if Eve would work "as a stenographer and expert typist for fourteen hours a day on average, Sundays and holidays included, every day in the year as Miss Brown has done."

But he would not consent to barring any of his "friends," such as Marie Aspiroz, from El Alisal. Eve's concerns about his friends were her problem. She has "for many years played to perfection her role of a patient and martyred angel wife, to her own convictions and of those who saw her only incidentally; whereas, as a matter of fact, she is of ungovernable and violent temper, insanely jealous, not only sexually but socially, and relentlessly vindictive and venomous toward those who shine beside her," Lummis wrote.

He went on to accuse Eve of a history of financial mismanagement. Every month for years she had exceeded the household grocery budget. She had always whined that he filled the house up with people and expected her to feed them on nothing. He had always replied, "No matter how many people are here, give them what that money will buy, and if they don't like it, nor get enough, let them go somewhere else." And yet she had continued to exceed her food allowance, threatening the family with financial ruin.

Another tendency had grievously damaged him in a more intimate respect, Lummis asserted in one of his more astonishing claims. "Being exceptionally amorous, and of that idle, luxurious and self-indulgent temperament which increases such desire, she taxed her husband's powers at the very outset when he was in the flush of his manhood, an athlete, living large out of doors and devotedly attached to her," Lummis asserted. "After they came to civilization in Los Angeles, and when he began to be confined to his desk with literary work, devoting his nights and days to mental labor, which tends to decrease a man's potencies, she began to develop a jealous monomania and believed and charged that his failure to satisfy her was due to attentions to other women—though she knew that he did not visit other women, and that after finishing his work at his desk at 3 or 4 o'clock in the morning, he slept on a hard cot in the attic. Ungratified desire, in combination with intense social jealousy, has been the foundation of her attitude of nagging, hatred, libel and antagonism during at least eighteen out of the nineteen years of their married life. For she not only charged him of wasting upon other women what she believed was her due, but by implication, innuendo, shrugs, references to other people and sometimes by direct accusation, conveyed to her fellow gossips her belief that her husband was a roving Lothario."

Lummis had spent an untold number of hours on this cross-complaint, judging from the multiple drafts of the lengthy document that he had in his files. With his incredible claim that she had made excessive sexual demands on him, wearing him out in the process, he was just getting warmed up.

Since her family history was relevant to the issue of whether she was fit to raise the children, he intended to prove that her brother Fred had committed suicide because he was detected embezzling and that her brothers Brose and Morrison were frequenters of saloons and brothels. Moreover, if their divorce ended up in court, he would prove "that she has been seen not only by the regular servants of the house, but by casual hirelings, embracing, kissing, and otherwise conducting herself with undue familiarity with Charles Amadon Moody, Carl Oscar Borg and Courteney DeKalb; that she has been seen standing in her bedroom in her nightgown with her arms around the shoulders of said Charles Amadon Moody and his arm around her waist and her head upon his shoulder." In fact, Eve "was in the habit (only lately discovered by me) of entertaining in her room Charles Amadon Moody, before she got up from bed in the morning and when she supposed and he supposed that her oldest son in the same bed with her was asleep."

Lummis had incontrovertible proof that his wife had for years been in the habit of giving Moody "hugs, kisses, and endearments in her bed chamber." And it wasn't just the testimony of numerous eyewitnesses. He had "obvious, unmistakable living proof"—the child known as Keith Lummis, ostensibly the son of Charles and Eve Lummis but in fact the spitting image of Charles Amadon Moody.

Lummis also said he would accuse Eve of neglect for allowing their old family friend, Doc Lund, to molest Turbesé.

Then he proceeded to hint at the fate that awaited Phoebe Hearst if Eve really wanted to make a fight of their divorce in open court. He had prepared and was ready to file a suit for loss of consortium against Hearst seeking $100,000 in damages. Her conduct in supporting Eve and two of his children amounted to a "millionaire kidnapping of my children," he explained. "I have the facts and documents in my possession proving conclusively that Mrs. Hearst has alienated the affection of these children from me, has procured them to disobey and hate me, has deprived me of their society and companionship and deprived them of my companionship and that sane and loving guidance which they so much need."

It didn't have to come to this, Lummis assured his wife. "First and last, this is to say that if you will cooperate with me for the good of the children, I shall continue my practice of holding you high before the public," he said. "If it's a fight, I shall fight to the last ditch—and when the last ditch is past, I shall go beyond it."

The enormous effort that Lummis had invested in these documents that he threatened to file paid off. She didn't file her complaint as she had threatened. Not long after she received his response, Eve's lawyers notified his lawyers that she would proceed with a divorce complaint "on grounds that are non-scandalous."

It took another two years to work out the complicated details of the division of property. But on June 13, 1912, Charles and Eva Lummis were officially divorced. The event was written up in a short item that appeared in the *Los Angeles Times*, the only newspaper clipping about the divorce that Lummis kept. Considering that the press had been so close to covering the most deliciously scandalous marital dissolution of the century, the story fairly drips with regret. "On the simple ground of failure to provide, without sensational allegations or courtroom pyrotechnics of any kind, Mrs. Eve Frances Lummis quietly obtained a divorce yesterday from Charles F. Lummis, former Public Librarian of Los Angeles," the *Times* reported.

A year later, Eve married one of the men she was accused of dallying with, Courtney DeKalb. As for Moody, his own wife, Ella, neither confirmed nor denied Lummis's allegation, which he had relayed to her in a letter in April. But if it were true, she replied, then "you are as much to blame for it as anyone because over and over again you turned to him to settle your family affairs which should have been assumed by no one but yourself. I have yet to know of an outsider mixing in any family affair without getting in as much of a tangle himself."[7] Six months later, Moody himself died under circumstances that strongly suggested suicide. Lummis never again insinuated that Keith was anyone's son but his own. And he later would often describe Doc Lund, the man he was prepared to accuse of child molestation, as his oldest and dearest friend.

The manner in which the divorce ended was at best a Pyrrhic victory for Lummis. When the dust had settled he was in a slow but inexorable decline. Not that he didn't try to change at least some of his bad habits. Before breakfast on October 28, 1910, Lummis resolved to quit smoking. He quit drinking two days later. At about the same time, he also decided to stop swearing. In his diary Lummis tracked his progress in honoring those pledges. He managed to stay off alcohol until the next

May 22, but he seems to have resumed smoking much sooner than that. Lummis had more success in curtailing the profanity. According to his diary, he made it all the way through 1911 with just one "By God" and one "Hell."

But there were plenty of other chickens coming home to roost. His notions about old California hospitality saddled him with a major burden at the end of 1910. Amate had finally died of cancer on October 26 of that year, leaving behind his wife, Elena, who was seven months pregnant at the time. She gave birth to a baby girl on Christmas Day. Lummis called her Panchita. Elena and Panchita were now his responsibility.

Both Marie Aspiroz and Gertrude Redit were also living at El Alisal at the time. Judging from the Greek notations in his diary, both were his lovers although neither officially knew about the nature of his relationship with the other. Marie, on whom he had bestowed the Indian name Wa-u-wi Wi-Wai, found out soon enough and left in a huff, causing Lummis much anguish. He was madly in love with her, he insisted in letters in which he denied her insinuations about "G" and begged her to return. She didn't. But Lummis managed to find plenty of other young, mostly willing women to satisfy a need for sexual intimacy that had become an obsession in the wake of the divorce.

Lummis found a large, regularly replenished supply of intelligent, adventurous young women at the summer sessions of the School of American Archaeology, a program that he had helped launch under Southwest Society auspices in association with the New Mexico State Museum. The sessions, held at Lummis's favorite ruin—Tyuonyi, in the Cañon de los Frijoles, which he had first seen in the company of the legendary Adolph Bandelier—cost ten dollars plus a dollar a day for food. They featured actual digging in the ruins, along with walking tours of the canyon with world-renowned experts, lectures by visiting professors on such things as Pueblo art or Indian cultures of the Southwest or the history of Mexico and Central America, and an excursion to the Santo Domingo pueblo for the annual Green Corn Dance. Lummis himself gave lectures on various topics, but his specialty was leading the singing at the big campfire each night.[8]

Lummis was known to keep a stash of liquor in his cave, and regularly had to chase off Indians who tried to slip in and sneak a drink. He also entertained female campers privately, though not always unnoticed by others. The director at one summer session fielded a complaint from other campers that they had been disturbed by the rhythmic squeaking of the bedsprings emanating from Lummis's quarters.

His joviality masked an inner anguish. As he noted in one of his letters to Marie Aspiroz, "All of the rats have deserted the sinking ship." He had suffered "desertion by all I love." But, he added, "I never shall fall down and cry. I'll meet my end alone but not afraid. There's no one else to forget & desert me except Quimu. I don't think he will."

Actually, Lummis wasn't so sure about that. Eve was desperate to get Quimu back. She had offered to abandon every other claim against her husband if he would give up the boy and let him join his brother and sister in San Francisco. Quimu professed his loyalty to his dad, but it's clear that a lot of what the child had to say in those days was reflected back from his needy father. One typed document in Lummis's files written in Quimu's name but quite obviously not in his voice begins, "Dear Life: I'm 'most Eleven, and Dad's Chum, and I take after him, Life and all. The Suffragettes never got me yet; but he says they will if I don't watch out, for no man-child is safe. You bet I'm watching. . . . I'd hate to have a Mamma like that. . . . If I have to get a wife, she's going to be an extra Dad to my kids and not any of these do-funnies that we ought to spank but dassen't."

Quimu's true feelings were more accurately reflected in some of his own attempts at ghost writing. He scrawled half a dozen notes on Sequoya League stationery that showed how upset and conflicted he was about the divorce. Lummis found them and kept them in his files. "Dear Mrs. Moody," one of them read. "Tell your husband to come down here. I will shoot 50 holes in him and feed his meat to the dogs. CF Lummis." Another read, "Dear Eve: Your husband is telling lies about me. He said I murdered Procopio. Charles Moody." And yet another: "Dear Eve: It is a shame your husband tells such lies. All men are that way."[9]

In the spring of 1911, when Lummis's anxiety about being abandoned by everyone was at a peak, he suffered a medical mishap that left him so dependent on his young son that he couldn't go anywhere without Quimu. He became ill during a six-week excavating trip to Guatemala. The School of American Archaeology had received a grant to excavate an eighty-acre site encompassing the Mayan ruins of Quiriguá, which were still almost entirely covered in jungle. Lummis went to chronicle the undertaking and to pitch in on the hard labor. While working to burn off underbrush and chop down hundred-ton mahogany trees without damaging the ruins, Lummis came down with a case of what he called "jungle fever." The chief consequence didn't become apparent until after he had returned to Los Angeles. He woke up one morning to find that he was completely blind.

After that, Lummis didn't go anywhere without a handkerchief wrapped ostentatiously around his head and Quimu to lead the way. Other than that, the blindness didn't stop him. One day Quimu led his father, who shuffled along behind with his hand on his son's shoulder, to the office of the architect who was in the midst of designing the Southwest Museum. As Lummis told it in his diary, the architect guided his fingers over the blueprints, "which I correct and rearrange to a large extent."

He continued to shave every day without a nick, and took to starting each diary entry by counting off how many consecutive times he had now successfully completed a "blind shave." He also kept up his daily practice of filling a page in his diary with small cursive script which somehow managed to stay between the narrow lines on the page despite his blindness. Lummis continued to write eight, ten, twelve letters a day. Most were dictated to a secretary, but many were written by hand. The only concession to, or sign of, his blindness was his use of pencil. "Excuse pencil—it's my only safe fist now," he explained in an April 23, 1912, letter to John Muir. "I've been blind over 9 months—it's that long since I've seen even my boy's face or any other of God's pictures. But I know nearly everybody by voice and took my 273rd blind shave today (no 'safety' and not a nick yet); and I'm happy and working as hard as ever, and better work; Quimu leads me everywhere I need to go (took me all over the mesas and cañons of N Mex); and in spite of my advanced age, I'm bully."

Mere loss of sight wasn't about to slow him down. Nor did it prevent him from returning with Quimu to the School of American Archaeology's summer camp. Lummis, who had acquired various nicknames the previous two summers including Chief Bronco Buster, Medicine Man, and Wakan Witshasha, acquired a new moniker in 1912, Cacique Ciego—Blind High Priest. He was so familiar with the layout of the thousands of individual cave dwellings dotting the wall of the canyon for half a mile that he could make a beeline for his favorite one simply on the basis of a description of the surroundings relayed by Quimu, known to the campers as the Barefoot One. Lummis still took photographs, with Quimu serving as his eyes, looking through the viewfinder, describing what he saw, and shifting the aim according to his father's direction. Lummis also was still attractive to certain of the female students, including one who once wrote him saying, "I would rather be unhappy with you than stolidly content with another man. This sounds like throwing myself at your head but I have to take my chances as you did and I am not afraid."

Turbesé once observed of her father's relations with women, "My father had the deadly gift of the Byronic lover. Tender, selfish, thoughtful, ruthless, broad, bigoted, the enemy of woman and her most ardent lover."

By the end of 1912 Lummis began to hint that his sight was coming back. Though most people around him had always seemed to take him at his word about his handicap, at least some were privately skeptical. John Muir, for one, wrote Lummis in early 1913, saying, "I'm glad to learn by your letter that you're getting back your eyesight. I never believed you had gone blind though you deserved a good warning eclipse for your insane night work."

But Lummis continued to wear the bandage, waiting for an appropriate moment to announce that he had been cured. It came the next March at a gala dinner put on by the Gamut Club. The guest of honor was Mary Garden, the famous soprano for the Chicago Grand Opera Company, and Lummis had the honor of presenting her with a bouquet of white roses and a poem. According to an unidentified newspaper clipping in one of Lummis's scrapbooks, "Miss Garden's real achievement of the evening was the miracle she performed in restoring the sight of Lummis, who for the occasion, removed the bandage which has kept him in darkness for two years, and even took off his amber glasses to look in Miss Garden's face when he addressed her. He said she is one of the last persons he saw before the light failed him, and now she brought the day again.

"The heartiness of the club's applause was too much for the endurance of the building, and a large pane of glass was shattered by the vibration." Two members were cut by flying glass.

Public accolades for Lummis were getting fewer and farther between by then. He was occasionally feted at dinners of civic groups such as the Gamut Club, where he was always introduced as an old pioneer, a relic of the rapidly receding past. Los Angeles had changed dramatically, and Lummis hadn't. A dusty frontier pueblo when he arrived, it was on its way to becoming Tinseltown. Lummis had begun to hate the burgeoning city, but there was no question of his leaving. He still had plenty of old friends around town, who were also showing their age, and he still regularly held Courts of El Alcalde Mayor, noises, and his annual party for March Hares, though for financial reasons he sometimes had to forgo an elaborate dinner. He also still had responsibilities to the several movements he had launched, though they were slowly but surely losing vitality.

The Landmarks Club survived into the 1920s, though it wasn't much more than a name on a letterhead for its final decade or more. Other groups had taken the lead in completing restoration of the Spanish missions and to Lummis's considerable annoyance were taking the credit for saving the architectural treasures from certain destruction. The Sequoya League was also fizzling out, although for a time Lummis continued to be perceived as someone who wielded clout in Indian policy circles. After Roosevelt finished out his second term and William Howard Taft became president in 1909, bureaucrats who had been both friendly and not so friendly to Lummis wrote him, pleading for recommendations, for whatever his word might be worth with the new president. Estelle Reel, for example, who was trying to hang on to her job as superintendent of Indian education, wrote Lummis in May of 1909, beseeching him, "I am in the midst of a bitter fight. . . . Oh please help me Mr. Lummis."[10] Lummis wrote President Taft a letter of unmitigated praise for Reel.

The league lost its platform in *Out West* when Lummis cut his ties to the magazine at the end of 1909. While Lummis continued for some time to talk about the league as if it still existed, it effectively had expired.

Both the Sequoya League and the Landmarks Club spent their final years in an embarrassing snarl of administrative problems as Lummis's attention was diverted to his crumbling marriage. People who tried to quit kept getting dunned for unpaid dues. People who had died kept getting letters for years despite attempts by their bereaved spouses to take them off the rolls.

In 1908 John Muir tried to pay his dues for all three of Lummis's societies twenty years in advance so that he would stop getting billed each year, but it didn't work. "Never a word from you these days except in a bothersome bill. I think I paid all those Indian and Archaeological things ten or twenty years ahead when I tried to start a self-preservation society." Paying the bills was taking up all his time, "so the thing must stop," he said. Muir had to repeat his plea several times over the next three years.[11]

One civic group that Lummis founded, the Southwest Society, did last, though it made its way into the future without him. The Southwest Museum, which still stands halfway between Pasadena and downtown Los Angeles, opened its doors to the public on August 1, 1914, on a site that Lummis had chosen, on a hillside above El Alisal. He was still secretary of the museum at the time, but resigned under fire less than a year later, an episode he once called "the greatest disappointment of my life." He had continued to try to dominate the organization even though people who had given it far more money had long since taken charge. He had worn out his welcome with his determination to force on the board his vision of such things as a string of branch museums scattered throughout the Southwest. By 1917 he was forced out of the Southwest Society altogether, and the museum gave him back El Alisal. The house was going to be the headquarters of yet another association that Lummis vowed to start, the Institute of the West. The museum board continued to pay Lummis a monthly retainer of one hundred dollars, out of pity more than anything else. And there was some talk that Lummis's new enterprise, which would be devoted to furthering scholarship and preserving the historical landmarks of California, Nevada, Arizona, and New Mexico, would maintain a loose affiliation with the museum. But the institute never got off the ground.

Lummis's writing career was also sputtering. *West Coast* magazine revived his old column, "In the Lion's Den," for a short while, but his heart wasn't in producing that column for a magazine that wasn't his own. When they announced the return of the Lion, the publishers of the magazine stated that a book featuring the best of Lummis's old "Lion's Den" columns would be out soon. But nothing more was heard of that. In fact, his output of books virtually ceased. After cranking out ten books in the phenomenally prolific 1890s, Lummis didn't produce another new book, except for reprints of previously published material, for twenty-five years.

Lummis dabbled in working on films in the earliest days of that medium. Some productions were even staged at El Alisal. But a man accustomed to having full control over his creative output wasn't cut out for the collaborative nature of that sort of work, as he revealed in a letter to Amado Chaves in 1917. Producers of a film version of Helen Hunt Jackson's novel *Ramona* had asked for his advice "and then did everything exactly as I told them not to," Lummis complained. "These Movie People are on the average the most conscienceless pirates I have ever met—and as you know I know the frontier, you can understand that I am saying something pretty strong."[12] Though actors Douglas Fairbanks, Mary Pickford, Will Rogers, and Harold Lloyd occasionally showed up for El Alisal noises, Lummis's opinion of the industry hadn't changed in the 1920s when a researcher from Universal Pictures wrote Lummis saying that a "great idea" had just come to her for a picture that would vindicate the American Indian. She wanted Lummis to drop by the studio for lunch to talk about it. He was one of a select handful of experts, including Collis P. Huntington, with whom the studio wanted to consult, she wrote.

Lummis responded promptly. "Of course a picture could be made showing the American Indian in his true light, and it could be made a very great thing—if done right. But I don't know of any film company that would think of doing it right," he remarked, citing several "idiocies" and "absurdities" that had made it onto the silver screen. Her plan to contact Huntington, he added, was "rather late—he died many years ago."[13]

For a few years midway through the 1910s, Lummis's byline returned to the *Los Angeles Times* on a regular basis after a thirty-year absence. He wrote a weekly column first called "Chile Con Carnage" and later called variously "I Know So," "I Guess So," and "I Wonder," which occasionally displayed flashes of the feisty old Lummis.

But in 1918, as World War I heated up, the U.S. Board of War Economies cut the supply of newsprint to papers. Harry Chandler warned Lummis in May, that come July, the *Times* would have to drop his column.[14]

Lummis's dream of publishing a multivolume encyclopedia of Spanish America covering the years 1492 to 1850 died a slower death. No commercial publisher would expend the large sum needed to produce such a specialized set of books. And Lummis never could find a benefactor to underwrite the project. Nothing would do more to strengthen ties between the United States and its Latin American neighbors than a greater appreciation among ordinary Americans for the Spanish heritage that had so enriched the nation, Lummis believed. But he could only watch in frustration as far more money than he would have needed to publish his encyclopedia was spent on a congressional goodwill tour of Latin America. His magnum opus remained locked up in the massive collection of tens of thousands of index cards in the attic of El Alisal.

Lummis continued to speak out at every opportunity about the glorious contributions of Spain in the New World—and he persisted in offering a slanted perspective that excluded any suggestion that the noble Spaniards ever did anything wrong. In a speech at the San Gabriel Mission just east of Los Angeles in 1913 on the two-hundredth birthday of Junípero Serra, the father of California's chain of missions, Lummis praised Spain's coloniztion of the Southwest as "one of the greatest achievements ever made by man in all his history."[15]

He went on, as usual, to put that rose-tinted view into the context of the treatment of natives by other European colonists and, after its formation, by the United States. Anglo-Saxon Americans killed off ninety percent of the three million Indians who had occupied the parts of the continent that they colonized, Lummis pointed out. "The conversion of the heathen never figured in our own pioneering," he said.

The sense of urgency that had originally motivated Lummis to preach that message had diminished by 1913. The anti-Spanish sentiment that had peaked during the Spanish-American War had died down, and so had the anti-Catholic sentiment that had been at a fever pitch during the heyday of the American Protective Association at the turn of the century. After sixty years of frustrated bids for entry into the Union, largely Spanish-Catholic New Mexico had finally attained statehood in 1912. And New Yorkers elected a Catholic governor in 1918, the popular Alfred Smith, who gained the Democratic nomination for president in 1928.

Lummis deserves part of the credit for slowly turning the tide of public opinion, the purpose of much of what he wrote about the Spanish in America. As Lummis explained in the preface to *The Spanish Pioneers*, first published in 1893, "The hopelessness of trying to get from any or all

English text-books a just picture of the Spanish hero in the New World made me resolve that no other young American lover of heroism and justice shall need to grope so long in the dark as I had to," he wrote. Though his portrayals of the Spanish were somewhat distorted, it was a corrective exercise on his part with a worthy objective. "In this country of free and brave men, race-prejudice, the most ignorant of all human ignorances, must die out," he noted in the preface. "We must respect manhood more than nationality, and admire it for its own sake wherever found—and it is found everywhere."

Lummis's work hadn't gone unnoticed in Spain. On March 15, 1915, King Alfonso XIII named him Knight Commander with the Star of the Royal Order of Isabel, an honor named after the queen who had sold her jewelry to finance Christopher Columbus's voyage. The award was in recognition of Lummis's lifelong crusade to win proper respect for the cultural contributions of the Spanish in North America. For the rest of his life, he had a new accessory for the costume he wore on formal occasions—the Grand Cross of the Order of Isabel la Católica, which hung on a ribbon around his neck.

Some of Lummis's critics claimed to notice another improvement in his appearance at about that time. Unkind rumor had it that emissaries of the king paid for new corduroys for Lummis, since the badly worn Spanish-style suits he was still wont to wear were an embarrassment to the image of Spain.

Lummis had completed much of the work for which he was knighted fifteen or twenty years earlier. But he was still showing signs of his old vitality, as indicated by a short item in the *Times* on May 5. "Charles F. Lummis, author, explorer, scientist, and discoverer, has made a new and most important discovery—vital to himself," the *Times* proclaimed. "He has discovered he is in love." The story went on to report that the fifty-six-year-old Lummis was getting married again. His third wife was going to be Gertrude Redit, the petite British secretary who had been entwined in the life of El Alisal since 1903 and a resident since 1910. She would turn thirty-seven on the day of the wedding, May 9. Though she was much younger than he, she was "old-fashioned in her ideas of the family and parenthood and duty to the community and to the world," Lummis said at the wedding, adding that she would bring new vitality to his lifelong crusades to preserve the missions, help take care of the Indians, and boost the Southwest Museum to worldwide prominence.

Unfortunately, Lummis's marriage to Redit began falling apart inside of two years, though it was pleasant for a while. After the wedding, "cielo" made a reappearance in his diary after a six-year absence, replacing the tawdry Greek code words that had tracked his extramarital affairs. But in March of 1917, Redit deserted Lummis, taking the first of several extended absences that would mark their marriage. She seems to have purposely picked a most inopportune time to walk out.

Lummis had granted her request for a vacation from the secretarial duties that she still performed, but she was supposed to find a replacement secretary before she left. Instead Redit departed unannounced without making any such arrangement, and on the very day that an important pair of visitors from Europe, the count and countess del Valle de Salazar, were due at El Alisal. Without a secretary to properly receive them, Lummis had to abruptly put off their visit that day. She left his daily journal, which he usually dictated to a secretary, "in the soup." Her abrupt departure also disrupted the new civic association that Lummis was trying to launch, the Institute of the West, which had to cancel a meeting because Gertrude hadn't finished typing up the Articles of Incorporation and Bylaws. She knew there was a big dinner for the count and countess on Sunday. And in yet another affront, "I was left neither with pajamas nor jeans ready to wear." He had to find a temporary secretary himself, getting "the usual 40 or so applicants." A Mrs. Alice Yates "got the undesirable job." She proved to be "one of the most amiable, and satisfactory, people that have ever been in the house in any capacity," Lummis said in a letter that August to Bertha, who had gotten married and moved away several years earlier. That opinion portended trouble with Gertrude when she returned six weeks later.

Yates turned out to be more than a temporary secretary. She was pregnant at the time, and her husband, a young doctor who didn't want children just then, abandoned her. Lummis loved children and already had seven-year-old Panchita on the premises. "That settled it in this orphan asylum," Lummis said. "I told her that as she had made good in the work, she could have a home here as long as she needed." Gertrude responded by conceiving "a violent and unreasoning dislike of Mrs. Yates—very much like Eve's anger if anyone else in the house got any attention except herself," Lummis told Bertha.

Yates certainly did get her share of attention. Every day Lummis took three flowers to her room, one for her and two more because she said she thought she was carrying twins. And "Old Papa Doctor" took her a basin of hot water every night because her feet were swollen.

When he wrote Bertha about the situation in August, Gertrude had just issued an ultimatum, stating that Yates would have to leave after she had her baby or babies, a demand that Lummis found intolerable. "I love G.—when she is sane," Lummis wrote. "I am not looking for any further wives nor any further scandals." But, he added, "by the Bones of God" nobody alive was going to dictate to him within the granite walls of the house he built, and no one was going to present him with any ultimatums.

Bertha's response four days later showed that she was no longer under her dear father's sway. "In the first place, I want you to realize that I'm with Gertrude—heart and soul. . . . When you call her 'slacker,' 'scrub,' etc., etc., it goes very decidedly against my grain, for if there was ever a girl of high ideals and fine principles, it is Gertrude," Bertha wrote. "If you let her slip away from you because of your own inability to appreciate the fineness and loyalty and love, why I'm sure I don't know whether I could forgive you."

She concluded, "I should think you'd begin to realize by this time, Father, that instead of <u>all of us</u> who have left you at one time or another being scrubs, etc., that perhaps there might be some fault in your nature which has driven us away from you."[16]

Alice Yates ended up staying after she had her child—just one, as it turned out—naming her Carlita, after Lummis. But Gertrude came back anyway, though she treated El Alisal as a convenient rooming house, maintaining a fitful relationship with her husband until 1923 when they separated for good.

Lummis, meanwhile, had bigger problems on his hands than women. He was falling into increasingly desperate financial straits. He dropped a hint about his situation in a letter to his old friend and onetime divorce lawyer Henry O'Melveny in the fall of 1918.[17] O'Melveny had apparently casually remarked some time before that he might be able to get Lummis a bucket of fingerling trout for the pond in his courtyard. Lummis reminded him of the offer: "Trout are the most important thing I know of in the world; and even when I'm dubious about where my next meal is coming from, the thought of having some trout under the spreading branches of the Alcalde Mayor gets right to the ventricles of my heart." He added, "I am pounding on all the doors that I can discover; but there seems to be Nobody Home." He had tried to sell one of his paintings by his old friend William Keith, to no avail. "I am pounding on the books—but none of them will do anything till next year. . . . I am convinced that I can write as well as I ever did; but I have had no 'Experiences in the Front Trenches'—and that seems to be the only thing that is welcome." If only he knew trout were on the way, he could fast and the others at El Alisal could suck their thumbs, Lummis told O'Melveny.

One of the doors he was insistently knocking on was that of Isidore Dockweiler, his other divorce lawyer and former head of the Library Board.[18] Dockweiler was living in Washington, D.C., at the time, and was a top official on the Democratic National Committee, with some influence in the administration of President Woodrow Wilson. "You inveigled me into becoming librarian. Please inveigle me again! Or help me to Get Inveigled!" Lummis wrote. "My only income is $25 for a column in the Sunday *Times* and it will be snuffed out July 1 under government orders to cut down on newspaper pages."

Lummis suggested that he might be right for a job in shipbuilding or railroading or conservation. Or as one in charge of a government library service providing books for the soldiers fighting in Europe. "Our boys . . . deserve something more than the offal of books from careless homes, and the weedings of worn-out libraries," Lummis said. He could "Man-ify the cantonment libraries." Indeed, there should be an Inspector General of Libraries for Troops, and he was the right person for that job. As if Dockweiler needed any reminding about Lummis's tumultuous years in the Los Angeles Public Library, Lummis added, "You will remember that I was not a Sweet Girl Graduate of a Library School—but that I was a Scholar and Frontiersman and a Two-Fisted, He-Person; and that I went to the roots of that Sissy Library, and made it, within two years, an Institution of Character, a He-Library, of which we were all proud. I knew books and I knew people—didn't I? And didn't I get them into a relationship never before dreamed of in this town?"

Dockweiler, who undoubtedly also remembered the venomous tactics that Lummis had employed in his divorce, replied diplomatically that he wasn't sure about the library idea. But perhaps there might be an opening in the federal Bureau of Public Information. "I shall, of course, go to bat on your behalf in the strongest possible fashion," he told Lummis.

More than six weeks passed before Dockweiler wrote again to say that unfortunately the Bureau of Public Information had just had its budget cut and was laying off, not hiring, people. "I will continue to plug and hope that I will be able to land something," Dockweiler said. Six weeks later Lummis wrote, "I don't aim to be a nuisance—but hope you aren't forgetting me. . . . For it's <u>critical</u> with me. I'm absolutely at the <u>end of my rope</u>. No telling how long it will be before my writing brings returns again and meantime, we prefer to eat. . . . I <u>know</u> that if you made a Head-on Collision with the federal building you could get me a temporary berth there. . . . I want to be of service—and I want to live!"

It was a sad plea coming from a man who had once been as filled with love of life and boundless optimism as Charles Lummis. He had been reduced to beseeching his wealthy friends for help in achieving bare subsistence. The Southwest that he had discovered years earlier, and its promise of a far more exalted existence rooted in the ancient rhythms of the earth, had long since vanished. He had written a lament for the passing of that era in 1905, before burgeoning modern cities had spread across the plains and paved roads filled with automobiles had covered the old trails as they had when he was begging Dockweiler for help in finding work.

"When I first stumbled upon the Southwest, more than twenty years ago, it was different," he wrote in 1905. "The stark peaks, the bewitched valleys were as now. As now, except that the Old Life had not yet fled from them. Across those incredible acclivities, where distance loses itself and the eye is a liar, the prong-horn antelope still drifted, like a ghostly scud of great thistle-down, five hundred a band. In the peaks, the cimarron still played ladder with the precipices; in the pineries, the grizzly shambled snuffling; and in green rincones where valley and foothill come together, and a spring issues of their union, there were lonely adobes, with a curl of friendly smoke from their potsherd chimneys—gray, flat little homes, bald without, but within warm and vocal of the Old Times when people sang because they Felt Like It.

"Today the antelopes are gone, the cimarrones have yielded up their wonderful coiled horns to adorn the walls of those who didn't kill them; the grizzlies are rugs for persons who couldn't shoot a flock of barns flying low; and the songs are almost as near extinction."[19]

When he hit bottom during the bitter years of World War I, his love of a heartfelt song seemed long forgotten. Lummis would have settled for some assurance about where he would get his next meal.

Chapter *13*

Last Stand Against the Indian Bureau

In the fall of 1920 a man named John Collier, his wife, three young sons, and five dogs left their home near San Francisco and headed south for a year-long camping trip in the mountains of Sonora, Mexico. Collier, a native of Atlanta, had arrived in California just a year earlier by way of New York, and had served as director of California's adult education system. But the legislature had cut off funding for his position after a conservative business group raised alarms about Collier's fascination with the Bolshevik Revolution that had recently toppled the Russian czar. Collier was no Bolshevik, but he had said the Russian Revolution was "the most important single sociological experiment of our time."[1]

Now he was out of a job, and not for the first time in his life. He had previously attempted to organize mutual aid groups among immigrants in the teeming tenements of New York, but that too had failed. At the age of thirty-six, having suffered more than his share of career disappointments, Collier decided it was a good time to take a break, and so he planned a long sojourn in Mexico before making his next move. The family didn't get very far. Before they had even left California, Collier received a letter from an old friend, Mabel Dodge, that prompted him to change his plans and eventually changed his life.

Collier had become friends with Dodge in New York City before World War I. He was civic secretary of the People's Institute, a group that urged immigrants to preserve their cultures and communal traditions.

She was the hostess of a weekly salon at her Fifth Avenue home attended by a stimulating collection of people ranging from avant-garde dancer Isadora Duncan and anarchist Emma Goldman to writers Walter Lippmann and John Reed. Collier was a regular at the gatherings, which continued until 1917 when Dodge moved to Taos, New Mexico.

Over the next several years, Dodge's letters to her friends, filled with rhapsodies about the radiant climate of New Mexico and the ancient, timeless culture of the native inhabitants of the Rio Grande valley, drew other members of her New York salon to Taos. Dodge went to work on Collier in her letter to him in the fall of 1920. She described a "magical habitation" on the edge of the little town that he just had to see, the ancient pueblo of Taos. Collier's plans were flexible. Taos sounded like as good a place as the Sonora wilderness to find himself. So instead of proceeding south he and his family headed east on a train bound for New Mexico, where they remained for nearly a year.[2]

Collier met regularly around Mabel Dodge's fireplace with other writers and artists, although he was never completely comfortable among the artists of the town. But he did absorb an interest in Indians, one of the major topics of conversation in Dodge's circle. One member of the Taos literati in particular, Mary Austin, was especially influential in inducing Collier to join a growing regional movement to protect and preserve Indian culture.

He quickly became a true convert to the cause. The more he learned about the Taos pueblo, the more he became convinced that the type of community he had tried to sustain among immigrants in New York, and later in California through his organizing activities in adult schools, already existed in America and had for centuries in the pueblos of the Southwest. Drawing in part from Frank Cushing, he formed a theory that the pueblo was an antidote to the alienating influences of modern life, and a model that all the world could emulate, which made the U.S. government's ongoing assault on the culture of the Pueblos that much more tragic.[3] Collier, then and there, had found a new calling in life—helping American Indians preserve their culture, for their own and everyone's sake.

In the fall of 1921 Collier moved his family back to California. He had accepted a teaching position at San Francisco State College, but Indian rights had become the primary focus of his life. And so, back in California, he looked up a man whose name kept coming up in that context in his conversations with Mary Austin and the Pueblo Indians he had met. The man was Charles Lummis.

Collier immediately took to the small, frail, sickly old man, who was in such poor health in the early 1920s that he seemed much older than his early sixties. Lummis and Collier found that they had much in common despite the difference in age. Collier too was born in the East in 1884, the year the twenty-five-year-old Lummis made his cross-country tramp. Both men had lost parents when they were young, though Collier's family history was more tragic than Lummis's. His father, a distinguished banker and lawyer, served as a reform mayor of Atlanta, but was caught in a financial scandal, leading to a family crisis that contributed to his mother's death from a drug overdose when he was thirteen. His father committed suicide three years later. Collier dealt with his personal grief in the same ways that Lummis had, by taking long hikes—in the southern Appalachian Mountains, in Collier's case—and by writing poetry. They both had a devotion to the cause of Indian rights and a special affinity with the Pueblos of the Southwest.

In his memoir *From Every Zenith*, published in 1963, Collier recalled his initial contacts with Lummis and the almost spiritual attachment he had to the older man. "As one might enter Chartres Cathedral, I often entered Charles Lummis's home; and there we were silent together," Collier wrote. "But in the Indian struggle . . . Lummis was not silent, but was a tongue of flame."

Isidore Dockweiler was never able to scare up a job for Lummis when he was so desperate for work in 1918. But Lummis had somehow survived the war years. He had shifted down into subsistence mode at El Alisal. He had cut back on parties, and when he had a group of friends over, he would schedule their arrival after the dinner hour. According to a financial ledger that he kept in 1919, his average daily expenditure for that year was $2.68. So he was able to cover his average monthly total of just over $80 with the monthly retainer of $100—"when I get it"—from the Southwest Museum. In addition, there were a "very few windfalls"—occasional royalty checks from books of his that were still in print, or proceeds from the sale of some photographs—but that extra income was quickly exhausted on incidental expenses.

And yet by 1920 things were looking up for Lummis. He had for the moment reconciled with Gertrude and with his children. Quimu, who had turned into a muscular, handsome, taciturn young man for whom fifteen words constituted a "torrent of language," was casting about for a career while still living at El Alisal. Keith, who had hardly known his father as a young child, came for visits. Turbesé and Bertha, who had cut their father off for periods of time in protest of his domineering way with his children and his women, were on good terms with him again and also visited from time to time with their husbands. And Lummis still had a vast, far-flung network of friends that he kept in touch with through his continuing obsessive outpouring of correspondence.

In 1920 a number of his most influential friends tried to get Lummis a position worthy of a man of his stature. The post of director of the Los Angeles County Museum had recently become vacant, and more than fifty leading citizens—including Henry O'Melveny, William Mulholland, and Will Rogers—signed a letter written by Harry Chandler, the powerful publisher of the Los Angeles Times, enthusiastically recommending Lummis for the job. "There is probably no man in this country so well qualified in every particular for the position sought," Chandler wrote.[4] It was a generous remark, and perhaps true with respect to the scope of Lummis's intellectual interests and his habit of devoting himself fully to a job. But given his temperament, reputation as an iconoclast, and penchant for personal excess, the board of a museum in a city as important as Los Angeles had become couldn't be blamed for steering clear of Lummis.

Indeed, word of strange doings at El Alisal regularly wafted out of the Arroyo, and it often seemed as if it were only a matter of time before the next scandal would surface. One cause for gossip in the early 1920s was Panchita, the daughter of the late Andalusian troubadour Amate. She had become a constant irritant around El Alisal as she entered adolescence. Neither she nor her mother, Elena, who had remained under Lummis's care since Amate died in 1910, took well to the rigid discipline and heavy load of chores, such as cleaning out the chicken coop, that Lummis imposed on the girl. She often sneaked away from home, skipped school, and made mischief around the neighborhood. She might dutifully complete her chores every day for a week, but then the next day she was "as lazy as ever," and the day after that was "lying about watering," Lummis recorded in his journal. One day she fiddled with a neighbor's car, disabling it, and on another, "Panchita bloomed in a new role—kidnapper." A frantic neighbor came to

El Alisal to say that her two-year-old child had reportedly been taken away by a "Mexican." Sure enough, it was Panchita, who insisted that the child had followed her—though witnesses reported that Panchita had taken the little girl parentally by the hand for a walk ten blocks away. Lummis eventually took to restraining Panchita in a harness that he called the "stay-here" whenever he and Gertrude left El Alisal on errands. In 1922 he came up with a more permanent solution. He shipped Panchita off to a boarding school at the convent in Santa Fe where he had recovered from his paralysis thirty-five years earlier.

The hint of scandal hanging over the place must have added a measure of excitement to the parties at El Alisal. Even through the lean years Lummis hadn't lost his knack for throwing a memorable soiree. On June 12, 1920, for the first time in a long time, Lummis held a full-scale noise at El Alisal. Gertrude helped send out invitations and coordinate the dinner for fifty-eight. The guest of honor was Ina Coolbrith, one of the most noted poets of the pioneer era in California literary history.

Lummis's own literary output had virtually ceased after his column for the *Times* was dropped during World War I. But in the 1920s his writing career got a breath of new life. He had tried in vain for years to find a publisher for a book of the Spanish folk songs he had been collecting since he arrived in the Southwest. In 1923, with a loan from a friend, Lummis published a songbook himself, lining up advance sales with a mass mailing of circulars. The book was a modest effort, just thirty-five pages long, but when it appeared that fall, *Spanish Songs of Old California* was Lummis's first new book in twenty-five years. Lummis managed to sell several thousand copies at $1.50, though he never got around to producing a volume two.

Lummis's moribund writing career got a bigger jump start in the early 1920s when the Century Company agreed to publish an updated version of his 1892 southwestern travel classic *Some Strange Corners of Our Country*. Writing was no longer the effortless exercise that it had been for Lummis earlier in his life. He was slow to produce a manuscript, and when he did, it was a five-hundred-page jumble of recycled essays, twice as long as it was supposed to be. Then he vehemently insisted that the book must have a hundred illustrations, while the publisher wanted thirty. Lummis's relationship with the Century Company devolved into endless bickering, which delayed publication even more, making

Lummis still angrier. "The unspeakable dotard at the Century Company has put it off for a year, on a pretext which I believe would be actionable, and all on account of a petty grudge," Lummis griped to Collier. The Century Company finally came out with the book, entitled *Mesa, Cañon and Pueblo*, in 1925.

In the meantime, Lummis had found more congenial employment as a writer, albeit in a position that must have taken him some time to reconcile himself to. The job was with a venture recently launched by the Santa Fe Railroad in conjunction with the Fred Harvey Company, which owned hotels and restaurants throughout the West. It was called the Indian Detour, a luxurious automobile excursion featuring a fleet of brand-new Packard Eight automobiles that carried passengers on "a glorious three-day motor outing through the storied heart of the Indo-Spanish Southwest, under ideal conditions and as a part of the transcontinental rail journey," a brochure for the Detour stated.

The excursions, which cost $45 for adults and $22.50 for children, took in many of Lummis's old haunts, from Frijoles Canyon and the Tyuonyi ruin, to Enchanted Mesa and Acoma, to the Laguna pueblo, where the tourists would be entertained with an authentic Indian dance. "At Albuquerque, there is ample time for rest and relaxation, after an unhurried Fred Harvey luncheon at The Alvarado, before setting out on the run to the large inhabited pueblo of Isleta a dozen miles to the south," the brochure continued. "The traveler has only to relax to complete the enjoyment of a memorable experience."

At one time Lummis would have been appalled at such a brazenly commercial scheme to ferry pampered tourists through the sacred lands that he had reverentially explored on foot in his youth. Throughout his life, he had regularly railed at each new innovation that reduced the discomforts of travel. In 1900 he had chastised the train passenger who "slips from Chicago to California in three days, keeps his Pullman curtains down (for fear he might accidentally learn something), reads a few trashy novels and grumbles at the difficulty of the trip." At that time, the legacy of the 100,000 or so men, women, and children who by his estimate had walked to California was still fresh, which in his view accounted for the vitality and spirit of boundless optimism for which the state was world famous. "Such men and women had juice in their veins that it will take two or three generations of cowardly and unweaned prosperity to lose altogether," Lummis wrote.

306

He eventually came to love racing through the deserts of the Southwest by train. But he kept a sense of connection to the land over which he was passing by whiling away the hours smoking cigars in the open vestibules between cars—that is, until the railways introduced new, improved cars. "I shall never forget his indignation when the Santa Fe installed Pullmans with closed vestibule platforms which made it impossible for him longer to indulge the almost sacred rite of sitting out on the steps and watching his beloved Indian country roll by," *Los Angeles Times* columnist Harry Carr recalled. When the railroad said the enclosures were intended to keep people from falling off, "his scorn knew no bounds." Anyone who would fall off a train was destined to die that way, he declared.

When the automobile came along, Lummis recognized that it could be a remarkably useful contrivance. In 1905 he marveled in his journal that thanks to an automobile he had managed to tour four potential sites for the future Southwest Museum scattered around the Los Angeles area all in one day. But he was worried about the impact of the automobile anyway. In a 1905 article for *McClure's* magazine about pioneer transportation in America, he lamented the fact that "in these degenerate days" a man "can hardly move himself without organized assistance." Lummis weighed in with additional objections in an essay for the January 5, 1911, issue of *Life* magazine entitled "Woman and the Motor Car." The twentieth-century woman, he complained, had become a "slave to the motor car—the great, luridly painted, furious, rankly odorous machine that now whizzes through the streets of every great city in the world. Everything that tends to feminine enjoyment must have the scent of gasoline in it." A lowly pedestrian couldn't even enter an inn or restaurant anymore without enduring the scorn of motorists. "Hungry chorus girls, devouring lobsters and champagne for breakfast, look pityingly upon him, while their escorts in coats and caps that make them look like animals pass jokes at the pedestrian's expense. The notion that one might prefer to walk is too absurd for consideration."

That was then. A decade later, years of uncertainty about where his next meal would come from, not to mention the toll of advancing years on his legs, changed Lummis's attitude. So when the Santa Fe Railroad offered him a position as a member of the Harveycars Courier Corps advisory board, he didn't agonize for long if at all before accepting. A number of enticing perks came with the job. He would get a pass to travel free of charge on the Santa Fe Railroad, free accommodations and meals at Fred Harvey hotels in Albuquerque and Santa Fe, an opportunity to take the Indian Detour excursions himself, and a chance to mingle with the famous Harvey Girls, as the tour guides for the excursions were called.

The job brought Lummis a modicum of financial relief. In fact, at one point Harveycars officials sent him a letter with an unsolicited extra thirty-five dollars, noting that in light of all the work he had done, the fee he had received was "hardly equitable." The money was welcomed with deep gratitude. But the bigger benefit of the job was that it allowed Lummis to spend more time in his beloved New Mexico, where he still had many friends.

His contacts throughout the Southwest would prove to be an invaluable asset to the younger man who was about to step into the shoes he had once filled, resuming the unfinished crusade he had started years earlier.

It was through Lummis's contacts in Los Angeles that John Collier got his first full-time job as an Indian rights advocate. A group of wealthy, politically active women in the Los Angeles area who had known and admired Lummis for years gave Collier his big break. Collier met his future employer, Stella Atwood, who chaired the Indian Welfare Committee of the General Federation of Women's Clubs, in 1921. But she didn't hire him until 1922 when Kate Vosburg, a Los Angeles philanthropist, agreed to pay for a field representative for Atwood's committee as long as Collier got the job. Vosburg was the daughter of a wealthy banker, Jonathan Slauson, who had been a friend of Lummis's since the 1880s and was the first president of the Southwest Society. An occasional guest at El Alisal noises, Vosburg had developed an interest in Indian affairs when she toured the Southwest in 1921 with a batch of letters of introduction from Lummis.

Before Collier made his first trip through the Southwest in the fall of 1922 in his capacity as the Indian Welfare Committee's investigator, he wrote Lummis. "Can you give me introductions to certain people— people who did everything in the world for Mrs. Vosburg on the strength of your introductions last year?" he asked.[5]

That summer Lummis had suffered a serious setback in his health. His body seemed to be revolting from the punishment inflicted by decades of overwork. An array of ailments descended on him all at once. When Collier wrote, Lummis was bedridden with rheumatism, cataracts, a severe cough, and other unidentified ailments. But he was almost never too ill to dictate a stirring letter. He obliged Collier with letters of introduction to thirty-four important people in Arizona and New Mexico. On his way to New Mexico, Collier dropped by El Alisal on September 13 to pick them up. "I was still in a state of coma, but roused enough to cheer him a little," Lummis reported in a letter to his children. But he couldn't muster the strength to sign the letters, so Collier had to do it for him.

"For the first time since any of us can remember there looks to be a reasonable chance to hope for a betterment of Indian conditions in the Southwest," said the letters introducing Collier.[6] "He is no tenderfoot nor wild theorist nor dreamer, but a fine fellow, earnest and sane and sympathetic, and a man of much weight. I am glad to vouch for him, and to ask you personally for my sake, and for your own sake as an American who would like to see our national record a little bettered, to give Mr. Collier every assistance in your power."

Lummis added a personal note to his closest friends. To Amado and Ireneo Chaves, Sol and Emil Bibo, and Judges A. J. Abbott and Alonzo Hubbell he wrote, "This is just what we have been looking for! Mr. Collier will warm your patriarchal heart; I want him to know you sturdy Old Timers and I want you to help him all you can in his quest."

"I want you to take my friend Mr. Collier right into your heart, and help him just as you would me," Lummis wrote Tuyo Abeita, one of the "little cautivos" whom he had liberated from the Albuquerque Indian School thirty years earlier. "He is on a great and important errand, and every Indian should help him in every possible way."

The imminent threat to the Pueblo Indians in the fall of 1922 was a piece of legislation called the Bursum Bill, introduced in Congress in 1921 by Senator Holm Bursum of New Mexico. It sought to put to rest a long-festering controversy over conflicting land claims by effectively validating virtually every disputed claim to Pueblo land by Anglo and Hispano settlers. The legislation proposed that the Pueblos be compensated with adjacent agricultural acreage from federal holdings, though in reality such lands didn't exist. Some of the non-Indian owners of parcels of reservation land had bought their property in good faith. But Collier estimated that seventy-five percent of the disputed claims to Pueblo land weren't based on legal title. And yet the Bursum Bill would have forced the Pueblos to forfeit the rights to a large portion of their best irrigated farmland.

Poor health forced Lummis to watch the battle against the Bursum Bill from the sidelines. As he told Collier in a letter in September 1922, he was down to ninety-four pounds and expected "a long siege before I am good for much."[7] But he was good for a long, scathing letter that month to the *Santa Fe New Mexican* about the history of the land conflict and about the "powerful and ruthless forces" behind legislation that "puts a knife to the throat of every pueblo in New Mexico." News of Collier's progress in fending off the bill cheered him up, he said in his letter to his protégé, which he concluded with the salutation he reserved for his personal heroes: "Power to your elbow."

Lummis's letters opened doors for Collier all across the Southwest. He visited seventeen of the eighteen pueblos, missing only Acoma. In each pueblo, he met with the local tribal councils to rally opposition to the Bursum Bill and support for an alternative measure that would create a commission to sort out conflicting land claims and pay adequate compensation for any lands that the reservations lost. Collier encountered stiff resistance from some of the younger "progressive" Indians who had attended government schools and who urged their elders to "trust the government." But on November 5, 1922, at a climactic meeting of the All Pueblo Council, a pantribal policy-making body created a year earlier, the 121 delegates were virtually unanimous in agreeing to wage an all-out fight against the Bursum Bill.

The council also agreed to send a delegation of Indians with Collier on a public awareness-raising trip to New York and Washington, D.C., in January. Collier and seven Pueblo Indians in feathered headdress, beaded moccasins, and blue blankets were a sensation on a visit to the New York Stock Exchange, where they sidestepped a prohibition against giving speeches by chanting songs and beating drums instead. The Pueblos got extensive, favorable coverage in the press. Meanwhile, in Taos, the literati were doing their part for the cause. British novelist D. H. Lawrence, one of the writers who had moved to Taos at Dodge's urging, wrote for the *New York Times* about the Bursum Bill, which he called a "Wild West scalping trick" on the Pueblos.

Collier made another trip to the East with a group of Pueblo dancers the following year, and opponents of the legislation kept up a drumbeat against it in the press. The campaign worked. On June 3, 1924, President Calvin Coolidge signed an alternative bill, the Pueblo Lands Act. It was far from perfect, in Collier's view, but it was vastly better than the Bursum Bill, assuring that the Pueblos wouldn't be summarily stripped of much of their best land.

Other battles were already brewing, in particular one over religious freedom for Indians and their right to continue certain ceremonial practices. Decades after Lummis had touched on the issue in his battles with Dorchester in the early 1890s and with Burton on the Hopi reservation just after the turn of the century, bureaucrats in Washington were still working themselves into a lather over one practice in particular: dancing. Secretary of the Interior Albert Fall and Commissioner of Indian Affairs Charles Burke launched a frontal assault on dancing and other native religious rituals early in 1921 with a directive called Circular 1665.[8]

"The sun-dance, and all other similar dances and so-called religious ceremonies, are considered 'Indian Offenses' under existing regulations, and corrective penalties are provided," the directive declared. Ceremonies that bring "pleasure and relaxation" were permissible. But any "so-called religious ceremonies" that include "the reckless giving away of property . . . frequent or prolonged periods of celebration . . . in fact, any disorderly or plainly excessive performance that promotes superstitious cruelty, licentiousness, idleness, danger to health, and shiftless indifference to family welfare" were punishable in the Bureau of Indian Affairs's reservation courts by fines and imprisonment of up to six months.

Two years later, concerned that many tribes were abusing the loophole that permitted recreational dancing, Commissioner Burke issued a much more restrictive Supplement to Circular 1665. Dances of any sort would henceforth be limited to one per month per district and could take place only in midweek during daylight hours. Moreover, no one younger than fifty could participate or watch.

Voicing his support for the policy, the new secretary of the interior, Hubert Work, said the bureau was simply trying to bring Indian ceremonies into "harmony with the forms of Christian religion which civilization has approved, from which our rules of life are drafted and from which our government is founded." The crackdown was for the Indians' own good, he added. Indian dances, which tended to exaggerate the Indian's sex impulse, he said, would "contribute to his spiritual and physical downfall."

311

Some of the Indians, particularly in the militant strongholds of Taos and Zuni, openly defied the bureau's edict. So in April 1924, a year and a month after issuing his ultimatum, Burke rolled into Taos intent on teaching the recalcitrant Indians a lesson. He announced that he would initiate criminal proceedings against parents at the two pueblos who were taking their children out of school at various times for religious training.

The policy's supporters trotted out some familiar, lurid stories about what the training entailed. A report written for the venerable Indian Rights Association by William E. Pussyfoot Johnson asserted that the Taos trainees were subjected to a two-year course in sodomy, and the dances they learned from their pagan instructors were more hideous than Hindu phallic worship. One of his Indian informants told Johnson that after one ostensibly sacred dance at Zuni, every girl who had participated became pregnant.

The most effective defender of the bureau's crackdown on Indian religion, however, was a group called the General Council of Progressive Christian Indians. Members of the group claimed they were the true victims of religious persecution perpetrated by their pagan neighbors. In a proclamation issued May 2, 1924, the group supported the bureau's crackdown on the "traditionals" at Taos. To be sure, the progressive Christians could claim the support of only about two thousand of the ten thousand Pueblos in New Mexico. The majority spoke two days later. At a meeting of the All Pueblo Council, seventy-four delegates voted unanimously to back the Taos and Zuni militants.

As the battle over Indian religious freedoms escalated, Collier was on the front line. But back in Los Angeles, Lummis had staged a recovery from the various ailments that had nearly killed him in 1922 and, to the extent that his frail condition allowed, was raring to join the fray.

To recuperate from the afflictions that had felled him in 1922, Lummis spent long periods of time at Camulos, where one of the del Valle girls still lived along with her American in-laws. Lummis celebrated his recovery at a Resurrection Barbecue held at Camulos on March 27, 1923. Many of his friends from Los Angeles traveled out to the Ventura County ranch for the occasion. For the first time ever, Lummis's House Book was temporarily removed from El Alisal and taken to Camulos so that the guests at the barbecue could inscribe it with their best wishes.

312

"Few return from so far down the Valley of the Shadow as I have fared in the last year—but few have such friends to win them back, or such a paradise for healing," Lummis wrote at the top of the page in the book opened for the occasion.

From paradise, he returned a few days later to a hornet's nest of strife at El Alisal. The source of conflict was the same as ever: secretaries and wives. Lummis had announced that Alice Yates would return to work as a secretary, a plan Gertrude vehemently opposed. Yates, whom Lummis had sheltered after she was abandoned, pregnant, by her husband in 1917, had been living in the San Francisco Bay Area, working for Lummis's friend David Starr Jordan. But that job had ended and so she had asked Lummis to take her in once again. Crediting her with an almost magical ability to awaken his creative impulse, Lummis said he would be delighted to take her back. A "new great Hope has sprung to life since you shook me with your wonderful and undreamed offer," he wrote, calling her Great Daughter Heart. "My creaky brain is already beginning to nimble up."[9]

Gertrude warned that there wasn't room enough at El Alisal for both women. Lummis responded by accusing her of succumbing to "insane" jealousy, but all the other women in his life seemed to be siding with Gertrude. Lummis's sister Harriet, for one, had tried to talk her brother out of his plan for Yates, only to be accused by him of harboring lurid fantasies.

"You are quite mistaken, Charlie, if you suppose that any of your sisters are women of filthy minds, looking eagerly for something obnoxious in clean and wholesome relationships," she replied in a sixteen-page letter in April.[10] "We are not champions of Gertrude particularly. . . . But if she planned to introduce into the family circle a man you distrusted and detested and who made no secret of the fact that he despised you, you would probably have something to say." As far as Harriet could tell, Yates was "one of the unscrupulous women who do not hesitate to break up a home when they can and is sufficiently dim to be very dangerous."

Even if he wasn't having an affair with Yates, others would think so, especially if her arrival prompted Gertrude to storm out, Harriet wrote. "You have, I know, many friends but you also have many enemies. . . . It would be unfortunate to give them such a weapon. All that has been unsavory in the past will be raked up and exploited."

No one was about to tell Lummis whom he could or could not welcome to the house that he built with his own hands as a refuge for Old
California hospitality. Yates soon returned and, true to her word,
Gertrude left, effectively ending their marriage. There were no laments
on either's part. As Lummis told his friend Edgar Hewett, "Gertrude
took her Kachina dolls and a lion's share of the property and went
north . . . to take a course in New Thought or something. Both of us are
perfectly satisfied with the arrangement."[11]

Alice and her six-year-old daughter returned triumphantly to El
Alisal, and lived there happily, for a while anyway. Yates made her exit
in an especially mean-spirited fashion on May 7, 1924. That night, the
Gamut Club held a gala dinner in honor of Lummis. They called the
occasion Lummis Night, club members carried the guest of honor
around the room on their shoulders, they all sang "Jolly Good Fellow"
to Lummis and gave raucous speeches recounting his lifetime of colorful exploits. He returned to El Alisal afterward to find that Alice had
"eloped" with a "snoopie-faced beachcomber" that Lummis had "harbored when he came begging for shelter," Lummis noted in his journal.
"And she had skinned me clean of papers, photographs and autographs
which I never recovered."

Yates's departure plunged Lummis into "a nightmare of incompetent
secretaries—NO secretaries—near-Secretaries—till a nervous man
would go crazy," he recalled in his memoir. He wasted a year trying to
find new secretaries who were up to the task of working for him, a
search made all the more difficult because by then he had a reputation as a "fiend for work" with lecherous tendencies. And the salary he
offered—twenty-five dollars a month plus room and board—wasn't
much of a draw. He touted the value of the experience of living at El
Alisal, but there were few takers. The disruption from not having a secretary was all the more tragic because at the time Lummis had "so many
books boiling" in his head. "While I can still do two men's work myself,"
he noted in his journal at the time, "this needs four."

Amidst all the turmoil at home, the Indian-religious-rights fight was
a welcome diversion for Lummis. He got his first chance to join the
battle in person in June of 1924, when the General Federation of Women's
Clubs held its national convention in Los Angeles. Lummis was invited
to speak to the assembly.[12] He praised the group for its role, through its

field representative John Collier, in helping defeat the Bursum Bill. But he urged the women not to drop their vigilance, as another battle was looming. "You have saved the Pueblo lands from direct assault," Lummis said. "Will you now save these lands from a more fatal indirect assault— an assault which strikes at the land tenure of the Pueblos through perse- cuting and outlawing their religions around which their tribal and economic life is organized?"

Lummis apparently wasn't prepared for one source of opposition he encountered at the meeting. A delegation of progressive Christian Indian women led by Mrs. Nina Otero Warren, a government Indian inspector from a prominent Spanish American family in New Mexico, showed up to voice their support for the government's crackdown on Indian religious practices. Lummis wrote a letter the next day to Amado Chaves seeking information on the background of Mrs. Warren, the bureau's "henchwoman," who was "doing a lot of harm to the Indian cause."[13] Any derogatory information Chaves might have provided would have come too late to prevent the damage that she and her entourage were able to inflict on Lummis's and Collier's cause. The pro- gressive Indian women were a sensation with the federation delegates. Dressed just like white women, their hair cut in the latest white styles, they spoke in eloquent English about their tribulations as Christians surrounded by painted heathens who wanted to drag them back into savagery.

Lummis fought back first by appealing to the federation members' womanly instincts. It was woman who had kept the home together from the dawn of the human race, declared Lummis, whose appearance no doubt set the convention buzzing with titillating stories about his own record at home. "She, better than anyone else, realized that without the Home, humanity would fall to pieces; and that without Reverence and Faith—which are Religion—Home itself must fall," Lummis said.

In case that soft approach failed, Lummis also launched a more aggressive counterattack. Warren's entourage, he said, consisted of "renegade hirelings of the Indian Bureau." It was absurd for them to sug- gest that pagans persecuted Christians in the pueblos because, while many Pueblos maintained their native religious traditions, they were at the same time "baptized, married, and buried in a Christian church."

The government's assault on the pueblos went beyond religion, Lum- mis believed. It was part of a brazen attempt to destroy their way of life in order to free up the valuable land that the tribes were locking up, he maintained. Responsible Americans should help the Indians "resist the efforts to turn them into drifting social half-breeds, slave-driven by the 6,000 Indian Bureau job-holders who make their living 'civilizing' the Indians," Lummis said in his speech.

Atwood's committee sponsored a resolution voicing support for Indian religious liberty. Lummis made a strong plea for passage of the measure. But the delegates soundly rejected it. Instead, they approved a bland resolution calling on President Coolidge to reorganize Indian affairs. The most devastating blow, however, came in another vote. The convention delegates removed Stella Atwood from her chairmanship of the Indian Welfare Committee because of the continuing controversy she and her committee had engendered.

Collier had seen the handwriting on the wall more than a year earlier. At a congressional hearing in early 1923, several hostile legislators had raked Atwood over the coals, accusing her of spending funds on Collier and his activities without authorization from the federation. Atwood's defenders replied that she had raised funds for her committee on her own, and her activities were no secret to the board or the entire membership. She had, after all, provided a running account in the federation's newsletter. Atwood survived the grilling, but she was wounded and would never recover.

In May 1923 Collier founded the American Indian Defense Association, based in New York. It would become one of the most effective Indian rights groups ever. As executive secretary of the new group, he was able to leave his post with the federation and continue his work without missing a beat. Helped by his growing national reputation, Collier raised funds and recruited volunteer lawyers from the highest echelons of progressive circles on both coasts and built an organization with more muscle than Lummis's Sequoya League ever had. When the women's federation terminated Stella Atwood, he hired her as secretary.

In its attack on Pueblo religious practices, the bureau had backed off momentarily in the summer of 1924. But the next summer, Burke returned to Taos, having identified a better target than the parents of truant children. The test case that the bureau selected this time concerned a whipping administered by peyote-using members of the Native American Church. Practitioners of the religion had punished two Indians for attending a ceremony in proscribed attire. Given a choice of paying a two-dollar fine or receiving one lash with a leather whip administered through clothing and a blanket, they chose the whipping. It later came out that they were bureau agents who had barged into the ceremony intent on provoking a response that would set up a legal challenge. Indian Bureau police immediately moved in and arrested the Native American Church leaders who had administered the punishment. They were charged with assault and battery and thrown in jail, but were immediately bailed out by Collier's defense association. The next day a judge repudiated the bureau's action, saying Congress intended for the pueblos to govern their own internal affairs.

Outmaneuvered once again, Burke responded with a new approach, drafting a bill that was introduced in Congress in early 1926. Called the Leavitt Bill, it would have abolished Indian customs governing marriage and divorce and solidified the authority of the reservation courts to police violations of so-called Indian offenses, including the restrictions on dancing and certain religious practices. At a hearing in February bureau officials defended the Leavitt Bill, saying it would help them prosecute "unlawful cohabitation, fornication, seduction, carnal knowledge, incest, polygamy, lewdness, soliciting females for immoral purposes, and desertion of wife." Collier matched that rhetoric with some loaded language of his own. The Leavitt Bill, he declared in a letter to the editor of a Montana newspaper, would bring "absolute ruthless, even fanatic oppression and enslavement."

In the summer of 1926, Lummis felt strong enough to make an extended trip away from Los Angeles. He headed for New Mexico for the first time in five years. His job with the Santa Fe Railroad's Harvey-cars division helped cover the cost. He stayed part of the time in the company's La Fonda hotel in Santa Fe and ate in the hotel restaurant free of charge. His only responsibility was to lecture the Harvey Girls on regional culture and history, try out the Indian Detour excursions, and attend a meeting of the advisory board.

His return to New Mexico attracted considerable attention from the press. Many of the reports commented on his shocking appearance. The last time he had been the object of sustained coverage in the local press decades earlier, he had been a "trained athlete," a fearless reporter with a rapier pen who didn't shy away from any story, and a crusader who couldn't be stopped even with buckshot. "And now was this Lummis, this little man, hardly able to drag himself to our door?" the *Santa Fe New Mexican* asked. The story went on to describe how Lummis came back to life that summer. The catalyst was an invitation from Hewett to Lummis to join an excursion by motorcar to archaeological sites in New Mexico and Colorado. "When they rolled out of town on the annual archaeological trip of 1,000 miles to ancient sites and living pueblos he lost that humped over, cadaverous look," the paper reported. "Every foot of the country . . . was familiar ground to him, some of it quite unchanged since he had last explored it, afoot or astride, with Bandelier, nearly forty years before. Revisiting wrought wonders. Before the joyous end he clambered up the difficult Old Trail to Acoma . . . chipper as a boy. And when he emerged from the warm embrace of an Indian friend of other days, 'Don Carlos' was himself again."

Later that summer he spent two weeks with Amado Chaves and his family in their cabin on the Upper Pecos River. He fished for trout, returning with a laughable string of a few small fry after a long day's effort, but having had the time of his life. He puttered around with river stones and mortar and built a fireplace in the Chaveses' log cabin. And he filled his lungs with the invigorating high plains air. In a thank-you note to Amado that he wrote after his return to Los Angeles, Lummis announced that the visit had so revived his spirits that he planned to make an annual pilgrimage to New Mexico. "Every year makes Los Angeles crazier and more crowded, but New Mexico is a bit of God's Grace in making a land so spacious (and so dry) that the hand of man shall never destroy it, nor much disfigure," he wrote.[14]

As it turned out, the trip had not been entirely for pleasure. In Taos, preparing to return home, he had learned about a meeting of Pueblo leaders that had been called by the Bureau of Indian Affairs. Elected representatives from all of the pueblos already met regularly under the auspices of the All Pueblo Council, which had been going strong for more than five years. Lummis knew immediately that the bureau's proposed meeting was a brazen scheme to co-opt the council, and he thought the Indians would recognize the ploy. But a number of Pueblos had agreed to participate, so the meeting was going to proceed as scheduled. Collier was back East, unable to make it to New Mexico, so Lummis decided to go. He phoned the man who was organizing the meeting on the bureau's behalf, Herbert J. Hagerman, a former governor of New Mexico˙then serving as a member of the Pueblo Lands Board, the panel set up by the Pueblo Lands Act to mediate property disputes, and asked if he could sit in. Probably hoping to avoid riling up the aging but still potentially dangerous agitator—and no doubt relieved that the much more vigorous Collier would not be on hand— Hagerman said Lummis was welcome to attend.

Lummis's suspicions about the bureau's intentions were confirmed soon after the two-day meeting got under way on November 15 at the government Indian school in Santa Fe. Hagerman, who was "one of the weakest faced men I ever saw, but nobody's particular fool, presided and talked very much, mildly and plausibly," Lummis noted in his journal. Hagerman said the government called the meeting because it wanted the Pueblos to have a chance to participate directly in the policy-making process. He insisted on calling the bureau-sponsored gathering "the All Pueblo Council." Hagerman disclaimed any intention to supplant the Indians' own council, but it was obvious to Lummis that the bureau intended to do precisely that. Before they responded, the Indians held a private caucus and invited Lummis, who proposed a novel counter-move. He suggested that the Indians could turn the tables on the bureau by agreeing to participate in the government's new council on the condition that all invitations to attend were relayed through their own All Pueblo Council, which would retain final authority to speak for the tribe on policy issues.

Expecting a rebuff, Hagerman was elated—and astonished—when he was told the next day that the Indians were prepared to join the bureau's council. "The government folks in general overwhelmed me with thanks for bringing the Indians into the fold," Lummis noted in his journal. He took some of the smile off their collective face, however, when they asked him to explain how he had persuaded the Indians to come aboard. "I told [the bureau officials] frankly that I did it only because I thought that then the Indians would have them 'in the door'," Lummis wrote. "That figure [of speech] is of the old frontier—when a man came out into the lighted door where he was where you could shoot him if you wanted to."

Lummis then proceeded to put Hagerman on the spot concerning the name he had claimed for his new group. "I took pains to drag in a remark that . . . of course the Government could not think of descending to plagiarize the name the Indians had made honorable for five years. I was sure the government would be ingenious enough to get a new name which would cover the ground without causing confusion," Lummis said. "Hagerman winced visibly; and floundered a good deal when he came to the point. He was inclined to stick to his first choice. But my little sarcasm had made that impossible . . . so he finally shuffled out that this new organization would be known as the United States Pueblo Indian Council."

With the government in an increasingly undignified retreat, Lummis completed his mastery of the meeting with a flourish. "I had suggested to Governor Hagerman at the noon recess that it would be a good deal more like an Indian Council if we smoked," he wrote in his journal. Hagerman was reluctant to give official permission to smoke in a government Indian school assembly hall, but he "intimated unofficially that there would be no objection if we burned the weed," Lummis noted. So after lunch, Lummis commenced the "blessing of tobacco," breaking out the supplies he had brought along—a carton of Camels and five or six sacks of Bull Durham tobacco with rolling papers. "I trotted up and down the aisles quite as if I owned the Government Reserve, passing cigarettes to fifty Indians at appropriate intervals. . . . The afternoon session was very much happier than any of the others. And discussion went much smoother."

That evening, with the assistance of "a borrowed stenographer," Lummis dictated a long letter to Collier explaining what had transpired.[15] In Collier's absence, he had made some controversial calls that Collier would have to live with, and he was a bit defensive about it. But Lummis hoped Collier would agree that his tactical ploy was the right move. He started his letter to Collier by "congratulating him on this great victory." The department "has put itself exactly where we would wish it," he wrote.

Collier wasn't convinced. In his response, he said he believed the Indians should have flatly rejected the bureau's invitation to participate in the new group. He asked Lummis to remain in New Mexico long enough to attend a meeting of the All Pueblo Council on December 10, and to meet him in Albuquerque the day before to discuss matters.

With a week to kill before that meeting, Lummis had time to reconnect with two friends from way back, Alice Rea and Tuyo Abeita. Alice, Eve's older sister, the woman who had mothered him in Isleta, nursing him back to health after he was shot, was living in a mud-chinked log cabin up behind Bosque Peak, not far from where Lummis had built a cabin for her long-dead husband Archibald in the summer of 1890. She was "lean as ever and a war map of wrinkles but with the old fire and the old twinkle in her eyes and an unmistakable trace of her former beauty," Lummis noted.

As for Tuyo, twelve years after Lummis had liberated him and the other Isleta children from involuntary confinement at the Albuquerque Indian School, he had enrolled at the Hampton Institute in Virginia on a letter of recommendation from Lummis and had stayed for four years. Now he was living in Albuquerque with a Scottish wife and children of his own. Lummis stayed with the Abeitas for several days, and got to meet Tuyo's oldest son for the first time since he was a baby. His name was Lummis Abeita. "I don't think you ever saw four lovelier children of one stock. Fine bodies, fine faces, perfect manners and great intelligence," Lummis wrote in his journal. "Lummis is ten and a beautiful boy one would be proud to have as a namesake."

Tuyo stayed up to talk with Lummis until 2:15 one morning. Lummis continued working on letters and his journal until the break of dawn. John Collier came by at 10 A.M. on December 8, but Lummis was no longer as resilient as he had been in his youth, when he could work until four or five in the morning and bound out of bed at six or seven as if he had gotten a full night's sleep. Collier was unable to rouse him. He returned at 12:30 to find Lummis still groggy but awake.

In their discussion, Collier made it clear that he remained deeply suspicious of the U.S. Pueblo Indian Council. Lummis explained that half of the Pueblos would have joined anyway and "the whole thing would have been in a mess." It was better to be inside and in a position to control the government's group, Lummis said.

Since Lummis had already told Hagerman what the Indians had decided to do, it was too late to back out anyway. At the meeting of the "genuine All Pueblo Council" on December 10, the sixty delegates formally endorsed the decision. Before the meeting adjourned, the council took one other vote that nearly moved Lummis to tears. Sotero Ortiz, president of the council, "said that he thought that this Council should vote thanks to God for sparing my life thus far, and thanks to me for helping them. And incredible as I would have thought for Indians, every last one got to his feet in a standing vote of thanks, without a moment's hesitation," Lummis wrote in his journal.

Lummis ended that trip to New Mexico with a stopover in Isleta. His contacts with the pueblo had diminished in the years after 1907 when the Isleta teenager Procopio was murdered at El Alisal. But the passage of time had healed that wound. Often when he passed through the Isleta junction on a train, he would wire ahead with news of his itinerary and a small crowd would gather on the depot platform to greet him, even if only for a few minutes. Now he was back in Isleta to stay for a few days, and Pablo Abeita found a room for him in his old homestead.

When Lummis got back to Los Angeles, he found a familiar set of problems waiting for him. He returned "to find my papers and everything in an awful mess" from yet another "absconding secretary." Almost immediately, his health once again began to deteriorate. His eyes were "as comfortable as a tooth ache," he told Collier in a letter: one had gone bad and the good one had "gone on strike" from working too hard to compensate.

But the trip had been an unalloyed success, not only because it had enabled him to renew his ties with his beloved New Mexico, but because he had helped the Pueblos gain the upper hand over the Indian Bureau. Collier conceded as much in a letter he sent to Lummis in January. "I thought that as a result of the last All-Pueblo Council meeting and other causes, the Bureau officers would be even chillier than usual in their manner," he wrote. "The opposite has been the case, and without yielding anything in the matter of our program, I have been able to get a few substantial concessions for the Indians."

Lummis responded two days later with some general observations from his decades of experience about how best to handle the Bureau of Indian Affairs.[16] "The worst scoundrels in the world are ninety-seven or ninety-eight percent human and decent. I am inclined to think that the Bureau people are no exception to this life long experience of mine," he wrote. "It takes a war to the knife to shake them out of their immemorial Bureau habit; it will take eternal watchfulness as long as there are Indians left with anything to administrate. But I doubt if we can hope for any real progress unless we accept in good faith any proffer on their part of cooperation in our aims for the betterment of the Indians; but of course if they want us to follow in their path in any respect, we let them Walk Ahead; we come trailing along after with the gun in our hands. I have known horse thieves and others to play entirely true as guides under these circumstances."

* * *

Lummis returned to New Mexico the next summer. He visited Tony and Mabel Dodge Luhan in Taos, Tuyo and his family in Albuquerque, and the Chaves family at their cabin on the Pecos. In September he attended another meeting of the All Pueblo Council. In the face of relentless opposition from Collier's group, the bureau had quietly withdrawn the Leavitt Bill from Congress. So for the first time since the council was created in 1921, there was no hostile federal legislation to fight off. The council could focus instead on practical concerns, such as how to control the unruly Rio Grande and cope with the problem of alkaline soil in the fields near the river. In an indication of the dramatically changed nature of the relationship between the Pueblos and the government, Collier had invited two agents of the bureau to attend the council meeting as observers. "They told the Indians that if they followed Collier they couldn't go wrong," Lummis marveled in his journal. "Most astonishing attitude for the Indian Bureau people! For most hate Collier like poison."

On his 1927 trip, Lummis stopped off once again at Isleta, where he stayed with Tuyo's nephew, Diego Abeita. He was a "young progressive" and "couldn't refrain from getting at me at once. He does not realize that their only salvation is to cling to their community life," Lummis observed.

The only other annoyance that Lummis encountered on that trip was a nagging sore on his cheek. He suspected that it was an infected spider bite. One doctor told him to treat it with hot towels. Three weeks later in Taos, on advice from another doctor, he tried mercurochrome, but it steadily got worse.

That aside, the trip to New Mexico once again had been a marvelous tonic. Back at El Alisal, Lummis was in a mood to celebrate. On October 22 he had a "Noise at Home-Coming." He had returned to his home but in another sense was "back from Home—from two months in New Mexico with my Pueblo Indians, that ancient Aristocracy which was ripe a thousand years before Columbus," Lummis wrote in the House Book. "They have been my brothers for forty-three years. They have no politicians, no newspapers, no taxes, no graft, no spoiled children, no ladylike men & roughneck women, no Birth Control, no divorce. They have Homes not filling stations." The select group of friends he had invited to the party were "those who shall help me readjust to this bedlam we welter in. . . . For the only people worthwhile are they that keep—so far as Civilization will let them—the ancient Human Nature of the First Americans."

Less than two weeks later, Lummis received disturbing news. The suspiciously quiescent Bureau of Indian Affairs hadn't stopped trying to undermine the Pueblos' political autonomy after all. As soon as Lummis and Collier returned to their respective coasts, the bureau had scheduled yet another meeting of its "bastard council," Collier wrote Lummis. And in flagrant disregard of its promise, it sent notice about the meeting to individual Indian leaders in each of the pueblos without contacting the All Pueblo Council.

Collier urged Lummis to send another round of letters warning the Indians of a plot. So Lummis immediately dictated a six-hundred-word message to his Pueblo friends.[17] "I trust that you will have [the bureau officials] understand that you will take no action in any matter at this Santa Fe meeting of the U.S. Pueblo Council, but will refer it to your own All Pueblo Council," Lummis wrote. "If the Bureau is afraid or unwilling to put its propositions to the Pueblos through this legitimate channel of the All Pueblo Council, and tries to push its plans through at its own hand-picked meeting, that is enough to show you that you should be afraid of their propositions."

Lummis was delighted with the news that reached him from New Mexico on November 9. The Indians hadn't wavered when pressed to take votes on issues presented by the bureau, insisting that they would have to take the matters up at the next meeting of their All Pueblo Council.

On that same day, Lummis also received another report that he had been awaiting. On November 3 he had gone to see another doctor about the sore on his face. "That was certainly some spider that drank from my blooming cheek way back in July!" he had observed in his journal that day. The doctor applied a local anesthetic and probed behind his cheek through an incision under Lummis's upper lip, extracting two chunks of bone for analysis. Lummis got the results on November 9. The "spider bite" was a malignant tumor. It had spread too far to eradicate. It would certainly kill him, though doctors would have to run more tests to estimate when.

Lummis recorded his thoughts about the news in his journal that day. "Well, I have my Ticket and Destination—but not my Train-time yet!"

he wrote. "I never was late for a train but once in my life—but I think perhaps I will miss a few on this Road. . . . I know of a lot more things that I want to do at this end of the line than at the other."

Ten days later he broke the news to Amado: "It is extremely doubtful whether I shall be able to get to N.M. next summer; the doctors promise me something entirely different than that, and a journey to a country which I don't believe is half as good as old New Mexico."[18]

Lummis soon learned that in the opinion of the doctors, he might last a year. That news forced him to make some decisions of a sort that he had never had to make before. No longer could he continue to allow himself to believe that if only he maintained a methodical pace for twenty hours a day, he could accomplish everything. He decided to concentrate whatever energy he had left on finishing three books— *Bronco Pegasus*, which would be a collection of his best poems, a new edition of *Spanish Pioneers*, and a new book of essays called *Flowers of Our Lost Romance*—and put aside just about everything else.

But first, he devoted some time to another priority: his family. Despite his deep emotional attachment to the concept, Family (which was often in uppercase when he wrote the word) had usually ended up well down on his crowded list of things to do. But all four of his children were with him for Christmas in 1927, the first time they had all been together since 1921 and only the second time since Eve left him. The House Book inscription marking the occasion read "It's a scattery world—but there's something in the Blood to pull us together now and then. For the second time in 20 years I have all four of my living children with me at one time, and it's a benediction. And [Quimu's wife] Betty to boot, and the two little granddaughters she has given me." It was signed by the children. No one else from the crowd of friends and acquaintances who usually packed El Alisal on special occasions was present.

In his final year, Lummis was a changed man in many respects. "Those close to him saw the impatient one becoming patient, the master of sarcasm become tender," Turbesé and Keith wrote in their book about their father. In an especially dramatic concession to circumstances, early in the new year Lummis gave up his lifelong obsession with letter writing. It wasn't an easy decision. His mind-boggling output of correspondence had kept him in close touch with dozens of dear friends and hundreds of acquaintances. Letters had often proved to be formidable weapons. In his declining years, when on occasion he had come so uncharacteristically close to losing the will to live, letters had kept him going.

One that came as quite a surprise—and that undoubtedly quickened his pulse at a memory from a summer long ago—had come out of the blue a few years earlier, in August of 1922.[19] It was from Emma Nourse, his summer love from the Profile House, the slight girl who became Bertha's mother. They had corresponded briefly a decade earlier on the occasion of Bertha's engagement to be married. But otherwise they had had no direct contact with each other since the summer of 1880. Forty-two years later she was writing to say she knew he had a wife but "shouldn't it have been me you had married on account of having Bertha? You did not want a bad woman for a wife did you—but I have been good since," Emma wrote. "Oh! Charlie if I could only see you it would do me a world of good." Her hair hadn't turned gray, she said, and she had no wrinkles. People thought she looked fifty. "I want you," Emma wrote. "You will think I am crazy but I am not." Little did she know that Charlie was down to ninety-four pounds that summer, virtually blind, for that matter half dead. His hair had gone completely white. His cheeks were hollow and his eyes had sunk into his head. People would have guessed he was eighty.

A few years later when he was feeling livelier, he engaged in a round of repartee with another old flame, his first wife Dorothea.[20] The occasion was a notice that Lummis had sent out in 1925 announcing that Quimu had a new son. Lummis included a photograph of Quimu, the baby, and himself, the beaming grandfather. Dorothea wrote back, "That is a most enchanting baby you and Kimu have conspired to produce. But wasn't there any mother? You do not say." Never one to let a jab like that go without a counterpunch, Lummis fired back, "I thought you had long ago graduated from that embattled attitude—which, after all, is not merely one of the reasons why women are inferior, but their own confession of the fact. An Equal never demands recognition." The picture "was not meant to be a genealogical tree of the Lummises, and I didn't include Quimu's mother nor his wife nor any of his sisters nor cousins nor aunts; not because I am ashamed of any of them but because I did not think them pertinent." Those who received the card did not know Quimu's wife, but since she had asked, Lummis sent Dorothea another picture of Quimu and his "fine wife."

Lummis had a more pleasant correspondence in his last years with Alice Rea.[21] She wrote in 1927 to order a copy of *Spanish Songs of Old California,* said she would love to see him again next time he was in New Mexico, and concluded with a word about Eve, with whom Lummis rarely communicated after the divorce. Alice made a point of telling him that Eve had told her she believed his best books would endure for generations.

He received an especially poignant letter when he was in the depths of depression in World War I, out of work and uncertain where his next meal would come from. It was from Mary Austin, another woman with whom he had had a prickly relationship.[22] Her mentally retarded daughter, Ruth, had just died in her early twenties of a bad case of flu. Lummis was one of the few people who had known of her condition and had not made Mary feel ashamed. His child Amado had been Ruth's only friend. She had previously told Eve the story she was writing to tell him, unsure if Eve had ever passed it on. She wanted to share it with him "for it is by mysteries such as these our life is kept from sterility," she wrote.

She proceeded to recall an incident that had happened on Christmas night of 1900. She had put Ruth to bed, leaving the door open a crack. A little while later, uncharacteristically, the little girl started talking to herself. When Mary went into the room, Ruth was sitting up in her bed and laughing.

"Amado is here," she told her mother in her broken words. "He want me to go a walk with him, a long, long way off."

"I didn't understand of course," Austin wrote Lummis. "I took it for a sign of developing intelligence." She left the room, and a few minutes later she heard Ruth call out, "Goodbye, Amado." Two days later Mary received a letter from Eve telling her that, at about that moment, Amado had died.

"We do not know what these things mean," Mary wrote, "but to me it has always meant the faith that back of her poor, imperfect body my child's soul waited its deliverance, and I am glad she will find one child who loved her in that country where they have both gone."

Lummis's files contained tens of thousands of letters. He kept carbon copies of his outgoing typewritten correspondence—and asked some of those he wrote by hand to return his letters for his safekeeping. He responded personally to just about every note he ever received. All told, his correspondence represented years of labor. He would need every last ounce of that sort of energy to complete three books in the final months of his life.

And so, early in 1928 he dictated a form letter, directing his secretary to send it in response to most letters he received.[23] "The state of Dr. Lummis' health, and the pressure of work he feels he must finish in the short span left, make it impossible for him to devote personal attention to his endless correspondence—as he did so generously for forty years," the letter stated. "In that term, the time, advice, expert information, that he gave out freely—mostly to strangers—would have added at least forty books to his list, all paying him royalties. His disposition is just as good, his intention to Pay his Fare in the world is just as strong, but—he has come to his limit. He bids me, therefore, to acknowledge your letters with such thanks as are due, and with his regret that he cannot answer you personally and as gladly as if he had nothing else to do in the world."

Lummis wrote very few letters after that, and while he still played host at an occasional noise at El Alisal, he declined most invitations for other social engagements. One request that he couldn't turn down was an invitation to speak to students at a Mexican American grammar school. He discussed with relish his plans for the occasion in his journal. "I expect I shall be the first person in the U.S. to tell them not to be bulldozed by the Gringos, not to let themselves be looked down upon; and to give them a few fistfuls of history to fling back in the face of any shallow parvenu Yankee that tried to high-hat them," Lummis wrote.

He also made exceptions to his no-correspondence rule when he thought a letter could help an old friend. In March 1928, for instance, he wrote Edgar Hewett about Fanny Bandelier, Adolph's widow.[24] He wondered if Hewett had any leads for a respectable job for her that matched her considerable skills as a scholar of Spanish American history. It was "one of the rottenest jokes in all the folly of Scholarship that this wonderful woman is left to eke out a living as if she were a cheap piano teacher," he wrote. "I'd hate to die leaving Fanny Bandelier out in the ungrateful cold."

Lummis would need plenty of help himself in finishing the books that he was desperate to complete, which would mean finding secretaries and editors who could put up with him. He had no time to spare for staff conflict.

A poet and occasional visitor to El Alisal named Henry Herbert Knibbs, known for his western-themed ballads, agreed to help Lummis finish *Bronco Pegasus*. "Harry Knibbs was out to the Noise the other night, and we had a fine time," Lummis noted that spring. "I am almost ready for the promised siege of Troy with him, where he is to come over and camp with me while we go over my poems, to see if he would include in the proposed book any that my modesty and good sense would lead me to throw away—or veto something which my own infatuations might lead me to include."

Lummis was undergoing lengthy sessions of deep radiotherapy treatment that left him exhausted. But when he could muster the energy, he and Knibbs would go over his poems line by line, agonizing in particular over his poem about Geronimo. Knibbs spent days on it, lobbying for deletion of three stanzas, particularly the one that Lummis insisted must come last. Lummis had a great deal of respect for Knibbs, calling him "one of the half dozen real poets left in this country," but Lummis won the argument.

Knibbs survived the ordeal, and *Bronco Pegasus* was completed on July 10. The next day Lummis started in on a new edition of *Spanish Pioneers*, and worked himself blind, according to a notation in his diary. On July 14 he had no whisky all day "for first time in months or a year." August 13 was a "Grand and Glorious Day!" he reported in his diary. "Houghton Mifflin accepts *Bronco Pegasus*!" Three days after that, he completed the revision of *Spanish Pioneers* and prepared to plunge into *Flowers of Our Lost Romance*.

Quimu and his family stayed at El Alisal that summer, providing Lummis with some respite from the grinding work. Quimu's oldest daughter, Patricia, turned three on August 19. "She has a great flair to call me Dr. Lummis now; and while I prefer 'Grandpa' the other sounds so demure and cunning that we will let it go at that," he wrote in his journal that day. A few days later he had a discussion with Quimu about the niche he wanted to carve in the outside wall of El Alisal facing the courtyard where he wanted his ashes to be placed along with those of his first son, Amado. Quimu took a drill and went to work on the project.

Meanwhile Lummis still had publishers to joust with and secretaries to keep on track in his bid to finish his life's work. He still showed flashes of his old temper when they let him down. When he received a copy of the latest edition of *Mesa, Cañon and Pueblo*, he was enraged by a line on the new jacket calling the book "The Classic Southwest History." That is "not only idiotic but a fake and I'll make them eat it," Lummis fumed.

Helen Wilson, Lummis's last secretary, handled the brunt of the labor of getting the *Flowers of Our Lost Romance* manuscript ready to send to the publisher. The book was a collection of essays selected from among dozens that Lummis had written over the course of his life. They needed to be retrieved from files, read to Lummis line by line while he dictated revisions, then retyped and edited and typed again. By the fall, Wilson was ill. She managed to stay with the job until September 1 when, ground down by months of relentless work, she told Lummis she couldn't go on and would have to quit. He argued with her but it was hopeless, he indicated in his diary.

By October his handwriting in his diary had begun to deteriorate. His entries grew shorter. But he still managed to jot down a peculiar assortment of details from his daily life, from the mundane to the momentous, as he had virtually every day since 1888. On November 3 he noted that he completed his 5,534th "blind shave," a practice of shaving with a straight-edged razor and no mirror that dated back to the time he went blind from jungle fever in Guatemala. It was an exercise in "self-control and handiness." On November 5 he played the guitar for fifteen minutes and on the next day he ate soup, toast, grapes, and Ovaltine, and with assistance from Harry Knibbs made it to the polls to vote. He made a point of noting "0 guitar" that day and every day for the next five days. On November 12 his diary entry, just a few lines long and barely legible, carried one discouraging note—"Cannot find secretary to take Helen's place. Nobody left."—but also the triumphant news that a copy of *Bronco Pegasus* had arrived via airmail from New York.

That night Lummis suffered a massive hemorrhage and slipped into a coma. His children said there were occasions after that when he would awake and talk lucidly for a while, but the diary he had kept for just short of forty-one years and the journal he had maintained for nearly as long fell silent. On November 17 a telegram reached El Alisal informing Lummis that *Flowers of Our Lost Romance*, finished by temporary secretaries recruited by Wilson, had been accepted for publication.

By then, all of Lummis's children had gathered at El Alisal to be with their father at the end. Turbesé played the guitar for him, which roused him on one occasion for long enough to join her in singing in a clear voice "Adios, Adios, Amores." On another occasion he murmured to her, "You are more precious than fine jewels." One day he demanded his trousers, put them on, and tramped in a circuit of the room before getting back into bed. One of the last things he said was overheard by Keith. "Make way!" he called out. "A Lummis in the field meeting all comers." On the evening of November 25, Lummis died.

He had left precise instructions about how his body should be handled. He wanted to be placed Indian-fashion between two redwood boards that he had selected himself. And he wanted to be wrapped in one of his favorite Indian blankets and cremated. For the memorial service in the courtyard at El Alisal, his body, thus prepared for the incorporating flames, lay in state under the spreading branches of El Alcalde Mayor. Scores of the most prominent old-timers in the city gathered for the occasion.

"Charles Lummis as a man was unique; his career was unique, and so was his funeral," a reporter observed. Señora Alma Real sang several songs in a moving cadence, including "La Hamaca," a Spanish ballad composed by Lummis, and the José Arias orchestra played plaintive melodies including "Adios, Adios, Amores." A succession of Lummis's closest friends offered testimonials.

John Collier wrote an epitaph for Lummis in the form of a poem, "The Indians' Charles Fletcher Lummis," that was published a week after his death in the *Los Angeles Times*. "Ah, much is told, much shall be told of you," it began, concluding with an image of Lummis "gone into the longed-for cloud" to gather with a band of Indians around a great drum.[25]

Lummis wasn't so sure where he would end up after death. Though he wasn't an overly religious man, he thought and wrote often about God, which he once defined, when pressed for a definition by a reader of *Out West*, as "the best we know." According to the writer John Steven McGroarty, Lummis had little faith in an afterlife, but he was open to the possibility. "I think his mind was poised to wait and see, and not to be afraid, no matter which way it might prove out," McGroarty said.[26] But certainly he wasn't in any hurry to find out. That was apparent in the epitaph he wrote for himself, a poem called "Top o' the Hill," which was read by one of his friends at his memorial service.[27] It summarizes the aim of his various lifelong crusades in a succinct phrase about how he sought to serve the future with the past. It is a triumphant poem about how he overcame sorrow and failure, made his dreams come true, lived the lives of many men. But as the opening lines make clear, he had a few more lives to live: "One rests here who still was young, still aflame with songs unsung."

Epilogue

On April 11, 1933, a group of men gathered at the White House to meet with newly elected President Franklin D. Roosevelt. The president had called the meeting to sort out a controversy over who should fill the post of commissioner of Indian affairs. According to the *New York Sun*, the controversy had turned into a modern-day Battle of Little Big Horn. "All the winds of patronage" strongly supported Edgar Merritt. He had little experience with or interest in Indians, but he was the brother-in-law of a powerful U.S. senator who had close connections with land, oil, and water-power companies. They had a lot riding on the selection of the person who would head an agency that controlled millions of acres of western land.

After hearing out Merritt's supporters, Roosevelt noted that "every highbrow organization in the country" fiercely opposed Merritt. So did Roosevelt's newly installed secretary of the interior, Harold Ickes. One of the first members of the American Indian Defense Association when it was formed in 1923, Ickes had made it clear to Congress that he wouldn't submit any further nominations for posts in his department until his choice for commissioner of Indian affairs was approved. His choice was John Collier.

In the showdown at the White House, Ickes prevailed, and nine days later Collier was sworn in. He moved into an office where even then the walls must have been ringing with curses against his old friend Lummis, who had died more than four years earlier. Collier filled the position for twelve years, transforming U.S. policy toward American Indians in the process. His tenure was certainly not without controversy. But the terms of engagement in the policy battles he waged from inside the bureau were dramatically different than before. The Indian Bureau had become the advocate of preserving native traditions. On the opposing side were vocal factions in many tribes that accused Collier and his bureau of trying to relegate Indians to a quaint state of backwardness.

As Kenneth R. Philp points out in *John Collier's Crusade for Indian Reform 1920–1954*, Collier pushed for day schools that taught Native American history even though some tribes favored boarding schools that taught patriotism and perseverance. At the Taos pueblo, he supported the Native American Church and its peyote-smoking rituals over the opposition of many Christian progressives in the pueblo. He advocated roadless areas on reservations, limits on timber harvests, and cuts in sheep and cattle herds that were overgrazing pastures, even though many Indians favored full-tilt production of their land, its future viability be damned. One of his primary goals was to establish democratic self-government among the tribes, though some weren't ready for autonomy.

It didn't help that Collier had an autocratic streak, which showed in his response to the resistance he encountered. Eventually even his friends in the Taos artist colony, including Mabel Dodge Luhan, turned against him.

The most significant reform during Collier's tenure, the Indian Reorganization Act of 1934, ended the half-century-old policy of allotment of reservation lands to individual Indians who could do with their parcels as they saw fit, even sell them to whites. Many progressive Indians, and old-line reform groups such as the Indian Rights Association, opposed the reorganization act, complaining that it would keep Indians tied to their reservations. Quite a few Indians thought Collier's ideas smacked of communism, socialism, and paganism. In the end, Collier learned the hard way that his idealistic view of American Indians as repositories of ancient wisdom about living in harmony was at best greatly exaggerated.

Collier clearly had his faults. But there was no comparison between his naïveté and bossiness and the ruthless insensitivity and arrogance of his predecessors, such as Lummis's old nemesis Commissioner Thomas J.

Morgan, who had coldly asserted in 1889, "The Indians must conform to 'the white man's ways,' peaceably if they will, forcibly if they must."

Collier's policies gave American Indians protection from the juggernaut of "the white man's ways." Whether they ultimately wanted to stay on the reservation or not, the end of allotment put the brakes on dispersal of tribal lands, preserving that choice for future generations. Reservations grew in size during Collier's tenure through strategic acquisitions and transfers of surplus federal lands. During the "Indian New Deal" that he presided over, native arts and crafts enjoyed a revival with government assistance. And the Bureau of Indian Affairs got a new look. The percentage of jobs in the bureau held by Native Americans more than doubled to sixty-five percent.

Lummis had always had little patience for theories, and so he, too, might have balked at some of Collier's attempts at social engineering. But the most lasting legacy of Collier's tenure was the simple notion that Indians were entitled to basic respect and the right to determine for themselves how they wanted to live their lives. That's what Lummis spent his life fighting for. The movement in that direction under Collier is part of Lummis's legacy as well.

The massive record that Lummis left of his life and times has by itself assured that he remains well known among academic historians of the era in which he lived. But Lummis has never gotten much credit from historians for the part he played in reshaping the U.S. government's Indian policies. In the eyes of many scholars, his antics overshadow his achievements.

Franklin Walker rather politely made the point in his 1950 book *Literary History of Southern California*. He mentions "the not unsubstantiated charges that [Lummis] was a poseur, a lecher and a drunkard." But Walker was willing to overlook all that, concluding that Lummis was "a man of extraordinary energy and great bravery, whose neuroses and enthusiasms, like those of many men who move mountains, were mutually stimulating."

Contemporary scholars have been more critical. They have zeroed in on the careless errors and factual discrepancies that are easy to find in Lummis's voluminous body of work. And they have disparaged his penchant for "self-glorifying purple prose," as University of Arizona professor emeritus James W. Byrkit put it in his introduction to *Letters from the Southwest,* a collection of the dispatches that Lummis wrote during his tramp across the continent. Byrkit concedes that "all of the cruel limitations to his image notwithstanding, the sum of his talents and achievements is overpowering." But he concludes, "A man of action, not of ideas, his credibility as a seminal figure was washed away in a torrent of superlatives and melodrama, travelogues and didacticism, hyperbole and simplistic observations. . . . More discriminating scholars rarely treat such products with kindness. Among serious historians, he has earned no more respect or recognition that any number of grade B (or worse) movie directors."

Lummis wouldn't be surprised that "serious historians" don't think very highly of him. He spent his life skewering the stuffy academic guardians of the "ologies," who seemed intent on keeping their "epoch-making research buried in sacrosanct reports for a few Bostonians." He was a popularizer more than a groundbreaking scholar, and regularly admitted it, deferring to the greater expertise of the many scientists he counted among his best friends. He regularly employed literary devices, creating composite characters, concocting dialogue, and re-arranging events for the sake of a better story, techniques that are quite common, if somewhat controversial, among reputable nonfiction writers these days. It was all for the good cause of instilling in his fellow citizens an appreciation for their nation's rich and diverse culture heritage of which many were entirely ignorant.

That central mission of his life helps explain some of his most notable peculiarities. His eccentric behavior and ostentatious outfits were partly the mark of a savvy salesman who depended on a precarious stream of revenue from books and freelance articles to make ends meet. But it was also a form of personal protest against silly prejudices toward people who are different, which was at the root of the racism and xenophobia that Lummis spent his life fighting.

When the novelist Hamlin Garland saw him in his worn-out corduroy suit and sweat-stained sombrero heading off to see the president in 1901, he had wondered whether Lummis was too eccentric for his own good. But ultimately he was sufficiently impressed with Lummis's achievements to be convinced that his legacy would endure. As he put it, "Vital, impulsive, stormy, and often unreasonable, Lummis talked and wrote and fought—building for himself a secure place in Southwestern history."

Notes

PROLOGUE

1. Garland, *Companions on the Trail* (1931), pp. 95–97, 99–100.

2. Review of Lummis's *Mesa, Cañon and Pueblo* in the *Los Angeles Times,* quoted in Gordon, p. 154.

CHAPTER 1

1. The document hereinafter called the "memoir" is an unfinished, unbound manuscript in multiple drafts, written by Lummis and partially edited by his daughter Turbesé Lummis Fiske. One version, parts of which carry the working title *As I Remember,* is at the Braun Research Library of the Southwest Museum in Los Angeles (hereinafter Braun). Large portions of the memoir also appear in a manuscript that Turbesé was working on when she died in 1967. Entitled *It Was Fun Being Lummis,* it is at the University of Arizona Library's Special Collections Department in Tucson. Part of Turbesé's manuscript, including many lengthy excerpts from the memoir, was completed and edited by her brother Keith Lummis, and published as *Charles F. Lummis: The Man and His West* (1975).

2. Undated, handwritten autobiographical essay, Charles Fletcher Lummis Papers (Collection 763), Department of Special Collections, Charles E. Young Research Library, University of California, Los Angeles.

3. The diary that Lummis kept for several months in college is at Braun.

4. The quotes from the diary of Lummis's mother come from Fiske, *The Man and His West.*

5. See the short biography of Otis in Spalding, *History and Reminiscences,* vol. 3, pp. 76–80, for a description of the publisher's early years with the *Los Angeles Daily Times.*

CHAPTER 2

1. Lummis wrote several different accounts of his 1884–85 "tramp" from Cincinnati to Los Angeles. Most of the quotations in this chapter come from his first version—the weekly letters he sent to the *Chillicothe Leader.* They have been compiled by James W. Byrkit in *Letters from the Southwest* (1989), an invaluable resource for determining what Lummis actually did and thought during his tramp. The *Leader's* headlines on Lummis's letters are quoted by Daniela P. Moneta in *Chas. F. Lummis: The Centennial Exhibition Commemorating His Tramp Across the Continent* (1985). Most of Lummis's *Los Angeles Times* articles about the tramp were written after the journey. They departed from the original letters to the *Leader* in ways that seemed designed to suit the interests of readers in Los Angeles. Lummis's book, *A Tramp Across the Continent,* published six years later, is the most fictionalized account of his trek. Lummis included a number of episodes from his subsequent trips to the Southwest, and other passages were embellished for dramatic effect.

2. Letter to Lummis from Mayne Reid, May 15, 1883, reprinted in Gordon, *Crusader in Corduroy,* p. 83.

3. Jesse Green has edited, and written informative introductions for, two collections of Frank Cushing's writings from his years among the Pueblo Indians of western New Mexico: *Zuni: Selected Writings of Frank Hamilton Cushing* (1979) and *Cushing at Zuni: The Correspondence and Journals of Frank Hamilton Cushing, 1879–1884* (1990).

4. Lummis, "The White Indian," *Land of Sunshine,* June 1900.

5. Joan Steele discusses Reid's background and explores his views on the Southwest and Native Americans in *Captain Mayne Reid* (1978).

6. Byrkit, *Letters from the Southwest,* is critical of Lummis, chastising him for his "self-gratifying purple prose." But Byrkit credits him with being much more receptive to Hispanic and Indian cultures than other nineteenth-century Anglo-American visitors to the Southwest. Gregg and Pike are quoted in Wilson, *The Earth Shall Weep,* p. 211.

7. Fiske, *The Man and His West*, p. 17.

8. Letter to Lummis from Dorothea Lummis, quoted in Fiske, *The Man and His West*, p. 23.

9. "A New Mexican Hero," *A New Mexico David*, pp. 190–217.

10. *Los Angeles Times*, May 17, 1885.

CHAPTER 3

1. Spalding, *Los Angeles Newspaperman*. Written in the 1930s, when Spalding was in his eighties, the memoir was published by the Huntington Library in 1961.

2. Lummis wrote the story March 1, 1885, as the last installment of his letters to the *Chillicothe Leader* from his tramp. It is reprinted in Byrkit. A somewhat different version of the story was published in the *Los Angeles Times*, January 1, 1886, p. 6.

3. Letter from Lummis to friends in Ohio, quoted in Fiske, *The Man and His West*, p. 37.

CHAPTER 4

1. Lummis's dispatches from Fort Bowie to the *Los Angeles Times* have been collected in two books: *General Crook and the Apache Wars* (1966), a volume edited by his daughter Turbesé, and a more thorough compilation, *Dateline Fort Bowie* (1979), edited, annotated, and with an introduction by Dan L. Thrapp. Lummis also collected copies of his own stories for the *Times*, the *San Francisco Chronicle*, and other papers, as well as other clippings about the Apache Wars, in one of the dozens of scrapbooks that he compiled. Braun, "Among the Apaches, Illustrated."

2. Crook's career as Indian fighter is recounted by his longtime aide John G. Bourke in *An Apache Campaign* (1886), about the 1883 pursuit of Geronimo, and *On the Border with Crook* (1891).

3. For background on the Apache War and the tribe's history, I am indebted to Terrell, *Apache Chronicle: The Story of a People* (1972), Utley, *A Clash of Cultures: Fort Bowie and the Chiricahua Apaches* (1977), and Faulk, *The Geronimo Campaign* (1969).

4. Beyond his newspaper dispatches, Lummis reflected on the fighting prowess of Apache warriors in a chapter in *The Land of Poco Tiempo* (1893) entitled "The Apache Warrior." Lummis also wrote an extended note about Apache fighters in *A Bronco Pegasus* (1928) to accompany his epic poem about Geronimo entitled "Man-Who-Yawns."

5. For an account of Crook's surrender negotiations with Geronimo, see Van Orden, *Geronimo's Surrender: The 1886 C. S. Fly Photographs* (1991), in which many of Fly's famous photographs are reprinted.

6. Letter to Lummis from Dorothea Lummis, undated 1886, Dorothea Lummis Moore Papers, Huntington Library, San Marino, Calif.

7. Lummis criticized Miles and credited Crook's tactics for the capture of Geronimo in "In the Lion's Den," *Land of Sunshine*, November 1895, p. 284.

CHAPTER 5

1. Bowman, *Los Angeles: Epic of a City* (1974), pp. 181–92, contains a concise history of the land boom of the 1880s.

2. Lummis recounted the conflict between Otis and Boyce in his memoir. Spalding also mentioned the conflict between the former partners in *Los Angeles Newspaperman*.

3. Lummis describes purchasing his first camera and his early experiments with the device in an article about a trip to Acoma published in late 1886 in the *Los Angeles Times*. "At Flagstaff: 'Lum' and 'Doc' Call upon the Cliff-Dwellers. . . . A Wrestle with Amateur Photography," undated clipping, "In the Land of Poco Tiempo, Illustrated," Braun MS.1 S1.

4. The story about how Dorothea kept a knife at hand out of fear of her husband was cited in Gordon, *Crusader in Corduroy*.

5. *Los Angeles Times*, July 1, 1887, p. 1.

6. Lummis reminisced about Otis in "One of the Old Guard," *Land of Sunshine*, January 1900; in a paper prepared for a gathering of *Times* employees in 1922, reprinted in *Crusader in Corduroy*, pp. 128–31; and in his memoir.

CHAPTER 6

1. Lummis described his battle with paralysis in the last chapter of *King of the Broncos* (1897), which was reprinted in an inspirational booklet entitled *My Friend Will* (1911).

2. The Amado Chaves Papers at the New Mexico State Library in Santa Fe (hereinafter Chaves Papers) include several dozen items that shed some light on the Chaves family's friendship with Lummis. For more on Lummis's friendship with Chaves, see Simmons, *Two Southwesterners: Charles F. Lummis and Amado Chaves* (1968).

3. The original volumes of the daily diary that Lummis began keeping in February 1888 are at Braun.

4. Lummis described life in the sheep camps in "New Mexican Folk-Songs," a chapter of *The Land of Poco Tiempo* (1893), and much later in his introduction to *Spanish Songs of Old California* (1923).

5. Patrick and Betsy Houlihan, *Lummis in the Pueblos* (1986), explore Lummis's career in New Mexico as a photographer of daily life among the Pueblo Indians.

6. Lummis collected many of his newspaper dispatches from New Mexico to the *Los Angeles Times*, the *Chillicothe Leader*, the *St. Louis Globe-Democrat*, and other publications, as well as news stories about contemporary events that interested him, in a two-volume scrapbook, "In the Land of Poco Tiempo, Illustrated," Braun MS.1 S1 and MS.1 S2.

7. "The Penitent Brothers," *Cosmopolitan*, May 1889. A slightly different version of the magazine article comprises a chapter of *Land of Poco Tiempo*. Marta Weigle's *Brothers of Light, Brothers of Blood* (1976) is a more objective treatment of the history of the Penitente sect.

8. Only a few original copies of the *Gringo & Greaser* are known to exist and most of them are in the New Mexico State Library in Santa Fe. The library also has a copy of a booklet by Peter Hertzog with biographical information about publisher Thomas Kusz and many excerpts from the paper.

9. The effort of the territorial legislature to prevent the alleged killers of Provencher from being held for trial is briefly discussed in Lamar Howard, "Edmund G. Ross as Governor of New Mexico Territory, A Reappraisal," *New Mexico Historical Review* 36 (July 1961): 204.

CHAPTER 7

1. For a history of the nearly four-hundred-year-old church in Isleta, see Montoya, *Isleta Pueblo and the Church of St. Augustine.*

2. For information on the history of the Pueblo tribe, I drew from Dozier, *The Pueblo Indians of North America* (1970), and Sturtevant, *Handbook of North American Indians*, vol. 9, *Southwest*, which contains a succinct history of the tribe in a

chapter by Marc Simmons, "History of the Pueblos Since 1821," and other chapters giving in-depth treatment to three of the pueblos that Lummis frequented, Isleta, Acoma, and Laguna.

3. Some demographic and economic data about the Rio Grande pueblos during the 1880s can be found in the brief annual reports filed each fall by the Indian agent for the pueblos and published as part of the annual Report of the Secretary of the Interior.

4. For a discussion of the social, political, and economic climate in Isleta when Lummis arrived, and for an account of his early relationship with the people of the pueblo, I am indebted to Professor Theodore Jojola, of the University of New Mexico in Albuquerque. Jojola's paper "Charles F. Lummis and American Indian Policy," prepared for the Charles F. Lummis Centennial Symposium at the Southwest Museum in 1985, is on file at Braun.

5. Lummis describes Rea's store, and the use of sheepskins as currency, in his description of the Day of the Dead in Isleta. He included the passage in *A Tramp Across the Continent*, though in fact he didn't visit Isleta on the Day of the Dead until several years after his tramp.

6. Letter from Amado Chaves, January 1888, Chaves Papers.

7. Letters from Dorothea Lummis to Lummis in New Mexico are reprinted in Fiske, *The Man and His West*, pp. 41–42.

8. Lummis collected many of the newspaper clippings about the attempt on his life—along with a piece of his hat pierced by buckshot and a sheet of newspaper splotched with his blood—in a scrapbook, "In the Land of Poco Tiempo, Illustrated," Braun MS.1 S1.

9. The letters between Lummis in New Mexico and Dorothea Lummis and Eve Douglas, then living together in Los Angeles, are at Braun, Keith Lummis Donation.

10. Lummis described his July 1891 recovery from paralysis in his memoir and in *My Friend Will* (1911).

CHAPTER 8

1. For biographical details about Bandelier and insights into his thinking, I am indebted to Lange and Riley, *Bandelier: The Life and Adventures of Adolph Bandelier* (1996), from which the quotations from Bandelier's journal are drawn. Lummis offered his own thoughts on Bandelier in "A Hero in Science," *Land of Sunshine*, August 1900, and his introduction to later editions of Bandelier's historical novel *The Delight Makers*.

2. In a letter to a friend telling of her negotiations with the publisher, Bandelier's widow revealed her thoughts about Lummis's customary attire. "I told Mr. Dodd yesterday a bit of my opinion of dear Lummis' outfit and he laughed himself sick," she wrote. Lange and Riley, p. 217.

3. A Tom and Jerry is a variation on eggnog most likely invented by Professor Jerry Thomas, a bartender at San Francisco's Occidental Hotel in the 1860s and author of *The Bartender's Companion* (1862).

4. Robert F. Gish, in his introduction to *Pueblo Indian Folk-Stories*, a reissue of Lummis's 1894 book *The Man Who Married the Moon*, gives a mixed review of Lummis's ethnological work, accusing Lummis of fabricating encounters with the Indians and inserting his character into the folktales. But Gish credits Lummis with preserving the vanishing oral literature of the Pueblos.

5. Lummis collected newspaper clippings about the Albuquerque Indian School controversy and Indian education policy in general in a scrapbook, "Newspaper Articles on the Treatment of Indians," Braun, Sequoya League Series.

6. For background on the Catholic-Protestant clash over Indian policy, and Indian education policy in general, I am indebted to Prucha, *The Churches and the Indian Schools, 1888–1912* (1979), and Hoxie, *A Final Promise: The Campaign to Assimilate the Indians, 1880–1920* (1984). Hoxie mentions Lummis only in passing, inexplicably portraying him as a racist who welcomed the extinction of the Indians.

7. Department of the Interior, *Report of the Commissioner of Indian Affairs*, by T. J. Morgan, annual report, 51st Cong., 1st sess., October 1, 1889, H. Ex. Doc. 11, p. 3.

8. Lummis wrote many magazine stories and books offering an idyllic view of life among the Pueblos. See, for example, "Among the Children of the Pueblos," *Harper's Young People*, November 4, 1890; "The Superior Race," *Drake's*, October 1889; "The Indian Who Is Not Poor," *Scribner's*, September 1892; and "My Real Brownies," *Land of Sunshine*, June 1897.

9. Department of the Interior, *Report of Superintendent of Indian Schools*, by Daniel Dorchester, annual report, 52d Cong., 2d sess., August 16, 1892, H. Ex. Doc. 1, pt. 5, II, p. 526.

10. For a laudatory account of the school, see Lillie G. McKinney, "History of the Albuquerque Indian School," *New Mexico Historical Review*, April 1945.

11. Department of the Interior, *Report of Superintendent of Indian Schools*, by Daniel Dorchester, annual report, 53d Cong., 1st sess., September 20, 1893, H. Ex. Doc. 1, pt. 5, II, p. 360.

12. Letter to Eve Lummis from Dorothea Lummis, May 29, 1892, Braun, Keith Lummis Donation.

13. Letter to Lummis from James Foshay, July 21, 1903, Braun, "Newspaper Articles on the Treatment of Indians."

CHAPTER 9

1. The document hereinafter called the "journal" is not to be confused with Lummis's diary. The journal, which was usually dictated to a secretary and typed, was a longer narrative about the events in his life, in contrast with the diary, which contained cryptic notes about the mundane details of his daily existence. In his later years, Lummis made multiple copies of his journal and circulated them among a small circle of family and friends. Originals of the journal are kept at Braun, and copies are housed at other libraries including the Special Collections department of the University of Arizona library in Tucson. A complete set of Lummis's journal covering the years from the late 1880s through 1928 has been copied onto sixteen rolls of microfilm, *Charles F. Lummis Manuscript Collection, Journal Series*, MS.1.

2. Adolph Bandelier's perspective on Lummis's sojourn in Peru, and the quotations from Bandelier's journals, come from Lange and Riley.

3. "Los Angeles: The Metropolis of the Southwest," *Land of Sunshine*, June 1895.

4. In each of his trilogy of books on California history, California State Librarian Kevin Starr discusses Lummis's role as a scholar and promoter of the region's Spanish heritage, concluding that it was in this field that he "made his most lasting contribution"; see *Americans and the California Dream* (1973), pp. 397–401.

5. Bingham, *Charles F. Lummis: Editor of the Southwest* (1955), gives a thorough account of Lummis's tenure as editor of *Land of Sunshine*, later renamed *Out West*. The quotations from Charles Willard's letters come from Bingham, p. 48.

6. Letter from John Muir to Lummis, June 11, 1895, Braun MS.1.1.3221A MF.R44.F595.

7. Letters from Jack London to *Land of Sunshine* associate editor Charles Moody, July 2 and December 15, 1902, Braun MS.1.1.2700 MF.R35.F699. Jack London's story for *Land of Sunshine* that netted him ten dollars was "The Sickness of Lone Chief," October 1902.

8. Bingham, p. 73.

9. Bingham has a mixed opinion of the magazine and of Lummis, who as a writer is "little better than second rate," in his view. Bingham unfairly accuses Lummis of avoiding controversial issues and asserts that for Lummis "the recent past in the Southwest was too sordid to touch." But he credits the magazine for the crucial support it provided three reform movements.

10. Lummis's description of the founding of the Landmarks Club is from his memoir, which is quoted extensively in Fiske, *The Man and His West*, chapter 18, "To the Rescue of the Missions," pp. 87–92.

11. Letter from Lummis to W. J. McGee, October 26, 1897, quoted in Bingham, p. 54.

12. For an example of respectful treatment of American Indian culture in Lummis's magazine, see the two-part series "Songs of the Navajos" by a pair of prominent ethnologists, the first by Dr. Washington Matthews, October 1896, and the second by John Comfort Fillmore, November 1896. The articles debunked the view that Navajo culture is devoid of poetic literature. The disagreeable "succession of grunts" described by others is actually a precious heritage of thousands of songs, Matthews wrote.

13. For a fuller account of the history of the house, see Apostol, *El Alisal: Where History Lingers* (1994).

14. Lummis wrote a detailed description of El Alisal and its history in a letter to the Los Angeles City Parks Commission on January 11, 1912. At the time, the city was considering condemning El Alisal and neighboring houses to expand a park. The letter is reprinted in Gordon, *Crusader in Corduroy*, p. 171.

15. Mary Austin offers some caustic observations of Lummis in her autobiography, *Earth Horizon* (1932), accusing him of drinking too much, sleeping too little, leaning on his wife's translation of Spanish historical documents, and attempting to make Austin his latest sexual conquest (p. 292). Sui Sin Far, the pen name for Edith Maude Eaton, was more complimentary about Lummis in her autobiographical essay "Leaves from the Mental Portfolio of an Eurasian," *Independent* 66 (January 21, 1909):125–32.

16. Copies of blank subpoenas served on invitees to Courts of El Alcalde Mayor, other invitations to parties, and the El Alisal House Book are at Braun.

17. Edith Pla is quoted in Fiske, *The Man and His West*, p. 164.

18. Letter to Lummis from W. C. Patterson, August 2, 1900, Braun MS.1.1.3477A MF.R48.F416.

19. Letters to Lummis from Caroline Severance, April 13 and July 26, 1900, Braun MS.1.1.3970A MF.R56.F21.

20. Roosevelt discusses his stint as a rancher in the Dakotas in his 1913 autobiography.

21. Correspondence between Lummis and Roosevelt, 1898–1901, Braun MS.1.1.3805A MF.R.52.F273.

22. Helen Hunt Jackson's *Ramona* (1884) offers a fictionalized account of the contented life of the Mission Indians under Spanish rule.

23. The quote from Horace Bell's paper the *Porcupine* comes from Wilson, *The Earth Shall Weep* (1998), p. 236.

24. The first article in *Land of Sunshine* to raise an alarm about the fate of the Indians at Agua Caliente was H. N. Rust's "A Fiesta at Warner's Ranch," April 1899.

25. The meeting at El Alisal and the new group's objectives were described in "A New Indian Policy," *Land of Sunshine*, December 1901.

26. Amado Chaves told of Lummis's visit to the White House in an October 2, 1926, letter to Laurence Lee, Chaves Papers.

CHAPTER 10

1. Hagan, *Theodore Roosevelt and Six Friends of the Indian* (1997), is an indispensable source of information on Indian policy during Theodore Roosevelt's presidency, Roosevelt's personal view of Indians, and the influence on his administration of advisors including Lummis, Hamlin Garland, George Bird Grinnell, and C. Hart Merriam.

2. Letter from Lummis to George Bird Grinnell, December 12, 1901, Braun MS.1.1.1805A MF.R24A.F84.

3. Garland tells of growing up in Nebraska and the Dakotas in his best-known book, *A Son of the Middle Border* (1925).

4. Correspondence between Lummis and Hamlin Garland, December 1901, Braun MS.1.1.1603A MF.R21.F514.

5. Letter from Lummis to George Bird Grinnell, January 2, 1902, Braun MS.1.1.1805A MF.R24A.F84.

6. *Out West*, March 1902.

7. Letter from Lummis to President Roosevelt, February 26, 1902, Braun MS.1.1.3805B MF.R.52.F285

8. Letter from Lummis to Phoebe Hearst, June 1, 1902, Braun MS.1.1.1982 MF.R25.F87.

9. Preliminary report of the Warner's Ranch Commission, Braun, Warner's Ranch Series.

10. Letter from Lummis to Senator Thomas Bard, April 29, 1903, Braun, Warner's Ranch Series.

11. The transcript of the April 16, 1903, meeting at Agua Caliente, and other material gathered by the Warner's Ranch Commission, is at Braun, Warner's Ranch Series.

12. Letter from Lummis to William Jones, April 18, 1903, Braun, Warner's Ranch Series.

13. Letter from Lummis to C. Hart Merriam, April 25, 1903, Braun MS.1.1.3060B MF.R42.F588.

14. Letter from Lummis to President Roosevelt, May 11, 1902, Braun MS.1.1.3805B MF.R.52.F289.

15. Letter from Lummis to John Muir, April 25, 1903, Braun MS.1.1.3221A MF.R44.F595.

16. Correspondence between Lummis and William Loeb Jr., March 1903, Braun MS.1.1.3060A MFR42.F488.

17. Letter from Lummis to C. Hart Merriam, May 2, 1902, Braun MS.1.1.3060A MFR42.F488.

18. Grant Wallace wrote two stories for *Out West* about the removal of the Indians to the Pala Valley: "The Last Eviction," July 1903, and "The Exiles of Cupa," November 1903.

19. Letter from Lummis to William Jones, May 30, 1903, Braun MS.1.1.2376B MF.R31F149.

20. Letter from Lummis to Senator Thomas Bard, December 31, 1902, Braun, Warner's Ranch Series.

21. Letter from Lummis to William Jones, March 1903, Braun, Warner's Ranch Series.

22. Letter from William Jones to President Roosevelt, June 23, 1903, Braun, Warner's Ranch Series.

CHAPTER 11

1. The Bureau of Indian Affairs's hair-cutting order was reprinted in *Out West*, March 1902.

2. Letters to and from A. H. Viets, A. C. Vroman, and Charles Burton, Braun, Sequoya League Series.

3. Letter to Gertrude Gates from her sister, Braun, Sequoya League Series.

4. Letter from W. J. McGee to Lummis, November 29, 1902, Braun, Sequoya League Series.

5. Correspondence between Gertrude Gates and Charles Burton, fall 1902, Braun, Sequoya League Series.

6. Letter from William Jones to Charles Burton, November 29, 1902, quoted in Hagan, p. 131.

7. Letter from President Roosevelt to E. A. Hitchcock, May 9, 1903, quoted in Hagan, p. 133.

8. Letters to Lummis from Charles Moody, July 27 and August 4, 1903, Braun MS.1.1.3157 MF.R.44F166.

9. Letters from Charles Moody to James E. Jenkins and Roberta Balfour, apparently with the Indian Bureau, August 12, 1903, Braun MS.1.1.3157 MF.R.44F170.

10. Lummis published Charles Moody's explanation of his change of heart in "Mr. Moody's Report," *Out West*, September 1903, p. 303.

11. Letter from Gertrude Gates to Lummis and Executive Committee of the Sequoya League, September 19, 1903, Braun, Sequoya League Series.

12. Letter from Lummis to C. Hart Merriam, August 1903, Braun MS.1.1.3060B MF.R42.F588.

13. Letter from William Jones to Charles Burton, September 5, 1903, Braun, Sequoya League Series.

14. Letter from President Roosevelt to E. A. Hitchcock, August 29, 1903, quoted in Hagan, p. 135.

15. Letter to Lummis from President Roosevelt, September 10, 1903, Braun, Sequoya League Series.

CHAPTER 12

1. Correspondence between Lummis and Bertha Lummis, 1904–5, Braun MS.1.1.2768A MF.R.36.F339. The files contain seventy-six letters dated between November 1904 and early August 1905.

2. Letter to Lummis from President Roosevelt, October 5, 1903, quoted in Hagan, p. 137.

3. Correspondence between Lummis and Jack London, March 1905, Braun MS.1.1.2700 MF.R35.F701.

4. Lummis tells the story of Pancho Amate in "The Last Troubadour," a chapter in *Flowers of Our Lost Romance.*

5. Lummis reports on the death of Procopio in his journal, August 23–26, 1907.

6. Documents, drafts of pleadings, and correspondence pertaining to the divorce of Charles and Eve Lummis is at Braun, Divorce Correspondence.

7. Letter to Ella L. Moody from Lummis, April 30, 1910, Braun MS.1.1.3158 MF.R.44.F186; reply from Ella L. Moody to Lummis, Braun, Divorce Correspondence.

8. Judd, *Men Met Along the Trail: Adventures in Archaeology* (1968), p. 141, depicts Lummis at the 1910 summer session at Tyuonyi, ensconced in the choicest cave, smoking Mexican cigars and playing Spanish and cowboy songs on his guitar until 3 A.M.

9. Letters from Jordan "Quimu" Lummis, Braun MS.1.1.2777B MF.R37.F664.

10. Letter to Lummis from Estelle Reel, May 13, 1909, Braun, Sequoya League Series.

11. Letters from John Muir to Lummis and the Sequoya League, 1908–11, Braun MS.1.1.3221B MR.R44.F623.

12. Letter from Lummis to Amado Chaves, Chaves Papers.

13. Letter to Lummis from Florence Wilson of Universal Pictures, April 6, 1925, and Lummis's response, April 9, 1920, Braun MS.1.1.4681 MF.R65.F112.

14. Many of the Lummis columns, as well as the letter from Harry Chandler, May 18, 1918, are collected in a scrapbook, "Chile Con Carnage and I Guess So," Braun MS.1 S12.

15. Lummis's speech about Junípero Serra in 1913 at San Gabriel Mission, Braun, Miscellaneous Manuscripts.

16. Correspondence between Lummis and Bertha Lummis, August 1917, Braun MS.1.1.2768P MF.R37.F115.

17. Letter from Lummis to Henry O'Melveny, September 16, 1918, Braun MS.1.1.3369D MF.R47.F218.

18. Correspondence between Lummis and Isidore Dockweiler, June 7–September 25, 1918, Braun MS.1.1.1146B MF.R15.F640.

19. "Catching Our Archaeology Alive," *Out West*, January 1905, p. 35.

CHAPTER 13

1. Kenneth Philp begins his excellent book *John Collier's Crusade for Indian Reform, 1920–1954* with a discussion of Collier's early years in Georgia and New York.

2. In an introduction to the 1987 edition of *Edge of Taos Desert* by Mabel Dodge Luhan, John Collier Jr. vividly recalls his family's arrival in Taos on Christmas Eve of 1920.

3. Collier fleshes out his theory about how the Indians of the Southwest are a repository of ancient wisdom about social organization in his article "Red Atlantis," *Survey Graphic*, October 1922, in *American Indian Ceremonial Dances* (1972), and in his memoir *From Every Zenith* (1963).

4. Letter from Harry Chandler to County Museum board, June 1920, reprinted in Gordon, *Crusader in Corduroy*, p. 127.

5. Letter from John Collier to Lummis, July 16, 1922, Braun MS.1.1.845A MF.R11.F357.

6. Letters from Lummis to various friends in New Mexico, September 1922, Braun MS.1.1.845A MF.R11.F357.

7. Letter from Lummis to John Collier, September 14, 1922, Braun MS.1.1.845A MF.R11.F357.

8. Philp offers an in-depth look at Circular 1665 and the crackdown on Pueblo religious practices in the 1920s.

9. Letter from Lummis to Alice Yates, March 25, 1923, Braun MS.1.1.4776 MF.R66.F124.

10. Letter from Harriet Lummis to Lummis, April 10, 1923, Braun MS.1.1.2774D MF.R37.F491.

11. Letter from Lummis to Edgar Hewett, April 3, 1924, Braun MS.1.1.2032N MF.R26.F156.

12. Lummis's testimony is excerpted in an American Indian Defense Association pamphlet on Indian religious rights, Braun, Miscellaneous Manuscripts.

13. Letter from Lummis to Amado Chaves, June 12, 1924, Chaves Papers.

14. Letter from Lummis to Amado Chaves, October 1926, Braun MS1.1.749E MF.R10.F445.

15. Letter from Lummis to John Collier, November 18, 1926, Braun MS.1.1.845C MF.R11.F421.

16. Letter from Lummis to John Collier, January 19, 1927, Braun MS.1.1.845C MF.R11.F421.

17. Letter from Lummis to "My dear Friends of the Pueblos of New Mexico," November 5, 1927, Braun MS.1.1.845C MF.R11.F421.

18. Letter from Lummis to Amado Chaves, November 19, 1927, Chaves Papers.

19. Letter from Emma Nourse to Lummis, August 1, 1922, Braun MS.1.1.3346 MF.R47.F20.

20. Letter from Dorothea Moore to Lummis, February 1, 1925, and Lummis's response, February 5, 1925, Braun MS.1.1.2771B MF.R37.F316.

21. Letter from Alice Rea to Lummis, January 1927, Braun MS.1.1.3671 MF.R50.F417.

22. Letter from Mary Austin to Lummis, December 28, 1918, Huntington Library (AU1139), San Marino, Calif.

23. Form letter from Lummis to Winona M. Wilson, February 29, 1928, Braun MS.1.1.4693 MF.R65.F176.

24. Letter from Lummis to Edgar Hewett, March 19, 1928, Braun MS.1.1.2032N MF.R26.F156.

25. The poem reads in part:

> Ah, much is told, much shall be told of you,
> You who wrought great the immeasurable tale
> Of Spain amid the hemispheres, who blew
> With trumpet-words life into ages pale. . . .
> Lummis has gone, has gone into the prime.
> Lummis has gone into the longed-for cloud,
> Has gone into the grass which answers prayer,
> Has gone where Indians around the great drum crowd.
> The world soul takes its own. Lummis is there!

Notes

26. Quoted in Bingham, p. 32.

27. The poem reads in part:

> One rests here who still was young,
> Still aflame with songs unsung;
> In his threescore years and ten
> Lived the lives of many men . . .
> Dreamed, and helped his dreams come true—
> There's so much for Dreams to do!
> Sorrow knew in every guise—
> Found it came to make him wise.
> Learned from Failure, all and each,
> What Success could never teach.
> Held the Old and faced the New,
> Questing only for the True,
> Serving the Future with the Past.
> Turned a quiet smile at last—
> As who should challenge the flickering heart:
> "We Had Our Share—Did We Do Our Part?"

Bibliography

.

A NOTE ABOUT ARCHIVAL HOLDINGS

The Braun Research Library of the Southwest Museum in Los Angeles holds most of Lummis's personal papers and photographic archives. The collection includes tens of thousands of items of correspondence, thousands of negatives including hundreds of five-by-seven-inch glass negatives that Lummis made in the late nineteenth century, Lummis's diary and journals, the files of his various historical preservation and Indian rights crusades, and many of the scrapbooks of newspaper clippings and assorted ephemera that Lummis kept throughout his life.

Some material from the Lummis archives has been microfilmed. The *Charles F. Lummis Manuscript Collection Correspondence Series,* MS.1.1, consists of sixty-six rolls of film containing correspondence and other items from four thousand individuals. It has been thoroughly catalogued in the invaluable three-volume *Finding Aid,* edited by Kim Walters and Richard Buchen and published by the Southwest Museum.

I have also quoted extensively from letters, manuscripts, and other documents in the archives of the Braun Research Library that have not yet been individually catalogued. They are identified by the name of the file series where those items can be found.

Other libraries where I found useful material about the life and times of Charles Lummis, and received courteous treatment from the staff, include the New Mexico State Library in Santa Fe, the Center for

Southwest Research at the University of New Mexico in Albuquerque, the Los Angeles Public Library, and the Department of Special Collections in the library at the University of California, Los Angeles. I found important holdings of newspapers from Lummis's era in the libraries mentioned above and also at the University of Southern California library's Regional History Center, the Special Collections Branch of the Rio Grande Valley Library System in Albuquerque, the Arizona Historical Society library in Tucson, and the Santa Fe Public Library.

SELECTED ARTICLES BY CHARLES LUMMIS IN HIS MAGAZINES

"The Spanish American Face." *Land of Sunshine*, January 1895.

"Los Angeles: The Metropolis of the Southwest." *Land of Sunshine*, June 1895.

"Just Climate." *Land of Sunshine*, October 1897.

"My Real Brownies." *Land of Sunshine*, June 1897.

"My Brother's Keeper." First of seven in a monthly series. *Land of Sunshine*, August 1899.

"The White Indian." *Land of Sunshine*, June 1900.

"A New Indian Policy." *Land of Sunshine*, December 1901.

"The Right Hand of the Continent." First of six in a monthly series. *Out West*, July 1902.

"Bullying the 'Quaker Indians'." First of three in a monthly series. *Out West*, June 1903.

"Catching Our Archaeology Alive." *Out West*, January 1905.

BOOKS BY CHARLES LUMMIS

Birch Bark Poems. Cambridge, Mass.: C. F. Lummis, 1879.

A New Mexico David. New York: Charles Scribner's Sons, 1891.

The Man Who Married the Moon. New York: Century, 1892. Reprinted as *Pueblo Indian Folk-Stories* (Lincoln: University of Nebraska Press, 1992).

Some Strange Corners of Our Country. New York: Century, 1892. Reprint, Tucson: University of Arizona Press, 1989.

A Tramp Across the Continent. Charles Scribner's Sons, 1892. Reprint, Lincoln: University of Nebraska Press, 1982.

The Land of Poco Tiempo. New York: Charles Scribner's Sons, 1893. Reprint, Albuquerque: University of New Mexico Press, 1966.

The Spanish Pioneers. Chicago: A. C. McClurg, 1893. Reprinted as *The Spanish Pioneers and the California Missions* (Chicago: A. C. McClurg, 1929).

The Gold Fish of Gran Chimu. Boston: Lamson, Wolffe, 1896.

The Enchanted Burro. Chicago: Way and Williams, 1897.

The King of the Broncos and Other Stories of New Mexico. New York: Charles Scribner's Sons, 1897.

The Awakening of a Nation: Mexico of Today. New York: Harper and Brothers, 1898.

The Landmarks Club Cook Book. Los Angeles: Out West, 1903.

My Friend Will. Chicago: A. C. McClurg, 1911.

Spanish Songs of Old California. Los Angeles: C. F. Lummis, 1923.

Mesa, Cañon and Pueblo. New York: Century, 1925.

A Bronco Pegasus. Boston: Houghton Mifflin, 1928.

Flowers of Our Lost Romance. New York: Houghton Mifflin, 1929.

COMPILATIONS OF NEWSPAPER ARTICLES BY CHARLES LUMMIS

General Crook and the Apache Wars. Edited by Turbesé Lummis Fiske. Flagstaff, Ariz.: Northland Press, 1966.

Dateline Fort Bowie. Edited by Dan L. Thrapp. Norman: University of Oklahoma Press, 1979.

Letters from the Southwest. Edited by James Byrkit. Tucson: University of Arizona Press, 1989.

OTHER BOOKS

Apostol, Jane. *El Alisal: Where History Lingers*. Los Angeles: Historical Society of Southern California, 1994.

Austin, Mary Hunter. *Earth Horizon*. Boston: Houghton Mifflin, 1932.

Bandelier, Adolph. *The Delight Makers*. New York: Dodd, Mead, 1890. Reprint, with an introduction by Charles F. Lummis, New York: Dodd, Mead, 1918.

Bingham, Edwin R. *Charles F. Lummis: Editor of the Southwest*. San Marino, Calif., Huntington Library, 1955.

Bourke, John G. *An Apache Campaign in the Sierra Madre*. Charles Scribner's Sons, 1886. Reprint, Lincoln: University of Nebraska Press, 1987.

———. *On the Border with Crook*. Charles Scribner's Sons, 1891. Reprint, Lincoln: University of Nebraska Press, 1971.

Bowman, Lynn. *Los Angeles: Epic of a City*. Berkeley, Calif.: Howell-North Books, 1974.

Brands, H. W. *T. R.: The Last Romantic*. New York: Basic Books, 1997.

Collier, John. *American Indian Ceremonial Dances*. New York: Bounty Books, 1972.

———. *From Every Zenith*. Denver: Sage Books, 1963.

Cushing, Frank Hamilton. *Cushing at Zuni: The Correspondence and Journals of Frank Hamilton Cushing, 1879–1884*. Edited by Jesse Green. Albuquerque: University of New Mexico Press, 1990.

———. *Zuni: Selected Writings of Frank Hamilton Cushing*. Edited by Jesse Green. Lincoln: University of Nebraska Press, 1979.

Dozier, Edward P. *The Pueblo Indians of North America*. New York: Holt, Rinehart and Winston, 1970.

Faulk, Odie B. *The Geronimo Campaign*. New York: Oxford University Press, 1969.

Fiske, Turbesé Lummis, and Keith Lummis. *Charles F. Lummis: The Man and His West*. Norman: University of Oklahoma Press, 1975.

Fleming, Robert E. *Charles F. Lummis*. Western Writers Series, no. 50. Boise, Idaho: Boise State University, 1981.

Garland, Hamlin. *Companions on the Trail: A Literary Chronicle*. New York: Macmillan, 1931.

————. *A Son of the Middle Border*. New York: Macmillan, 1925.

Gordon, Dudley. *Charles F. Lummis: Crusader in Corduroy*. Los Angeles: Cultural Assets Press, 1972.

Hagan, William T. *Theodore Roosevelt and Six Friends of the Indian*. Norman: University of Oklahoma Press, 1997.

Hertzog, Peter. *The Gringo & Greaser*. Santa Fe, N.Mex.: Press of the Territorian, [1964].

Houlihan, Patrick T., and Betsy E. Houlihan. *Lummis in the Pueblos*. Flagstaff, Ariz.: Northland Press, 1986.

Hoxie, Frederick E. *A Final Promise: The Campaign to Assimilate the Indians, 1880–1920*. Cambridge: Cambridge University Press, 1984.

Jackson, Helen Hunt. *A Century of Dishonor: A Sketch of the United States Government's Dealings with Some of the Indian Tribes*. New York: Harper & Brothers, 1881. Reprint, Norman: University of Oklahoma Press, 1995.

————. *Ramona: A Story*. Boston: Roberts Brothers, 1884. Reprint, New York: Signet, 1988.

Jordan, David Starr. *The Days of a Man: Being Memories of a Naturalist, Teacher and Minor Prophet of Democracy*. 2 vols. Yonkers-on-Hudson, N.Y.: World Book, 1922.

Judd, Neil. *Men Met Along the Trail: Adventures in Archaeology*. Norman: University of Oklahoma Press, 1968.

Lange, Charles H., and Carroll L. Riley. *Bandelier: The Life and Adventures of Adolph Bandelier*. Salt Lake City: University of Utah Press, 1996.

Luhan, Mabel Dodge. *Edge of Taos Desert: An Escape to Reality*. New York: Harcourt, Brace, 1937. Reprint, Albuquerque: University of New Mexico Press, 1987.

Moneta, Daniela P., ed. *Chas. F. Lummis: The Centennial Exhibition Commemorating His Tramp Across the Continent*. Los Angeles: Southwest Museum, 1985.

Montoya, Joe L. *Isleta Pueblo and the Church of St. Augustine*. Isleta Pueblo, N.M.: St. Augustine Parish, 1978.

Philp, Kenneth R. *John Collier's Crusade for Indian Reform, 1920–1954*. Tucson: University of Arizona Press, 1977.

Prucha, Francis Paul. *The Churches and the Indian Schools, 1888–1912*. Lincoln: University of Nebraska Press, 1979.

Reid, Mayne. *The White Chief: A Legend of North Mexico.* New York: De Witt, 1860. Reprint, Ridgewood, N.J.: Gregg Press, 1968.

Roosevelt, Theodore. *Theodore Roosevelt: An Autobiography.* New York: Macmillan, 1913.

————. *The Winning of the West.* 4 vols. New York, London: G. P. Putnam's Sons, 1889–96. Reprint, Lincoln: University of Nebraska Press, 1995.

Simmons, Marc. *Two Southwesterners: Charles F. Lummis and Amado Chaves.* Cerrillos, N.M.: San Marcos Press, 1968.

Spalding, William A. *William Andrew Spalding: Los Angeles Newspaperman.* San Marino, Calif.: Huntington Library, 1961.

Spalding, William A., ed. *History and Reminiscences, Los Angeles City and County, California.* Los Angeles: J. R. Finnell and Sons, 1931.

Starr, Kevin. *Americans and the California Dream, 1850–1915.* New York: Oxford University Press, 1973.

————. *Inventing the Dream: California Through the Progressive Era.* New York: Oxford University Press, 1985.

————. *Material Dreams: Southern California Through the 1920's.* New York: Oxford University Press, 1990.

Steele, Joan. *Captain Mayne Reid.* Boston: Twayne, 1978.

Sturtevant, William C., ed. *Handbook of North American Indians.* Vol. 9, *Southwest.* Washington, D.C.: Smithsonian Institution, 1979.

Terrell, John Upton. *Apache Chronicle: The Story of a People.* New York: World, 1972.

Utley, Robert M. *A Clash of Cultures: Fort Bowie and the Chiricahua Apaches.* Washington, D.C.: National Park Service, 1977.

Van Orden, Jay. *Geronimo's Surrender: The 1886 C. S. Fly Photographs.* Tucson: Arizona Historical Society, 1991.

Weigle, Marta. *Brothers of Light, Brothers of Blood: The Penitentes of the Southwest.* Albuquerque: University of New Mexico Press, 1976.

Wilson, James. *The Earth Shall Weep: A History of Native America.* New York: Atlantic Monthly Press, 1998.

Index

Index

Index

Index

Index